Imagining Boston

Augustus Saint-Gaudens
THE SHAW–54TH MEMORIAL, 1897
Boston Common
(*Photo by Clive Russ*)

Imagining Boston

A LITERARY LANDSCAPE

SHAUN O'CONNELL

BEACON PRESS　　　BOSTON

Beacon Press
25 Beacon Street
Boston, Massachusetts 02108-2800

Beacon Press books
are published under the auspices of
the Unitarian Universalist Association of Congregations.

97 96 95 94 93 92 91   8 7 6 5 4 3 2

Text design by Dede Cummings

Library of Congress Cataloging-in-Publication Data

O'Connell, Shaun.
Imagining Boston : a literary landscape / Shaun O'Connell.
    p.   cm.
Includes bibliographical references and index.
ISBN 0-8070-5102-0
1. American literature—Massachusetts—Boston—History and
criticism.   2. Authors, American—Homes and haunts—Massachusetts—
Boston.   3. Literary landmarks—Massachusetts—Boston.   4. Boston
(Mass.)—Intellectual life.   5. Cities and towns in literature.
6. Boston (Mass.) in literature.   I. Title.
            PS255.B6025   1990
    810.9′3274461—dc20   90-52588
                CIP

For Dorothy,
fellow pilgrim across the symbolic landscape of Greater Boston—
from Marlborough, to Cambridge, to Sudbury.

For our children,
Michael, Liam and Kathleen—
make way for the ducklings!—
who accompanied me on the Swan Boats in Boston Garden,
who carried away their own versions of the Boston Idea.

Contents

Preface   ix

1   Approaching Boston   1

2   Hawthorne's Boston and Other Imaginary Places   18

3   Boston, The Right American Stuff   74

4   Irish America's Red Brick City   108

5   Black Boston's Books   141

6   Boston Manners and Morals   172

7   Boston's Sphere of Influence   206

8   A New England Genius   266

9   Boston, City of Spirit and Flesh   304

Notes   333
Bibliography   373
Credits   391
Index   393

Preface

M Y FIRST, halting effort to "do" Boston writers appeared
in a 1975 essay for *Boston Magazine,* "The Infrequent
Family: In Search of Boston's Literary Community." I wondered
there whether Boston could justly claim such a community. "The
moral," I invoked Henry James, "is that the flower of art blooms
only where the soil is deep, that it takes a great deal of history to
produce a little literature, that it needs a complex machinery to
set a writer in motion."[1] Did Boston possess enough history and
sufficient machinery to create a community of writers? In a Boston
pub I asked John Updike, an accomplished writer who was then a
Bostonian, what he thought. Updike had his doubts; however,

ix

when we emerged from the pub and walked along Beacon Street, Updike was struck with the way Robert Lowell's poetry and prose had defined our perceptions of the surrounding symbolic sites of Boston: the Garden, the Common, and the Hill. After much reading and interviewing, I found traces of the literary community in the gathering of writers and the tributes they paid to one of their own, recently deceased poet Anne Sexton, at memorial ceremonies held at Boston University's Marsh Chapel, in the fall of 1974. The literary community registered its presence in the characteristic Boston mode: threnody.

This study is less concerned with the literary community, a magnetic force of support and influence, than it is with images and ideas of Boston and surrounding communities: emblems and visions of place created by Greater Boston's writers, writers who have invented and extended America's sense of the city upon a hill. Yet, trace elements of a literary-academic-cultural community were crucial to my conception and completion of this work.

I thank the following colleagues and friends for their help: Fuad Safwat, Dean of Graduate Studies and Research at the University of Massachusetts at Boston, who invited me to deliver a lecture on Boston, in the spring of 1986, as part of the University's Distinguished Lecture Series. Padraig O'Malley, editor and Irish cultural historian, for publishing a version of this talk, "Imagining Boston: The City as Image and Experience," in *New England Journal of Public Policy,* in 1986. The West End Branch of the Boston Public Library, for inviting me to deliver five lectures, on "Beacon Hill Authors," in the spring of 1986. John Tobin and the Northeast Modern Language Association, for inviting me to deliver the Keynote Address at NMLA's spring, 1987 meeting: "Boston: The City as Image and Idea." Neal Bruss, Director of Graduate Studies in English at UMB, for inviting me to speak on "Reimagining Boston," in the 1988 Graduate English Colloquium Series. Dan Wakefield, a self-determined Boston writer, who urged me to submit a book proposal, based upon my lecture and essays, to Beacon Press. Wendy Strothman, Director of Beacon Press, for accepting and shaping this proposal, and for her unfailing encouragement and guidance. Thomas N. Brown, distinguished historian, Joel Blair and Edwin Gittleman, fellow investigators of the city's typological emblems, for reading and responding, with telling suggestions, to portions of this work-in-progress. Duncan Nelson, sensitive reader, for his editorial eye. William Barker, master builder, for apt source suggestions. My students at UMB and Harvard Extension School for contributing to my understanding of Greater Boston writers. Finally, I thank my mentors and friends at the University of Massachusetts, Amherst who showed me the power of thought and language: Doris Abramson, Jules Chametzky, and Sidney Kaplan.

FOR most of my life, but for a few years in Cambridge, I have lived twenty to twenty-five miles west of Boston, in towns along the Old Post Road, a road built upon the original mail route between New York and Boston. From Marlborough, a factory town, then from Sudbury, a suburban town, I have long commuted to Cambridge and Boston. As a result, I have developed what might be called a visitor's imagination of the city. When I drive east on Route 2, from Concord to Cambridge, I ascend a high hill in Belmont where, coming down the other side, I am often struck with wonder at the sight of the metropolis spread out beyond: for a moment the city, including Cambridge, lies fair and shimmering, another Oz, its buildings caught in sunlight or shining by night, a city poised at the edge of the ocean, where America began. Though I know it is a "city of neighborhoods," a community long sensitive to territorial distinctions, my Boston is one place: its boundaries blur into unity, its many stories weave into one narrative.

Marlborough was another story. A tight little town of fifteen thousand (though it declared itself a city in 1890), my Marlborough was marked by labor strife and muffled class-ethnic tensions. (Even Marlborough's Catholic community was separated into three churches: Irish, Italian, and French. Catholics and Protestants kept to themselves. The ruling elite was aloof, country club centered.) Boston lay beyond the horizon to the east, a place which we visited rarely, for brief escape—usually to see the Red Sox or the Braves play baseball—from the closed system of Marlborough, my version of John O'Hara's Gibbsville. Like O'Hara, I too saw my hometown from an insecure, Irish-American, middle-class point-of-view.

In the late nineteenth century Marlborough's leaders—Yankees, Unitarians, Republicans, capitalists—failed to sustain a secularized version of the Puritan cultural tradition, failed to fuse piety with profit. Though they professed values of religion, education, and progress to the immigrant Irish and French Canadians employed in their shoe factories, when economic times got tough, manufacturers like S. H. Howe forced their workers to accept pay cuts and broke their unions.[2] After a strike in 1899, some two thousand workers, most of them Irish, were driven from the town, their places taken in the shoe shops by Italian immigrants.[3] As a boy, I encountered evidence of lingering hard feelings—a heritage of exploitation, strikes, lockouts and strikebreaking—among these groups, though no one told me why.

I was reared in Marlborough, at midcentury, by a Yankee uncle, who had left his family's farm to work in the shoe shops as a boy, and an Irish-American aunt; thus I was shaped, I now understand, by several strains of Greater Boston culture: Irish-American status anxiety, Yankee rigidity, and a failed version of the Boston Idea—work, community, service, spiritual quest—in a town of atrophied economic and cultural opportunities. In my day, either you worked in the declining shoe and box factories or you left town.

My Marlborough was embodied in two cultural symbols, both suggesting lost mission. As a boy I explored the teetering shell of the once-magnificent Williams Tavern, and wondered what to make of this diminished thing; its guests, including General Washington, were not only long gone but also quite forgotten by the city. That Post Road tavern, along with other historically resonant emblems, was razed to serve the commercial passions of "Marlboro," as it is now usually spelled. First a used-car lot, then a fast-food restaurant occupied the tavern site, overlooking Lake Williams. However, my Marlborough was defined not only by what it threw away but also by what it held onto. When I was a high school student, an extant historical artifact teased my imagination. Loitering on Main Street with other corner-boys, I often wondered about the John Brown Bell, which hung outside the American Legion Hall, on a Main Street building, above Bibbie's Pool Room. A local funeral director was named John Brown, but why, we wondered, would he have a bell? That bell, I later discovered, had been rung by the abolitionist militant, John Brown, at Harper's Ferry, to signal a slave uprising in 1859. Then it was stolen by Union soldiers of Company One, Thirteenth Massachusetts, Marlborough young men who fought Confederate forces at Harper's Ferry in 1861.[4] Those symbols of cultural dislocation, the razed tavern and the stolen bell, came to represent Marlborough for me when I left town. However, apart from four college years in Amherst, three military years in Savannah, Georgia and frequent stays in Ireland, I never went far from Greater Boston. Perhaps, I now see, I never wholly left, for I have sought in Boston the sense of the past, the presence of mission, the sustaining emblems of culture and the spirit of place I found missing in Marlborough.

Marlborough, I now understand, had a compensatory subtext to its story of failed mission. Those nineteenth-century secular Puritans—those Howes, Bigelows, and Morses, those suburban Yankees who were pledged to foster the Boston mission—did not entirely fail. They contributed, for example, portraits of the New England Fireside Poets—Bryant, Longfellow, Lowell, Whittier— to the high school. As a student in Marlborough High School in the early 1950s, I stared at those portraits, repelled by the poets' grim visages, but I was also stirred by curiosity to read some of their works. Those nineteenth-century civic capitalists also dedicated the Marlborough Public Library to "a higher plane of intellectual thought and moral culture," as a trustee wrote in 1878. The library's periodical reading room would serve to introduce Marlborough's youth to the town fathers' notion of culture: earnest, pious, uplifting. Boys would come into the reading room merely to glance at the "illustrated papers," wrote a trustee in 1884, but some might stay on and "become readers of a good class of literature."[5] As a boy, in the early 1950s, I too went into the Marlborough Public Library's periodical room to glance at my era's "illustrated papers"—*Life, Look, The Saturday Evening Post*—and stayed on, in a sense, to become, as its founder had hoped, a reader of "a good class of literature," some of it written by those Fireside Poets, who came to seem less grim and more thoughtful. The Puritan mission of cultural purpose, then, works in mysterious ways, even casting its shaping influence upon hesitant young men from bookless homes and muffled communities.

Marlborough has now gone its own, original way, and it has renewed its sense of mission. The city, which it now truly is, has demonstrated an amazing degree of economic resilience and cultural adaptability. In the 1980s a new north-south interstate highway, Route 495, which cut through Marlborough and intersected with the east-west Post Road, attracted high-tech/computer firms, an industry which inspired the "Massachusetts Miracle." The Marlborough of my youth—inward-turning, economically depressed, tense with invidious distinctions—became a modern boomtown—open, acquisitive, inventive. Tracy Kidder's *The Soul of the New Machine*, a study of the development of a new computer by a fledgling firm located on former farmland, became the emblematic book of the new Marlborough. Kidder caught the moment of transition from old to new Marlborough, indeed between two distinct eras of Greater Boston's cultural history, in one striking passage. In the early 1980s, Route 495 traversed

some of the ghost country of rural Massachusetts. Like Troy, this region contains evidence of successive sackings: in the pine and hardwood forests, which now comprise two-thirds of the state, many cellar holes and overgrown stone walls that farmers left behind when they went west; riverside textile mills, still the largest buildings in many little towns, but their windows broken now, their machinery crumbling to rust and their business gone to Asia and down south. However, on many of the roads that lead back behind the highway's scenery stand not woods and relics, but brand-new neighborhoods, apartment houses, and shopping centers. The roads around them fill up with cars before nine and after five. They are going to and from commercial buildings that wear on their doors and walls descriptions of a new enterprise. Digital Equipment, Data General—there on the edge of the woods, those names seemed like prophesies to me, before I realized that the new order had arrived already.[6]

By then I was living in Sudbury, a sprawling, former farming community which was fast becoming a bedroom suburb for those, like me, who commute to Boston for work and urban culture, or others who drive to Marlborough for a career in "high tech." Sudbury Town, a model "Puritan Village," once encompassed the territory which became Marlborough. Sudbury was settled in 1637 by English Congregationalists, who envisioned a cooperative, communal settlement, whose citizens shared the town's common land, "forever." However, from 1655 to 1657 a controversy broke out between town elders, dedicated to the founders' communal values, and younger settlers, who petitioned for private ownership of lands. In Sudbury, as in Boston, just as John Cotton had feared, economic self-interest was eroding communal accord. After much painful disputation at town meetings, the dissenters were allowed to separate and to found a new community: Marlborough.[7] New Canaan lay ever westward for these Puritan property developers. I see now that I have moved eastward—from Marlborough to Sudbury to Boston—to track their story, to understand their mission as it has been reflected in successive generations of Greater Boston's writers.

Sudbury's story was different from Marlborough's, for Sudbury has better preserved its historical emblems. Sudbury's First Parish Church—its graceful Meeting House, located in the town's center, was built in 1797—embodies much of Greater Boston's religious history. Founded in 1640, it remained Congregational for nearly two centuries; then, in 1839, it became, as it is today, Unitarian.[8] A few miles away stands the Wayside Inn, along the original Post Road, though traffic has been rerouted away from the inn. This inn, first built in the late seventeenth century, has long served as a stopover for travelers between New York and Boston. In the nineteenth century it was Howe's Red Horse Inn, until it fell into disrepair. Henry Wadsworth Longfellow's *Tales of a Wayside Inn*—written in nostalgia for a lost, idyllic America, during the Civil War—revived interest in the inn, which reopened as the Wayside Tavern and is now known as "Longfellow's Wayside Inn." In 1923 Henry Ford, also hankering for an idyllic version of the American village his autos were fast making obsolete, bought and refurbished the Inn. After a fire in 1955, the National Trust for Historic Preservation restored the inn. Today it is both an inn and a restaurant; it is a tourist attraction, along with a grist mill, a one-room schoolhouse, and a non-denominational chapel, built by Ford. So Sudbury, despite its many mini-malls, arrayed along the Old Post Road, and its proliferating and pricey housing market, sustains its covenant with Greater Boston culture through its preservation and use of valuable symbols which invoke time past in time present: the First Parish Church and the Wayside Inn.

Both Marlborough and Sudbury were products of the Boston Idea of community, culture, and spiritual quest. Both of these former Puritan villages lie well within Boston's extensive sphere of influence. The flower of Boston's art is deeply embedded in Boston's history; its root-system extends in all land directions. Marlborough, where I grew up, served as a model of cultural fragmentation, loss, and renewal; Sudbury, where my wife and I have reared our children, served as a model of cultural preservation and separation. When I travel to the city—as I do to teach, at the University of Massachusetts at Boston or at Harvard Extension School, to meet friends, or to seek my own renewal in Cambridge-Boston's cultural resources—I, as they say, "come from" Marlborough and Sudbury. Whatever route I travel into the city, whatever way I imagine Boston, it stands as a city upon a hill, still—cohesive, coherent, and continuous.

1

Approaching Boston

Every continent has its own great spirit of place. Every people is polarized in some particular locality, which is home, the homeland. Different places on the face of the earth have different vital effluence, different vibration, different chemical exhalation, different polarity with different stars: call it what you like. But the spirit of place is a great reality.

—D. H. LAWRENCE,
"The Spirit of Place,"
Studies in Classic American Literature

BOSTON holds a high, though precarious, place in the American mind. The first true city of the new world, built on a narrow peninsula, between ocean's edge and the wilderness, Boston has long stood as the embodiment of the American dream of freedom from Europe's dark past and the promise of American life, both to generations of newcomers from the old world and to pilgrims from every part of the new land. If New York has symbolized, in F. Scott Fitzgerald's words, "a fresh, green breast of the new world," the nation's heart, Boston came to represent its head, the national citadel of culture and moral purpose.[1]

The city has also embodied a darker side of the American char-

acter—a puritan streak which has punished dissenters, expelled
rebels from the community's narrowly defined, ideological covenant, and systematically excluded its racial and ethnic minorities.
From its founding in 1630, Boston has been variously seen as the
stern moral conscience of the nation, as an arena of American
political conflicts, and as a norm—not always celebrated—of propriety in manners, morality, and literature. Above all, Boston has
never ceased to *mean*, to embody symbolic resonance, to contain
a special spirit of place. Literature has been the primary mode in
which the idea of Boston has been articulated and re-created in
arresting metaphors.

Of course other American cities and regions have developed
compelling bodies of literature, from Walt Whitman's New York,
to Sinclair Lewis's midwestern Main Street, to Wallace Stegner's
true West. However, regionalism has been a diminishing force in
an increasingly homogenized America. Only the literature of the
South—centered in the popular mind in Margaret Mitchell's Atlanta, but more deeply rooted in Faulkner's Yoknapatawpha
County, Mississippi—and the literature of Greater Boston—centered in Hawthorne's Boston but radiating throughout New England—retain an enduring spirit of place in the American psychic
map. Both in Hawthorne and in Faulkner, and present also in those
whom they influenced, we discover a sense of the past as a living,
shaping presence; in the literature of both regions we encounter
a sense of original sin, but also a concern for moral mission, salvation
for the individual and the community, a vision of the future of the
Republic—all embedded within original prose narratives or poetic
formulations.

In "A Study in Denudation," George W. Pierson bemoaned the
decline of New England regionalism, yet even he concluded that
"as a region of the heart and mind, New England is still very much
alive."[2] Indeed the heart and the mind are the right places to look
for New England's identity or the Boston Idea. When C. Vann
Woodward set out in "The Search for Southern Identity," he decided that "their unique experience as Americans" gave Southern-
ers a distinctive region.[3] The same might be said of Greater

Bostonians, though their "experience" should be broadened to include literature, which codifies the experiences of heart and mind. The spiritual autobiography—with its formal variations: the diary, the journal, the jeremiad, the romance, the novel, the lyric poem, the dramatic monologue—became the characteristic regional mode, for it best reflects the Puritan and post-Puritan idea of life as an individual and collective quest for realization and salvation. As Augustine's *City of God* provided the topographical metaphor for the Boston Idea, so too does his *Confessions* provide a model for the regional articulation of spiritual quest. Life's journey (*peregrinatio vitae*) results in a spiritual crisis, a passage from an old to a new life, an acknowledgement of God's design. Even when they dispensed with a Christian framework, Boston writers have bent this form to their purposes for three centuries.

A strain in the American character has been shaped by the repudiation of place and time. Like Huck Finn, when times got tough we have lit out for the territories, seeking new lives on the frontier. Like Henry Ford, when the past haunted us we have declared that history is bunk. Yet, when Henry Ford decided to pay homage to idyllic, pastoral America, he was inspired by a writer, Henry Wadsworth Longfellow, and a New England village, Sudbury, thirty miles west of Boston. Longfellow's *Tales of a Wayside Inn* (1863) commemorated an eighteenth-century Post Road inn as the site of travelers' tales of adventure. The tales are framed by a nostalgic recollection of great days gone, "when men lived in a grander way / with ampler hospitality." Longfellow evoked "a region of repose," far from railway noise, where guests could rest and let their imaginations roam.[4] Inspired by similar dreams of a lost American pastoral simplicity, in 1923 Henry Ford restored the Wayside Inn and built a chapel and a grist mill nearby. Thus literature, profits from industry, and nostalgia combined to convert this New England village into a theme park. In Greater Boston, as in the American South, despite vast changes, literature links us with our past and reminds us of our place.

Boston: city of the bean and the cod, the Puritan and the Brahmin, the Yankee and the Celt, the Red Sox and the Celtics. Boston:

the City upon a Hill, the Athens or Sparta of America, the Hub of the Solar System. Boston: the next parish and the new frontier, where Europe and America meet. Boston: New England's capital city, commercial and cultural center. Boston: a city of myth and mutability. Boston: the battle ground and common ground for ethnic groups, races, and classes. Boston: the heart and mind of a New England network of imaginary cities—places persuasively envisioned and perpetually reimagined in poetry and prose.

Boston's unique literary heritage—from John Winthrop's articulation of Boston's promise as a "City upon a Hill" to Robert Lowell's denunciation of Boston's "savage servility"—defines the city. America's foremost city of words, Boston has, in turn, articulated the nation's sense of the past, mapped its symbolic landscape, and shaped its moral quest. Though lately mythologized as a city whose great days and great writers are long gone, Boston continually renews and reinvents itself in language—in compelling metaphors, powerful poems, and useful fictions. Boston is no closed book. Indeed, Boston remains an open diary, in which successive generations make entries; a book of common prayer, in which Greater Bostonians leave their marks and define Boston's place in the American myth.

THE City upon a Hill has been Boston's central, recurrent image, established at its founding and abiding today, positing an elevated, spiritual, fixed *place*. Other analogies amplify and modify. The designation of Boston as the American Athens or Sparta—Gilbert Stuart and Samuel Adams, representing Boston's art and politics during the Revolutionary era, debated this—was an effort to convert Winthrop's spatial and spiritual vision into cultural terms.[5] "Hub of the solar system"—a semi-facetious phrase formed by Oliver Wendell Holmes in 1858—is a hyperbolic trope that suggests American commercial and social energies which actually deserted Boston after the Civil War.[6] However, above all, it is the "City upon a Hill" metaphor which, though Boston has expanded and subdivided, reminds Bostonians of who they believed they were, an image which stands as a vision of what they might yet become. Adopted from Matthew 5:14—"Ye are the light of the world. A city that is set on a hill cannot be hid"—this figure illustrates Boston's commitment to communal cohesion and purpose. This image—at once literary, political, and spiritual, a trope which anticipates the city's achievements of the imagination—lies at the heart of the matter of Boston. It both inspires and haunts Boston as a vision of polity and purpose.

However, no single hill, indeed no single ideology, could adequately represent it. No other American city has so dramatically redefined its boundaries and rearranged its topography (with successive territorial appropriations, water diversions, and landfills) in shapes of evolving self-conceptions. The opening sentence of Walter Muir Whitehill's marvelous evocation, *Boston: A Topographical History,* catches the mutable spirit of the city: "Boston, which now appears to the casual visitor to be built upon a solid segment of the Massachusetts coast, was in the early seventeenth century a hilly peninsula, almost completely surrounded by water."[7] Thus the city has been a poem, regularly revised and amplified by its citizens: an urban *Leaves of Grass.* These citizens were long cramped into close surroundings, restrictive forms, by theocratic and commercial purposes, on a narrow peninsula—a near island barely linked to the mainland by a "neck," mud flats, and salt marshes.[8] As Boston expanded in territory, population, and self-conception, it has had more to battle over; at the same time, residents' sense of themselves as one people, as Bostonians—or as members of smaller communities which define themselves in relation to the evolving idea of Boston—has been steadily renewed by its writers: those who chart the topography, trace the genealogies, and keep the commemorative albums of Boston's tense family histories.

IN the late years of the twentieth century, Boston has gone far in redefining itself as a tolerant city, in reinterpreting its often divisive past. In the mid-1970s Boston was torn apart by racial, class, and ethnic conflicts surrounding the federal court-ordered integration of the Boston public schools. In 1985, however, Anthony Lukas published a book on this subject which offered a redemptive myth of place, reflected in his title, *Common Ground*.[9] The black, the Irish-American, and the Yankee families he chose for examination are presented, as Emerson might say, as representative men and women of Boston in a narrative of artfully arranged juxtapositions, a narrative which forms a pattern: a unity which transcends each group's special interests. Locked in conflict—the Boston Irish even divided against themselves—during those tense days of "forced busing," these groups, in Lukas's reconstruction, pursue similar goals, each group trying to protect its community values, to provide a better education for its children, and to defend its visions of Boston. Divided by ethnic and racial differences, picket lines, and Boston's tactical police during the school integration crisis, these families unite on Lukas's pages. *Common Ground* stands as a heartening parable of transcendence for Boston's painful recent history. Not for the first or last time, a book serves as an anodyne for Boston pains, provides a healing vision of cultural unity.

"Boston is in need of a new history. The old one—handed down from the 19th century—is more trouble than it is worth," concluded Boston historian Thomas N. Brown, after reading *Common Ground*.[10] The mounters of the 1986 Museum of Fine Arts exhibition, *The Bostonians: Painters of an Elegant Age, 1870–1930*, also believed that Boston needed a revised history of its art and artists.[11] The core of the exhibit focused upon the Boston school of painters: Edmund C. Tarbell, Frank Benson, William Paxton and others, artists who flattered Boston society with elegant portraits early in this century. These painters were aristocrats and antimodernists who omitted poverty and ethnicity from their stylish portrayals of Brahmin felicities: they limned slim women trying on hats or packing trunks for ocean voyages, dining, resting in bed, posing on North Shore porches or patios. However, the exhibit included many painters of greater range, artists whose identification with Boston was marginal, brief, or painful. Winslow Homer, for example, who did not live in Boston after he was twenty-three, was represented because he, in the words of Trevor Fairbrother, catalog editor, was "in tune with Boston, . . . his temperament was New England in character, and his social outlook was that of a New England gentleman."[12] Childe Hassam's properly included *Boston Common at Twilight* (1885–86) evokes a shimmering, placid, idealized Boston, but he *left* Boston in 1889 to further his career in New York; later Hassam contributed to the famous, modernist Armory Show of 1913 in New York, which the Boston school of his day mocked. Maurice Prendergast—an Irish-American who was born in St. John's, Newfoundland, a man who worked in Boston selling fabrics in a dry-goods store—may have been, as Fairbrother says, "the only Boston artist of his generation to take a truly important place in the new art of the twentieth century," but his works, along with his brother's great frames, were not exhibited at the MFA in his lifetime. "You can't get a picture into the Boston Museum except you [*sic*] antecedents date back to the Mayflower," said Prendergast.[13] He too was prominently displayed in the revisionist MFA show. The MFA justly determined that the covenant of Boston painters should be extended to the previously unsainted.

The last painting in the MFA show, John Whorf's *North End, Boston* (1936) is in jarring contrast to Boston school decorum. In an impressionistic, Hopper-like scene, Whorf portrayed a parked car and a jumble of fire escapes, building fronts, and signs—"Hotel," "Louis Levy"—in vivid colors and blurred shapes. *North End, Boston* depicts a realistic city of poverty and ethnic identity, a scene which the original Boston school chose to exclude from their gentlemanly art of invidious distinctions. Though Boston's art history was highly discriminatory—modernists, Jews, and Irish need not apply—the recent MFA show became an equal-opportunity celebrator of various local talents. The MFA exhibit reflected the *actual* range of achievements, styles, and visions in Boston's past. The *idea* of Boston painting, like the idea of Boston itself, has thus become more expansive, inclusive, and various. Boston's present residents—who reflect greater ethnic, racial, and cultural diversity—responded enthusiastically to the MFA exhibit, to this new history of themselves, just as they did to *Common Ground*. Boston seemed finally willing to accept and transcend its past of division and exclusion, to include all of those whose efforts and imaginations shaped its history. Boston presented America with a fresh image of itself—a revised sense of the past, a renewed promise for the future.

As Boston has reassessed its history of discrimination in racial and class relations, and broadened its notion of Boston artists, so too should the cast of Boston writers be reconsidered. Though often divisive, subversive, or satiric, these writers are also joined on common ground, for they renew the myths and meanings by which the city lives in the American mind. The Boston school of writers is wider than previous views of it in our literary histories. Boston's *place* in the American scheme and dream, its "different vibration" reflected in its literature, deserves renewed attention. Boston articulated an unattainable ideal of community and culture; Boston writers have preserved that vision for all Americans.

BOSTON was always more than a settlement upon a hilly, seaside peninsula. It was a city imagined into being. John Winthrop established the anticipatory mode in 1630, in "A Model of Christian Charity," a sermon he delivered aboard the *Arbella* before settlers arrived on the Shawmut peninsula, in the bay of what they called New England, a world away from old England. Winthrop's sermon defined the mix of idealism and anxiety which characterizes later conceptions of Boston. Anticipating and shaping the new world in his rhetoric, Winthrop tried to head off factional disputation by invoking the requirements of love and community as a Christian duty.

> We must delight in each other, make each others' conditions our own, rejoice together, mourn together, labor and suffer together: always having before our eyes our commission and community in the work, our community as members of the same body. . . . For we must consider that we shall be like a city upon a hill, the eyes of all people are upon us.[14]

Winthrop sought a new world to serve as a redemptive model for the old world.[15] Corrupt Londoners would fix their eyes in awe upon all that the colonists would build. Therefore Boston's residents, Winthrop insisted, must fulfill their covenant with God. If they remained united in high purpose, God would protect them and their posterity; if they fell apart and failed their mission, God would punish them and destroy their city.[16] The passage of Winthrop's settlers from England to America was prefigured by the Israelites' passage across the Red Sea; thus Boston became another Promised Land. Because he knew its *type* (its biblical model), Winthrop knew Boston, its landscape and its communal character, before he set foot on the narrow peninsula. He willed the new world's city upon a hill into being. To apply a line from Robert Frost, "the land was ours before we were the land's."[17] Boston existed as pure, exalted *idea,* derived from these dissenters' and separatists' faith in the promise of American life.

Four centuries later, Boston still applies Winthrop's words as a standard of measure. "The strength of his Puritan beliefs resonates across the centuries," noted an editorial in *The Boston Globe* on the four hundredth anniversary of Winthrop's birth. The editorial also went on to praise John F. Kennedy's "city on a hill" speech to the Massachusetts Legislature, just before his inauguration as president in 1961; Kennedy too had invoked Winthrop as a model and a guide, a man "who established a standard of intelligence and rectitude that is as relevant today as it was in 1630," concluded the *Globe*.[18] In life and literature, Boston's airs are thick with metaphors and models by which we may understand, judge, and reimagine this city. From the first, Boston claimed an exalted vision—the promise of spiritual fulfillment, individual and communal, in America.

THE New England mind derives from a tension between freedom and control. Implicit in the city-on-a-hill image are contradictory pulls toward liberty and coercion. Perry Miller, historian of New

England's intellectual history, held that a "ruthless individualism was indelibly stamped upon the tradition of New England."[19] Conscience was the free man's guide, a conscience institutionalized in Congregationalism. The principle of individual consent—each citizen must make his or her own covenant, or not—was at the center of the regional tradition, a principle well articulated by successive generations of Greater Boston's writers. On the other hand, Michael Zuckerman, historian of tyranny in New England towns, underscored the coercive side of the Puritan tradition, whose aim was "consensual communism," and whose social structure was "in a very real sense, a totalitarianism of true believers."[20] Both strains within the New England mind—the warring impulses between commitments to individual freedoms and community obligations— are evident in *The Scarlet Letter* and other Boston books. Boston: an emblematic city, where personal moral meaning and social purpose are at constant issue.

Boston has not lived up to Winthrop's great expectations. No earthly place could. The city has not become the inward-and-upward turning community he desired, a Puritan Zion; rather, it has spread, divided, and discovered its identity in diversity. Fittingly, Boston was actually a city of several hills, particularly what was called Trimountain, which encompassed Pemberton (later Cotton Hill), Beacon, and Mount Vernon. On the north end of the peninsula, Copp's Hill stood sentry; on the south end, Fort Hill marked land's end. For 150 years the colonists settled on the level ground of their narrow peninsula, but the hill at city center, later leveled into the squat and pricey Beacon Hill we now know, stood as their image of affirmation and ascent. Sentry Hill, the high central peak of Trimountain, was named from the 1634 order of the General Court that "there shalbe forthwith a beacon sett on the sentry hill att Boston, to give notice to the country of any danger."[21] Within fifteen years of the Bay colonists' arrival, the hill, the Puritan Acropolis—which, for most, was too steep to build upon—became Boston's mighty fortress. "For over fifty years Boston was a homogeneous Puritan community," wrote Whitehill, "in which the leaders of the Massachusetts Bay Company did what they had a mind to do."[22] Indeed "mind"—ideology: presumption and projection—was a central instrument of Boston's power, as became clear in the banishment of Anne Hutchinson for heresy seven years after Boston's settlement.

Bostonians quickly strained the territorial and ideological bounds of Winthrop's theocracy. Antinomian separatists warred with the Congregationalist establishment, shaping an enduring Boston dialectic. Dissenters lost that battle; they were banished or punished, suppressed by the coercive force of polity, but, by the mid-nineteenth century, those who advocated diversity had found their place in an enlarged and revised Boston. By then the original Congregational consensus had broken down and former fortresses of Calvinism, King's Chapel and Harvard, had fallen to Unitarianism, articulated by William Ellery Channing of the Federal Street Church.[23] Calvinists met this "new Arminianism" by founding Andover Theological Seminary and establishing the Park Street Church. Ralph Waldo Emerson repudiated "Channing Unitarianism" in 1832, when he resigned his pastorate in the Second Church of Boston. Anglicanism retained a presence in Christ Church and Trinity Church. Amazingly, even Catholicism took hold in Boston, serving newly arrived strangers in a strange land.[24] By then Nathaniel Hawthorne, in literary Boston's most resonant work, *The Scarlet Letter*, had dramatized the erosion of polity and the grip old ways have upon all residents. At the same time, Emerson, Boston's philosopher king, and Henry David Thoreau, his disciple, urged Greater Bostonians to release themselves from precedent and redeem their lost selves in Nature—woods, rivers, and ponds just outside Boston. If Boston is an idea, it is as well a divided mind, teeming with visions and revisions. If Boston is a place, it is as well a projection of images and values into other imaginary places: North, South, and West of Boston.

BOSTON began in high purpose and great expectations; it expanded beyond its natural geographic bounds and its original self-conceptions over three and a half centuries. However, after the arrival of the Irish immigrants in great number in the 1850s, and the Civil War, Boston lost its pivotal position in the culture and the economy of America; thereafter, a note of remorse for great days gone characterized many of Boston's remembrances of things past. In *The Bostonians* (1885), Henry James contrasted the times of noble causes before the war with his own era of postwar cranks and manipulators. In *The Rise of Silas Lapham* (1885), William Dean Howells dramatized conflict between a cultural aristocracy which had lost its will to rule and a willful, new-rich business class which lacked the capacity for culture. In *The Education of Henry Adams* (1907), Henry Adams described his miseducation, his preparation for first-family culture and power in a Boston which ignored his kind. In *The Last Puritan* (1937), George Santayana described a desiccated Boston ascendancy whose representative man declines to narcissism and courts death in World War I. In *The Late George Apley* (1937), John P. Marquand viewed Boston's ruling class with a satire so gentle that it is Apley's nostalgia for his own class's lost vitality that most engages us. In *Boston Adventure* (1944), Jean Stafford evoked a smothering world of perverse privilege among Boston's best, adventureless families. She wrote this novel while married to Robert Lowell, descendant of one of Boston's first families and relative of those family and city poets, James Russell Lowell and Amy Lowell. Robert Lowell registered his protest against Boston's gentility and conformity in a satiric prose meditation, "91 Revere Street," and in many other works, particularly *Life Studies* (1959) and *For the Union Dead* (1964). Elizabeth Hardwick was married to Lowell when she wrote her dismissive essay, "Boston: A Lost Ideal" (1959). Howells, Stafford, and Hardwick were outsiders who came to Boston with high expectations shaped by the cultural deprivations of the American West or South. Edwin O'Connor, from nearby Rhode Island, incorporated into his fiction the perspective of the Irish-American immigrant; his view, particularly in *The Last Hurrah* (1956), is also suffused with regret for fled glories. *Last* and *lost* are characteristic qualifying adjectives in Boston's literature. However, the works which embody this myth of decline and fall often also portray a saving grace in the city, a hint of hope for its future. They constitute a record of literary achievement which, paradoxically, revitalizes the city's imaginative contingency. From evocations of what once was, laments for what might have been, played off against what the city has so inescapably become, Boston renews its covenant with its betrayed, unrealized, or fading faiths. Boston, then, begins as a utopian vision and persists as a misplaced but recoverable ideal; either way, Boston remains an act of mind, a creation of the literary imagination.

For some critics, Boston abandoned the thrust of its original faith, faith both in its powers of articulation and in the guiding hand of God. Van Wyck Brooks, in *The Flowering of New England*, described his Boston in autumnal terms. "What has once been vital becomes provincial; and the sense that one belongs to a dying race dominates and poisons the creative mind."[25] In *The New England Conscience*, Austin Warren wrote, "in the twentieth century, Boston, 'the metropolis' of New England, looks backward, *preserving* the historic churches, houses, and patriotic monuments of an earlier time; or it looks inward and outward, seeking a faith to replace the faith of the Fathers."[26] In *After Strange Fruit*, P. Albert Duhamel argued that Boston, after World War II, went from repressive to permissive, from moral to amoral, from mannered to shocking.[27] In *The Problem of Boston*, Martin Green mourned the passing of a golden age of civility and culture.[28] In Green's reading, Boston, in the second half of the nineteenth century, "became progressively more malformed and dysfunctional, a caricature of the earlier ideal." By 1900 Boston was "ordinary." Green's lost ideal of Boston was a unified, coherent society, held together by a faith in its own perfectability, which produced a great culture, evidenced by its literature. Industrialization and immigration destroyed this polity, wrote Green. The veneration of gentlemanly values among the ascendancy dissipated the creativity of its citizens. After 1845— that is, after the beginning of Ireland's potato famine, which resulted in massive emigration to Boston—Boston sank, like Atlantis. By the Gilded Age, Green argued, immigrants—mainly the Irish, through their political machine—had "destroyed the Yankee culture" in Boston.[29]

This is a partial, distorted, and selective, though widely held vision of Boston as an American Rome, a city in long decline and fall from glory days. Perhaps Boston needs not so much a new history as a new look at its old history, particularly at many of the lively imaginings which were shaped into works of art while this Boston school of critics was holding funeral services for the city. Far from being depleted, Boston remains a city of immigrants, a port of entry for those from Europe, Africa and, most recently, Asia, those newcomers who seek to realize the American dream. As Whitehill put it, "the history of Boston is one of successive European migrations and of what those people did in their new home."[30] It still is, though new Bostonians do not only arrive from Europe. Though decline has been a pervasive myth among those critics who have shaped America's understanding of Boston, it is far from the whole story. Boston, for example, was *not* a unified culture, a place of polity, in the eyes of its writers during the days which F. O. Matthiessen called the *American Renaissance*.[31] Emerson became an outcast and a radical in the eyes of the Unitarian establishment after his 1838 Harvard Divinity School Address. Thoreau was thought a crank and a nag in Concord and Boston. Hawthorne repudiated old *and* new Boston. Margaret Fuller tested Boston, found it wanting, and left for New York. All four condemned Boston for its social and moral failures. That is, the city's best writers have long been dissenters from the narrow, censorious, smug, mercantile, and mannered idea of Boston. Their works testify not to communal affirmation but to the characteristically Bostonian, creative tensions between the one and the many. Of course much has changed since these writers' day, but Boston has lost neither its moral character nor its literary inventiveness. Writers continue to create a convincing sense of place, to renew the image of Boston, often in elegies and denunciations, the preferred local modes.

While Boston did lose its dominance in American literature—exactly, says Alfred Kazin, when William Dean Howells left Boston and his post as *Atlantic Monthly* editor, in 1881, to go to New York to write for *Harper's*—and Boston lost its economic centrality, the city became, in compensation, a more open, lively, and various culture, particularly in its arts and letters.[32] New voices shook the calcified world of Brahmin money and culture. Black, ethnic, and women writers described *their* Bostons, only blocks away but worlds removed from Brahmin Beacon Hill. Writers from the Boston ascendancy, particularly T. S. Eliot and Robert Lowell, reimagined Boston in the metaphorical landscape of literary modernism; other writers moved to Boston, from the American provinces and from abroad, to stake their claims upon its resources, to add to its holdings, to modify and extend its great tradition of literary achievement. As a result, Boston, covenant and concept, has been renewed from within and without. John Updike, for example, has honored Boston literary figures in luminous essays; he has reworked Hawthorne's *Scarlet Letter*, the central literary myth of Boston, into three of his own fictional designs.[33] Boston, then, remains malleable in the competent and creative hands of its writers. Boston renews itself in our imaginations through and beyond those who criticize or satirize it in essays, autobiographies, diaries, letters, novels, stories, and poems. The Boston tradition, with all of its history of exclusion and invidious distinctions, is based not only upon a site of past glories and sins; it is based as well upon the vision of an expansive and salvific city upon a hill.

Boston's errand into the wilderness is central to the American dream. (Both "errand" and "wilderness" begin as facts and become figures of speech, notes Perry Miller.)[34] Boston's ability to perpetuate its promise may depend upon its ability to recognize and renew its past, to remember the unrealized dreams recorded in its literature, to create from a new, more humane history of itself a renewed promise for America. Faulkner teaches us that the past is not over: in *Absalom, Absalom!*, Quentin Compson thinks *"maybe nothing ever happens once and is finished."*[35] As long as it remains vivid and viable in our minds, Boston's past persists, Boston's future is promising. The distinction of Boston's literature is that it is still happening. The *idea* of Boston—which includes the goal of a cohesive community, a sustained moral mission, and trials of faith on a symbolic landscape—has spread beyond the city's boundaries, even beyond that area of Boston's immediate influence, Greater Boston, to all parts of the Republic.

AFTER he discovered that the home of his youth, on Ashburton Place behind the State House, had been razed at the turn of the century, Henry James wrote a moving meditation on his lost Boston in *The American Scene*. On Charles Street, at the base of Beacon Hill, restless ghosts from Boston's past confronted him.

> Such was the condition of the Charles Street ghosts, it seemed to me—shades of a past that had once been so thick and warm and happy; they moved, dimly, through a turbid medium in which the signs of their old life looked soiled and sordid.[36]

Half a century later, after excavations for an underground garage had torn open the Boston Common, Robert Lowell wrote "For the Union Dead," a poem which mourned Boston's lost idealism, symbolized by Augustus Saint-Gaudens's relief which pays tribute to Colonel Robert Gould Shaw and the black soldiers of the Fifty-Fourth Massachusetts Regiment who died at Fort Wagner, South Carolina, in July 1863.

> Their monument sticks like a fishbone
> In the city's throat.
> Its colonel is as lean
> as a compass-needle.[37]

Though James and Lowell saw the Bostons of their adult years as lesser places than the Bostons they remembered, their literary images of noble, forgotten, or betrayed ghosts granted the city a renewed sense of itself and another chance to live up to its ideals. Boston absences resonate symbolic presences. Winthrop bravely projected Boston's future; James and Lowell were haunted by its lost past: either way, worlds of words showed Boston an alternate version of its present condition. Boston writers have long served as compass needles, showing the way, comparing the noble missions of dead Bostonians with their failed successors, measuring the city's falling-off, reviving Bostonians' best sense of who they are and where they should be going. In this study of Greater Boston's poems, stories, journals, and other prose forms, America may reencounter and renew its sense of the nation's first city, a place of fact tempered by imagination. No longer the lofty and righteous peak of moral and literary excellence it once proclaimed itself, Boston, now a more tolerant and various place, still stands as America's City upon a Hill.

2

Hawthorne's Boston and Other Imaginary Places

T HE VISION of Boston as an act of mind is articulated most
forcefully and self-consciously by Nathaniel Hawthorne. His
sense of a haunted, sin-ridden land in need of redemption was
questioned, amplified, and modified by his peers and neighbors in
and around Boston and Concord: Ralph Waldo Emerson, Henry
David Thoreau, Margaret Fuller, and others. Far to the west,
Hawthorne's neighbor in the Berkshire Hills, Herman Melville,
seized upon Hawthorne's "power of blackness" for inspiration while
writing *Moby-Dick;* decades later, a few miles away from Melville's
former farm, Edith Wharton's dark New England tales were also
inspired by Hawthorne. Thus the story of literary Boston—its sym-

bolic presence and its influence in space and time—properly begins with Hawthorne and extends through his circles of contemporaries and followers: other writers who, like Hawthorne, shaped our understanding of the New England mind, centered in Boston.

THE tale of Hester Prynne, Hawthorne insists in "The Custom-House," the preface to *The Scarlet Letter*, was transported in a bundle of papers from Boston to Salem by Jonathan Pue, an eighteenth-century Salem customs officer; abandoned at his death, they lay hidden until Hawthorne, a nineteenth-century Salem customs officer, discovered them, embellished them, and incorporated them into the form of a romance. The secret history of Boston, then, Hawthorne purports, is preserved, abandoned, rediscovered, and published by the combined talents, authentic and invented, of these Boston-Salem authors. In fact, this Boston is an imaginary place, located in the mind of Nathaniel Hawthorne. Indeed Hawthorne, it has been said, invented our conception of New England Puritanism. So complained Samuel Eliot Morison: "Hawthorne, more than any man, was responsible for the somber picture of early New England dear to popular illustrators, and already embalmed in tradition."[1]

In *The Scarlet Letter* Hawthorne presents the Boston of the 1640s as a tiny and tight settlement of single-minded ideologues, huddled together on a narrow peninsula. Two places defined the character of Puritan Boston's concerns with death and judgment, both secular and divine: the wooden prison, already weather-stained, its ironwork rusting in the harsh New England air, and the community's first burial ground. These stern images are qualified, in a dialectic of Boston imagery, by the rosebush, a "sweet moral blossom" in Hawthorne's symbolic landscape, which blooms beside the prison door. Either the product of "Nature," which was more capable of pity than the Puritans, or a magical growth "that had sprung up under the footsteps of the sainted Anne Hutchinson," who had been banished for heretical thinking in 1638, the rosebush represented the passion and compassion of his persecuted heroine,

Hester Prynne.[2] Through such images, *The Scarlet Letter*—written in the middle of the nineteenth century, but looking back to the first days of the Bay Colony, and still influential as a literary model throughout the twentieth century—serves as a powerful parable of Boston, place and character. Beyond local concerns, Hawthorne dramatized the American conflict between community cohesion and individual freedom. Hawthorne articulated metaphors by which Boston can be both understood and reimagined. Fittingly, his romance was set in Boston's center city, on the downslope of Beacon Hill; more than any other work, his fiction defines Boston's troubled heart of the matter.

The Scarlet Letter is a parable of the Puritan errand into the wilderness, the Boston idea of communal salvation which calcified into coercion. As the fanatical founders judged Hester—for her infidelity, which resulted in a child, Pearl, and for her refusal to reveal the name of her lover—so do we, seeing Puritan powers through Hester's pained and courageous perspective, judge them. Against their claims for Puritan polity, Hawthorne set Hester's desire for Emersonian independence. America's head, driven by mission and submission, wars with its heart, fired by passion and rebellion.

For a while Hester thought she and her secret lover, Rev. Arthur Dimmesdale, could break Puritan Boston's hold. "Doth the universe lie within the compass of yonder town, which only a little time ago was but a leaf-strewn desert, as lonely as this around us?" she asks him. They might find freedom deeper into the wilderness, she pleaded, or they could follow "the broad pathway of the sea," back to England. Timid Dimmesdale protested that he was powerless to leave, but Hester insisted, invoking an Emersonian injunction to self-realization as her justification: "Begin all anew!"[3] However, subsequent events—her lover's public confession and death, along with the complicity of Roger Chillingworth, her tortured husband, in that death—teach Hester that she *is* Boston, the place that made her. Long after Dimmesdale's death, Pearl, by then a rich heiress, asks her mother to join her in Europe. Though Hester did leave Boston for years, she returned to spend the rest of her life amid those who had named her with a scarlet letter and those whom, in turn, she redefined by her presence.

Hester belonged in Boston. She was the Puritan community's representative woman and Boston was her defining place. "There was a more real life for Hester Prynne, here, in New England, than in that unknown region where Pearl had found a home. Here had been her sin; here, her sorrow; and here was yet her penitence," comments the narrative voice.[4] Elsewhere, she would have no identity, no clear persona; finally, Hester accepts Boston as her fate. It only remained for Hester to shape Boston's character and future, through her example.

Though Hawthorne, like Hester, escaped from his home place, he remained for most of his life within a thirty-mile radius of Boston, with Salem, Concord, and West Roxbury at its periphery; one hundred miles west of Boston, Hawthorne found refuge in still another Massachusetts place, Lenox. In England he sought his "old home," but Hawthorne, like Hester, always returned to the original place which shaped him, Greater Boston, the place which, in turn, more powerfully than any other author, he defined.

In "The Custom-House," Hawthorne debated his ambivalent attitudes towards Salem. As a sense of sin held Hester in place— "Her sin, her ignominy, were the roots which she had struck into the soil"—a sense of sinful family heritage also held Hawthorne to his native ground.[5] Even after he left, Hawthorne defined himself in terms of his family history in Salem, as he suggested in an autobiographical sketch: "I was born in the town of Salem, Massachusetts, in a house built by my grandfather, who was a maritime personage."[6] Salem, that north-shore town which had fallen upon hard times, still gripped him with a "sensuous sympathy of dust for dust."[7] Hawthorne (who changed the spelling of the family name) was possessed by the moral fervor of his ancestors, particularly his great-great-great grandfather, William Hathorne, who persecuted Quakers, and William's son, John Hathorne, magistrate at the Salem witch trials of 1692.

Nathaniel Hawthorne altered the family name, but he took his ancestors' shame on himself and he wrote so that their curse might be removed.[8] Thus, both "The Custom-House" and *The Scarlet Letter* serve as his expiation. The sins of long-dead fathers from Salem, and mothers from Boston, are revealed and exorcised in parables. Puritan persecutions—adultery in Boston, witchcraft in Salem—are reimagined from the point of view of their victims and descendants. The original sin of moral righteousness has laid its curse upon the land. Salem is a particularly blighted example for Hawthorne, so it must be exposed and expelled.

Looking back to a time which foreshadowed his time, Hawthorne sought not only to delineate the Puritan mind but also to portray the national character. That is, Hawthorne accepted the original notion of an errand into the wilderness, but he rethought its implications. The builders of the Bay Colony were guided by missionary zeal and righteousness. They evolved the myth of the New Israel, the idea of America as a nation bound by a special covenant with God, but for Hawthorne their righteousness had become tyrannical. Yet, through Dimmesdale's final sermon and Hester's ministry to Boston women, Hawthorne suggested that the fate of America depends upon sustaining the founders' idealism, however compromised, though their original restrictive covenant must be expanded by a greater tolerance for human weakness. *All* of Boston's citizens must be covenanted. At the same time, Boston's citizens must *not* begin all anew; rather, following Hester's example, they must return, to redeem the old. Boston, despite its official repressiveness and the backsliding of some of its citizens, remained for Hawthorne the center of a worthy mission, the site of great moments and expectations.

Hawthorne imagined his ancestors' suspicion of him, "a writer of story-books! What kind of a business in life,—what mode of glorifying God, or being serviceable to mankind in his day and generation,—may that be?" These single-minded Hathornes could never understand their descendent, who treasured his artful ambivalence, but Nathaniel Hawthorne was determined to know them. His mission in *The Scarlet Letter*, then, was to explore and explain their world, through the story of Hester Prynne's persecution, so that he could be released from its thrall, so that its curse might lift from his land. Then Hawthorne could move on from this "worn-out soil" to more fertile landscapes of the imagination. He declared his separate peace with Salem and with the whole Puritan history of the region in *The Scarlet Letter*. "Human nature will not flourish, any more than a potato, if it be planted and replanted, for too long a series of generations, in the same worn-out soil."[9]

Hawthorne's separation from Salem was long, painful, and artistically productive. After graduation from Bowdoin in 1825, Hawthorne spent much of the next thirteen years as a dedicated Salem recluse who occasionally lapsed from isolation into travel or gregariousness. "The obscurest man of letters in America," by his own testimony, Hawthorne stayed within his own family—he lived with his mother and two sisters—slowly developing his art of fiction.[10] He seldom left the house, "except at twilight, or only to take the nearest way to the seashore,—the rocks and beaches in that vicinity being as fine as any in New England."[11]

Though Hawthorne was attached to Salem by long family lines (the early Hathornes were Puritan judges; the later Hathornes, including the author's father, were seamen; the Mannings were businessmen), he seldom spoke well of his home place, calling it "joyless," with "chill east winds" in its social airs as well as in its weather.[12] "It was only after his return to Salem," said his sister, Elizabeth, "and when he felt as if he could not get away from there and yet was conscious of being utterly unlike everyone else in the place, that he began to withdraw into himself."[13] She took out some twelve hundred volumes for him from the Salem Athenaeum.[14] In worlds of words, then, his lonely readings and his writings, Hawthorne became a psychic voyager, shipping out from Salem. On 25 October 1836 Hawthorne, as yet unknown, confirmed his mission and practiced his self-irony: "In this dismal chamber FAME was won. (Salem, Union Street.)"[15] By withdrawing to an imaginary world, Hawthorne prepared himself to seize the attentions of the real world, beyond Salem.

Hawthorne learned to see Salem slant in his night journeys. Across the North River, in the water's reflections, he perceived an image which inverted the town, which he converted into a romance. "The picture of the town perfect in the water,—towers of churches, houses, with here and there a light gleaming near the shore above, and more faintly gleaming under water,—all perfect, but somewhat more hazy and indistinct than the reality."[16] Literal, flawed Salem became insubstantial, perfectible; all was absorbed into a romantic image in young Hawthorne's grasping imagination. But he could not so easily dream away Salem's reality.

When he was preparing to leave Salem for Lenox in 1849, Hawthorne told his old Bowdoin friend, Horatio Bridge, "I detest this town."[17] He must have thought that he had made a clean break when he wrote *The Scarlet Letter*, but Salem would haunt him again in *The House of the Seven Gables*.

HAWTHORNE was far more intrigued by Boston. He saw Boston from quite different perspectives as he passed through the city or looked down upon it. Though "an anti-urbanist," like his Blithedale/Brook Farm pilgrims, Hawthorne was also drawn to views Boston offered to the voyeur.[18] On 22 June 1835 Hawthorne, then only thirty, visited an estate on Cotton Hill, which was then being leveled, its earth hauled away as landfill for the base of Beacon Hill. After the arrival of the railroad, most of Boston's Trimountain was reduced. Cotton Hill, its eastern peak, long the home of spacious houses and formal gardens, was the last to go.[19] When Hawthorne climbed the narrow path that led to the top, he stood on the highest point in this city upon a dwindling hill. Boston was spread before him, a symbolic landscape available for gloss.

> It gives an admirable view of the city, being almost as high as the steeples and the dome of the State house, and overlooking the whole mass of brick buildings and slated roofs, with glimpses of streets far below. It was really a pity to take it down. I noticed the stump of a very large elm, recently felled. No house in the city could have reared its roof so high as the roots of that tree, if indeed the church-spires did so.[20]

Hawthorne here had an eye for ironic juxtaposition—the tree stump elevated over the city's roofs: nature over civilization—and urban depletion. He would develop this topsy-turvy, backside, inside-out view of a diminished Boston in several works.

Hawthorne's most telling tale of Boston, "My Kinsman, Major Molineux," is a surreal night-journey version of his own wonder when visiting the city.[21] Set in prerevolutionary Boston, young Robin, son of a rural clergyman, seeks his kinsman, who will show the lad the ways of the world. Not satisfied with his placid, rural life, Robin lusts for Boston's city lights. He arrives by ferry, then walks into the city, "with as eager an eye as if he were entering London city, instead of the little metropolis of a New England colony." Robin loses his way; the city turns into a hostile maze in which he is enclosed. Finally Robin sees Molineux, who has been tarred and feathered, presumably for his royalist sympathies, sitting in a cart, mocked by citizens. Robin finds he cannot go home again.[22] Having renounced his innocence when he left his rural haven, Robin discovered more than he bargained for in Boston: there drama, mystery, and sin trap him and transform him into one of the tainted citizens of the new democracy.

In "The New Adam and Eve," Adam and Eve confront a city in which other people have disappeared, though urban structures remain intact; Boston again offers its institutional and cultural emblems for the puzzled contemplation of innocents abroad in its mysterious, circuitous streets. Adam and Eve recoil from Boston's "squareness and ugliness," from its "unrenewed decay" and class distinctions.[23] Finally they find refuge in Cambridge's Mount Auburn Cemetery. Only there, paradoxically, is the city blessed.

In "Sights from a Steeple," Hawthorne returns to the elevated, panoramic perspective mode of his notebook entry on Cotton Hill.[24] The narrator of this story seeks transcendence, his moral elevation over the world. However, this Paul Pry spends most of his time in the steeple contemplating the world he has just renounced. The country may be a more wholesome and natural place, but the city clearly provides a more interesting theater for the aloof, prying eye. Adam and Eve found sanctuary in a cemetery; the narrator of "Sights" found serenity in a steeple; however, Robin, on its populated ground, is trapped in Boston's dark streets.

Hawthorne was intrigued by Boston for the moral tests it offered. His Boston was an artificial creation which encouraged greed, lust, and power. It was a destructive element for post-Edenic innocents. At the same time, his narratives tell another story between the lines. Boston, for his camera-eye, was a challenge to the imagination, a place where humans, released from the safety and serenity of their rural homes, might heighten and intensify their responses, find and lose themselves.

HAWTHORNE was always sensitive to place, though typically ill at ease wherever he lived; his notebooks are rich with observations on Boston, particularly during 1839 and 1840 when he worked at the Boston Custom House and dutifully recorded many of his mundane business activities. Hawthorne also continued to search for the most informing and revealing perspectives for viewing Boston, suggesting that the truth of the city resided in some special combination of the perceiver and the object perceived.

In May 1850 Hawthorne found an observation point on Boston which yielded a telling epiphany of place: "I take an interest in all the nooks and crannies and every development of cities; so here I try to make a description of the view from the back of windows of a house in the centre of Boston, at which I glance in the intervals of writing." Hawthorne viewed the backs of houses facing Temple Place from his boardinghouse on West Winter Street. He was particularly drawn to the open spaces between dwellings, where birds gathered and trees flourished. Hawthorne was also charmed by the sight of grapevines, delighted that Madeira would be made "here in the heart of the city, in this little spot of fructifying earth, while the thunder of wheels rolls about it on every side."[25] Boston's intoxicated soul was located in its secret gardens.

When Hawthorne wrote *The Blithedale Romance* (1852), a satirical novel based upon his stay at Brook Farm, the utopian community in West Roxbury where he stayed for eight months between the spring of 1841 and the spring of 1842, he included this rear-window perspective on Boston. The Paul Pry narrator of *Blithedale*, Miles Coverdale, leaves the utopian community during a season of chill weather; back in Boston, staying in a boardinghouse, drinking his sherry-cobbler by the fire, Coverdale enjoys the backside view of spacious and fashionable residences, convinced that "realities keep in the rear, and put forward an advance-guard of show and humbug." For Coverdale, who discovers he can spy upon some of his fellow utopians, who are staying at a hotel across the back-yards from Coverdale's lodging, the city scene become a theatrical set; the opening and closing of window drapes mark scenes and acts.[26] At his rear window, Coverdale is the audience to the drama of private lives, which reveal Boston's dark secrets.

Hawthorne, like Coverdale, began his own stay at Brook Farm with high hopes. "I am transformed into a complete farmer," Hawthorne bragged to his fiancée, Sophia Peabody, in May 1841.[27] However, his resolve quickly faded, and his tone turned satiric when he learned that Brook Farm would not, as he had hoped, provide a proper setting to write and create a life with his wife. The work was painful, leaving his imagination drained. His ambivalence was embedded in the pages of *The Blithedale Romance*. There Coverdale too left Boston, thinking it all artifice, but, in the midst of his Blithedale labors, he came to miss the pleasures of urban civilities. "What, in the name of common-sense, had I to do with any better society than I had always lived in!"[28] Hawthorne insisted that Brook Farm was also a mere "theater," a realm of romance, at once "a day-dream, and yet a fact," located somewhere "between fiction and reality."[29] However, Hawthorne failed, as he had with Salem and Boston, to convert Brook Farm, confining and exacting in fact, into pure romance.

The Blithedale Romance climaxes in a grotesque drowning. The passionate feminist, Zenobia, based loosely upon Margaret Fuller, whose emotional and political intensities made Hawthorne recoil, yielded to the thrall of unrequited love for Hollingsworth, a stern reformer, so she drowned herself in the Charles River. Coverdale concludes that she drowned under the spell of an "Arcadian affectation." Curiously, too, Margaret Fuller would drown, her life eerily imitating Hawthorne's art, when the ship on which she was returning from Italy sank, though, unlike Zenobia, Fuller was no slave of ideology or passion.

Hawthorne took the description of Zenobia's death from his journal entry of 9 July 1843, a report on his participation in the search for a young woman who drowned herself in the Concord River. The girl of nineteen "was of a melancholic temperament, accustomed to solitary walks in the woods"; thus she was Hawthorne's alter ego. Along with Ellery Channing, Hawthorne joined the search for her body. When she was discovered by a probing pole, and hauled to the surface, Hawthorne was overcome. "I never saw or imagined a spectacle of such perfect horror."[30] The event, for Hawthorne, was a revelation: neither the Concord girl nor Zenobia could see the horrific results of her romantic gestures. Hawthorne's dream of pastoral felicity, like his failed dream of urban bliss, may be an Arcadian affectation, a romantic spell which blinded him to harsh realities.

Curiously, Hawthorne recorded the event of the drowned girl during his happiest years, while living in Concord; he later recalled it when he wrote his novel of disillusionment over the Arcadian experiment at Brook Farm. As the symbolic woods of Boston offered dangerous, passionate release to Hester Prynne, so did the serene woods and rivers of Concord and West Roxbury remind Hawthorne that there is a *memento mori* at the heart of nature, human and pastoral. Neither Boston nor the seemingly safe havens surrounding the city could provide a home for Nathaniel Hawthorne. Though an anti-Puritan revisionist, Hawthorne found his world resembled the moral landscape, the testing grounds, of his ancestors.

HAWTHORNE came closest to finding his true home, his spiritual and physical place, in Concord during the years (1842–1846) when he and his bride, Sophia Peabody, lived in the Emerson-Ripley house, which Hawthorne called "The Old Manse," the name it still bears. Concord then had settled from its fervor during the Revolutionary War into a placid, rural community, where two sluggish rivers, the Sudbury and the Assabet, form the slow-moving Concord River. In Concord farmers tended and sold their crops; under its elms, in brick and clapboard homes and in huts by Walden Pond, Concord writers prepared other nourishing goods for the Boston market.

In the Old Manse, to which the newlyweds came on their wedding night, Hawthorne was transported out of a commonplace world into another realm, a world of imaginative and sexual release. The new home of Sophia and Nathaniel Hawthorne had been arranged for and spruced up by devoted Transcendentalists. Emerson and Elizabeth Hoar, the fiancée of his late brother Charles, had suggested the site; Thoreau planted a garden for them and helped select their furniture; Sophia's sister, Elizabeth, hired a servant to cook and clean.[31] Hawthorne embraced his new life, as he noted only a month after his arrival. "We have been living in eternity, ever since we came to this old Manse."[32] Sophia became the Eve to his Adam during their self-elected solitude in this Eden, where he could pick apples and pears from trees he neither planted nor tended. "The man has reached a region of repose," wrote his son, Julian.[33]

For all that, the Manse challenged Hawthorne with its tradition of ministerial presences; for three generations, Emersons and Ripleys had written their sermons in the second-floor, northwest study, where Hawthorne would compose his "idle stories." Hawthorne found the study was "blackened with the smoke of unnumbered years, and made still blacker by the grim prints of Puritan ministers that hung around." Against these inhibitions and prohibitions, Hawthorne set his mental and physical energies. Hawthorne removed these "bad angels" and brightened the room with paint and paper. He replaced the stern Puritan visages with a print of a Raphael Madonna "and two pleasant pictures of the Lake of Como." A bronze vase, a gift from Margaret Fuller, held ferns and another held flowers, "always fresh."[34] Hawthorne thus transformed the

Manse's study from what would have been a proper setting for the composition of *The Scarlet Letter* into a bright and cheery space with touches of the aesthetic, the heretical, and the international to further detach himself from an oppressive sense of the Puritan past. In this "delightful little nook," Hawthorne took inspiration from the example of Emerson, who had also explored worlds elsewhere while inhabiting the Manse.

Born in Salem, Hawthorne came of age in Boston, realized his mission in West Roxbury, then entered a new life, with his new wife, in literary Concord, his occasional haven. Yet, even in Concord, a metaphor of the Emersonian vision of benign nature, Hawthorne encountered his heart of darkness, his Arcadian affectation.

RALPH WALDO EMERSON, Concord's first citizen, looked above and beyond Hawthornian emblems of darkness and sin. Emerson and Hawthorne lived in the same village—indeed, at different times in the same house—but each saw a different world. "The least change in our point of view gives the whole world a pictorial air," writes Emerson in *Nature*. Concord, like Boston, is made and remade in their informing imaginations.[35] For Hawthorne, America was a dark past which must be evoked and exorcised. For Emerson, "America is a poem in our eyes."[36] Emerson was another John Winthrop, another discoverer of America, another definer of its mission. But Emerson calls for a colony of scholars (poets, prophets), not, like Winthrop, a community of saints. Emerson's community is populated by individuals. "A nation of men will for the first time exist, because each believes himself inspired by the Divine Soul which also inspires all men."[37]

Born in Boston on 25 May 1803, Emerson was the son of Rev. William Emerson, pastor of the First Church of Boston, one of the founders of the Athenaeum and *The Monthly Anthology*. Thus Waldo, as he then liked to be called, was born one of Boston's elect, defined by a world of Unitarian-Federalist values. As a boy he was forbidden to play in the streets, lest he be assaulted by the

"rude boys" who came from Windmill Point, or get caught up in
the ritual battles between ruffians from South Boston and the West
End.[38] Educated at Boston Public Latin School and Harvard,
Waldo escaped Boston in long visits to Concord, particularly after
his father's death in 1811. At the house which his grandfather had
built, hard by the Revolution's rude bridge and the Concord River,
Waldo entered another world: fixed, coherent, continuous. If Boston meant a succession of temporary, rented homes during Ralph's
childhood, Concord meant family stability, rooted in history.

Emerson was a thirty-one-year-old widower in 1834, when he
and his mother came to live, as boarders, in the manse owned by
his step-grandfather, Rev. Ezra Ripley. After Rev. Ripley's death
in 1841, Waldo, who had resigned from his position as Unitarian
minister in the Second Church of Boston in 1832, paid tribute to
his step-grandfather, but at the same time he distanced himself
from his ancestor's Puritanism.

> Ezra Ripley was identified with the ideas and forms of the New
> England Church, which expired about the same time with him, so
> that he and his coevals seemed the rear guard of the great camp
> and army of Puritans, which, however in its last days declining into
> formalism, in the heyday of its strength had planted and liberated
> America.[39]

Two hundred years after Anne Hutchinson was excommunicated
from Boston's First Church, Emerson identified himself with this
persecuted, antinomian rebel, setting himself against his father's
condemnation of Hutchinson and countering his father's defense
of John Winthrop, who banished her.[40] Both Emerson and Hawthorne, then, tried to deflect their families' Puritan heritage, embedded in the house where they lived and wrote, so they might
form their own original relationships with the universe.

Emerson's philosophical and aesthetic values also drove him to
detach himself from any particular place, to generalize, so he would
never represent Concord in the rich detail of his disciple, Thoreau;
nor would Emerson bring to his home territory the vivid sense of

place as fate that characterizes Hawthorne's writing. Indeed, Emerson's journals have little to say about his year in the Ripley manse. There he occupied a life of the mind at some remove from his physical sphere. When, for example, he was asked to prepare a "Historical Discourse" for the town anniversary in 1835, Emerson wondered, "Why notice it?"[41] Yet Emerson did notice it and he did write the historical discourse, as requested, for the hills and trees of Concord gripped him, however much he tried to transcend their earthly attractions. His "Concord Hymn: Sung at the Completion of the Battle Monument, July 4, 1837," commemorates the famous historical moment—which, according to questionable legend, was witnessed by his grandfather, William Emerson, from the manse's study window—and places that event deep in nature imagery and Concord consciousness.

> On this green bank, by this soft stream,
> We set to-day a votive stone;
> That memory may their deed redeem,
> When, like our sires, our songs are gone.[42]

Nature (1836) was Emerson's first major publication, a work composed in the study occupied before him by Emerson and Ripley ministers and after him by Hawthorne, a romancer whose works Emerson never appreciated. In the same small room, Emerson and Hawthorne wrote works which spoke to different sides of the American character: Emerson's vision of light, optimism, and faith in the future contended with Hawthorne's pessimism, darkness, and obsession with the past. However, Emerson and Hawthorne, both inheritors of the Puritan tradition, looked to decipher the symbolic design beneath the surface of things in sedate Concord or commercial Boston.

In *Nature*, the philosophical basis for all of his subsequent works, Emerson appropriated the Concord landscape to his conscious design, utilizing its emblems for his thematic ends: nature and spirit are one, each separate person is joined in the universal. This essay served as a model for Thoreau, who became Concord's greatest land speculator, though his holdings were staked out in his mind. Thoreau must have been struck by the passage in which Emerson surveyed Concord's landholdings: "There is a property in the horizon which no man has but he whose eye can integrate all the parts, that is the poet. This is the best part of these men's farms, yet to this their warranty-deeds give no title." Emerson urged his readers to lift their eyes, to dissolve the getting-and-spending world around them, to become, like him, "a transparent eyeball, . . . part and parcel of God," not defined by land parcels.[43] In *Nature* Emerson revealed the deep and lasting effects of Concord. Fresh from its vernal woods, in the study overlooking the river, Emerson was inspired to urge his readers to look *through* the lovely fields of Concord, to a greater world within and beyond. Concord became Emerson's symbolic landscape for his spiritual quest—his mode of "enchantment and deliverance," in the words of Alfred Kazin.[44] However, Emerson's spiritual quest follows the model of Wordsworth's *Prelude* more than Augustine's *Confessions*. For Emerson, as for Wordsworth, Nature replaces God; man is reborn through imagination—with the artist as priest—rather than faith.

For all his commitment to transcendence, however, Emerson was not above a canny land deal. In his journal entry for 15 August 1835, he noted "I bought my house & two acres six rods of land of John T. Coolidge for 3500 dollars." In this house on the Cambridge Turnpike, the principle route between Concord and Boston, Emerson lived until his death in 1882. Emerson left his handsome home involuntarily only once, when fire drove the Emersons out. His journal entry for 24 July 1872 tersely notes, "House burned."[45] His neighbors, including Louisa May Alcott, helped rescue the Emerson family heirlooms and his precious books. Their home uninhabitable, the Emersons retreated to the family haven, the Old Manse, for a brief stay; then they left for Europe. When the Emersons returned, in May 1873, they were greeted at the Concord train station by a brass band playing "Home, Sweet Home," and a gathering of Concord citizens followed the open barouche which carried them home. A floral arch had been constructed over their front gate; rows of schoolchildren sang as Emerson and his wife discovered their house had been restored; even his books were returned to their proper places. Bronson Alcott presented Emerson with a leather-bound copy of his *Concord Days*, a fitting reminder that Concord was, indeed, Emerson's sweet home.[46] This fire and its aftermath serve as an apt Emersonian parable, confirming his optimism, his idealism, and his union with Concord's citizens.

Concord was a pastoral retreat for Emerson, an alternative world from Boston. For Emerson, and for many of his ideological disciples in Concord and at Brook Farm, the discussion of proper sites for the conduct of a good life was not new. Boston, for them, became what London had been for their Puritan ancestors: a center of commerce, decadent arts, and corruption, the Sodom from which to separate. As Winthrop and his colonists sought to convert the landscape they were to call Boston into a city upon a hill, repudiating London, so too would Emerson and other Corcordians seek to make their village into an exemplary and cautionary option to Boston.

When Emerson was a boy, Boston still possessed rural traits: he pastured his mother's cow near Beacon Street. However, after the railroads arrived in the 1830s, Boston grew crowded, urban.[47] In 1815, when Emerson was only twelve, he felt enclosed in Boston's center city, when his mother rented a house at the foot of Beacon Hill. Confined with bronchitis, Emerson described in verse his view of Boston from a basement window, to his brother Edward, who was away at Andover Academy. The juvenile verse reveals Emerson's lifelong reservations about Boston: it is crowded, confining, dirty.

> The Wide Unbounded Prospect Lies before Me
> Imprimis then, a dirty yard
> By boards and dirt and rubbish marr'd
> Pil'd up aloft a mountain steep
> Of broken Chairs and beams a heap
> But rising higher you explore
> In this fair prospect wonders more

Upon the right a wicket grate
The left appears a jail of State
Before the view all boundless spreads
And 5 tall Chimnies lift their lofty heads.[48]

Emerson's youthful vision of the heart of Boston bears a striking resemblance to the Boston of *The Scarlet Letter*, also circumscribed by a jail and a burial ground (the Old Granary Burying Ground); this Puritan tone persisted in public hangings, still held on Boston Common in Emerson's time. Young Waldo saw Boston as a mountain of dirt. Mounds of rubble served Emerson as a proper emblem of Boston, as heaps of dirt from the excavation for an underground garage would later serve as a fitting symbol of Boston for Robert Lowell. Emerson was looking at the result of the project (1810–16) to cut down the top of the hill, on which a beacon had so long stood, for real estate development.[49] That is, young Waldo contemplated evidence of the transformation of the errand into the wilderness from its original religious purpose to newly discovered commercial possibilities.

Yet Boston also offered Waldo opportunities for imaginative release. While he was a student at Latin School, assigned to write a theme a week, he had an epiphany of the immensity of the heavens above Boston Common, which may have developed into his image, in *Nature*, of the "transparent eyeball."[50] In December 1834, Emerson recalled this moment in his journal: "I do not cross the common without a wild poetic delight notwithstanding the prose of my demeanor."[51] This led to a passage in *Nature* in which Emerson discovered a redemptive element in Boston Common, an open and natural space in the midst of the city.

Crossing a bare common, in snow puddles, at twilight, under a clouded sky, without having in my thoughts any occurrence of special good fortune, I have enjoyed a perfect exhilaration. I am glad to the brink of fear. In the woods, too, a man casts off his years, as the snake his slough, and at what period soever of life is always a child. In the woods is perpetual youth.[52]

Boston Common, then, prefigured Concord as an alternative world representing youth, exhilaration, and openness to natural impulses, in contrast to the Boston which removed its beacons, leveled its hills, and confined its youth to dismal views.[53] The best that Boston could offer was an epiphany in which Emerson saw his place in the vast universe, and a setting where he could contemplate building his own world. That world would be better made in Concord.

Yet Concord was only twenty miles from Boston; traffic passed Emerson's home constantly, between the village and the city. Sometimes he was part of it, for both sides of the debate over the good life had to be kept alive in his mind. The Concord writers did not stray far; they returned to Boston frequently to enjoy its culture and to confirm their prejudices against it. Only Thoreau would attempt to cut off contact with the city. Emerson invited Thoreau to join him in dinners with important figures, like James Russell Lowell, but Thoreau declined: "I am engaged to Concord & my very private pursuits by 10,000 ties, & it would be suicide to cut them."[54]

Emerson maintained his ties to Boston culture. He was a central figure in various literary clubs: Town and Country, Atlantic and the Saturday Club, made famous in Oliver Wendell Holmes's *Autocrat of the Breakfast Table* (1860). If Concord was a place where the mind was elevated to higher considerations, Boston was the place where Emerson tried out his ideas in lecture form, as he noted in his journal, in 1839: "For the five last years I have read each winter a new course of lectures in Boston, and each was my creed & confession of faith."[55] Those deliberations resulted in ten lectures on "The Present Age," delivered at Boston's Masonic Temple, between December 1839 and February 1840, lectures in which Emerson, neither Whig nor Democrat, identified himself with the party of the future. Boston, then, held opportunities for cultural and political contact, particularly during the abolitionist years, for Emerson. Boston remained the site of ancient idealism of purpose, which, in "Boston Hymn," Emerson invoked in the midst of the Civil War, a poem he read in Boston's Music Hall on 1 January 1863: God's missionaries into the wilderness must struggle to "unbind the captive, / So, only ye are unbound."[56] Emerson, almost against his will, had to acknowledge that Boston was still America's city upon a hill. "I do not speak with any fondness, but the language of coldest history, when I say that Boston commands attention as the town which was appointed in the destiny of nations to lead the civilization of North America."[57]

However, when Emerson discovered moral compromise, which he saw in Daniel Webster's 1850 support of the Fugitive Slave Act, he blamed Boston for the silence of its leading citizens. "It is now as disgraceful to be a Bostonian as it was hitherto a credit."[58] He admitted that the city held attraction for men of genius, that only in the city could you find significant cultural institutions, so he granted that every man should live *near* the city.[59] However, Emerson, that occasional commuter, was convinced that "the dear old Devil kept his state in Boston."[60] Boston was his Vanity Fair, a place where men and women frittered away their lives on inessential matters. In one striking reflection, he dismissed the typical life cycle of Boston with the melancholy of Shakespeare's Jaques.

> Life in Boston: A play in two acts, Youth & Age. Toys, dancing school, *Sets*, parties, picture galleries, sleighrides, Nahant, Saratoga Springs, lectures, concerts, *sets* through them all, solitude & poetry, friendship, ennui, desolation, meanness, plausibility, old age, death.[61]

Though Hawthorne and Emerson saw the world through different eyes, they agreed that Boston was a drama of artifice. However, for Henry David Thoreau Boston was no play; rather, it was a penal colony, east of Eden.

IN August 1844, Emerson prepared to read his "Discourse on Emancipation" in the Concord Town Hall, but the selectmen would not allow the meeting-house bell to be rung. Characteristically, Thoreau defied their edict, came forward and rang the bell to summon the villagers.[62] Emerson, in his eulogy after Thoreau's death in 1862, said he "was a born protestant."[63] Thoreau repudiated not only Boston, but the Concord social establishment, defiantly ringing their bells of consciousness and conscience. As Emerson scorned Boston's commercialism for Concord's serenity, symbolized by his grand house and land holdings on the Cambridge Turnpike, Thoreau rejected Concord's houses and properties for occupancy of a defiantly humble hut at Walden Pond. "What does our Concord culture amount to?"[64] Little in Concord's community stirred his admiration. Walden, on the other hand, was his Wordsworthian landscape of poetic inspiration. "This is our lake country," said Thoreau.[65]

"Mr. Thoreau," wrote Emerson in his tribute, "dedicated his genius with such entire love to the fields, hills and waters of his native town, that he made them known and interesting to all reading Americans, and to people over the sea."[66] Concord, the Concord of natural facts and transcendent emblems, was Thoreau's world. Emerson called attention to Thoreau's touching idea that most of America's flora could be found in Concord. Why travel, when one could find the essential world in Concord's woods, fields, and streams? "The landscape lies fair within."[67] Thoreau walked to its rhythms and floated upon its currents, seeking his true self.

"I have travelled a good deal in Concord," wrote Thoreau at the beginning of *Walden,* "and every where, in shops, and offices, and fields, the inhabitants have appeared to me to be doing penance in a thousand remarkable ways."[68] More than anyone else—more than Emerson, the Sage of Concord; more than Alcott, author of *Concord Days*—Thoreau *is* Concord. Surveyor and psychic land-speculator, Thoreau laid claim to its streets, fields, woods, and rivers; he studied its various life-forms with passionate intensity. Ellery Channing tells us that "Concord, the phrase *local associations,* or the delightful word *home,* do not explain his absorbing love for a town with few picturesque attractions beside its river."[69] Hawthorne went beyond Concord to other nations and Emerson saw beyond Concord to wider worlds, but Thoreau knew the lay of its land with a tracker's knowing eye. Emerson, though older, yielded to the authority of Thoreau's knowledge of Concord's fair fields. "He knew every track in the snow or on the ground, and what creature had taken this path before him. One must submit abjectly to such a guide and the reward was great."[70] Concord was Thoreau's natural habitat; there he thrived and served as a cautionary figure on constant patrol on his home ground. "Concord is the oldest inland town in New England," wrote Thoreau, "perhaps in the States, and the walker is peculiarly favored here."[71] From Concord, Thoreau could travel to the ends of the earth or to the heart of the matter. At his death, Thoreau's final words were, "one world at a time."[72] Concord, with all of the vast implication he saw in this then tiny Massachusetts village, was the center of Thoreau's world.

Yet Thoreau's Concord had no defined boundaries; in Concord he could contemplate the universe, within and without. "At the heart of his Journal is Concord," writes William Howarth, "the place that he came to see as a microcosm, a whole earth living in organic harmony."[73] As Leo Marx notes, Thoreau occupied a "symbolic landscape," particularly in *Walden*.[74] His hut stood between Concord village and the outer reaches of the American wilderness. Like Hester Prynne before him, Thoreau lived outside the town, at water's edge, so he too was able to go farther out or deeper in, as his spiritual quest moved him.

In 1841, while others were moving from Concord and Boston to Brook Farm, Thoreau, seeking his proper place, moved to the Emerson house, into a tiny room next to Waldo and Lidian's huge bedroom.[75] In 1844 a fire set by Thoreau and Isaac Hecker accidentally burned three hundred acres of Concord's woods, making his fellow townsmen as suspicious of him as he was of them. Perhaps, as has been suggested, the fire was Thoreau's unconscious act of aggression against a hostile community.[76]

However, Thoreau soon found a way to celebrate Concord's woods and waters, imaginatively to reforest the village landscape, at the same time that he repudiated its citizenry and made a house of his own. During the year of Thoreau's fire, Emerson bought woodlots on the slope of Walden Pond, planning to build a cabin for himself.[77] But it was Thoreau who realized this dream by translating an Emersonian image into a Thoreauvian fact. On 4 July 1845, Thoreau moved into his hut at Walden Pond, an act of dissent against the Mexican War, the annexation of Texas, and a rejection of the commercial impulses of his fellow townsmen.[78] Even more, it was a move to discover the divinity within himself, in a proper setting.

Walden begins and ends with a repudiation of civilization, symbolized by Concord and Boston. Thoreau mocks those who waste their powers by getting and spending, but he adopts their commercial imagery. "I plan to build me a house which will surpass any on the main street in Concord in grandeur and luxury, as soon as it pleases me as much and will cost me no more than my present one."[79] (He spent $28.12½ cents in construction costs!) The body of *Walden* traces a quest which carries Thoreau farther than Concord, where his family lived; farther than Cambridge, where he had resisted Harvard's idea of education; or farther than Boston, where he had lived as a child, where he occasionally returned to reaffirm the sanctity of his alternative world in Concord. At Walden he found transcendence: a new life, a recovery of his lost life.

> When I was four years old, as I well remember, I was brought from Boston to this native town, through these very woods and this field, to the pond. It is one of the oldest scenes in my memory. And now to-night my flute has waked the echoes over that very water. . . . I have at length helped to clothe that fabulous landscape of my infant dreams, and one of the results of my presence and influence is seen in these bean leaves, corn blades, and potato vines.[80]

Art (the flute) reawakens memory of his transforming passage to a "fabulous landscape," which is made real by his farm labors. Concord, then—the town he measured, planted, surveyed, and interpreted—was a creation of Thoreau's imagination. At Walden Pond Thoreau reached inward, downward, to a hard place, where he was in touch with essentials; his was a quest to find the spirit within the body, the transcendent vision inside the ordinary place.

Throughout *Walden* Thoreau defines his mystic quest—"I long ago lost a hound, a bay horse, and a turtledove, and am still on their trail"—in counterpoint to civilization and its discontents in Greater Boston. Despite his attractions to foreign parts, he searched the landscape near at hand. "Walden wears best, and best preserves its purity." Within the boundaries of Concord, in the midst of his life, Thoreau found his true self, without a guide, in the woods; he *placed* himself at the pond, in whose reflections he saw his true self, the sky, and the universe which opened above and beyond. Walden was inviolable, despite intrusions by woodchoppers, Irishmen, and the railroad. The Maker "rounded this water with his hand, deepened and clarified it in his thought, and in his vision bequeathed it to Concord."[81]

After his successful spiritual quest to the center of Walden and himself, Thoreau held out the promise of transcendence to all, including deluded Bostonians and corrupt Concordians.

> There is not one of my readers who has yet lived a whole human life. These may be but the spring months in the life of the human race. If we have had the seven-years' itch, we have not seen the seventeen-year locust yet in Concord. . . . We know not where we are.[82]

Henry David Thoreau, who centered himself in Concord, place and idea, lived a whole human life, knew who he was, knew *where* he was.

HAWTHORNE liked Thoreau, though the naturalist puzzled the novelist. Hawthorne decided that Thoreau was best met in his natural environment, the open air—they would skate and boat together on the Concord River—and concluded that Thoreau might benefit from leaving Concord, "for, morally and intellectually, he does not seem to have found the guiding clew."[83] Thoreau seldom went far or long from Concord, but Hawthorne did, so this journal entry tells us more about Hawthorne's restless search than it does about Thoreau. If Thoreau possessed the guiding clew, knew his *place*, Hawthorne never found his true home.

For Hawthorne life in the Manse was a kind of Eden, but he could not find means to support his family in Concord. In 1845 the Hawthornes were forced to leave, when Samuel Ripley, son of Ezra Ripley, decided to take possession of the family home. However, Hawthorne preserved the myth of Concord as Eden in his preface to *Mosses from an Old Manse,* which was written just after his expulsion from the garden, during his return to the Salem rooms on Herbert Street, where he had spent so many years dreaming of literary success.[84] Hawthorne, it seems, could not free himself from Salem any more than Hester Prynne could detach herself from Boston.

In March 1846, Hawthorne was nominated by President Polk for the position of Surveyor of the Custom House of Salem. Hawthorne had hoped to be able to combine work with writing, but he soon found this difficult, just as he had found the combination of farming and writing impossible at Brook Farm. Apart from journals and letters, he wrote little for the three years he spent in the Salem Custom House. However, after his dismissal in 1849, he quickly wrote the story of Hester Prynne, which obliquely was his own story.

The success of *The Scarlet Letter* allowed Hawthorne to leave Salem at last, though Hawthorne would compose a final myth of his hometown. In the summer of 1850, Hawthorne moved his family to Lenox, in the Berkshires of western Massachusetts, where he wrote *The House of the Seven Gables*. This tale of long-buried crimes and sudden punishments in Salem contrasted with the beauties of Lenox. "It is a brilliant and generous landscape," wrote Henry James in his 1879 monograph on Hawthorne, "and thirty years ago a man of fancy, desiring to apply himself, might have found both inspiration and tranquility there. Hawthorne found so much of both that he wrote more during his two years of residence at Lenox than at any period of his career."[85]

Throughout the latter months of 1850, Hawthorne worked on

his manuscript near a window, through which he could see Monument Mountain, though his inner eye was on Salem. *The House
of the Seven Gables* is another act of exorcism, another effort to
set aside the haunting memories of Salem's past and his family's
history. Hawthorne contrived his tale as a parable, with a moral:
"the truth, namely, that the wrong-doing of one generation lives
into the successive ones."[86] From his pastoral retreat in Lenox,
Hawthorne portrayed a world of remembrance and guilt, but his
fiction neatly sets all to right.

Melville would see in Hawthorne "a touch of Puritanic gloom,"
a "great power of blackness" which "derives its force from its appeals to that Calvinistic sense of Innate Depravity and original
Sin."[87] Reading these words in the midst of composing *The House
of the Seven Gables*, Hawthorne may have recoiled from Melville's
shrewd analysis; the sunny conclusion of Hawthorne's novel may
be Hawthorne's forced effort to dispel the gloom that Melville
ascribed to his character.

The Salem house which stands at the center of *The House of the
Seven Gables* represents regional and family heritage. This blackened, rotting structure, the site of crimes, the repository of secrets,
symbolizes, like the scaffold in *The Scarlet Letter,* the blighted
promise of American life. As F. O. Matthiessen has said of Hawthorne, "unlike virtually all the other spokesmen for his day, he
could never feel that America was a new world."[88] The house is
also a mirror which reflects the faces of those who gaze upon it.
The gabled house is a site where forces of light and darkness,
optimism and pessimism, promise and defeat contend.

The wooden, peaked house on Pyncheon Street held a tale of
two families: the Maules, the original owners, and the Pyncheons,
the appropriators. The Maules place a curse on the Pyncheons and
their house which takes two centuries to dispel. "The very timbers
were oozy, as with the moisture of a heart. It was itself like a great
human heart, with a life of its own, and full of rich and somber
reminiscences."[89] The house, at once cold countenance and warm
heart, serves as a moral emblem; it reveals the costs incurred when
love is sacrificed for power and privilege. Yet at the end of the

novel the curse is magically lifted and the warring families are united. In his final fictional treatment of Salem, Hawthorne set out to reveal the sins of the fathers in the lives of their descendants, but he ended with a work which reflected what Sophia called "dear home-loveliness and satisfaction."[90] In Lenox, Hawthorne willed the belief, embodied in *The House of the Seven Gables*, that he could transcend his Salem history; he determined to dispel the power of blackness, to live a new life of light and promise.

THE small, red house which the Hawthornes occupied in Lenox seemed cramped to James's eye, but it presented a splendid vista of mountains, lake, and valley. Hawthorne grimly joked that their house resembled the Scarlet Letter.[91] In this tiny home, he adapted dark images of Boston into bright visions of the Berkshires.

As Hawthorne, the pessimist, engaged Emerson, the optimist, in indirect debate in Concord, so too did he meet a worthy philosophical opponent, Herman Melville, in the Berkshires. However, here Melville was the nay-sayer while Hawthorne was forcing his writings into strained optimism. Hawthorne's encounter with Herman Melville, each validating the other's vision, was determining in shaping a truly American literature, a literature which takes its life from American scenes and experiences, a literature which D. H. Lawrence said embodied the "spirit of place." Indeed Melville could not think about Hawthorne without invoking a New England place. "The orchard of the Old Manse," wrote Melville, "seems the visible type of the fine mind that has described it."[92]

Hawthorne met Melville on 5 August 1850. Both joined a climb of Monument Mountain, along with Evert Duyckinck, a New York publisher, Mr. and Mrs. James T. Fields, Oliver Wendell Holmes, those Boston literary worthies, and others. Hawthorne and Melville hit it off, though Hawthorne must have been surprised by the intensity of Melville's response, published two weeks later in Duyckinck's *Literary World*, a long review-essay, "Hawthorne and His Mosses."

Melville invented a persona, "a Virginian spending July in Vermont," for his appreciation of Hawthorne, to establish tone and distance. "A papered chamber in a fine old farm-house—a mile from any other dwelling, and dipped to the eaves in foliage— surrounded by mountains, old woods, and Indian ponds—this, surely, is the place to write of Hawthorne."[93] The meaning of place was central to the Melville–Hawthorne relationship during the period when they lived six miles apart in Western Massachusetts. Both men chose the Berkshires as a congenial retreat to recompose their lives and works. Both responded to the drama of the countryside: fields of grass that rippled like the ocean to Melville, violent storms which drove residents into inward isolation, mists and fogs which teased their imaginations.

In his rapturous essay, Melville detects in Hawthorne "a blackness, ten times black." Further, Melville's Hawthorne represents the true American spirit: adventurous, brave, able to face and name the worst. Beneath the surface of his works, placid and charming, lies a fierce, demonic mind. Behind the bucolic balm of a summer season in New England, Melville suggests a secret terror, a vision of evil which Hawthorne confirms. This is the "shock of recognition" which Melville felt in Hawthorne's art. For Melville, Hawthorne was an American Shakespeare, an embodiment of the genius of American place. "The smell of your beeches and hemlocks is upon him; your own broad prairies are in his soul; and if you travel away inland into his deep and noble nature, you will hear the far roar of his Niagara."[94]

Melville, projecting his own persona upon his new friend, wished to see Hawthorne as a possessed visionary, but Hawthorne's *A Wonder-Book for Girls and Boys* shows his determination to recompose himself into a benign tale-teller, to find a new Eden. In "Tanglewood Porch," the book's introductory chapter, Hawthorne appropriates the Lenox landscape to his idealizing imagination. On a warm, Indian-summer day, "a merry party of little folks, with a tall youth in the midst of them," gathers beneath the porch at Tanglewood.[95] Mist covers the ground, converting all into a shimmering, pastoral vision, an appropriate setting for magical tales.

To tell these tales to the assembled children—Primrose, Periwin-
kle, Sweet Fern, Buttercup and others—Hawthorne invented a
persona utterly different from Melville's tortured romancer. Hawthorne's narrator, young Eustace Bright, is all light and cheer.
While the merry group journeys into the Lenox countryside, Eustace serves as a reassuring guide who shapes local legends with
compassion and sentiment.

The volume of stories has charm and shows the delight with
which Hawthorne quickly composed, free from his characteristic
self-conscious and haunted voice. However, the cheery chatter of
Eustace is strained and cloying, suggesting the costs of such an act
of ventriloquism for Hawthorne. When Eustace tells the children
about other authors who live nearby, for example, Hawthorne re-
duces his own and Melville's literary efforts to the level of childish
amusements. "On the hither side of Pittsfield sits Herman Melville,
shaping out the gigantic conception of his 'White Whale,' while
the gigantic shape of Graylock looms upon him from his study-
window." Eustace speaks of Hawthorne with mock warnings, par-
odying Melville's assessment. "Our neighbor in the red house is a
harmless sort of person enough, for aught I know, as concerns the
rest of the world; but something whispers to me that he has a
terrible power over ourselves, extending to nothing short of annihilation." Primrose calls such talk "nonsense."[96] Indeed it is, for
Hawthorne's *Wonder-Book* has no "terrible power" of annihilation
over anyone. This whimsical book may, in fact, have been Hawthorne's way of denying Melville's attributed power of blackness.
Having confronted and exorcised his past in *The House of the Seven
Gables,* Hawthorne invoked a reassuring pastoral, a myth of idyllic
childhood, in *A Wonder-Book.* In western Massachusetts Hawthorne and Melville parried myth and countermyth, debating what
the world means, through symbol-laden literary encounters.

ON the hither side of Pittsfield sat Melville, extending his own
black powers in *Moby-Dick,* during a period when he was most

and the maimed Mattie are sentenced to a dreary half-life together, trapped in rural poverty and mutual recrimination. Like Melville's Marianna, Wharton's characters can only dream of escape from their rural prisons.

Despite its more temperate seasonal setting, *Summer* provides no possibility of release from confinement for local residents, though Wharton's stern vision is modified. Charity Royall, a romantic young girl who dreams of escape, is seduced, made pregnant, then abandoned by a smooth-talking architectural historian, visiting the village from the city. Charity is rescued by her guardian who marries her and takes her back to North Dormer. Looming over the village is the Mountain, where illiterate and incestuous mountain-folk show their scorn for civilization; there Charity was born. Beyond the village lurk seducers and deceivers. Charity comes to see that North Dormer is a sanctuary between predatory worlds.[110]

Written during the Great War, *Summer* embodied Edith Wharton's struggle with the dark forces which undermined civilization. In *Ethan Frome* and *Summer*, Edith Wharton found her Congo, wrote her *Heart of Darkness*, illustrated and confronted her "horror."[111] Echoes of *The Scarlet Letter* also resound in *Summer*. In both novels a lonely young woman finds forbidden love outside the boundaries of a stern community, with a man of higher social station. In both novels a romantic and rebellious young woman chooses to remain in her censorious community, to reconcile herself to her assigned place in life. After her own bitter divorce and disappointed love affair, after seeing the ravages of unleashed passions in the Great War, Edith Wharton found, as did the hero of her novel *The Age of Innocence* (1920), that "there was good in the old ways" of even the most restrictive social arrangements, even in a stark New England village.[112]

Boston was a peripheral place in Edith Wharton's map of imagination. The city is satirized in *The Age of Innocence* as a place where rigid social proprieties are still observed in the late nineteenth century, while New York was open to novelties, though Boston is also the site where the novel's illicit lovers declare themselves. Though New York and Newport composed the principle theater of Edith Wharton's fictional world, it was rural, inland New England that shaped her moral imagination. Drawing upon her own domestic anxieties, her observations and her readings, particularly in Hawthorne, she refuted the myths of pastoral beneficence which were celebrated in other local colorists' purple prose, and she countered the legend that she wrote about New England from the point of view of an outsider.[113]

OF course Edith Wharton *was* an outsider to Boston culture. Though Wharton did articulate myths of isolation in rural New England villages, we must return to Hawthorne's era, to the exemplary lives and writings of Lydia Maria Child, Harriet Beecher Stowe and the New England "local colorists," Elizabeth Peabody, Margaret Fuller, Julia Ward Howe, and Louisa May Alcott for a clearer sense of what Boston *meant* to gifted, though thwarted, women of Greater Boston.

Boston women have long been clear about the condition of women. If the informing parable of Anne Hutchinson did not make Boston women's frustrations sufficiently lucid, Abigail Adams's declaration of gender rights to John Adams, written just after the British occupation of Boston was lifted in 1776, did. In forming a "Code of Law" for the new Republic, Abigail Adams urged John to

> Remember the Ladies, and be more generous and favourable to them than your ancestors. Do not put such unlimited power into the hands of Husbands. Remember all Men would be tyrants if they could. If particular care and attention is not paid to the Ladies we are determined to foment a Rebellion, and will not hold ourselves bound by any Laws in which we have no voice, or Representation.[114]

In various literary forms, Greater Boston's representative women found it necessary to revive Anne Hutchinson's legend and to renew

Abigail Adams's reminder that Winthrop's ideal of "justice and mercy" should apply to all of its citizenry.

THOUGH she was short, plump, and plain, Lydia Maria Child towered over the Greater Boston of her day, particularly during the decades before the Civil War, when she fought with her writings and made other gestures of protest against slavery.[115] She was born Lydia Maria Francis in 1802, just outside Boston in Medford. The daughter of a shrewd businessman, she turned against middle-class privilege, became a teacher and used her domestic arts to extend privileges and rights to others. She embodied the Puritan zeal and moral authority of Boston's founders, shaping her prose to public purpose.

By age twenty-two she became a best-selling author in Boston, publishing a romantic novel, *Hobomok*. The story tells of a noble Indian, his white wife, who was an apparent widow, their baby and the Indian's noble sacrifice of his family to his wife's first husband, a white man who arrives to reclaim his lost wife.[116] Readers enjoyed the novel's romantic story, but racial tolerance was Child's real theme. Though generalized in setting, Child's *Hobomok* and *The Rebels*, which followed in 1825, began a tradition of New England "local color" literature, a genre which women would dominate, for it stressed, argues Josephine Donovan, "a counter world of their own, a rural realm that existed on the margins of patriarchal society, a world that nourished strong, free women."[117] Child's *First Settlers of New England* and *Souvenir of New England* confirmed this genre. However, it was more as a dedicated feminist and abolitionist than as an accomplished novelist that Child made her mark on her day. *The Frugal Housewife* (1830) was published two years after Lydia Maria Francis married David Lee Child, a lawyer and social activist. This work, a combined cookbook and household manual, was designed to empower intimidated housewives to take their lives into their own hands and minds. Frugality and practicality should be national ideals, argued Child, particularly in education. Her treatise on domestic economy was, then, a revolutionary document. "Some will think the evils of which I have been speaking are confined principally to the rich; but I am convinced they extend to all classes of people."[118]

Child and Margaret Fuller, who was eight years younger, developed their feminist principles and literary tastes in frequent discussions. Child provided a worthy example for Fuller. In a letter of 1827 Child wrote the seventeen-year-old Fuller on woman's independence, a woman's need to reach beyond passionate love and Ellery Channing's opinions of Bonaparte.[119] Both Child and Fuller were inspired to emulate Goethe, a model of intellectual and artistic attainment. Child joined Fuller's "Conversations," a circle of concerned women who met regularly in Boston. Both women combined political commitment with polemical skills in their writings.

It is as a passionate antislavery advocate that Child is best remembered, particularly for her 1833 composition, *Appeal in Favor of That Class of Americans Called Africans*, a document which not only dramatized the horrors of slavery for captive Africans but explored its demeaning effects upon slave owners.[120] As Fuller's feminism would point out the degrading effects of prejudice upon women *and* men, so too does Child's abolitionism show that slavery eroded *white* culture at the same time it inflicted evils upon blacks; furthermore, she argued, better-motivated free labor would result in greater profits for plantation owners. Thus political purpose, private morality, and profit combined, in her mind, to close the case against slavery.[121] In *The Scarlet Letter* Hawthorne persuades us to witness Puritanism from the eyes of its victim, a free woman; Child's writings evoke the informing perspective angles of other victims: slaves and housewives.

Her antislavery opinions caused a sensation in establishment Boston, where Child lost her reputation as a harmless and popular romancer. Thus her principles hurt her income—she had to leave *Miscellany*, a journal which she had been editing for fifteen years—and diminished her readership. However, Child was not intimidated by the crowd which smashed the window of William Ticknor's Old Corner Bookstore because the *Appeal* was on display. "I would not exchange the consciousness [of racial justice] for all Rothschild's wealth or Sir Walter [Scott]'s fame."[122]

Lydia Maria Child's influence was both immediate and lasting. Wendell Phillips, at age twenty-two, read her *Appeal* and committed himself to abolitionism. Her husband helped form the New England Anti-Slavery Society and she was the director of the Boston Ladies' Anti-Slavery Society. Charles Sumner was inspired by Child's passionate intensity and became her friend. Her correspondence with Sumner reveals her political commitment and her frustration at restrictions imposed upon her as a woman. After Sumner was beaten by Preston Brooks in the Senate and John Brown attacked proslavery settlers at Pottawatomie, Kansas, Child wrote to Sumner, "at times my old heart swells almost to bursting, in view of all these things; for it is the heart of a man imprisoned within a woman's destiny."[123]

After a stint as a journalist in New York, Child returned to the Boston area—living in West Newton, then in Wayland—where she became deeply engaged in the Abolitionist activities of the 1850s: denouncing The Fugitive Slave Law and Daniel Webster, hiding escaped slaves in her homes, writing propaganda. When Child offered to nurse John Brown, sentenced to death for the raid on Harper's Ferry (Brown rejected her offer), she combined her anti-slavery commitment with domestic feminism and spiritual values.

Child was always looking for ways to convert her beliefs into worthy, effective deeds. She edited *Incidents in the Life of a Slave Girl,* by "Linda Brent" (actually by Harriet A. Jacobs), a former slave, and she edited the *National Anti-Slavery Standard.* She mourned the death of Robert Gould Shaw and worked to raise money for a Shaw memorial on Boston Common. After the Civil War she compiled *Freedman's Book* (1865), an anthology of verse which included contributions from Whittier and Stowe as well as hymns and tales describing and praising black contributions; she then underwrote the book's publication by Boston's Ticknor and Company. Thus her career had both symmetry and consistency.

Her early *Frugal Housewife* was written as a support manual for gender "slaves" and her *Appeal* against racial slavery; late in a career which combined domesticity and literary success, she addressed the needs of the freed slave. Throughout her life she translated Boston's moral conscience into passionate and worthy words and deeds.

THOUGH Harriet Beecher Stowe lived most of her life well beyond the territorial pale of Greater Boston, she expressed the New England mind in her life and works. Daughter of Lyman Beecher, a Presbyterian minister who denounced liquor and Catholicism in Boston, she was born in Litchfield, Connecticut, in 1811. Her brother, Henry Ward Beecher, became a charismatic preacher and a fiery antislavery crusader. She was married in Cincinnati and later took up residence in Brunswick, Maine and Andover, Massachusetts to be near the schools at which her husband, Calvin Stowe, a minister and a theologian, taught. Finally, she settled again in Connecticut, in Hartford. However, her family's Puritan heritage and her husband's background—he grew up in Natick, just outside Boston—shaped her New England identity. Though little concerned with Boston as a symbol, Stowe helped define America's vision of the New England village.[124]

Stowe's major works illustrate the shift in the New England mind from the Calvinist insistence upon sin and predestination to evangelical Christianity's emphasis upon redemption. *Uncle Tom's Cabin* (1852) is a parable of Christian suffering and sacrifice, a call to redemption, as the extended prayer in the novel's "Concluding Remarks" indicates.[125]

Stowe's New England stories combine a vivid sense of local place and a revised version of Calvinist values. *The Minister's Wooing* (1859), set in Newport, Rhode Island, portrays a number of women who reject Calvinism while they retain a Christianity of compassion.[126] In *Oldtown Folks* (1869), a novel based in part upon her husband's childhood experiences in Natick, Stowe set out to define the New England character in a village parable. To understand New England is to understand America, reflects Horace Holyoke, her fictional version of Calvin Stowe:

> New England has been to these United States what the Dorian hive was to Greece. It has always been a capital country to emigrate from, and North, South, East, and West have been populated largely from New England, so that the seed-bed of New England was the seed-bed of this great American Republic, and of all that is likely to come of it.[127]

For Stowe, then, New England embodied America's moral mission. It remained for her, as it had for Hawthorne, to redefine the nature of that mission, to remove it from Puritanism's dark hand and to infuse it with evangelical Christianity's hope for the future. She showed this, as had Hawthorne, by rewriting the history of a New England town. Her Oldtown, Massachusetts is portrayed in "the ante-railroad times—the period when our own hard, rocky, sterile New England was half Hebrew theocracy, half-ultra-democratic republic of little villages," separated from Europe, yet "burning like live coals" with "individual life."[128] The novel's complex plot traces two orphaned children, Tina and Harry, who eventually receive a worthy education, mainly from other women, in this democratic, post-Puritan, preindustrial, model American village, an idyll. "An Arcadia," Josephine Donovan calls it, "where patriarchal tyrannies such as Calvinism were overcome, and where women were free to develop their potential and form strong friendships with one another."[129]

The New England local colorists—Stowe inspired Sarah Orne Jewett and Mary E. Wilkins Freeman—portrayed a world apart from Boston, the regional center of political and commercial power. In their works, Stowe, Freeman (*A New England Nun*), Jewett (*The Country of the Pointed Firs*), along with Elizabeth Stuart Phelps and Rose Terry Cooke became early American realists, anticipating Howells and James.[130] The New England village became their testing ground for democracy. The family was the telling social model and educational opportunity was their crucial concern. They described a world where women could discover rooms and develop views of their own. [131] Their fictional models served to remind New England of the price of Puritan polity; they also reminded the region to honor its long-held ideals by remembering the ladies.

THOUGH women were not accepted as members in the Boston Athenaeum, Lydia Maria Child was inspired by the example of Elizabeth Peabody to demand access. There Child, Peabody, and Fuller studied, absorbing all they could from Boston's cultural font, translating the learning and lessons they found into reformist literature in support of childhood education, abolitionism, and feminism.

With good reason Elizabeth Palmer Peabody has been called an "American Renaissance Woman."[132] For most of the century she sustained an impressive pitch of intellectual and moral energy in Greater Boston before she died in 1894, at age ninety, and was buried in Concord's Sleepy Hollow Cemetery, taking her place with other, better-known writers who shaped our understanding of Greater Boston. She was a teacher, an educational reformer, a member of Emerson's Transcendental Club, a publisher, a patron of the arts and struggling artists, a biographer, a polemical essayist, an antislavery crusader and a women's-rights advocate. A Boston woman for all ideological seasons.

Elizabeth Peabody came from a family of strong, influential women. She was taught in a school founded in Salem by her mother, who believed that educated women were necessary to redeem society. "The higher interests of society must be cared for by women," Elizabeth wrote in 1882. "That is, literature, art, and all the virtues and graces that make society progressive spiritually, morally, and intellectually."[133]

The Peabody sisters—Elizabeth, Mary, and Sophia—were representative women who, despite being relegated to a secondary station in Boston culture, "showed the way" for future feminists.[134] Mary married Horace Mann and devoted herself to educational reform, writing a series of stories—*The Flower People* (1838) was the first—stories which were designed to help children learn through closer contact with nature. Mary Mann also wrote *Christianity in the Kitchen: A Physiological Cookbook*, a work which combined recipes for physical and spiritual transformation.

Sophia was a painter, but she suffered so much from headaches that she became a shy recluse. When a Salem neighbor, young Nathaniel Hawthorne, visited the Peabody home in 1837—he was invited by Elizabeth, who admired the few stories he had published—Sophia was unable to come downstairs to meet him. However, after hearing from Elizabeth that the budding author resembled Byron, she made certain she was present when he called again and she seldom was separated from him for the rest of his life. Nathaniel and Sophia rescued each other from debility and obscurity in one of the few happy marriages in American literary history.

Elizabeth was given to "causes": both people—Hawthorne, Mann, Emerson—and social issues. At age sixteen she founded her own school in Lancaster. Then she became a devotee of William Ellery Channing, the embodiment of Boston Unitarianism, for she too held reason superior to revelation. Elizabeth expressed her tribute in *Reminiscences of the Rev. William Ellery Channing* (1880). She joined Amos Bronson Alcott in 1834 at his Temple School, a radical experiment in education which held the child to be divine, though she withdrew when she decided that Alcott was a manipulatory mortal. Her *Record of a School* is an enthusiastic, sometimes confusing account of her faith in the transforming powers of education. Every soul, she held, like every plant, "has a form, a beauty, a purpose of its own" and requires special nurturing.[135] She helped develop literary Boston when she arranged Hawthorne's Custom House position and when she underwrote the publication of the *Dial*.

In 1860 Elizabeth Peabody established the first kindergarten in America, on Beacon Hill. Here as elsewhere she attempted to translate ideas into action, to realize herself by releasing the potential in others, from Nathaniel Hawthorne and Margaret Fuller, whose careers she aided, to school children. Her bookshop on West Street became a center of intellectual activity—a "Babel of talkers" is how the ironic Hawthorne put it—for Boston.[136] Her account of the Brook Farm experiment was an enthusiastic endorsement. Cities were "absurd," she declared—"they originated not in love, but in war"—but the pastoral landscape of West Roxbury would encourage a "true life," full of health and culture. "The lowing of cattle is the natural bass to the melody of human voices."[137] Though she was mocked for her enthusiasms and her stylistic hyperbole (she would be satirized by Henry James in *The Bostonians*), Elizabeth Palmer Peabody, it should be said, reflected the whole moral history of Boston in her exemplary life and works.

WHEN Elizabeth Peabody left Alcott's Temple School, Margaret Fuller took her place, though she too left him after a few months, when Alcott could not pay her. Fuller, like Peabody, was also a devotee of the aging Channing and took his reformist optimism to heart. "I accept the Universe," said Fuller, an affirmation of faith.[138] All that remained was for Boston, the Hub of the Universe, to accept Margaret Fuller.

She was born in Cambridgeport, in 1810, the daughter of domineering Timothy Fuller, who controlled her education. She wrote approvingly, in the third person, of her special status in Boston-Cambridge: "With men and women her relations were noble; affectionate without passion, intellectual without coldness. The world was free to her, and she lived freely in it."[139] By her midteens she had defined her goal: "a life of letters."[140] By then her father had decided that he would rather she became a proper young lady. Though no women and few men had yet led a life of letters in America, she never wavered. Boston inspired in Margaret Fuller great expectations, but Boston also limited her options.

For Margaret Fuller a life of letters had to be centered in Boston or Cambridge. Translator of *Eckerman's Conversations,* she needed high talk to sustain the life of the mind. Visiting Concord to "kindle her torch," she found particular inspiration in Emerson's words and presence.[141] Fuller and Emerson were opposite natures, fire and ice, as Julia Ward Howe noted. "While Mr. Emerson never appeared to be modified by any change of circumstance, never melted nor took fire, but was always and everywhere himself, the soul of Margaret was subject to a glowing passion which raised the temperature of the social atmosphere around her."[142] They embodied the emotional extremes of the Transcendental movement. Though this opposition was the source of personal tensions, particularly for Fuller, it resulted in important works which, among other things, helped give Concord its lasting literary identity.

Fuller was one of the few women included in Emerson's group of Transcendentalists and she became the editor of the *Dial* (1840–42). The "Prospectus" for the *Dial* declared this would be "A Magazine for Literature, Philosophy, and Religion, . . . a medium for the freest expression of thought on the questions which interest earnest minds in every community."[143] The introductory announcement, written by Fuller, then rewritten by Emerson, placed the *Dial* in an imaginary garden, where time's shadow measures "what state of growth is now arrived and arriving."[144] The journal lasted only four years, showing strain and confusion of purpose from the beginning. It was, Emerson recalled forty years later,

> rather a work of friendship among the narrow circle of students than the organ of any party. Perhaps its writers were its chief readers; yet it contained some noble papers by Margaret Fuller, and some numbers had an instant exhausting sale, because of papers by Theodore Parker.[145]

Under Fuller's editorship, important essays by Thoreau, whose talents she cultivated, Emerson, Alcott, Parker, and Peabody were published. The *Dial* gave the Transcendentalists national attention, though some of it was mocking, and provided Fuller with an opportunity to develop her powers as an editor and writer.

In the *Dial* she published "The Great Lawsuit: Man vs. Men. Woman vs. Women" in 1843, an essay which insisted upon equality and woman's independence. In this essay Fuller also utilizes pastoral imagery, implicitly repudiating Boston and validating Concord. "The tree cannot come to flower till its root be freed from the cankering worm, and its whole growth open to air and light."[146] The "cankering worm" is the state of inequity between the sexes. More specifically, it is the false assumption of justified inequities which Fuller attacks. Men must realize their unity with women. "Male and female represent the two sides of the great radical dualism. But, in fact, they are perpetually passing into one another. Fluid hardens to solid, solid rushes to fluid. There is no wholly masculine man, no purely feminine woman."[147] The *Dial* gave Fuller editorial power and literary prestige, though little money, so she had to move on.

Elizabeth Peabody's book shop on West Street also served as a theater and platform for Fuller's arresting voice and ideas. A women's group was founded in 1839, led by Fuller and including the Peabody sisters and others; here, women who had been denied Harvard and the pulpit could talk freely about the condition of women in America. Men were trained to use their educations, while women were educated "for purposes of display," said Fuller.[148] Her goal in these "Conversations," which lasted four years, was to change all that, to free women from their social constraints, to give them voice, to grant them power. If such a plan failed in Boston, she said, it could not succeed anywhere.[149]

Her plan did not succeed in Boston, either for women in general or Fuller in particular, though she went far in showing the way women should travel in their quest for self-realization.

From a very early age I have felt that I was not born to the common womanly lot. I know I should never find a being who could keep the key to my character; that there would be none on whom I could always lean, from whom I could always learn; that I should be a pilgrim and a sojourner on earth, and that the birds and foxes would be surer of a place to lay the head than I.[150]

Emerson recoiled from Fuller's passionate intensity and Boston restricted her range of thought and action. So in 1844 she left for New York, to write for Horace Greeley's *Tribune*. In 1845 Greeley published Fuller's *Women in the Nineteenth Century*, an expansion of her *Dial* essay and an elaboration of the theme that both women and men were trapped by socially determined sexual stereotypes.

Literary Boston never quite knew what to make of Margaret Fuller. When, after her death, Emerson, J. C. Clarke, and W. H. Channing edited her *Memoirs* (1852), they made her over into a model of self-consuming passion, another Zenobia. Yet, as Perry Miller notes, "they could comprehend that in Margaret they had an authentic American version of a romantic heroine."[151] In her conversations and her example, she redefined women's image in America. As Paula Blanchard puts it, "this much she had achieved in Boston."[152]

In a review of Emerson's *Essays: Second Series*, Fuller *placed* Emerson, and by implication herself, within the New England mind, in a paragraph which at once acknowledges and illustrates her regional identity and her sometimes ponderous but always powerful prose.

> If New England may be regarded as a chief mental focus to the New World,—and many symptoms seem to give her this place,—as to other centres belong the characteristics of heart and lungs to the body politic; if we may believe, as we do believe, that what is to be acted out, in the country at large, is, most frequently, first indicated there, as all the phenomena of the nervous system are in the fantasies of the brain, we may hail as an auspicious omen the influence Mr. Emerson has there obtained, which is deep-rooted, increasing, and, over the younger portion of the community, far greater than that of any other person.[153]

Margaret Fuller was of course speaking for herself, admitting Emerson's influence upon her; however, her training in Boston and Concord gave her sufficient voice and courage to strike out on her own, in literary New York and in revolutionary Italy. Her career rearticulated the Boston tradition defined by Anne Hutchinson and Hester Prynne—other women of passionate thought and action who insisted upon their own original relationships with Boston values.[154]

WHEN Julia Ward Howe recalled her arrival in Boston after her European honeymoon with Samuel Gridley Howe, head of the Perkins Institute for the Blind, the first scene which came to her mind was Margaret Fuller "holding her friends in her well-remembered conversations."[155] On the centenary of Fuller's birth, Howe wrote a poem of tribute in which she glossed Fuller's drowning not as an Arcadian affectation but as a divine strategy for immortality.

> So He who laid our Pearl
> Deep in the sapphire sea
> Keeps her rare essence in the cup
> Of immortality.[156]

In a biography Howe defined her debt to Fuller's exemplary life. "As a woman who believed in women, her word is still an evangel of hope and inspiration to her sex."[157] As a feminist intellectual who fought for social justice in a variety of causes, Margaret Fuller showed Julia Ward Howe the Boston Way.

Howe, who came from New York, was open too to other Boston influences. Her husband was a devoted reformer, though women's rights was not one of his causes, so their marriage grew strained. Emerson of course shaped the Boston mind, including hers, in the era of transcendentalism and abolitionism. Dr. Channing's sermon on a "divine love" which included *all* men, white and black—and which came to imply for Howe all *women* as well—was a revelation for this young bride. "The doctrine was new to me, but I received it gladly."[158] Indeed she became, in residence and ideology, a true Bostonian.

At first Howe felt excluded by Boston's chilling social system. One day, passing Boston's Charitable Eye and Ear Infirmary, she said "Oh, I did not know there was a charitable eye or ear in Boston!"[159] However, her increasing involvement in Boston's causes of the era, abolitionism and feminism, won her acceptance, particularly among political activists like Garrison, Phillips, and Sumner. After her composition of *The Battle Hymn of the Republic* (published in the *Atlantic Monthly* in February 1862), she spoke *for* Boston's moral values. Like Harriet Beecher Stowe, Julia Ward Howe appropriated the moral righteousness of New England Puritanism and modified it with feminist compassion for society's victims. As Edmund Wilson has noted, her poem, set to the tune of "John Brown's Body," was a parable of Puritan New England's idealism. Christ may have "died to make men holy," but it was up to "us"—Boston's young men, like Colonel Shaw and his troops—to "die to make men free." Wilson parodied the *Battle Hymn* in a flip paraphrase: "now come on, New England boys, get in step with the marching God! If you succeed in crushing the serpent [the Confederacy], God will reward you with 'grace.' "[160]

Following the Civil War Howe devoted herself to lecturing and organizing for feminist causes, particularly to the founding of the New England Women's Club and the New England Suffrage Association (both in 1868). While women should maintain a proper home, they must look beyond the boundaries of home, "with a tolerance of things foreign to their individual experience."[161]

After her husband's death in 1876, Howe's home at 241 Beacon Street became a literary and cultural center of Boston. There she greeted Oscar Wilde during his Boston visit in 1882. There she argued with Thomas Wentworth Higginson over the propriety of her granting Wilde a charitable eye and ear.[162] In the words of one devotee, her home was "the meeting-place of the choicest spirits, literary, musical, artistic and scientific."[163] Inspired by Boston's moral idealism and literary models, Julia Ward Howe became Boston's cultural defender and moral guide, reminding Bostonians that they were obliged to ascend the heights and live by the lights of their moral topography.

And let our Boston, from her heights,
Match with her hills the virtues three,
And crown them, as with beacons bright,
With Faith and Hope and Charity. [164]

As it was for Henry Adams, life in Greater Boston for Louisa May Alcott was a double thing. She too was divided between Boston and a nearby, idyllic village: not the Adamses' Quincy but the Alcotts' Concord. However, this child of the Transcendentalist movement did not, like Emerson and Thoreau, reject Boston for its crass commercialism in favor of Concord's pastoral felicities. Though Alcott drew upon her childhood for *Little Women* (1869) and other works which solidify the myth of Concord as a place of family love and youthful innocence, she wrote these works *in* Boston. Meg, Jo, Beth, and Amy March learn the importance of domesticity, work, and love in Concord, but they prepare themselves for lives beyond the village. Alcott associated Concord with women's labor and a repression of the spirit, while Boston—"my beloved old town whose very dirt is interesting to my eyes"—represented energy, culture, and opportunity. [165]

Her father, Amos Bronson Alcott, was a utopian visionary, driven by a Transcendentalist modification of the Puritan impulse to establish a city upon a hill. When he arrived in Boston, a poor pedlar from Connecticut, in 1828, at age twenty-eight, he discovered his mecca. "It is the city that is set on high. 'It cannot be hid.' It is Boston." [166] His Temple School in Boston, a private academy located at the Masonic Temple on Beacon Street, was based upon the Romantic assumption of childhood innocence and the power of imagination to shape the world. [167] Love was his answer to the world's problems. His utopian community at Fruitlands (1844) was designed to be a new Eden for his "Consociate Family." Vegetarianism, labor, and love would bring about a "Concordium." However, Bronson Alcott's ideas frequently went bust, for he was both strikingly impractical and committed to control as much as he was to love; none of his visions accounted for the costs exacted upon his own family of long-suffering, overworked women. His devoted daughter, Louisa, satirized the Concord dreamers and mocked the Fruitlands experiment, suggesting "Apple Slump" would be a better name for the colony in "Transcendental Wild Oats."[168] Louisa May Alcott recoiled from Concord, a town which, in her view, was more interested in tourists than in feminists. She preferred Boston to Concord, the gritty actual to the lost ideal.

Alcott's Boston meant labor—she was a domestic servant in 1850—but it also meant culture—the theater, lectures, and sermons—and personal drama: even the Boston Fire of 1872 thrilled her. Above all, Boston meant opportunity, a place where a woman could make a career despite discouragements. In 1854 she brought her essay, "How I Went Out to Service" to James T. Fields, esteemed Boston publisher, but Fields told her she could not write.[169] By the end of that year, however, Alcott published *Flower Fables,* dedicated to Emerson's daughter, a collection of fairy tales based upon stories which had been told to Louisa by Thoreau.[170] Thus Alcott learned how to exploit her Concord experience in order to achieve success in the Boston publishing world. *Little Women, Little Men* and other works further idealized Concord, but Alcott used the profits from these writings to create an independent life for herself—although she continued to support her feckless father and other family members—in Boston. There she was "uplifted," first by listening to others lecture, finally by creating her own world of words. "Boston is nicer & noisier than ever," she wrote in 1856, when she was nearly twenty-four and on her own in Boston. She went for walks "to see pictures, get books, or eat goodies," then returned to her boardinghouse, to "my quiet garret to write & dream in."[171] Boston became the place where Louisa May Alcott realized her Concord dreams.

Alcott's 1873 novel, *Work: A Story of Experience,* explored the possibilities of self-realization for unmarried women.[172] Her heroine, Christie Devon, is an orphan who leaves behind the rigors of the farm for a new life in the city. Like Alcott, Christie goes into domestic service and finds it demeaning; she considers a stage career but finds it immoral; she becomes a shop laborer; finally she joins an association of working women. Alcott's "story of experience" led her to discover satisfying arrangements beyond marriage and rural domesticity. However idyllic was the life of the Marches in Concord, Jo too put aside childish things and became a writer in the city in *Little Women*. However wholesome was rural life for Christie, she abandoned it to realize herself in the city in *Work*. For Louisa May Alcott, Concord was a dream and Boston was an exciting, if exacting, reality.

Alcott, inspired by *Pilgrim's Progress*, saw her life as a quest. "For little tripping maids may follow God," she wrote in her preface to *Little Women*, "along the ways which saintly feet have trod."[173] Margaret Fuller saw herself as "a pilgrim and a sojourner on earth." Elizabeth Peabody, too, saw the world in the terms of Christian allegory. In 1839 she wrote to her sister Sophia from Concord: "Here I am on the mount of Transformation, but very much in the condition of the disciples when they were prostrate in the dust."[174] Stowe and Howe touched the heart of the nation in works which combined Puritan conscience with Christian compassion. All of these women were, of course, children of the anti-Puritan, Unitarian enlightenment, but Boston still taught them to see the world in terms of spiritual quest. Boston encouraged more than it delivered to these gifted women; however, each made her mark on the city and each enlarged the possibilities for women who came after them. Each of them recomposed herself and redefined her world in words. Child, Stowe, Peabody, Fuller, and Alcott were part of the domestic reform movement of their day: they praised *both* family commitment and individuality for women as a means to redeem society. Though Boston discouraged them, dismissed them, or parodied them, in time Boston heeded its representative women and honored them. From the democratic New England village of Stowe to the vital city center of Alcott, they gave us fresh versions and revived visions of Greater Boston.

IN the fall of 1851, after a dispute with his landlord over access to an apple orchard, Hawthorne removed his family from Edenic

Lenox, which had turned into his own Apple Slump. He then rented the home of his brother-in-law, Horace Mann, who had been elected to Congress, in West Newton. There, near Boston and West Roxbury, he wrote *The Blithedale Romance,* his anti-idyll.

When Hawthorne moved his family back to Concord, in the spring of 1852, after seven years' absence from the village, he sought once again to establish a permanent home, to find a proper place for himself. He bought a Concord house, on the Lexington Road, a house which had been previously owned by the Alcotts. Bronson Alcott's wife, Abba, with assistance from Emerson, had purchased what was then called "Hillside" in 1845, after the failure of Fruitlands. Alcott had planted a garden and expanded the house by adding sheds to its sides and a fragile summerhouse behind. Louisa May Alcott was twelve when they moved in; she would use the house as a setting for *Little Women*. But by 1848 the Alcotts gave up on this makeshift home and moved back to Boston. Hawthorne, too, would attempt renovations in a futile effort to bring the house to the shape of his imagination.

Hawthorne renamed his new Concord home the "Wayside" because it was so close to the busy road. Further, Hawthorne gave it life in language by incorporating the Wayside into his introduction to *Tanglewood Tales,* a companion volume to his *Wonder Book* of classical tales and legends for children, reviving Eustace Bright as the alleged author. When Eustace visits Concord, Hawthorne affects shame while showing Bright his humble dwelling and tame surroundings. Yet Hawthorne defends his placid life and setting, so different from the challenge and scenic grandeur of the Berkshires. "But to me there is a peculiar, quiet charm in these broad meadows and gentle eminences."[175] He even convinces Eustace, his Berkshires alter ego, that the realm of romance can be glimpsed in Concord. However, it is not certain Hawthorne long persuaded himself.

In his new home Hawthorne immediately found himself in the tense world of pre–Civil War politics when he agreed to write the campaign biography of his friend and Bowdoin classmate, Franklin

Pierce. After Pierce's election, Hawthorne, seeking financial stability, accepted an appointment as American Consul at Liverpool.
He was away from Concord until 1860.

Hawthorne's *Our Old Home* (1863), a reminiscence of his years
in England, dramatized his restless search for a true home. In his
"Pilgrimage to Old Boston," in Lancashire, a record of his visit in
the spring of 1857, Hawthorne recorded a rare epiphany of heart's
ease, recalling the day when he discovered his ancient roots and
made his final peace with his Puritan heritage; he even forgave
Salem. When he walked along the river, in this English town that
gave rise to many of the Puritans who settled Hester Prynne's
Boston, Hawthorne felt briefly at home. "I thought of Long Wharf,
and Faneuil Hall, and Washington Street, and the Great Elm, and
the State House, and exulted lustily,—but yet began to feel at
home in this good old town, for its very name's sake, as I never
had before felt, in England." Indeed he had never felt so at home
in America. Distance lent romance to America's Boston. The English church had been razed where John Cotton, once an ally of
Anne Hutchinson, had preached; but Hawthorne loved Old Boston
for the ways it reminded him of an idealized New Boston, "my
own dear native place."[176] Hawthorne *placed* himself in a Boston
of the mind.

When Hawthorne returned to his actual native place in 1860,
however, he was not happy. It was hot and oppressive on that June
day when the Hawthornes arrived by train at Concord station. "It
is dangerous to have a home; too much is required of it," concluded
his son.[177] While civil war loomed, Hawthorne turned his attentions
inward, to reshaping the Wayside and to recovering his waning
creative powers. He added Italian marble fireplace mantles and
carved wooden gables as window and door frames. A tiny doorway,
between beams, was made to connect their bedroom, part of the
original house, with the addition—a hall and wing for daughter
Una.

Hawthorne's principle effort at house reconstruction was, symbolically enough, a tower—a place of ascent and isolation where
he could gain an elevated, Paul Pry view of the world. Anticipating

Yeats, Hawthorne imagined his writing would be revitalized in a three-story tower whose top floor served as his study; from his stand-up desk, near the window, Hawthorne could look west, toward the Berkshires. However, though he forced himself to spend time there daily, his tower study turned out to be oppressive and unproductive: too hot in the summer and too stuffy in the winter. The tower symbolized Hawthorne's lack of ease in the house, in Concord, in America, perhaps even in this world. Still, in his tower Hawthorne converted his English notebooks into *Our Old Home* and made his final efforts as a novelist.

Hawthorne was unable to complete *Septimus Felton*, a romance based upon a local legend told to him by Thoreau, about a former owner of Hawthorne's house who believed he would never die. Perhaps Hawthorne found the notion incredible, even for a romance. Hawthorne was unable to shape a fitting myth of place in his tower study in the Wayside. While the Civil War was fought, Hawthorne's health diminished, along with his ability to focus upon the writing of fiction. Restless, he left Concord to visit Beverly, on the North Shore, and New York. In the spring of 1862 Thoreau died, but Hawthorne, unlike Emerson, was unable to write a tribute. After the death of his friend and publisher, William Ticknor, Hawthorne tried to escape depression on a trip with his friend, former president Franklin Pierce. At the Pemigewasset House in Plymouth, New Hampshire, Hawthorne himself died on 18 May 1863. Perhaps a room at an inn, accompanied by the college friend and mentor both men of another age, was a fitting place for him to die. For Hawthorne, who cared so much about place, whose works shape our sense of several American places, never found his home.

In death, however, Hawthorne became a permanent part of the landscape of Concord. Longfellow's moving funeral elegy so places Hawthorne.

> The lovely town was white with apple-blossoms,
> And the great elms o'erhead
> Dark shadows wove on their aerial loom
> Shot through with golden thread.[178]

Contemplating the burial site at Sleepy Hollow Cemetery, Longfellow sought Hawthorne's face, but only "an unseen presence filled
the air, / and baffled my pursuit."[179] Having given imaginative life
to Salem, Boston, Brook Farm, Concord, and Lenox, Hawthorne
discovered the certainty of place, the realized idea of home, only
in Sleepy Hollow, as in one of his tales Adam and Eve found their
ease only in Mount Auburn Cemetery. Having repudiated his Puritan heritage, Hawthorne's life became an unfulfilled quest for lost
coherence, for abandoned place and purpose.

Nathaniel Hawthorne engaged in the debate among his peers
over the symbolic significance of places in and around Boston. His
works *place* Boston in the American mind and conscience. Hawthorne revived the Puritan notion of place as symbolic landscape
for spiritual quest, though he multiplied the possibilities of goals
and moral implications. Hawthorne's art and vision extended to
the Berkshires, where literary Boston met literary New York in
the person of Herman Melville. Hawthorne's influence extended
further, beyond his own day, and inspired, among others, Edith
Wharton, whose dark New England novels derive from Hawthorne's "Ethan Brand" and other tales. Curiously, only the women
in Hawthorne's circle—Elizabeth Peabody, his sister-in-law; Margaret Fuller, his inspiring and threatening friend; Louisa May Alcott, his young Concord neighbor, all women who met formidable
obstacles in the region—had a good word for Boston, where they
felt liberated from domestic, village roles. *All* of these writers,
however, saw Greater Boston, urban and pastoral, as a vital symbolic center of literary, political, social, and spiritual activity. Each
of them shaped a plausible myth of Boston and helped renew its
spirit of place.

A century after his death, the ghost of Nathaniel Hawthorne still
haunted the local landscape and the minds of Boston writers. Just
as Hawthorne suggests he went upstairs in the Salem Custom
House to discover a record of Boston's archetypal parable, so too

did Robert Lowell travel to Salem in search of his literary ancestor. His poem, "Hawthorne," is a tribute to an alter ego. At first Lowell found nothing in Salem's circuitous streets. "You'll walk to no purpose / in Hawthorne's Salem." Then Lowell had a sudden vision of Hawthorne the dour customs officer.

> His head
> bent down, brooding, brooding,
> eyes fixed on some chip,
> some stone, some common plant,
> the commonest thing,
> as if it were the clue.
> The disturbed eyes rise,
> furtive, foiled, dissatisfied
> from meditation on the true
> and insignificant.[180]

As Lowell makes clear, Hawthorne taught us to see worlds of implications in local grains of sand.

3

Boston,
The Right American Stuff:
WILLIAM DEAN HOWELLS
AND HENRY JAMES

WILLIAM DEAN HOWELLS came to Boston from the American heartland in 1860, in search of a literary culture; he remained to shape and redefine that culture; from his Boston base he became the "Dean" of American letters, the most influential novelist, critic, and editor of his day. He met Henry James, who was poised to fly past the Boston nets, but Boston was the heart of Howells's America. Like his fictional hero, Silas Lapham, Howells could be called one of the "Solid Men of Boston," a representative man who reshaped America's vision of the city.[1]

In 1987 Harvard celebrated the 150th anniversary of Howells's birth with ceremonies and an address by John Updike.[2] Updike implied his debt to Howells in his conclusion. "Howells's agenda remains our agenda: for the American writer to live in America and to mirror it in writing, with 'everything brought out.'" In Howells's own words, he "wrought in common, crude material, . . . the right American stuff." Updike concluded, "It is hard to see, more than eight decades later, what else can be done."[3]

The common, crude material of Howells's most impressive fiction was found in Boston and Cambridge. Howells *and* James discovered the right American stuff in Greater Boston.

HOWELLS was only twenty-three when he first traveled by stage, through "summer sweetness," to Concord in 1860. He was full of bright prospect and ecstatic to have arrived at last at his true home, a place already well composed in his teeming literary imagination. Approaching Hawthorne's house, the Wayside, the polite but determined young man from Ohio feared that the shy romancer might flee into his eccentric tower. However, Howells met a genial and receptive Hawthorne. They climbed a hill behind the house, overlooking Concord, and sat on a log while Hawthorne smoked a cigar; he asked Howells about the American West, "which he seemed to fancy much more purely American, and said he would like to see some part of the country on which the shadow, or, if I must be precise, the damned shadow, of Europe had not fallen."[4] Though Howells, forty years after the event, still registered his acquired gentility in his diction, he discovered on his first visit that New England writers were quite real, surprisingly colloquial—not proper plaster busts suitable only for worship. For example, Hawthorne told him that New Englanders were, as often charged, guilty of a coldness of character. Hawthorne's bold comments must have amazed young Howells, who had been drawn to Boston from Ohio in search of the city's genteel, European-influenced culture. These words stuck in Howells's mind all his life; indeed they would help to define his own literary mission, for he would come to agree with Hawthorne's view of New England and its citizens. Perhaps Hawthorne sensed a disciple, for he wrote on the back of his card, "I find this young man worthy," as Howells's introduction to Emerson, who lived just up the Lincoln Road.[5]

Before he met Emerson, Howells visited Thoreau, a man whom he admired as much for supporting John Brown as for writing *Walden*. But Thoreau was characteristically cool. They sat in chairs set against walls, the width of the room representing the emotional distance between them.[6]

The visit to Thoreau may have made Howells wary of Emerson. Though Emerson greeted this eager young man at the door of his imposing colonial home, the visit did not go well, perhaps because Emerson said he thought Hawthorne's *Marble Faun*, a romance which Howells admired, "a mere mush"! Though Emerson granted Howells a garden tour and a dinner, then more literary talk in his famous study, Howells never relaxed; indeed, he felt patronized by the sage of Concord. Howells may have seen in Emerson something of that New England coldness of character which Hawthorne had noted. For reassurance, that evening Howells revisited Hawthorne, who was again willing to stroll and talk with this young man from the American provinces who was seeking his place in the Boston literary world.

Howells's first visit to Boston was filled with similar emblematic encounters, for his was nothing less than a literary pilgrim's progress, in which he set off in quest of a celestial city of culture. Forty years later, Howells was sufficiently detached from his smitten first impressions to place the moment in the context of a national literature.

> Boston stood for the whole Massachusetts group, and Massachusetts, in the literary impulse, meant New England. Certainly the city of Boston has distinctly waned in literature, though it has waxed in wealth and population. . . . I arrived in Boston, however, when all talent had more or less a literary coloring, and when the greatest talents were literary.[7]

Nothing was more telling in Howells's literary education than his mixed impression of Concord writers, whose books introduced him to new ways of thinking about his American material and whose personalities qualified some of the esteem in which Howells had held them. This visit began a process of gradual adjustment in Howells's vision, a modification of his original myth of the Boston-area literati, a coming to terms with what Leon Edel calls Howells's passion "to become a Boston Brahmin."[8] The three men he met in Concord had passed their best writing years. Within four years, Thoreau and Hawthorne would be dead, while Emerson, who lived for another twenty-two years, grew increasingly detached. Yet, Howells's visit to Concord would confirm his impression that American settings and Boston writers were, as Hawthorne had said of him, "worthy." Like Henry James, Howells would take up and redirect the New England literary tradition, in part by reimagining local people and places in fiction and criticism.

More than a century after Howells's first visit to Concord, John Updike claimed William Dean Howells as a worthy model for his own career. The local literary ambience drew both writers from points west to settle in the area and compose fictions which reconfigured our idea of Greater Boston.

HOWELLS understood that New England in general and Boston in particular were acts of the mind, images and visions of consciousness. In a series of novels, particularly *The Rise of Silas Lapham* (1885), essays, and reminiscences, Howells came to terms with the idealized Boston of his imagination and translated it into the language of literary realism. Henry James, for whom Boston and New England were familiar sites best imagined at a distance, wrote about the region in several fictions and composed one of the finest novels on Boston and Cambridge, *The Bostonians* (1886); then he reimagined the settings of his youth in meditations written late in his own life, particularly in *The American Scene* (1907). The debate between Howells and James over what James called "the art of fiction" was joined in Boston, a symbolic site in art and life for both writers of the American scene.[9]

If Boston was Howells's Celestial City, it was, at times, James's City of Destruction. When they met in 1866, Howells had at last returned to settle in the city for which he felt he had long been destined. (Between 1861 and 1864 Howells, who had written a campaign biography of Abraham Lincoln, was the United States Consul to Venice. In 1866 he became assistant editor of the *Atlantic Monthly*.) By then James had seen enough of Boston.

James had been living for two years in a house in Ashburton Place, behind the Massachusetts State House. It was a site of overbearing symbolism, "where the mouth of the Common itself uttered promises, more signs and portents than one could count."[10] James wanted a new literary life in Europe. As Leon Edel put it, "If Howells reached from Ohio to Boston, Henry was reaching out from Boston towards Europe."[11] Boston, then, was the site of the brief encounter between Howells and James; the city remained a touchstone in each man's life and art.

ON the brink of their great careers, it was, as Howells remembered it, a very heaven to be young and in Cambridge, walking along North Avenue, talking about books with Henry James.

> We seem to have been presently always together, and always talking of methods of fiction, whether we walked the streets by day or night, or we sat together reading our stuff to each other; his stuff which we both hoped might make itself into matter for the *Atlantic Monthly*, then mostly left to my editing by my senior editor Mr. Fields. I was seven years older than James, but I was much his junior in the art we both adored.[12]

Sometimes James joined the Howells family for dinner at their home on Sacramento Street, or they walked to Fresh Pond, then surrounded by woods, where they watched skaters in winter or boaters in summer while they talked about literature. In fact, as Howells notes, the imagery of his memory of these days centers upon *walking*, motions through American space. An apt image, for both young men were in transit, questing for success as artists. These two writers, best noted for their interior scenes from domestic life, were then open to the urban and the pastoral: the American scene, centered in Boston.[13] Boston was the primary source of Howells's inspiration, the place where, James recalled, "we knew together what American life *was*—or thought we did, deluded though we may have been!"[14] James was passing *through* Boston, moving toward his siege of Paris and London.

HAD the American Athens not existed, Howells would have had to invent another literary shrine. This intensely bookish, largely self-taught son of a printer transformed himself into "the passionate pilgrim from the West [who] approached his holy land at Boston." His small literary circle in Columbus had worshiped literary New England, declaring the *Atlantic Monthly* their holy book. All of Howells's first impressions of Boston were based upon the proposition that "there is no question but our literary centre was then in Boston."[15]

So too believed Kitty Ellison, heroine of *A Chance Acquaintance* (1871), Howells's first fictional definition of the character of Boston, though his heroine never arrives in the city.[16] This is a novel, written only a few years after Howells's arrival, in which a representative figure of democracy from the American West, a female alter ego, begins to retrace his journey east to America's cultural mecca. Her Boston meant culture, political idealism, and democracy. However, she comes to discover that Boston meant more, and less. *A Chance Acquaintance*, then, is a novel about *imagining* Boston, about Boston as idealized image and compromised reality.

The action of the novel centers upon Kitty's flirtation with Arburton, a Boston aristocrat who is "often mistaken for an Englishman," in the European ambience of Quebec.[17] Arburton— handsome, mannered, wealthy, cultured—seems the embodiment of her dream of Boston. Kitty's aunt affects an injured ankle so the young couple can be thrown together.

Howells told James of his intentions in writing *A Chance Acquaintance:* "I conceived the notion of confronting two extreme
American types: the conventional and the unconventional."[18] Kitty
and Arburton take their places, then, as factors in an argument
within Howells's mind about the character of both his native
grounds and his new found land. While Kitty idealizes Boston
(indeed, she sees Arburton through a nimbus of noble associations),
he literally cannot imagine Eriecreek, New York, her home. "Mr.
Arburton brought his fancy to bear upon Eriecreek, and wholly
failed to conceive of it."[19]

Though Arburton, a man of emotional and sexual repression, is
attracted by Kitty's western sense of freedom, he reveals his timid-
ity and self-centeredness when he fails to introduce her to aristocratic Bostonians they chance upon, because he thinks Kitty is
dressed in a fashion too common for their tastes. Quickly, her
romantic conception of Boston is tempered by her realistic appraisal
of this smug Bostonian. "This new Boston with which Mr. Arburton
inspired her was a Boston of mysterious prejudices and lofty reservations, . . . not in the least the Boston of her fond
preconceptions."[20]

Though Howells pulled his punch against Boston in *A Chance
Acquaintance* by modifying Arburton, some of the author's friends
were puzzled by this mildly anti-Boston novel, written by the young
westerner to whom they had given the keys to their kingdom.
Oliver Wendell Holmes complained that Arburton was "not quite
the kind of Bostonian one could wish to be," but then he gave
Howells the benefit of the doubt, a way out. "I understood, of
course, that he was *a* Bostonian, not *the* Bostonian," said Holmes.
Howells, keeping his reservations to himself, "could truthfully answer that this was by all means my own understanding too."[21]
However, *A Chance Acquaintance* established the Howells habit
of cool consideration of Boston, his ambivalent home as found.

HOWELLS'S Boston spread well beyond the city limits. "I would
have the reader always keep in mind the great fames at Cambridge

and at Concord, which formed so large a part of the celebrity of Boston."²² For Howells Cambridge stood for literature, the life of the mind, while Boston meant society, a world of old money and new ambitions.

Cambridge was Howells's home for seven years; then he moved to Boston's Louisburg Square in 1883. Howells delighted in the Cambridge literary luminaries of the 1860s, a list which included Louis Agassiz, the James family, James Russell Lowell, Henry Wadsworth Longfellow, Charles Eliot Norton and others. The land was so thick with writers that Bret Harte, a fellow westerner, told Howells, "Why, you couldn't fire a revolver from your front porch anywhere without bringing down a two-volumer!" However, it was impossible for Howells to mock the writers' paradise he found in Cambridge, though he too saw Cambridge in death imagery. "Being the wholly literary spirit I was when I went to Cambridge, I do not see how I could have been more content if I had found myself in the Elysian Fields with an agreeable eternity before me."²³ As much as Howells yearned for the cultural authentication that, as a young man on the rise, he had associated with Cambridge-Boston, as an achieved author-editor he was stifled by Boston propriety, inhibited by the persona of the high-minded, Boston man of letters—a persona which he adopted.

Forty years later, long released from these tensions of cultural and personal identity, Howells could recall with wonder those cold nights he walked back from Longfellow's Craige House—where he had discussed his host's translation of Dante—along the icy streets, through the cold Cambridge air, to his "carpenter's box" on Sacramento Street, a few miles away. "I was as if soul-borne through the air by my pride and joy, while the frozen blocks of snow clinked and tinkled before my feet stumbling along the middle of the road. [This was] the richest moment of my life."²⁴

In his early publications on Cambridge, however, Howells registered walks of a different direction and implication. Having "done" Niagara Falls and Quebec through the eyes of fictional characters in two novels, Howells then wrote up his own travels through the less picturesque but no less fascinating streets of Cambridge in *Suburban Sketches* (1871). In these pages Howells set forth for a journey of discovery in "this heavenly weather, which the Pilgrim Fathers, with the idea of turning their thoughts effectually from earthly pleasures, came so far to discover." In this sportive tone, Howells, a playful Christian in a suburban *Pilgrim's Progress*, mediates between earthly observations and their moral implications. "There is a Slough of Despond in full view, and not a delectable Mountain to be seen, unless you choose so to call the high lands about Waltham."[25] Yet his walk, or quest, ended in disappointment because Howells confronted the disturbing Irish settlers of North Cambridge, a people he could not convert into his fancy. Though Howells's commitment to literary realism carried him farther into the undiscovered country of immigrant life than any other writer of his day, his failure to fully accept their presence indicated his hesitations over ordinary life in nonliterary Boston-Cambridge.

Near the vast brickyards of North Cambridge, Howells encountered "Dublin," a settlement of hovels surrounding a graveyard. Women grieving for a dead child might have appeared picturesque in some Italian village, but here "I was now merely touched as a human being, and had little desire to turn the scene to literary account."[26]

Howells feared the Irish, thinking it far more likely that he would encounter a rebel, "a Whiteboy, or a Pikeman," than "a scholar or a saint" hidden away in "Dublin." "Dublin," which has an "appalling" depth of mud and "number of little ones," suggested that "sometimes [it] appears probable, such increases shall—together with the well-known ambition of Dubliners to rule the land—one day make an end of us poor Yankees as a dominant plurality."[27] That is, he feared the Irish would transform the character of *his* Cambridge, make it unknowable. Irish Cambridge, the right stuff of American realism, was too much for Howells.

Howells sought escape from these bleak visions. Back along the avenue "the Mansard-roofs look down upon me with their dormer-windows, and welcome me back to the American community."[28] After his failed quest through the "Dublin" of North Cambridge, where he had been beyond the "American" boundaries of his circumscribed imagination, Howells retreated into the Hawthornian delights of a second-hand curio shop, the realm of literary romance, where he allowed his fancy to have full play.

Howells was unable to resolve his attitude toward his adopted home. Boston-Cambridge-Concord inspired Howells's imagination with its literary associations. However, the gritty world of Irish immigrants tested his geniality and his claimed appreciation of the commonplace details which composed American life. By 1869 Howells was thinking about leaving Cambridge because, as he wrote to Henry James, with assurance of agreement, "all Ireland seems to be poured out upon it, and there is such a clamor of Irish children about us all day, that I suspect my 'exquisite English,' as I've seen it called in the newspapers, will yet be written with a brogue."29 As James would later fear that Yiddish-speaking immigrants would transform the language, Howells recoiled from the differently accented English speech of the Irish. *He*, after all, had an investment in the best Boston English, which he could perfectly mime.

THERE was, as his affection for Hawthorne indicated, always a bit of the romancer contending with Howells's commitment to realism. Like Hawthorne, he both sought and was repelled by the picturesque in Boston. Howells's Boston is a problematic place. He celebrated its literary resonance but he recoiled both from the Boston ascendancy's exclusiveness and the Boston immigrants' demands for democratization.

Yet, by Howells's own standards, he would not be a true writer until he could "do" Boston. A decade had passed since he attended the famous dinner at Parker's, with James Russell Lowell, James T. Fields, and Oliver Wendell Holmes, when the Autocrat foresaw Howells's future by saying to Lowell, "Well, James, this is something like the apostolic succession; this is the laying on of hands."30 Howells had inherited the *Atlantic Monthly* and he had been accepted into the privileged circle of Boston's literary luminaries, whom he had once admired from afar. However, he would not take full imaginative possession of Boston until he placed a mature work of fiction within its environs. That he did by writing *The Rise of Silas Lapham,* one of Boston's touchstone books.

Before he wrote this novel, Howells treated Boston glancingly in *A Modern Instance* (1882); there Howells moves a young couple, Bartley and Marcia Hubbard, from Equity, Maine (characterized by snow and "arctic quiet") to Boston, where they unsuccessfully try to assimilate.[31] Bartley throws himself into Boston's cosmopolitan ways so completely that he loses his moral bearings, becoming an unprincipled journalist, a drinker, and a philanderer. Boston for Marcia is too free, too much an open invitation to self-destruction for naive, rural folk. For all of its frozen dreariness, Equity is preferable, so she returns home. Boston constitutes the destructive element—*A Modern Instance* centers on their divorce—for these formerly good country people.

By the time he wrote *The Rise of Silas Lapham,* Howells was a fully assimilated Bostonian. In an 1884 letter to Henry James, Howells wrote with excitement and hyperbole about buying "a house 'on the water side of Beacon.' "

> The sun goes down over Cambridge with as much apparent interest as if he were a Harvard graduate: possibly he is; and he spreads a glory over the Back Bay. . . . Sometimes I feel it an extraordinary thing that I should have been able to buy a house on Beacon str. . . . Drolly enough, I am writing a story in which the chief personage built a house "on the water side of Beacon," and I shall be able to use all my experience, down to the quick. Perhaps the novel may pay for the house.[32]

During and after the Civil War, Boston expanded by filling in its Back Bay, along the Charles River. Boulevards designed after those in Paris attracted gentry and social climbers to the "new land," which was geographically and culturally contiguous with Beacon Hill. Holmes, Howells's Back Bay neighbor for three years, pointed out that fourteen towns and "three conspicuous monuments" could be seen from their homes.[33] On the waterside of Beacon Street Howells, like Holmes, was centered, "rooted," as Yeats prayed his daughter might be, "in one dear perpetual place."[34] Yet, his novel suggests he must have wondered how well he fit in and how much he was paying to live there. Howells might have recalled Thoreau's reflection on economy: "the cost of a thing is the amount of what I will call life which is required to be exchanged for it, immediately or in the long run."[35] The view over the Charles River from Beacon Street was costly, an expense of spirit, Howells's novel makes clear.

Howells brought a double perspective to *Silas Lapham:* the insider's view of the Coreys, a Boston Brahmin family, and the outsider's view of Silas Lapham, a newcomer on the rise. Try as he might, Silas could not, as outsider Howells had, bridge the gap between Boston's two cultures. Indeed, *Silas Lapham* should be read as a parable in which Howells contrives a moral test for those driven by upward mobility, those who have, as he writes of Silas, *"a cloudy vision of something unpurchasable."*[36] The grand Beacon Street house, with its water-view and all of its associations of status attainment, was an image of the unattainable dream of Silas Lapham, who anticipates Jay Gatsby in his inchoate desires and his petty purchases.

In the opening pages of the novel, this successful paint manufacturer from Lumberville, Vermont is interviewed by the cynical Bartley Hubbard, a journalist from Equity, Maine, whose joshing— "Your money or your life"—establishes the terms of Silas's trial of character in Boston. Silas says "so you want my life, death and Christian sufferings, do you, young man?," nearly realizing what is at stake.[37] Bartley was willing to make any trade for a successful life in Boston, but, in the end, Silas refuses to sell his soul. A spiritual journey underlays this novel's realistic surface.

Boston, in *Silas Lapham,* is an allegorical territory which provides the occasion and setting to test character and mission. Silas is compromised by the open opportunities presented in Boston and he too is driven back to Vermont. In Boston Silas overreaches himself socially and financially; then, as though he were unconsciously contriving a way out of the bind in which he had placed himself, he accidentally sets fire to his uninsured, nearly completed $100,000 house, an "accident" which assures Silas's downfall and precipitates his departure from Boston. Is the fire unconsciously set up by Silas to release him from status anxieties, or contrived by Howells to show that few outlanders should presume to join the socially elect of Boston? After the fire Silas's house looms with the gothic horror of Poe's House of Usher. "The windows looked like the eye-sockets of a skull down upon the blackened and trampled snow of the street."[38] Boston figures as Silas Lapham's *memento mori*.

The Laphams had lived for twelve years in Nankeen Square, in Boston's no longer fashionable South End. Their planned move across town, riverward to the newly developed Back Bay, is a natural step in the Lapham plan of upward mobility, but, as Kermit Vanderbilt has pointed out, passages which were included in the *Century* magazine serial version, later deleted from the published novel, reveal that the Laphams are fleeing their new South End neighbors, immigrant Jews! (A few years later, George Apley's father would flee the South End when he saw a man, probably an Irish workman, walking the streets without his coat. The South End was too *exposed* to invasion, while Back Bay was protected by the Charles River and Beacon Hill.) Silas explains to his wife: "You see, they *have* got in—and pretty thick, too—it's no use denying it. And when they get in, they send down the price of the property."[39] If it is not the Irish of Cambridge, it seems, it is the Jews of Boston who threaten felicity and property values for the outlanders who set out to transform themselves into proper Bostonians.

The Brahmin line, as embodied by the Coreys, who live in Bellingham Place at the base of Beacon Hill, has traded enterprise for culture; culture, then, became their citadel against threatening intruders, though the Coreys are a benign model of Brahmin exclusiveness. Silas Lapham seeks the stamp of Corey culture, an impossible goal, for Silas cannot assimilate their sophisticated style; he cannot even quite get his large hands into saffron-tinted gloves before a Corey dinner party, where he drinks too much and embarrasses himself. Young Tom Corey, a more positive realization of the representative Boston young aristocrat than Arburton, seeks to revitalize his line—first by joining Lapham's business and then by marrying Lapham's daughter, Penelope.

Howells shaped his myth of Boston's future with an optimistic eye toward the modification of class antagonisms. The marriage of Tom and Penelope does unite the families, but they discover there is no proper *place* for them in Boston. Howells left them in Mexico at novel's end. He allowed Silas no choice but to return to his homestead in Vermont. Silas might have saved himself had he been sufficiently unscrupulous to sell some land—land he knew would soon be bought cheaply by the railroad—to some unsuspecting English utopians. However, Silas would not do what Bartley Hubbard would have done: victimize naive newcomers in order to save himself. Rather, Silas chooses the moral life over financial self-interest, though in Howells's world of literary realism that choice also means that he must go home again, a broken man. Yet, for Silas Lapham all is not lost. There remains a muted life for him in Vermont, after his defeat in Boston. He and his wife "found it easier to leave it for the farmstead in Vermont than it would have been to go from that home of many years to the new house on the water side of Beacon."[40] It is better to go home again than it is futilely to seek entry into Boston's Brahmin world. Howells's *The Rise of Silas Lapham* shows how hard a place Boston can be, particularly to the naive newcomer who lacks the language of Boston culture. It is droll indeed that the profits from the sale of this popular novel did help pay for the Beacon Street house of William Dean Howells, who was agile, if ill at ease, in several languages and cultures.

Unlike Silas Lapham, William Dean Howells conquered Boston and Cambridge, becoming both a cultural and a financial success, before he moved on to other challenges in New York. Yet even while he took full possession of his adopted city, he was easing away from its grip. Van Wyck Brooks argues that Howells "was in Boston provisionally":

The truth was that Howells was really at home in the superworld of art and was only a sojourner in any other country. He was detached wherever he was, as a writer should be, and he might have said, with Bernard Berenson, "I am a stranger everywhere."[41]

But Howells, like Berenson after him, developed his consciousness of art in Boston and carried the city around, a shrine in his head, for the rest of his life.

THE *Minister's Charge* (1886) stands as Howells's long farewell to Boston. This would be "a Boston story with a vengeance," Howells said, anticipating the attack by antirealists upon his inquiry into the underclass of Boston. Like James in his London novel, *The Princess Casamassima*, Howells was interested in "doing" his city, in the style of Balzac. Howells's novel would be an exercise in realism which traced his "pathetic country boy" through the streets of Boston, perhaps in recollection of Hawthorne's "My Kinsman, Major Molineux." Howells, having "done" middle- and upper-class Boston, would here go downward, he told a Boston newspaper, to complete his picture of "the most interesting town in the world."[42] After that novel, Howells would close his books on Boston until his elderly remembrances of Boston past.

In *The Minister's Charge* Lemuel Barker, an up-country farm boy from pastoral Willoughby Pastures, wants to be a poet, so he seeks his literary fortunes in Boston; but eventually he, like other Howells provincials, is driven back to his humble home. After he arrives and is conned out of his money on Boston Common, a policeman wisely says, "Get out o' Boston, anyway, wherever you go or don't go. . . . It's a bad place."[43] When the young man finally takes this advice, the novel's narrator assures us that Barker marries and lives happily in Willoughby Pastures, finally free of delusions that he might attain literary acceptance in Boston. As with Marcia Hubbard and Silas Lapham, it is not the gap between classes which holds them back—for Howells would have us believe in a beneficent ascendancy—but something lacking in the outsiders' natures.

Provinciality, sensuality, and a degree of vulgarity are, it seems, bred in the bone of these decent but simple country people. Howells prefers to hint at a biological-regional determinism rather than blame Boston society for its hostility to outlanders, though the Boston ascendancy clearly preferred Barker only as an alternative to the incoming Irish hordes. So suggested a Brahmin benefactor, Charles Corey, who saw Barker's departure as Boston's loss. Boston is left open to the hungry Irish, who were laying siege to the contracting world of the waning Brahmins.

WILLIAM DEAN HOWELLS never wholly gave himself over to Boston. Citizen of the country of art, Howells seized upon, then transcended Boston culture. Born in the American West, he came of age culturally during his years in Europe. Boston was his point of cultural intersection, his adopted, uncommon ground, but Howells, for all his devotion to the details of place, remained essentially a man without a country.

Mark Twain often expressed an ambivalence about Boston which Howells suppressed. Twain, who lived in Hartford, midway between New York and Boston, liked to visit Boston. However, once in Boston, Twain acted out his bad-boy role. In April 1875, Twain and Howells, behaving like barely grown-up versions of Huck and Tom, failed to complete the journey from Cambridge to Concord for Centennial celebrations of the American Revolution. When they tried to lie their way out of their absence by saying that they had attended, they were found out. "I think the humor of this situation was finally a greater pleasure to Clemens than an actual visit to Concord would have been," concluded Howells, registering his own satisfaction obliquely, through his description of Twain, whose persona allowed him to be prankish in Boston.[44] The incident stands in delightful parody of Howells's first, star-struck visit to Concord, fifteen years earlier.

Howells was sympathetic when Twain embarrassed himself at a dinner in honor of John Greenleaf Whittier's seventieth birthday, held at the Hotel Brunswick in December of 1877. There Twain told a tall tale about three boozy visitors—he named them Emerson, Holmes, and Longfellow—to a miners' camp in the Sierra foothills. The visitors took over the cabin, Twain said, ate the miners' food, drank their liquor, and cheated them at cards. " 'I'm going to move,' a miner said to Mr. Twain. 'I ain't suited to a littery atmosphere.' "[45] Howells recalls that he stared at his plate in shame as Twain's comments puzzled and hushed the gathering. Still, Howells understood both sides, the embarrassment of the offended Brahmins and the strained humor of Twain; both Twain and Howells showed the Westerners' suspicion and nervous hostility toward the intimidating Eastern literati.[46]

Like his novels' ambitious heroes, Silas Lapham and Lemuel Barker, Howells should be seen as a man, divided between two worlds, whose crisis came to focus in Boston. However, unlike these failed social-climbers, Howells was strengthened by his success in Boston. Twain pulled him toward the American heartland—with its humor and realism—and James pulled him toward the international scene—with its irony and romance. Howells combined both worlds in the offices of the *Atlantic Monthly* and in his estimable Boston fiction. His fiction broadened Boston's literature to include the point of view of these young men and women from the American provinces.[47] In turn, Howells's fiction revised and revived America's vision of Boston.

THOUGH he celebrated Boston throughout his life and tried to put the best face upon his Brahmin benefactors, Howells grew weary of the city's cultural demands and felt constricted by its literary expectations. Finally he, too, was not cut out for Boston's "littery atmosphere." Boston, he decided, preferred a literature of men whose faith was Unitarian, whose art was Puritan. Boston practiced an art "marred by the intense ethicism that pervaded the New England mind for two hundred years, and that still characterizes it." Bostonians pointed morals in all they did. "Sometimes they sacrificed the song to the sermon, though not always, nor nearly always. It was in poetry and in romance that they excelled; in the novel, so far as they attempted it, they failed." Even his beloved Hawthorne, who, it might be said, had opened the door of the house of fiction to Howells, revealed the regional limitations.

> New England, in Hawthorne's work, achieved supremacy in romance; but the romance is always an allegory, and the novel is a picture in which the truth to life is suffered to do its unsermonized office for conduct; and New England yet lacks her novelist, because it was her instinct and her conscience in fiction to be true to an ideal of life rather than to life itself.[48]

For Howells, Boston and New England constituted a personal romance and challenged his commitment to literary realism. He never quite combined the two, in his life or art. Yet Howells's fiction and criticism fixed his ambivalent Boston in the American mind.

HENRY JAMES agreed with Howells's view of Hawthorne. "It cannot be too often repeated that Hawthorne was not a realist," wrote James of Hawthorne, the author whose existence and productions *meant* New England to James. James had his own reservations about Hawthorne, particularly about the underlying Puritanism of *The Scarlet Letter*, "in the very quality of his own vision, in the tone of the picture, in a certain coldness and exclusiveness of treatment."[49] Yet Hawthorne was a figure of central importance to James throughout his life, for Hawthorne showed James, as he had showed Howells, the way: one could be an American artist.

In 1879, living in London, James sought to define his own relations with American place, largely Boston, in a monograph on Hawthorne, written for an English audience. It is a curious document, full of James's pride in Hawthorne's achievement and marked by fond patronizing of Hawthorne's provincialism. James's Hawthorne is intensely *local*. "The cold, bright air of New England seems to blow through his pages." The more dreary the setting, the stronger the hold it had upon him.[50] James sympathized with Hawthorne's problem in making fiction out of such unpromising places. James's America is full of empty spaces for the inquiring artist, a nation which possessed no

> ivied ruins; no cathedrals, nor abbeys, nor little Norman churches; no great Universities nor public schools—no Oxford, nor Eton, nor Harrow; no literature, no novels, no museums, no pictures, no political society, no sporting class—no Epsom nor Ascot![51]

Such a list, with its own ironic hyperbole, playfully indicts American life for all it lacks, though James adds his own crucial qualification. "The American knows that a good deal remains; what it is that remains—that is his secret, his joke, as one may say." The ironic secret, which James understood, is that American isolation stirred Hawthorne's imagination, which played "among the shadows and substructures, the dark-based pillars and supports, of our moral nature."[52]

Throughout his study of Hawthorne, James vacillated between praising America as a fertile landscape of imagination and faulting his country as a cultural desert. James noted the characteristically Bostonian gatherings of Elizabeth Peabody, Hawthorne's sister-in-law, whom, in the character of Miss Birdseye, James would both satirize and honor in *The Bostonians*. Joined by Margaret Fuller and others, Elizabeth Peabody would bring out Flaxman's *Designs for Dante* for the evening's discussion by high-minded Bostonians. The idea of such an evening chilled James, who did not, it seems, contemplate Dante discussions with the same delight Howells found in his evenings at Craige House with Longfellow and his circle. Perhaps, for James, it was not Dante, not even the company, but the *place* which suggested to him "the lonely frigidity which characterized most attempts at social recreation in the New England world some forty years ago." All of this evoked for James a vision of pathos and isolation from his "initiated," European perspective. Yet James found a redemptive element to Hawthorne's provincialism in *The Scarlet Letter:* "the best of it was that the thing was absolutely American; it belonged to the soil, to the air; it came out of the very heart of New England."[53] However scornful he became, James never ceased to identify himself as an American, a Bostonian.

In *Hawthorne* Henry James established his own national and literary lineage by at once acknowledging and freeing himself from Hawthorne's patrimony. James would choose the international scene as his imaginative landscape. In the Brunswick Hotel, Boston, in November of 1881, James confided to his notebook his life choice. "My choice is the old world—my choice, my need, my life."[54] James's choice *for* the "old world" was also a defiant choice *against* the known world of Boston, where he felt his talents were wasted.

> Here I sit scribbling in my bedroom at a Boston hotel—on a marble top table!—and conscious of a ferocious homesickness—a home-sickness which makes me think of the day when I shall next see the white cliffs of old England loom through their native fog, as one of the happiest of my life![55]

This entry was written on a visit home, two years after James attempted to come to terms with Hawthorne, the provincial American.

> I have insisted upon the fact of his being an intense American, and of his looking at all things, during his residence in Europe, from the standpoint of that little clod of western earth which he carried about with him as the good Mohammedan carries the strip of carpet on which he kneels down to face Mecca.[56]

James did not wish to bear the burden of American soil across international boundaries. Europe was filled with marble top tables on which he might write. In England James mocked Hawthorne's provinciality but James knew Hawthorne's "secret." James would not find it so easy to dismiss memories of Hawthorne's mecca: Boston and its surrounding territories.

THOUGH as a young man James could not wait to leave Boston and Cambridge for wider worlds in Europe, as an old man, writing in London, he recalled the days of his youth in Boston with gratitude for their transient sweetness. He recalled, for example, the times Emerson had visited the James home to talk with the elder Henry James. "The wonder of Boston was above all just then and there for me in the sweetness of the voice and the finish of the speech." Though James, like Hawthorne before him, berated Boston for its thin cultural soil, in his late years James revealed the extent to which Boston had prodded his imagination as a site with problematic possibilities for the artist's grasping imagination. "Boston was in a manner of its own stoutly and vividly urban, not only a town, but a town of history."[57] James faulted Boston for its narrowness of cultural choices, its aesthetic drabness, its discouragement of aesthetic impulses, even its wintry weather, but in a Proustian passage on dining at Parker's restaurant James reverses himself on all these points.

> Parker's on the whole side of the joy of life *was* Boston—speaking as under the thrill of early occasions recaptured; Boston could be therefore, in the acutest connections, those of young comradeship and young esthetic experience, heaven save the mark, fondly prepared or properly crowned, but the enjoyed and shared repast, literally the American feast, as I then appraised such values; a basis of native abundance on which everything else rests.[58]

Boston, then, was both Henry James's bitter pill and his moveable feast.

JAMES had taken a far more caustic tone toward Boston during the early and middle years of his career. In *The American* (1876) Christopher Newman, a rich American businessman in Paris in search of a wife, becomes annoyed when another American speaks disparagingly of American cooking. Newman wished him "carried home in irons and compelled to live in Boston—which for Newman

94

was putting it very vindictively."[59] James, intoxicated by his own liberation, suggested through Newman that Boston is a prison.

In *The Europeans* (1878) James reversed Newman's journey of discovery. Instead of dramatizing the revealing journey of a wealthy American going to Europe to find a wife, *The Europeans* shows an impoverished American woman who has long lived in Europe, Madame de Cintre, along with her brother, Felix Young, coming to Boston in search of security and marriage. However, they are assaulted by a May snowstorm which casts a pall on their plans, just as the spring snow in *The Blithedale Romance* had foredoomed the mission of Hawthorne's utopians. As James's novella opens, the recently-arrived brother and sister look down upon Boston's grim emblems from their room in Parker's Hotel.

> A narrow grave-yard in the heart of a bustling, indifferent city, seen from the windows of a gloomy-looking inn, is at no time an object of enlivening suggestion. . . . The window-panes were battered by the sleet; the headstones in the grave-yard beneath seemed to be holding themselves askance to keep it out of their faces. A tall iron railing protected them from the street, and on the other side of the railing an assemblage of Bostonians were trampling about in the liquid snow. Many of them were looking up and down; they appeared to be waiting for something.[60]

Indeed, as it turns out, Madame de Cintre is also waiting for something that will never come in Boston. Though the weather suddenly turns beautiful and Madame de Cintre and Felix find their way to a serene New England village, where they meet a variety of local types, she has no more luck in breaking through the emotional chill of New England ways than Newman had in penetrating a French family sanctuary in *The American*, though Felix does win the hand of a worthy young woman. In a manner similar to Howells's heroes and heroines who fail in Boston and return to northern New England, Eugenia de Cintre returns to Europe, "deciding that the conditions of action on this provincial continent were not favorable to really superior women. The elder world was, after all, their natural field."[61]

In "A New England Winter" (1884) James took a softer view. In this story a presumptuous and affected young painter, with the extraordinary name of Florimond Daintry, who is visiting Boston, violates local mores by making advances to a proper Bostonian, a married woman named Mrs. Mesh. Eventually, lest he become enmeshed, Florimond is sent back to Paris by his mother, where he and his behavior obviously belong, in "the elder world." For all that, during his stay Florimond is struck by the beauty of Boston: the large windows of Beacon Street invited exposure and mixed public and private spheres. James allows Daintry to evoke Boston with a rapturous, painterly eye.

> The upper part of Beacon Street seemed to Florimond charming,—
> the long, wide, sunny slope, the uneven line of the older houses,
> the contrasted, differing, bulging fronts, the painted bricks, the tidy
> facings, the immaculate doors, the burnished silver plates, the de-
> nuded twigs of the far extent of the Common, on the other side;
> and to crown the eminence and complete the picture, high in the
> air, poised in the right place, over everything that clustered below,
> the most felicitous object in Boston—the gilded dome of the State
> House.[62]

Even in James's chill, proper Boston, transient beauty could be found.

IN *The Bostonians* James planned to do Boston in, but qualifying voices from the city, from his family and from his own mind turned on him and James reconsidered; in the end, his novel defends Boston, its peculiar ways and prickly values, against the greater dangers of siege by intruders.

At first James planned it to be "a remorseless exploitation of Boston," as he wrote to Thomas Sergeant Perry in the spring of 1884, when he had committed himself to serialization of the novel in *Century Magazine*.[63] James had spent many months in Boston between 1881 and 1883, years when both his mother and his father died. By then well established in London and in his career, James could cast a quizzical eye back upon the city of his youth, treat it as proper material for his mature fiction. He stayed on during his mother's illness and death, a period when Boston assaulted his imagination, no matter how much he tried to deny it. "Boston is absolutely nothing to me—I don't even dislike it. I like it, on the contrary; I only dislike to live there." He walked from his rooms on Mount Vernon Street to Parker's for breakfast and, after a day's writing, to Cambridge, "across that dreary bridge whose length I had measured so often in the past," for dinner at the family home on Quincy Street. "In the evening I walked back, in the clear, American starlight."[64]

James left after his mother's death, but he had to return to Boston in late 1882 when his father died. He stayed on again, caring for his sister Alice in the new James home at 131 Mount Vernon, on Beacon Hill. Again James confronted Boston, in "A New England Winter." More and more, Boston came to mean winter and death for James. Crossing the streets of Boston and Cambridge, James must have recalled his walks and talks with Howells, some two decades before, when they discussed native and expatriate fictions; now James was taking a Howells tack, determining "to write a very *American* tale, a tale very characteristic of our social conditions, and I ask myself what was the most salient and peculiar point in our social life. The answer was: the situation of women, the decline of the sentiment of sex, the agitation on their behalf."[65]

Abolitionism and feminism had long been advocated by leading Boston women: Elizabeth Peabody, Margaret Fuller, Louisa May Alcott and others. Boston's feminism stirred concerned responses within the establishment of male writers. Francis Parkman, for example, denounced "pregnant writing" and local novelists adapted to an audience largely composed of women.[66] Fortunately, James had a more considered response.

Henry James was able to see the world from the eyes of young women who sought freedom, as he demonstrated in *Daisy Miller* (1878) and *The Portrait of A Lady* (1881). His sympathy for women's point of view extended to his own family. By the time of his return,

James's brilliant and afflicted sister had developed a special relationship with Katharine Loring, a lively and resourceful young woman from Beverly, Massachusetts. Though Alice had long been a semirecluse and was frequently bedridden, she grew energetic and outgoing in the company of Katharine. In time Alice and Katharine developed what was called a "Boston marriage," a relationship similar to the well-known and accepted union between Sarah Orne Jewett and Annie Fields, the widow of publisher James T. Fields; these women lived together in harmony in the Fields home on Charles Street.[67] "I verily remember being struck with the stretch of wings that the spirit of Charles Street could bring off," wrote James, after visiting them.[68] James was fascinated by the Fields-Jewett "marriage," and came to accept a similar arrangement within the James family home. As he noted in his plans for *The Bostonians*, "the relation of the two girls should be a study of one of those friendships between women which are so common in New England." On the Alice-Katharine relationship James came to see, as he wrote to his aunt Kate after his sister and her friend had come to visit him in Europe, that there was "a kind of definite understanding between them," and "we must accept it with gratitude."[69] For James, feminism and lesbianism offered the material for a parable of place: "The whole thing [must be] as local, as American, as possible, and as full of Boston: an attempt to show that I *can* write an American story."[70]

IN *The Bostonians* James presents the city through the eyes of Basil Ransom, Confederate veteran and lawyer, who arrives from Mississippi to visit his cousin, Olive Chancellor, a Beacon Hill feminist, and to advance his fortunes. James is ironic about Basil, "our panting young man" who "was conscious at bottom of a bigger stomach than all the culture of Charles Street could fill," and he mocks Ransom's romantic view of Boston. His "artistic sense . . . had not been highly cultivated," James wryly reminds us. An outlander, like so many of Howells's heroes, Ransom discovers the emblems of culture, which he had so hungrily imagined, on Beacon Hill. "The general character of the place struck him as Bostonian; this was, in fact, very much what he had supposed Boston to be."[71]

Ransom, seeking to take possession of this world, briefly considers marriage to Olive, but he quickly realizes she is "unmarried by every implication of her being." He gives Adeline Luna, Olive's worldly sister from New York, longer consideration before he discovers the true object of his affection, Verena Tarrant, a young and gifted speaker for feminist causes. Ransom meets her when he is brought by Olive to a gathering of reformers, at which Verena speaks. Olive, too, is swept away by Verena. Olive "had found what she had been looking for so long—a friend of her own sex with whom she might have a union of soul."[72] Ransom also sees in Verena a figure he might shape. Olive, who detests men and agitates for women's rights, and Ransom, who detests feminists and seeks to silence Verena, have conflicting politics but similar goals. James's novel of Boston focuses upon a triangular struggle between two ideologues for power over virginal Verena, an empty vessel.

The hostess of the gathering at which Olive and Ransom hear Verena speak is Miss Birdseye, a character apparently based upon Elizabeth Peabody. In Boston in James's day, Elizabeth Peabody could still be seen, bustling about the streets, too busy doing good works to bother with her appearance, too kindly to dislike.[73] James treats Miss Birdseye harshly, however, offering her as a model of diminishing reformists' zeal in Boston. James sums up her character and her era in one memorable image: "She was heroic, she was sublime, the whole moral history of Boston was reflected in her displaced spectacles."[74] At its worst, James's Boston in this novel was a struggle of conflicting sexual-political positions. At its best James's Boston is presented as a decrepit site of irrelevant idealism.

William James, reading serial installments of *The Bostonians*, thought, as he wrote in a letter from Cambridge to his brother in London, it was a "bad business" to caricature Elizabeth Peabody as Miss Birdseye. William noted that their aunt Kate and other Bostonians had also complained. Henry responded petulantly to this charge, first denying that he had Miss Peabody in mind, then granting that he had taken the detail of those symbolic spectacles from Miss Peabody and placed them on Miss Birdseye, finally insisting that there was nothing critical in the characterization in any case. Sensitive to Boston's criticism, however, in later magazine installments of the novel-in-progress James added details to Miss Birdseye's background to distinguish her from Miss Peabody, making Miss Birdseye, for example, an abolitionist who "had roamed through certain parts of the South, carrying the Bible to the slave," which Miss Peabody never did.[75]

Still, Boston remained annoyed by what James had written about its revered characters. James could not understand why readers in Boston and London could so admire Howells's *Silas Lapham* but then condemn *The Bostonians*. "They don't revile Howells when he does America, and such an America as that, and why do they revile me? The 'Bostonians' is sugar-cake, compared with it."[76]

Certainly James's evocation of the death of Miss Birdseye could be called "sugar-cake," if it were not so moving. When she quietly passes away, surrounded by her disciples, in the tranquil setting of Marmion (actually Marion, on Buzzards Bay), near Cape Cod, even Ransom, that unreconstructed Southerner and ideological foe of everything Miss Birdseye stood for, is moved, seeing her as a "battered, immemorial monument" to the lost "heroic age of New England life."[77] James had evidently changed his mind about Miss Birdseye and thus qualified his satire of the tradition of moral-political idealism which she represented. James's ambivalence toward Miss Birdseye symbolizes his unresolved attitudes toward the strengths and limitations of Boston culture.

The struggle of displaced sexual aggression between Olive and Basil announces a new, more savage age. What once was noble and selfless in Boston has grown debased and selfish; idealism has become appetite. The city has retreated into a spiritual paralysis which is symbolized by its stone-cold weather and its impoverished cityscape. In a key scene Olive stands with Verena outside the Charles Street house, on a dark and wintry evening. Olive draws her cloak around Verena and makes the young woman vow she

will never marry.[78] In James's Boston, fierce, feminist separatism
vies with brutal, masculine domination.

In the novel's climax, Ransom is determined to stop Verena's
long-awaited speech at Boston's Music Hall and capture her for
himself. "The city of Boston be damned!," he shouts at Olive, his
real foe. The novel concludes with Verena crying, Ransom's cloak
enclosing her, and Olive Chancellor alone, finally prepared to speak
in her own voice, to face the audience of expectant Bostonians.
Even Ransom is momentarily touched by Olive's courage and the
graciousness of the audience, which had been long awaiting Verena.
"Ransom, palpitating with his victory, felt now a little sorry for
her, and was relieved to know that, even when exasperated, a
Boston audience is not ungenerous."[79] Thus James concluded his
novel with a conciliatory tribute to Bostonians. In the process of
writing *The Bostonians*, James may have learned that there was
good in Boston's old ways, particularly when seen in opposition to
the rapaciousness of outsiders like Basil Ransom. Boston's "secret"
was its saving remnant of character.

The Bostonians begins in denunciation but resolves in reconciliation. As bad as Boston has been, that tight little island community
remains a city of values and courage. James's Boston is a landscape
of seekers who bear the burden and the purpose of Puritan forefathers. Many have lost their way, but no Bostonian matches Basil
Ransom in a vulgar exercise of the will. Foolish, idealistic, kind-
hearted Miss Birdseye evokes an era of honorable self-sacrifice and
principle which is diminished but not forgotten. Curiously Olive
Chancellor, so severely satirized, becomes something of a heroine;
forced to renounce possessive love, she is prepared to address
Bostonians, presumably on the topics of social relations, their covenant, and Boston's future, their mission. She has the potential to
become another Hester Prynne! James does not carry her that far,
but he does present a Boston which has been filled-in, like its Back
Bay—a city resonant with social discriminations and ideological
variations, a site of significant quests, a stage for social comedy and
personal tragedy, a city that has turned away from its noble mission

but a place which has never ceased to embody momentous meaning for its citizens or for its artists.

WHEN James returned to America at age sixty in 1904, after twenty years' absence, he saw a transformed America through mature eyes and described it with a sure narrative voice; he had in the new century already completed *The Ambassadors, The Wings of the Dove,* and *The Golden Bowl,* works which portrayed Americans in search of culture in Europe. James, in his own words, "was to return with much of the freshness of eye, outward and inward," necessary to compose his "gathered impressions" into a sustained meditation upon his native land, *The American Scene.* James there includes chapters on New York, Washington, and cities of the South, but he was appalled by the height of the new buildings, the brashness of tone and the extent of commercialization in America, particularly in New York, where he found that both his boyhood home, on Fourteenth Street, and his birthplace, near Washington Square, had been leveled for new construction. All the more, then, Boston and other New England places attracted his attentions. No longer was Boston the site of his youthful exile from the bright lights of Paris or London. Now it reverberated with eloquent memories, "instant vibrations, to a past recalled from very far back; [he] fell into a train of association that receded, for its beginnings, to the dimness of extreme youth."[80] America had destroyed many of its nineteenth-century emblems, but Boston remained much as it had long been, a reminder of personal and national histories.

When he came to Cambridge, James was pleased to find "the rich old Harvard organism brooding," as ever, though a wall literally and symbolically separated the Yard from the city. But "the light of literary desire" had declined in Cambridge, James observed.[81] Passing Elmwood and Craige House, those grand manses which stood as memorials to the literary communities surrounding Lowell and Longfellow, James mourned the disintegration of a more coherent and homogeneous Cambridge. (Elmwood and Craige House, eighteenth-century structures identified with royalty and revolution, became literary centers, each a home of a Cambridge "fireside" poet, in the nineteenth century.) James walked, as he had in the 1860s with Howells, again to Fresh Pond, "to recover— some echo of the dreams of youth, the titles of tales, the communities of friendship, the sympathies and patience, in fine, of dear W. D. H.," but Howells had long ago removed himself from the Cambridge scene and the old ambience was lost.

After trips to New York and the west, James returned to the heart of his America, Boston, where he released his felicitous memories against the harsh impression of a larger, brassier, richer Boston. Could his precious impressions of old Boston withstand the realities of the new Boston? "Can one *have*, in the conditions, an impression of Boston, any that has not been for years as inappreciable as a 'sunk' picture?—that dead state of surface which requires a fresh application of varnish."[82]

Again walking up Beacon Hill, James was heartened to find that things were much as he had remembered them from his youth. "A great raw clearance had been made" at the top of the hill for the expansion of the State House, but James was pleased to discover that Ashburton Place, exposed by the destruction of surrounding houses, still stood, though others nearby had been torn down. This house—one of "the pair of ancient houses" which stood apart from the rest, where he dreamed of his life as an American novelist, where he heard of the deaths of Lincoln and Hawthorne—still stood, an emblem of precious perseverance in a transformed landscape: "the history of something as against the history of nothing" had been sustained.[83]

James placed this "conscious memento" next to his heart, like a folded pocket handkerchief, he said, and set forth for a month of travel, gathering more American impressions; but when he came home again, to Ashburton Place, in search of renewed memories, he found that his former house *had* been destroyed to make way for new construction. His return was "a justly-rebuked mistake." History was unmade, with a pickaxe. James's "small homogeneous Boston of the more interesting time" was gone forever.[84] Foreign voices and tall buildings had transformed even his Boston.

Boston, the bigger, braver, louder Boston, was "away," and it was quite, at that hour, as if each figure in my procession were there on purpose to leave me no doubt of it. Therefore I had the vision, as filling the sky, no longer of the great Puritan "whip," the whip for the conscience and the nerves, of the local legend, but that of a huge applied sponge, a sponge saturated with the foreign mixture and passed over almost everything I remembered and might still have recovered.[85]

James was not impressed by the new Boston Public Library building—designed by Charles F. McKim, opened in 1895—and he was dismayed by the glittering shops along Park Street. All was driven, he decided, by the same lust for money which he saw everywhere in America.

From the top of Mount Vernon Street, James could see that Boston had spread far to the south, where many Irish immigrants had settled. He recalled an earlier, tighter, more harmonious city, "exempt as yet from the Irish yoke."[86] Recoiling from Boston's new European immigrants, James took refuge in Isabella Stewart Gardner's newly opened Fenway Court, where, witnessing her collection of European art, James paradoxically could feel the old Boston of his youth. As Howells retreated into a curio shop after witnessing the shock of discovering "Dublin" in North Cambridge, James found a haven from modern Boston—brash, booming, ethnic Boston—in Mrs. Gardner's anachronistic palazzo in Boston's Fens.

JAMES had a bit more success in finding a remnant of American culture in Concord and Salem than he did in Boston. Unlike the shifting identities of other American cities, "Concord, Massachusetts, had an identity more palpable to the mind, had nestled in other words more successfully beneath her narrow fold of the mantle of history than any other American town."[87]

Like Howells, who came from Columbus, Ohio, first to Salem then to Concord, forty-five years before, James returned from England and went to Concord, then to Salem, to confirm an image of permanent place, and to retrieve old impressions from his youth. James walked to the bridge over the Concord River, the site of the beginning of the Revolutionary War, though James's associations were less military than literary. He visited the Old Manse nearby, where both Emerson and Hawthorne had lived, and he brooded upon the abilities of these writers to articulate an American spirit in their letters. For all that, James found the Old Manse a diminished emblem, "disconcertingly free of the ornamental mosses scattered by Hawthorne's light hand," a "shrunken historic site."[88] Symbols of the past James sought had either been destroyed, like his Ashburton Place house, or they had become museum pieces for tourists, like the Old Manse.

In Salem James was similarly disappointed. Seeking Hawthorne's House of the Seven Gables, James was put off when he asked directions from a young man who replied in Italian! Like seeing the razed house in Boston, hearing Italian in Salem exploded James's illusion of a homogeneous New England. James realized what he had come for and what he could not find. He had failed in his "search again, precisely, for the New England homogeneous—for the renewal of that impression of it which had lingered with me from a vision snatched too briefly, in a midsummer gloaming, long years ago."[89]

Yet James, in his meditation on Greater Boston places, does not conclude that one cannot go home again. Though "the place was not quite what my imagination had counted on," he searched on in Salem, as he had in Boston and Concord, for the redeeming image, the hidden sign that the world he had known still lived, despite its contemporary, "polyglot air." He continued to examine "the Salem Witch House" until he decided that its value resides in its endurance, its antithesis to surrounding modern structures, its preservation of "the mystery of antiquity." As James walked the neighborhood of Hawthorne's birth, he discovered a "small, Hawthornesque world, keeping the other, the smoky modernism, at a distance." A boy appeared, a "sympathetic American boy," James significantly notes, who pointed out the room in which Hawthorne had been born. James decided the boy was "the very genius of the place, feeding his small shrillness on the cold scraps of Hawthorne's leavings and with the making of his acquaintance alone worth the journey."[90] Though Hawthorne was gone, his presence still lived in the Salem streets where James, his imagination reinvigorated, rediscovered his place in the American scene. All was not, after all, lost.

HENRY JAMES and William Dean Howells left Boston in their lives and their arts. Yet they returned to Boston, in fact and in fiction. James and Howells met at the moment when the homogeneous ethnic and literary culture of Boston was breaking up, so they identified their own youthful literary expectations with the region's lost literary coherence. Yet both novelists carefully and eloquently recorded Boston's social and psychological shifts in the decades after the Civil War, even into this century. Therefore, whatever their reservations, they continued to shape the evolving image of Boston and showed it to be a steady source of inspiration. Boston embodied ideals and ideas worthy of their arts of fiction. Howells and James thus revitalized the "great tradition" of Boston letters in their myths of a city whose best days, they believed, were gone.

Their most revealing Boston books, *The Rise of Silas Lapham* and *The Bostonians*, portray a staid, sterile ascendancy which repels outsiders who come to Boston in search of culture. However, in each novel there is a saving grace. Marriage between an aristocrat and an outsider, Tom and Penelope, is for Howells a bridge between the classes of a divided city and a symbol of hope for the city's future. James's qualified tribute to Miss Birdseye and his portrayal of Olive Chancellor's belated discovery of her own voice are moments which, beneath his satire, acknowledge that Boston has had and might yet again have a worthy mission. In both novels Boston is a city of depth, history, and mystery beyond outsiders' capacities to understand. They know its secret. As such, Boston was rich soil for these novelists. Howells and James composed fictional parables which show spiritual quests—the struggle for personal and communal renewal—at the heart of what matters in Boston.

Both Howells and James admired and learned from Hawthorne, another novelist whose best work criticizes a city he would redeem. Hawthorne found Howells "worthy" and provided the young westerner with a model of the dedicated literary life. Hawthorne also showed young Henry James that an American could be an artist. Even more important, Hawthorne taught James how to see *through* the world, the interplay between surface and substance. James recognized that "the latent romance of New England" was Hawthorne's inspiration. "The secret play of the Puritan faith" served as a prod to Hawthorne's imagination to see beyond the world's surface to its symbolic implications. "The artist's imagination had to deck out the subject, to work it up, as we nowadays say; and Hawthorne's was—on intensely chastened lines—equal to the task." So, too, were the imaginations of Howells and James.[91]

4

Irish-America's Red Brick City:
EDWIN O'CONNOR'S BOSTON

The first night I sat down with Ronald Reagan in the White House, the president wanted to hear all about James Michael Curley, the four-time mayor of Boston who was immortalized in The Last Hurrah, *by Edwin O'Connor's famous novel about politics in Boston.*

—THOMAS P. O'NEILL,
Man of the House

AFTER Edwin O'Connor, not yet fifty, died in March of 1968, *The Atlantic* mourned his loss as "a death in the family." As a poorly paid reviewer for the *Boston Herald*, O'Connor had been aided by Edward Weeks, editor of *The Atlantic*. Weeks arranged to have O'Connor edit *Treadmill to Oblivion* in 1953, a memoir of early radio days by Fred Allen, who has been called the most popular Bostonian between Emerson and Kennedy.[1] Thus two Irish-Americans, Allen and O'Connor, who did much to shape the nation's conception of the Boston Irish—from "Allen's Alley" to City Hall—were supported by *The Atlantic*, that jewel in the crown of Boston Brahmin culture.

The Atlantic, wrote a later editor, Robert Manning, was O'Connor's "club" on Arlington Street, the place where he would drop in when he lived in his furnished rooms on Marlborough Street, "a few steps from our door." After *The Last Hurrah* became a financial and critical success, O'Connor moved, but not far from the center city of his imagination. In Boston he always lived within the elegant circle of Beacon Hill and Back Bay: on Beacon Street, then on Chestnut Street, finally back on Marlborough Street, where he bought a mansion across from his old rooming house. Throughout these moves, he came to *The Atlantic* daily, full of wit and charm. "He would deliver a marvelous story with a mimicry that was devastating but never unkind, or shift his big frame into a brief soft-shoe to the humming of 'Keep working, keep singing America!,' " recalls Manning.[2] Edwin O'Connor struck Bostonians as a gracious, smiling, public man, a winning Irish-American who was at ease in the cultural center of his elected home: Boston.

In the office of the editor of *The Atlantic*, at the time of O'Connor's death, stood a bust of William Dean Howells, the editor who gave the magazine its character and class, next to a window overlooking the Public Garden and, beyond, downtown Boston, his elected home. Edwin O'Connor and William Dean Howells were both ambitious young men who left their cultural provinces—Howells from Columbus, Ohio; O'Connor from Woonsocket, Rhode Island—to seek their fame and fortune in the Athens of America. Both men wrote novels (most notably Howells's *The Rise of Silas Lapham* and O'Connor's *The Last Hurrah*) which defined Boston as a symbolic, value-laden place where newcomers were ill at ease. Though these writers owed much to *The Atlantic*, each grew restive with Boston's cultural limitations. Howells left Boston for New York; O'Connor died in Boston, but part of him had already transcended the place he never named in his fiction, his red brick city.

Edwin O'Connor's fiction is characterized by an ambivalence toward those places which meant most to him. He was born in Providence in 1918, the son of Irish-American parents, a doctor and a teacher; he came of age in Woonsocket—a qualified idyll. Of Woonsocket O'Connor wrote, "to see it is not to love it."[3] Though

O'Connor loved Boston from the first moment he saw it, his works
are marked by a curious detachment from the city he seldom left,
a reluctance to commit either himself or his central characters to
any earthly place, even Boston.

In an upper middle-class, Yankee area of Woonsocket, O'Connor
grew up far from the roiling social and political world of Irish-
Americans he would discover in Boston. "I wanted to do a novel
on the whole Irish-American business. What the Irish got in America, they got through politics; so, of course, I had to use a political
framework."[4] Boston gave Edwin O'Connor his subject and theme:
the buoyant rise and sad demise of Irish-American culture.

O'Connor's achieved works of fiction—*The Last Hurrah* (1956),
The Edge of Sadness (1961), and *All in the Family* (1966)—articulate
a telling myth of Irish-American life in Boston, his original fictional
landscape.[5] As Edmund Wilson put it, "the Irish Catholic world
of Boston . . . had never before been exploited with this seriousness, intelligence and intimate knowledge."[6] Boston, however, was
a mixed blessing for his characters, a place where they could fulfill
the economic and political promise of America, but a place which
also tried their souls. "The whole Irish-American business" for
O'Connor became a parable of quest, hollow fulfillment, and defeat.
O'Connor's Boston fails to bring together its diverse citizenry into
a single community; in turn, his own people fail to fulfill their
city's high promises. Yet Boston teaches his representative Irish-
American characters to distinguish between worthy and unworthy
values.

Edwin O'Connor's fiction stands as his oblique spiritual autobiography: the discovery of his true subject—the record of his own
kind, the story of their religious and political seizure of a city—
and his renunciation of the city which tested his Irish-Americans:
Boston. Like other writers, O'Connor was both inspired and disappointed by the city upon a hill; he took to heart its lasting lesson:
the need to quest for spiritual transcendence.

BOSTON did not welcome Irish Catholics, though the city required their labors. In turn, Irish Catholics battled Yankee-Brahmin Boston, though the immigrants often adopted New England values. The immigrant Irish sought "room at the top" of the city upon a hill through education, thrift, and hard work, those Yankee values, as a popular verse of the turn of the century shows.

> Fancy the world a hill, lad,
> Look where the millions stop;
> You'll find the crowd at the base, lad,
> There's always room at the top.[7]

If Boston's first families, who lived at the top of Beacon Hill, reminded the Irish immigrant of their former Anglo-Irish landlords, the Boston Lowells, Cabots, and Lodges also served as their models of American propriety and achievement. As though both groups were trapped on an island, rather than crowded onto a peninsula, the Yankee-Celt encounter grew into a grudging marriage of convenience, driven by necessity, often acrimonious, but also not without respect, even love. Though their relations have been characterized by vacillation between separation and integration, Boston has been recomposed and revitalized by this Yankee-Celt passion play. "What is remarkable about the immigrant peoples—not Irish only, but all," writes Thomas N. Brown, "is the readiness with which they have adopted the Yankee past as their own and have become attached to the old places."[8]

For two centuries Catholics were persecuted in Boston, a city which tolerated an annual event called "Pope's Day," when unruly parades from the South End and North End met, battled, then joined in burning their effigies of the Pope. Finally, General George Washington ordered the Continental Army in Cambridge to cease "that ridiculous and childish custom."[9] By the 1830s Boston's Catholic population numbered 8,000, a threatening mass to Yankee residents. Lyman Beecher preached that Catholicism was incompatible with democracy because the Pope controlled the thoughts of his flock. A campaign against Catholics by "Native

Americans" set the background for the burning of the Ursuline Convent, Charlestown, in 1834. Francis J. Grund, one of the few native Bostonians who took a sympathetic interest in the fate of the Irish newcomers, warned them to remain orderly and to seek their place in Boston through the political system.[10] Boston's growing Irish-Catholic community took this advice with a vengeance in the next century.

When the Cunard Line opened regular, inexpensive, transatlantic steam service in 1842, Irish peasants from Cork, Kerry, Galway, and Clare flooded Boston's docks. In the midst of Ireland's Great Famine, thirty-seven thousand immigrants arrived in Boston in 1847. Between 1845 and 1855 the population of Boston increased by a third: fifty thousand of Boston's hundred sixty thousand citizens were Irish. In *Letters on Irish Emigration,* Edward Everett Hale called this "the most remarkable social phenomenon of our time."[11] For those who were optimistic, the Irish newcomers represented an opportunity for the revitalization of Boston culture. Ralph Waldo Emerson saw in them the possibilities of "a new race, a new religion, a new state, a new literature."[12] On the other hand, ascendancy voices felt their identities, even their lives, threatened by immigrants. "We are vanishing into provincial obscurity," said Barret Wendell of Harvard. "America has swept from our grasp. The future is beyond us."[13] The Irish had their Brahmin defenders, including Thomas Wentworth Higginson, abolitionist and soldier, self-described "Protestant of the Protestants," who had witnessed the bigotry of mob action when, as a boy, he saw a mob burn the Ursuline Convent.[14] But the stronger voice of Henry Cabot Lodge, scholar and statesman, dominated the discussion of Irish immigrants. They were, he said in 1881, a "very undesirable addition" to Boston, for they were "hard-drinking, idle, quarrelsome, and disorderly," a people "always at odds with the government."[15] A *fin de siècle* sense of loss pervaded the Brahmin community late in the nineteenth century and, curiously, still offered a rationale for Boston's alleged demise into the 1960s.[16]

Culture remained the issue for the Boston Irish for a century: the preservation of its own Irish-Catholic cultural identity against the counterpressures of a Yankee-Brahmin Boston culture. Each newcomer, Oscar Handlin states, "suffered a thoroughgoing physical metamorphosis," and faced "the necessity for a radically different cultural orientation."[17] Most of the Boston Irish sought refuge within their own community, but many tried to emulate the ways of the Boston ascendancy. Catholics were divided over the issue of parochial schools as a means of preserving Catholic values and resisting Yankee indoctrination.[18] This division of class and values *within* the Boston Irish population persisted for a century, climaxing in the controversy surrounding federally ordered integration of Boston's public schools in the 1970s. In his discussion of that ethnic and racial drama, J. Anthony Lukas singled out the acrimonious exchanges between Judge J. Arthur Garrity and James J. Sullivan, attorney for the Boston School Committee, as an informing parable in which two sides of the Irish-American community were set against each other. Garrity represented middle-class aspirations, while Sullivan remained loyal to "his clan, his turf, his blood" in 1974. "Indeed, the struggle in Arthur Garrity's courtroom that year often resembled an Irish morality play, fought out between various conceptions of what it meant to be Irish in contemporary Boston."[19] It has long been difficult to reconcile what it means to be Irish with what it means to be a Bostonian.

THE Boston Protestant ascendancy had a far different notion of what constituted *culture* than did the Irish newcomers. In his "Discourses in America," Matthew Arnold articulated a formula which educated Bostonians took to heart: the aim of culture is "*to know the best which has been thought and said in the world,*" not to practice sectarian celebration.[20] Those who did not "know" were philistines. It was just here that Bostonians found immigrants lacking, so culture became a Brahmin refuge and a barricade against immigrant encroachment upon *their* Boston. In the personas of "Bridget," the housemaid, and "Paddy," the tender of horses and furnaces, the Irish were accepted in Brahmin houses.[21] However, proper Bostonians were offended by boisterous Irish wakes and sports—John L. Sullivan, the "Boston Strong Boy," embodied "Mick" pugnaciousness—and they were fearful of the Irish immigrants' love of marching (forming militias) and their "monster" field days at Franklin Park. With their own habits, rituals, religion, and societies, the Boston Irish inhabited a separate world of values in a divided city.[22] On the other hand, what Bostonians saw as expressions of culture seemed to challenge the identities of immigrants. "The few Irishmen conscious of Boston's contemporary literature," writes Oscar Handlin, "were shocked and antagonized by its rational romanticism, regarding it as exclusively Protestant, overwhelmingly English, and suspect on both grounds."[23]

The Catholic church and ward politics, institutions which Edwin O'Connor would make central to his fiction, were the cultural strongholds of the Boston Irish. Religion and politics, more than the arts, reinforced their cultural identity and provided them access to Boston's power structure.

CONSIDER Saint Stephen's Church, in the city's North End, as a symbol of evolving religious and cultural identity in Boston, an emblem of conflict and cohesion. The church, founded as the Middle Street Meeting House, has stood on the same site, now Hanover Street, since 1714. It was rebuilt in 1730 as the New North Congregational Society, whose membership included Paul Revere. Indeed, Paul Revere is said to have cast the bell that adorned the "New North" church when it was extensively redesigned in 1804 by Charles Bulfinch; he was inspired by Italian Renaissance models, which he adapted to Boston tastes, using Doric columns and red brick facing. Soon the church was rededicated as the Second Church, Unitarian. In 1862, after Irish immigrants had overwhelmed the North End and its former residents had escaped to other parts of the city, the church was bought by the Archdiocese of Boston and renamed Saint Stephen's. Late nineteenth-century photographs show elaborate decorations and murals, evidence of its transformation from Protestant to Catholic hands.

So Saint Stephen's must have looked when, in February of 1863, John Francis Fitzgerald—future mayor and grandfather of President John F. Kennedy—was brought there to be baptized. Doris Kearns Goodwin speaks of the attraction that this church held at that time for the uprooted peasants of Ireland and their American-born children. It was their cultural sanctuary. "For the sheer beauty of the church building alone opened up to them, as to all their neighbors in the North End, an inner world of sounds, smells and sights in stark contrast to the world outside." In Saint Stephen's all the Fitzgerald children were baptized and received their first communion. When, on 1 January 1906, John Fitzgerald became the mayor of Boston, the pastor of Saint Stephen's offered a prayer at his swearing-in ceremonies. For the Kennedys, indeed for most of the North End Irish, Saint Stephen's became "a second home," a symbol of their presence in Boston.[24]

By the middle of the twentieth century—the North End long since having shifted from an Irish to an Italian population—Saint Stephen's had fallen into disrepair. Extensive restorations were then undertaken at the direction of Richard Cardinal Cushing, an intimate of the Kennedy family who offered prayers at both John Kennedy's presidential inauguration in 1961 and at his funeral in 1963. Though Cardinal Cushing was a Boston Irishman with little claim to cultural sophistication, he converted Saint Stephen's from a Catholic fortress into a graceful, ecumenical emblem for Boston. Catholic ornamentation was stripped or subdued and the church was returned to its original Bulfinch design, even to the restoration of its grand chandeliers; after this work, the church displayed its original clean, curving lines, with stark contrasts of polished wood and white walls. Saint Stephen's became an exemplary fusion of Boston's dominant heritages. Cardinal Cushing showed that the two cultures—Protestant and Brahmin, Irish and Catholic—can successfully merge in a work of art.

JOHN BOYLE O'REILLY was the most distinguished writer to emerge from the Boston Irish community in the last decades of the nineteenth century. More than any other man, he attempted to bridge the cultural gap between Irish and Yankee citizens, to fuse religion and politics in his art. He spoke for and to his people's gratitude and patriotism in Boston.

O'Reilly's past had been circuitous. Born in Ireland, in 1844, he was court-martialed for plotting nationalism while a member of the Tenth Hussars; then, as a Fenian he was banished to a penal colony in Australia in 1867. O'Reilly eventually escaped and assumed his identity as an American with an unambiguous passion: "we can do Ireland more good by our Americanism than by our Irishism."[25]

O'Reilly spread his views—selling the Irish immigrants to Bostonians and American patriotism to the newcomers—when in 1874, at age thirty, he became editor and co-owner of *The Pilot*, an Irish-American newspaper, a position he held until his death in 1890. In Boston he was helped to his editorial post by Dr. Robert Dwyer Joyce, author of *Ballads of Irish Chivalry*, and Patrick Collins, future mayor of the city, illustrating the increasing power of Boston's Irish counterculture.[26]

Founded in 1838 as an immigrant press, "an *Irish* and *Catholic* journal," *The Pilot*, "the Irishman's Bible," has long been the official organ of the archdiocese of Boston. Under Patrick Donahue, its owner, *The Pilot* served to bind the Irish-American community in Boston, particularly through its column, "Missing Friends," where families and loved ones who had been scattered by their crossings from Ireland were reunited.[27] *The Pilot*'s original purpose persists: "the elevation of the Irish character in this country, the Independence of Ireland, and the overthrow of sectarian prejudice."[28]

John Boyle O'Reilly, though fiercely anti-British, attempted to accommodate the immigrant Irish to Anglophile Boston culture. He played down Irish cultural separation and stressed the tradition of Irish-America's steady, unquestioning patriotism. O'Reilly's poem "America" (1882), read at the reunion of the Army of the Potomac, celebrated the "two clasping hands" of North and South, a subtle vaunting of his toleration and reconciliation themes. It was pronounced "the greatest poem I have ever heard" by U. S. Grant, who was present for the reading. John Greenleaf Whittier honored

"America" for its "poetic beauty as well as [its] noble enthusiasm of patriotism." O'Reilly was also invited to write a poem for the dedication of Plymouth Rock in 1899.[29] He was even invited to join that Brahmin literary sanctuary, the Tavern Club. O'Reilly was praised by Brahmins, like Higginson and Oliver Wendell Holmes, who said he was "thankful that you are with us as a representative Americanized Irishman." O'Reilly, then, was honored not so much for his poetic talents, his *cultural* achievements, as for his patriotic and chauvinistic sentiments.[30]

Indeed O'Reilly's claims to a poetic achievement were slight. His poetry was the conventional jingly and jingoistic verse of the day. "The Exile of the Gael" illustrates:

> No treason we bring from Erin—nor bring we shame
>   nor guilt!
> The sword we hold may be broken, but we have not
>   dropped the hilt!
> The wreath we bear to Columbia is twisted of thorns,
>   not bays,
> And the songs we sing are saddened by thought of
>   desolate days.
> But the hearts we bring for Freedom are washed in the
>   surge of tears,
> And we claim our right by a People's fight outliving a
>   thousand years![31]

The kind of Americans O'Reilly wished his people to become was made clear in "A Philistine's View," an essay which supported the middle-class reader who prefers "proper" fiction. "Being a Philistine myself, I vote with him."[32] That is, O'Reilly proclaimed himself to be that very person, the philistine, or narrow moralist, who was held up by Arnold as the model of one who is deficient in liberal culture and general enlightenment. Caught in a paradox, O'Reilly would not have his idea of culture defined by an Englishman, though in every other way O'Reilly shaped his values to conform to the conservative Boston literary establishment, which derived its notion of culture from Arnold. On the other hand,

O'Reilly's advocacy of labor legislation and his outrage over racism made him a political progressive.[33] Thus he spoke with one voice in *The Pilot* and another voice in the Tavern Club. O'Reilly was a representative Irish-American of his era, stretched by conflicting cultural claims. The tensions he tried to resolve may have led to his death, perhaps a suicide, at age forty-five. Buried under a megalith in Brookline's Holyhood Cemetery, O'Reilly also is honored by a memorial in Boston's Fenway. Sculpted by Daniel Chester French in 1896, O'Reilly is there depicted with Erin and her sons, Courage and Poetry; Celtic carvings form the background.[34] John Boyle O'Reilly is deservedly honored, for he was the first Irish-American writer both to break into the inner sanctum of Boston culture and to make Boston culture attractive to the Irish.

REPRESENTATIVE figures from Irish Boston's religious and political past illustrate that community's range of response, from their quest for acceptance to their spiritual transcendence of Boston, in the "next parish" west of Ireland.

John Bernard Fitzpatrick, who became third bishop of Boston in 1846, worked to reconcile hostilities between the two cultures during a period in which Catholics were persecuted; he also spread the influence of the Catholic church in New England. Fitzpatrick's Boston, whose streets he loved to walk, whose citizens respected him, became a city of greater tolerance and diversity. William Cardinal O'Connell, archbishop of the Boston diocese (1907–11) and later Cardinal (1911–44), also identified with Boston's moneyed Protestants, but Cardinal O'Connell had a constricting effect on Boston Catholics, enforcing a censorious sectarianism upon his flock. Despite his acceptance of Brahmin values—only wealthy and educated Catholics were entitled to "high culture," he said—he also believed that "the puritan has passed. The Catholic remains."[35] However, O'Connell tried to remake Boston into a city of Catholic Puritanism. Richard Cardinal Cushing (1944–70) shared his predecessors' territorial imperative and their patriotic anticommunism, but he was far more open to new modes of expression within his church, his flock, and his city. Cushing modeled himself more on Fitzgerald than on O'Connell. Taken together, Boston's Catholic church leaders gave a fuller voice and a more secure identity to the Boston Irish at the same time they addressed the ambivalent relationship between the Yankee and the Celt. Boston, a city founded by English Puritans, gradually redefined itself to include Irish Catholics.

Boston's Irish politicians fought on both sides of the cultural struggle, defending the preferences of their constituents while aspiring for acceptance in Brahmin circles. Hugh O'Brien, Boston's first Irish mayor (1884–88), for example, raised funds for the completion of the Boston Public Library, which he saw as "a monument to our intelligence and culture," but he also ordered Boston's libraries closed on St. Patrick's Day. He advocated wage and election reforms, improved public utilities systems and, characteristically, completed a bridge across the Charles River to link sections of the city from Dorchester to Cambridge. Fourteen years after O'Brien's defeat, Boston elected its second Irish-born mayor, Patrick A. Collins, another figure of cultural reconciliation. "In American politics we are Americans, pure and simple," said Collins.[36] O'Brien and Collins illustrated the opportunities available in Brahmin Boston to those who could at once represent the interests of their community and acknowledge the worth of Boston's cultural establishment. However, when power passed to Boston-born, Irish-American mayors, a new, more aggressive and less cultivated voice emerged to speak for the community. Politics ceased to be a means toward cultural union and instead became an end, Irish power, in this increasingly fragmented city. John Fitzgerald, from the North End, was elected mayor of Boston in 1906. His two terms were marked by vast spendings on public works, corruption, and charm from the man who sang "Sweet Adeline" and built a political machine.

An incident from the Fitzgerald era illustrates the conjunction of religion and politics in Irish Boston, a revealing moment which eventually resulted in a work of art. Cardinal O'Connell brought pressure upon Mayor Fitzgerald to refuse permission for his daughter, Rose, to attend Wellesley College, a symbol of Protestant aristocratic culture. Instead, O'Connell insisted that Rose enroll in the Academy of the Sacred Heart, which she did in 1907. Seven decades later, despite all the other trials she had endured, Rose Kennedy still found this painful. "My greatest regret is not having gone to Wellesley College," she confessed.[37] Rose Fitzgerald Kennedy here expressed the desire for social acceptance and respectability which only a Seven Sisters college could confer upon a daughter of Boston's Irish immigrants. At Wellesley College Rose had hoped to learn the ways of the world and to make a place for herself in it, just as Joseph Kennedy had sought acceptance and contacts at Harvard. Later her husband would respond to social rebuffs against the Irish with anger, but Rose was always puzzled and pained by rejection. She once asked a Harvard student from a Brahmin family, a friend of her sons, "When are the nice people of Boston going to accept us?"[38]

In 1987 Rose Kennedy's crisis became the subject of a dramatic monologue written by Molly Manning Howe, founder of Cambridge's Poets' Theater. (As her name suggests, Molly Manning Howe—an Irish actress and playwright who married a Bostonian—combined Boston's two cultures; she also contributed to its arts.)[39] Howe composed a drama about Rose Kennedy's disappointment at missing her chance to attend Wellesley College. *Go Lovely Rose* offers rare insight, in part because it is from a woman's point of view, into the costs exacted by Boston's cultural tensions:

> Rose may have been the most intelligent of all the Kennedy family, and she might have made a difference in the world. As a girl she was dying to stretch her wings. She could have been somebody. But it was snatched away from her. Her father betrayed her, put her in that terrible convent school. And she still carries the scar.[40]

Go Lovely Rose was produced at the John F. Kennedy Library, located in Dorchester, near the streets on which the Fitzgeralds had once lived. In the first scene young Rose is thrilled by the chance to attend Wellesley College, to realize her potential as an independent woman, but then, in the second scene, she is crushed by the news that Cardinal O'Connell and her father have decided her fate: she must learn how to be a good Catholic mother at Sacred Heart. Finally, in Howe's dramatic monologue Rose is at once acquiescent to their demand and defiant in the way she will carry it out: she will, she vows, become "the mother of kings"! These words, her exit line and the drama's climax, resonated in the Library dedicated to John F. Kennedy and housing, as well, a tribute to Rose's other fallen son, Robert Kennedy. Suddenly, the achievements of the Kennedy sons could be seen as evidence of Rose Fitzgerald Kennedy's frustration and displaced ambition. As in so many other local political legends, history is here reinvigorated, even reinvented, in the imagination of a Boston writer.[41]

Rose's father, "Honey Fitz," was succeeded by James Michael Curley, who dominated Boston politics for the first half of the twentieth century, serving eight years in Congress, sixteen years as mayor of Boston and two years as governor of Massachusetts. He also served two jail terms! Curley perfected and exploited the art of combativeness to the delight of his Irish-American constituents and the consternation of his critics. Both the product of his harsh environment and the creation of his own creative imagination, Curley's image ranges from the rogue saint of his flattering self-description in his autobiography, *I'd Do It Again*—where he is the "champion of the oppressed and underprivileged"—to the exploitative man of power without vision in William V. Shannon's *The American Irish*.[42]

Even Curley's house became an ambiguous legend. In 1915 Curley moved his family into a large, new, gracious Georgian Revival home, overlooking Jamaica Pond, which has been called the sapphire in the "Emerald Necklace" of Frederick Law Olmstead. Though Curley earned only ten thousand dollars annually in salary, the house and lot cost sixty thousand dollars. Contractors explained that they had built it for the mayor at no charge because it was a "demonstrations house"! His people called it the "shamrock house," because shamrocks were carved into its shutters. The Curley house stands as an emblem of the aggressive arrival of the Irish-American in the heart of Brahmin Boston.[43]

In his autobiography, Thomas P. "Tip" O'Neill, former Speaker of the House, includes two pictures of himself with James Michael Curley. In the first photograph, the young O'Neill—upright, stern, and staring off into the middle distance, dressed in a double-breasted suit—stands beside the buoyant governor Curley, whose shrewd eyes are fixed upon the camera. In the second, the elderly Tip, rumpled and laughing, sits on the memorial bench dedicated to Curley behind Boston's City Hall, apparently conversing with Curley's bronze statue, which sits attentively posed in perpetual gaze upon anyone who chooses to share his bench. In these two pictures, James Michael Curley is transformed from a posing politician into an icon of the imagination, a figure who promises to be alert to whatever you might say about yourself—and even more attentive to whatever you might say about him.

Curley lives on as an ambiguous image. Tip O'Neill affirms, then blurs the distinction between Curley as man and Curley as legend. *"The Last Hurrah,* as good as it is, doesn't begin to do justice to its subject. But what novel could? There are times when real life throws up characters who are more fantastic than any that are found in books. When the good Lord made James Michael Curley, He broke the mold." However, O'Neill then places Curley in the mythic mold of the rogue saint. "Curley was a great Irish folk hero." O'Neill's anecdotes enforce this legend. When they were asked to work together to collect money for the poor with the Boston *Post* Santa, O'Neill, then a novice at politicians' ways, accepted contributions, putting money in the pot, but he was shocked to discover that Curley was dipping into the pot, giving the money away to cronies and constituents nearly as fast as O'Neill was collecting it! But the rogue had a heart. When Curley saw city hall scrubwomen on their knees, he ordered long-handled mops. And the rogue was sage. When Curley saw an up-and-coming young politician like O'Neill, Curley offered pithy advice: "Son, it's nice to be important. But remember—it's more important to be nice." Central to O'Neill's version of the Curley myth is the former mayor's selfless disdain of personal profit. "Despite all the money that Curley was able to steal, he didn't have a quarter when he died." Selflessness apparently mitigates dishonesty for O'Neill. Whatever Curley did he did for his friends or for his people! Above all, this Curley was the glory of his Irish-American constituents, who admired him and his grand house as sources of ethnic pride; Curley personified their arrival in Boston. "The Yankees look down on him as a shanty-Irish rogue, but Curley did a tremendous amount of good for the people of Boston," concludes O'Neill.[44]

William Shannon, the late journalist and former ambassador to Ireland, also saw Curley as a rogue, but Shannon insists Curley was a destructive influence upon the Boston Irish. Shannon's Curley was driven by nothing more ennobling than "a fierce, unfocused instinct for personal power." He gave voice to previously suppressed discontents within the community by exploiting the hostilities between Celts and Yankees. "He solved nothing; he moved towards no larger understanding; he opened no new lines of communication."[45]

In his novel of the Boston Irish, *Mortal Friends* (1978), James Carroll also portrays Curley as a man darkly driven by an unfocused lust for power. At one point the novel's hero discovers that Curley "embodied the Irish and loved them, but he would do anything in his pursuit of power, even hand over his own to Beacon Hill Brit bloodhounds."[46]

Curley's first biographer, Joseph F. Dineen, in *The Purple Shamrock* (1949), a book published in the year in which Curley was defeated in his campaign to be reelected mayor, is less judgmental in its tracing of Curley's rise and its attendant costs. (In his 1936 novel, *Ward Eight*, Dineen sympathetically portrayed the era of the Boston Irish ward boss.)[47] Dineen's Curley was "the last of the political buccaneers, ungovernable, unmanageable, irrepressible, incorrigible, apparently indestructible."[48] James Michael Curley has receded into myths, codified in bronze and words.

Such was the immediate literary and political context available to Edwin O'Connor when he appropriated Curley as a model for Frank Skeffington in *The Last Hurrah*. By the mid-1950s, Curley's political day was past. During his fourth term he had served five months in the Federal Correctional Institute in Danbury, Connecticut for mail fraud, until he was pardoned by President Truman, though Congressman John F. Kennedy, Curley's successor in the eleventh congressional district of Massachusetts, refused to sign the petition for his pardon. By the time O'Connor fictionalized his career, Curley had been defeated three times in his effort to regain the office of mayor of Boston; his style seemed crude in the television age of Kennedy. After *The Last Hurrah* was published, Curley was worried about the way Bostonians would respond to the novel's hero; Curley even threatened to sue O'Connor.

However, it soon became clear to Curley that readers had great affection for O'Connor's fictional mayor, Frank Skeffington. Encountering Curley on a Boston trolley, O'Connor hesitated to speak because Curley had filed his suit against O'Connor's publisher and the movie company which planned to make a film of the novel. To O'Connor's surprise, Curley motioned him over. " 'You know,' confided the former mayor to the novelist, 'the part of your book I liked the best was when I was dying.' "⁴⁹

Curley quickly exploited his identification with Skeffington by publishing an autobiography, *I'd Do It Again,* a book which reveled in his triumphs over Irish and Brahmin adversaries, justified his misdeeds and struck a rare note of conciliation. As an elder statesman of Boston, he could now, he noted, meet Ralph Lowell on friendly terms in the Harvard Club; the dark days of discrimination were past. Now the feuds were over and "the Lowells and the Cabots speak to the Curleys."⁵⁰

Myth and fact merge in the Curley legend. During his political career the *Boston Globe* had criticized Curley so consistently that his son, Frank Curley, a former Jesuit priest, refused to read the newspaper for four decades. Yet when the Curley mansion, at 350 Jamaicaway, was put up for auction by the Oblate Fathers in early 1988, Frank Curley consented to a *Globe* interview, during which he praised O'Connor's novel. "He may have done some of his writing at the Ritz-Carlton bar," said Frank Curley of O'Connor, "but he did his research in all the barrooms around town, especially

Southie, because he would go in and buy drinks for old codgers there, and get them started telling stories."[51] Then the *Globe* editorial page further enforced the Curley-as-Robin-Hood legend by taking the editorial position that the city of Boston should raise money "to save a home where so much Boston political history was made," the Curley manse. "Champions of the little people are few. Until [Raymond] Flynn was elected [mayor of Boston], little people had not had a vigorous advocate in City hall since Curley's last mayoral hurrah in 1949."[52]

In April 1988, the city of Boston purchased the former home of James Michael Curley for $1.2 million. Only the churlish would point out that the city had by then paid for the house *twice:* once through builders' kickbacks, in return for city contracts during the Mayor Curley era, then again through direct purchase in Mayor Flynn's day!

WHEN Edwin O'Connor decided to write up "the whole Irish-American business," he drew upon all this: the religious, political, class, and cultural history of the Boston Irish. In doing so, O'Connor provided a parable of loss which would influence others' interpretations of Irish-American experience. For example, in 1960 Daniel Patrick Moynihan saw the election of John F. Kennedy as a "last hurrah" for Irish-American politics in America.[53] The assassination of Kennedy in 1963 reinforced this mode of wistful remembrance, particularly in Boston, where the Kennedy family is a political institution. From their emigration (their "exile") from Ireland, many Irish in America have cultivated this sense of loss. Their history of defeat and occupation in Ireland and their Catholic world view, argues Kerby A. Miller, "provided an ideological defense against change and misfortune, and the basis for a nationalistic assertion of Irish identity."[54] Boston encouraged Irish-American defensiveness, confirmed their defeatism, and enforced their ethnic cohesiveness; at the same time it provided paradoxical opportunities for their worldly success and their abandonment of ethnic identity. Even their success suggested their cultural limitations, for the Boston Irish often settled for security over self-development. In the words of Dennis P. Ryan, "the Boston Irish as a group were particularly short-sighted in opting for secure but financially dead-end jobs as government employees and union wage earners, rather than taking advantage of more remunative and prestigious opportunities in business and the professions."[55]

Edwin O'Connor celebrated the values that sustained the Irish-Americans in their long seige on Boston's sanctuaries of power and privilege: their pride, loyalty, combativeness, energy, and wit; above all he delighted in their *talk*, full of blarney and bluster. But O'Connor also detached himself from mere ethnic chauvinism, for his Irish-Americans are finally consumed by the same values which nourished them. Either they abandon their identity or they harden into chauvinism and blind allegiances. Even their talk declines into cant: bullying and verbal lunacy. They have no future in the city, only memories. In Edwin O'Connor's world, those who have no connection with their cultural heritage are hollow men; on the other hand, those who immerse themselves wholly in their Irish-American identity lose themselves in the parochial. His best men draw vitality from their ethnic and urban heritage, but they also realize that there are greater worlds beyond. Edwin O'Connor's novels provide the urban landscapes and dramatic occasions for men—O'Connor inadequately represents Irish-American women—who were wedged between cultures, men trying to define themselves in relation to their family, their Irish-American community, and their city: Boston. Significantly, O'Connor never identifies his red brick city as Boston, though *The Last Hurrah*, *The Edge of Sadness*, and *All in the Family* could be set nowhere else. Though he was a literary realist in the manner of Howells or James, though he was determined to "do" Boston, O'Connor remained detached in his portrayal of place—Boston, his adopted, if temporary, home.

O'CONNOR'S myth of the Boston Irish moves from celebration to renunciation, a motion illustrated in his three major works. In the main plot of each, an aging Irish-American makes a final gesture of personal and cultural affirmation, his "last hurrah"; then he exits, having become a myth. In the subplots of these novels, younger Irish-Americans, through whose eyes the aging patriarchs are seen, return to the place of their childhood, their elders' city, to become caught up in the Irish-American tribal world and to bear witness to the final arias of its chieftains. These centers of consciousness— in *Sadness* and *Family* they are the novels' narrators—confront the full force of Irish-American life and culture, religious and political, a world best conveyed in talk. Each of O'Connor's heroes traces his cultural roots, makes his separate peace with his heritage and serves as a go-between for the reader, who is carried deep into the heart of the Irish-American landscape.

The Last Hurrah deserves to be Edwin O'Connor's most popular work, for it is his sunniest novel, though it too is edged with sadness. This novel dramatizes a reconciliation, even before John F. Kennedy's election made ethnicity chic, between America's common readers and the previously suspect world of Irish-American politics. The plot alternates between the last campaign and the final days of Frank Skeffington, seventy-two-year-old mayor of "The City," and the cultural initiation of Adam Caulfield, Skeffington's nephew, a college-educated Irish-American who is newly arrived in the city, a young man who is barely aware of his heritage.

On his deathbed Skeffington affirms his life. (When one of his enemies, thinking the old mayor had fallen forever silent, gloats, saying that Skeffington might live his life differently if he had it to do over, Skeffington rallies, shouting *"The hell I would!"*[56] Characteristically, James Michael Curley appropriated and slightly revised this defiant phrase for the title of his autobiography, *I'd Do it Again*.) Adam, who stands by the dying Skeffington, comes to respect the mayor and to accept the heritage of Irish-American politics and culture. Both plot lines serve to reconcile the reader with a reputedly corrupt—at the least an ethnic political tradition dependent upon what George Washington Plunkett called "honest graft"—and archaic political tradition.[57]

At first Adam is put off by the comic grotesques of this ethnic world. When Skeffington brings him to Knocko Minihan's wake, for example, Adam is shocked at the irreverent attitude toward the deceased, a political hanger-on. Delia Boylan, an elderly woman who never misses a wake, judges the aesthetics of the corpse with cool professionalism: "He looks grand with the cheeks all puffed out, don't he?" Delia, however, makes it clear that her respect has nothing to do with the deceased, for she has no use for Knocko: "He was mean as a panther, but good luck to him."[58] Adam—a pallid chap who makes his living by drawing cartoons for a city newspaper—thinks Skeffington is misusing the wake as a campaign rally, but eventually Adam comes to realize that the Irish-American wake, including its drinking and politicking, serves as an important ritual of ethnic, cultural affirmation, a ceremony of renewal for community cohesion.

The wake scene is a parable of reconciliation, a brief illustration of the pattern of the whole novel. Skeffington blackmails the greedy undertaker into charging only thirty-five dollars for the lavish funeral he had planned to impose on Knocko's confused widow, using his mayoral power in an arbitrary, illegal, and benevolent fashion. At the same time Skeffington presents her with a thousand dollars out of his own pocket (but how did it get *into* his pocket?), justifying Irish boss politics as a triumph of compassion over ethics. Like Delia Boylan, Adam studies the flaws in his people, but he finally wishes them well. Tellingly, the Boston Irish-American community is most vividly realized—at once comic, devious, and sentimental, awash in wild talk—at a wake.

The Last Hurrah celebrates Skeffington and "*his* city, the wonderful, old, sprawling chaos of a city, whose ancient tangled streets and red bricks and ugly piles of quarried stone had held his heart forever."[59] Yet the city also has a destructive element, both for Skeffington and for the Irish. In the end, the city, to which he gave his heart, takes Skeffington's life and steals the soul of his people: Skeffington has a heart attack after being rejected by a duped electorate. Though he would do it all over again, the Irish-American mayor was finally undone by the city which made him, the city which he remade.

He knew it block by block, almost building by building, and while there had been population shifts, he had noted each one in detail. As the Yankees had moved in indignant retreat before the Irish, as the Irish had done likewise before the Italians, as if much smaller invasions of Greek, Syrian and Chinese had worked their minor dislocations, Skeffington had marked them all with sustained care, losing interest only when the migrants passed beyond the city limits, and so beyond the local vote.[60]

The Last Hurrah, as its title indicates, is a novel of cultural limitations and loss. It satirizes the Boston Brahmins, who are caricaturized as selfish and hypocritical. Cabel Force had had Skeffington's mother arrested for stealing, though he paid her slave wages and *expected* the Irish to steal, so that his presumptions about their character deficiencies might be confirmed. Norman Cass is a banker who hates the Irish and his son is a fool whom Skeffington can use to blackmail Cass. But O'Connor is far more interested in examining his own kind than he is in satirizing the Boston ascendancy. The whole novel, form and content, is an extended Irish wake. Skeffington's followers are comic characters and cranks, but they lack vision; they cannot see beyond the next election. O'Connor's irony, inspired by Evelyn Waugh, reveals their limited goals and values. "And if a reward were not perpetual, it was the best that could be expected on this earth. It was a reward good for four years, until the next quadrennial election; no reasonable politician could hope for more."[61] When Skeffington loses, they have nothing to live for, for they had invested their spirit in the mayor. Some of Skeffington's Irish-Americans found a home in their city, but they grew self-centered, ethnocentric, and obsessive as a result; others abandoned the city and their roots for suburbanization. O'Connor, however, is less interested in the Irish-American voters, who seem easily led by manipulatory television images of Skeffington's opponent, than he is in the aging mayor. In the end, Skeffington is forgiven because his day is deemed to be past. Surely a hasty judgment.

In 1987 Boston elected an Irish-American mayor—Raymond L. Flynn, from South Boston, who promised to restore Boston's neighborhoods, even its deteriorating bath houses, built by Mayor Curley. Irish-Americans still controlled Boston's school committee, its city council, its police, and its bureaucracy. Further, these Irish-Americans thrive in a city all but free from ethnic, if not racial, hostility. An ironic term, "CWASP" (Catholic White Anglo-Saxon Protestant), has even been devised to account for a telling phenomenon: how "Catholic boys from Boston neighborhoods are now in the power elite once reserved for only their Yankee cousins."[62]

The Last Hurrah, then, is a premature elegy for a lost world of Irish-American assertiveness which, purportedly passing away at the very moment when both Adam and the reader discover it, is glazed with sentiment, though O'Connor's working title had been *Not Moisten an Eye*. O'Connor celebrates Irish-America for the wonder of its arrival and its endurance, but he criticizes his people for their narrowness of vision and mourns the passing of their contingency. The novel is an elegy for the depleted character and the lost mission of a people.

Yet *The Last Hurrah* also demonstrates the vitality of Irish-Americans in an unnamed city, unmistakably Boston, and examines their emblem of achievement, a city hall which was "a lunatic pile of building: a great, grim, resolutely ugly dust-catcher," much like Boston's old city hall. Ugly though it was, some defenders saw in its "inefficient tangled warren the perfect symbol for municipal administration."[63] This city hall, in fact and in imagination, particularly suits O'Connor's vision of a Boston Irish political administration, an emblem of the Irish immigrants' experience in Boston.[64] It was a world, for all its humor, well-lost.

THE *Edge of Sadness* extends Edwin O'Connor's art of fiction and amplifies his myth of culture and place. Again an aging Irish-American patriarch, here Charlie Carmody, commits himself to a final gesture of self-affirmation: for his eighty-second birthday party Charlie reunites his family and the son of a friend, a priest. When Father Hugh Kennedy attends the gathering, he too becomes reinvolved in the Carmody family drama and, like Adam Caulfield, he becomes further initiated in Irish-American ways.

Father Hugh is "a muffled man," a fifty-five-year-old whiskey-priest who is holding himself together lest he fall off the wagon. After he lost his Irish-American parish, he was appointed pastor of Old Saint Paul's, a drafty, derelict church, "built like an armory," in an area of the city which has lost both its Irish population and much of its dignity.[65] Father Hugh Kennedy's encounter with Carmody restores the priest's dignity and prepares him for his final journey, to God's heavenly city. While *The Last Hurrah* mythologizes Boston's Irish-American political heritage, *The Edge of Sadness* treats Boston's Irish-American religious tradition.

Lying upon what he presumes to be his deathbed, after he has received the last rites, Charlie Carmody admits he is a hated man to Father Hugh. He blames his brutalizing Irish-American background.

> I came out of nothin'; you know that. My pa laid pipe in this city twelve hours a day and got paid a dollar for doin' it; we didn't any of us starve but we came damn close to it. And when I was on my way up, d'ye know how many around here gave me a break? Not a soul. Not a livin' soul. But I got there all the same, and once I did I gave them no more breaks than they gave me.[66]

O'Connor, in this dramatic monologue, catches the strain of bitterness which lies beneath the surface of ethnic and racial relations in Boston. Yet Charlie wants absolution from Father Hugh; Charlie wants the son of his old friend to say that Charlie was admired by Hugh's father, an honorable man. Hugh knows how much his father disapproved of Charlie, that combative Mick, but the priest shows mercy; he lies, creates a myth of consolation for Charlie, just as Skeffington had fabricated Knocko Minihan's nobility. Hugh invokes Irish blarney to counter Charlie's tirade and helps ease the death of this bitter man. Irish mist glazes harsh moral truths.

Though offered his old parish, Father Hugh decides to stay at tatty Saint Paul's, where he can connect with his poor parishioners and seek "the Richness, the Mercy, the immeasurable Love of God."[67] Finally he will not allow himself to be trapped inside any earthly place, not even the place he loves best: the Irish-American parish which gave him identity. O'Connor's hero is a man between worlds in this novel of qualified renunciation. As in *The Last Hurrah*, his hero again takes, as they say in Ireland, his "last look around" his beloved city and reflects upon all that it means before he prepares himself for his journey to another, better world. Another version of Boston is here repudiated for God's heavenly city.

IN *All in the Family*, his last complete and his finest novel, Edwin O'Connor makes his most eloquent statement about the power of place to define ethnic, family, and personal character. The place, though again unnamed, is clearly his adaptation of Boston, the same red brick city which Skeffington ruled. In fact the narrator, Jack Kinsella, served as Skeffington's last secretary; now, at age forty-nine, a successful author of mystery-suspense stories, he returns to the city of his youth when Charles Kinsella, his cousin, is elected governor. Jack experiences a rush of love for his city, a renewed sense of place, but not without ambivalence. "So I was bound here, it was a pleasant place to live, and yet it—and those who lived here—had been sold down the river time and time again. Politically it was a mess, and close to being a disaster."[68] Jack Kinsella's musings about his city foreshadow central questions in the novel. Can community here exist for Jack, who has been cut off from his Irish-American heritage since the death of his father? Can family here exist for Jack, who has been alone since his wife left him for another man? Is there *any* city, any earthly *place*, where a man might live a worthy life?

The political branch of the Kinsella clan illustrates O'Connor's lessons on cultural heritage, community, and family. Charles's election, for example—by the Kennedy-like "improbable coalition" of interest groups, radical and ethnic voting blocks, idealists and hacks—suggests that change is possible in this corrupt state. So believed Phil Kinsella, Charles's brother, who was Jack's cousin and closest friend. Phil, who acted as his brother's conscience, told his cousin, "there had been Adlai [Stevenson], there had been Jack [Kennedy], and now there was Charles."[69] That sentence is clearly designed by O'Connor to suggest that the Kinsellas are *not* a fictional representation of the Kennedys, despite the obvious resemblance between those smooth, cautious, ambitious media politicians, Charles Kinsella and John Kennedy; despite the further resemblance between those tough, loyal, moralistic brothers, Phil Kinsella and Bobby Kennedy. Clearly the Kinsellas *are* O'Connor's loose version of the Kennedys. To further the parallel, both families are ruled by strong-willed patriarchs, rich founding fathers who sought family validation through the political achievements of their sons. Friends of O'Connor report he worried that *All in the Family* would be seen as a *roman à clef*, which is exactly how it was read by reviewers.[70] Edmund Wilson was right when he said this novel portrays the "Ivy League generation of Boston Irish," or "the Kennedy generation which stands somewhere between the old Irish world of Boston and the new world of cocktails and enlightenment."[71]

This novel *should* be read as a critical satire both on the Kennedy family and the Boston Irish. The novel raises some of the same questions about the Kinsellas that Garry Wills poses in *The Kennedy Imprisonment*, where the Kennedys are portrayed as a family encased within a glossy image of their own contriving, a family controlled by a lust for power and recognition. O'Connor's Kinsellas and Wills's Kennedys are trapped inside self-serving myths of family unity and public service, myths which grew increasingly separate from truth, myths which imprisoned and finally divided both families. Neither O'Connor nor Wills acknowledge the political idealism inspired by the Kennedys, particularly for the Boston Irish. In *All in the Family* O'Connor repudiated the Irish-American political process, which he sentimentalized in *The Last Hurrah*. *All in the Family* is O'Connor's separate peace with Boston and, with his sudden death, the novel stands as his final statement—his last, faint hurrah—on his own kind.

O'Connor makes clear that the Kinsellas are *too* loyal to their family values. They were cut off from the city they presumed to rule, when Charles was mayor, and the state they claim to serve, when he is governor. Jimmy, the family patriarch, denounces their hometown, presumably Boston, in a wild, Irish-American rant:

> that deadhead burg they would have given back to the moths fifty years ago only the moths wouldn't take it! With those cold codfish Yankees that have to be warmed up before they can even be buried! And all those cornball Harps that keep moaning about what the APA's did to poor old Al in the last election, and about how John Jo Donovan could become Sewer Commissioner if only his brother the foot doctor would play Waltz-Me-Around-Again-Willie with fat Billy O'Brien, and about how Sister Mary Theresa of the Holy Angels gave the back of her hand to the bishop when he opened the new parish hall last Saint Cantaloupe's Day! I can hear it all now, right down to the last thick Mick syllable![72]

The comedy of *The Last Hurrah* turns spiteful in *All in the Family*.

Jimmy Kinsella repudiates both the Yankee and Celtic traditions of his Boston-like city, just as had Joseph P. Kennedy. The Kennedys, like the Kinsellas, were caught in a cycle; in the words of Doris Kearns Goodwin, "rebuffed by the Brahmin world, the family closed up within itself; but the more they banded together, the greater the anger and the envy they aroused." As a result, like the Kinsella children, "the Kennedy children became natives of the Kennedy family, first and foremost, before any city or any country."[73] After he was refused membership in a country club in Cohasset, a Yankee summer retreat, in 1927, Joseph Kennedy moved his family from Boston to New York. Later he cited Boston's Brahmin prejudices as his reason.

> I felt it was no place to bring up Irish Catholic children. I didn't want them to go through what I had to go through when I was growing up there. . . . They wouldn't have asked my daughters to join their deb clubs; not that our girls would have joined anyway— they never gave two cents for that society stuff. But the point is they wouldn't have been asked in Boston.[74]

Yet, unable to free himself from painful memories of rejection, ten years after he had moved his family out of Boston Kennedy returned to chastise the Boston Irish for their lack of cultural ambitions, for not giving "two cents" for Brahmin "society stuff." Addressing the Clover Club at the Hotel Somerset in Boston on Saint Patrick's Day in 1937, Kennedy said that too many of the Boston Irish had suffered by "not possessing family tradition adequate to win the respect and confidence of their Puritan neighbors."[75] Garry Wills suggested that the Kennedys were at best "semi-Irish" and more than semidetached from their Boston base after Joseph Kennedy's move. His children did not grow up in Boston, did not know the city, did not marry Irish spouses, and did not belong to a local Catholic parish after they left Brookline. Exactly the same can be said of the Kinsellas, another family characterized by isolation, as Jimmy's crazed denunciation of local clans indicates. The Kinsellas, like the Kennedys, illustrate a politics of family rather than the old-style, Boston politics of clan, as practiced in fiction by Frank Skeffington and in fact by both James Michael Curley and John Fitzgerald.

In *All in the Family* John Kinsella soon sees the limits of the family style when Phil and Charles split. The brothers disagree because Phil thinks Charles is sacrificing principle for ambition, while Charles thinks Phil wants to make him into a moral crusader. When Phil appeals to their father for help, Jimmy sides with Charles, deeming disloyalty on any grounds as evidence of Phil's actual madness. Jimmy, a petty and self-pitying Lear, rails, "My whole life was my family! And now I can say only one thing about my family: to hell with it! Because I haven't got it any more."[76] O'Connor's Irish-America has become a land where brothers divide and parents betray their young. Though Jack Kinsella was able to put his far more tentative family back together, *All in the Family* remains Edwin O'Connor's parable of qualified renunciation.

IRISH literature is characterized by a vivid sense of place. When Patrick Kavanagh titled a poem "Epic," he had specific "important places" in mind: "That half a rood of rock, a no-man's land / Surrounded by our pitchfork-armed claims."[77] Yet the sense of place is ambivalent in Kavanagh, for the County Monaghan landscape which shaped him produced not only beauty, evoked in his novel *Tarry Flynn*, but also spiritual impoverishment, described in his long poem *The Great Hunger*.[78] Similarly, a commitment to place cuts two ways in the fiction of Edwin O'Connor. His heroes are drawn to their red brick city, but they are also wary of being swallowed by its pulls of political, religious, and ethnic commitments. Perhaps O'Connor's Irish-Americans hold a buried memory of their betrayal by the land they had loved and lost, Ireland, particularly during and after the Great Famine of the 1840s, when so many thousands of the Irish fled to America in search of a better life. O'Connor's heroes refuse to surrender themselves to their "important places." On the other hand, his characters suffer if they remain isolated from the place which shaped them. Boston, or its fictional simulation, makes and unmakes O'Connor's Irish-Americans. The city delivered less than it promised, leaving its pilgrims in quest of a better place, another world. O'Connor, said Daniel Aaron, was no mere local colorist. Rather, he was one of those "who have moved from a parochial sphere into a universal one."[79]

AT his death Edwin O'Connor left the fragmentary beginnings of a promising work on the last days of a Cardinal. The chapter opens with the Cardinal, a priest for fifty years, experiencing an epiphany of place. As he has his breakfast, he momentarily feels

> that if he so wished he might rise from the table and with a springy, hard-muscled step walk right out of the house and into the morning, and then walk and walk, as fast and as far as he liked. Probably through all those old parts of the city where he'd once known all the buildings and most of the people . . . but where he hadn't been now for years, and where he would continue to walk, noting changes, making plans, observing but unobserved, and then at the end of

the day coming back home, tired, yes, but not really tired—the pleasant lassitude of the athlete in training—, and curiously satisfied, just as if the whole world was once again before him, long and still undefined and full of all sorts of possibilities.[80]

But the Cardinal is eighty years old, hardly able to make such a tour of his red brick city. During the day, he discovers that he has little time to live, so he must put aside his musings and prepare himself for another world. His last look around can only occur in memory and imagination. As such the Cardinal's reflection perfectly illustrates Edwin O'Connor's theme that place is important, defining, and stirring; yet place, for him, is also transient and far less important than preparation for the final journey. Boston is best invoked in the mind as image and idea.

ARTHUR SCHLESINGER, JR. notes that Edwin O'Connor's "Beacon Hill apartment had an almost monastic air, especially in the cell-like bedroom where a simple crucifix hung above what can only be described as a pallet."[81] In the midst of elegant Beacon Hill—that Protestant-Brahmin stronghold, the beauties and pleasures of which delighted him, from the Garden to *The Atlantic*—O'Connor shaped a symbolic monk's beehive hut, like those along the Kerry coast, within his bedroom, his place of writing and thinking, his site of description and renunciation of the world beyond his window. He needed Boston—its institutions, characters, and culture—for his fiction, just as his Irish immigrants needed Boston to establish their place and presence in America. But it was not enough. Edwin O'Connor's Irish-American Boston was a wonder and a delight, but it was also a dangerously absorbing place, a world which his most sympathetic heroes wished to engage and then transcend.

Had O'Connor lived to see the conclusion of Thomas P. O'Neill's career, recorded in the pages of O'Neill's political memoir, *Man of the House*, he might have thought better of the likelihood of honor in Boston's Irish-American politics. First elected as a Massachusetts representative in 1936, O'Neill retired as Speaker of the

House of Representatives in 1987, after half-a-century of unbroken public service. O'Neill's name is inscribed both upon a library at Boston College, from which he graduated in 1936, and a federal office building in Boston. "Tip" had come a long way from North Cambridge, where his grandfather settled, near his job in the brickworks and "Dublin," the land beyond "America" which had appalled Howells.

When O'Neill spoke at Harvard's 350th anniversary celebration in 1986, he recalled the days he had spent at Harvard, mowing the grass in the Yard, as a boy. O'Neill, in his dictated memoir, evoked an incident from this period to frame his remembrances of cultural deprivation.

> On a beautiful June day, as I was going about my daily grind, the class of 1927 gathered in a huge canvas tent to celebrate commencement. Inside, I could see hundreds of young men standing around in their white linen suits, laughing and talking. They were also drinking champagne, which was illegal in 1927 because of Prohibition. I remember that scene like it was yesterday, and I can still feel the anger I felt then, almost sixty years ago as I write these words. It was the illegal champagne that really annoyed me. Who the hell do these people think they are, I said to myself, that the law means nothing to them?[82]

This incident served as an epiphany for O'Neill, similar to those transfiguring moments of class consciousness experienced by John Fitzgerald and Joseph P. Kennedy in life, as well as Frank Skeffington and other O'Connor heroes in literature. O'Neill, though no stranger to the sometimes questionable methods of Boston's Irish politicians, devoted his long career to "work and wages" for his constituents. Recalling his exclusion from that Harvard tent in 1927, O'Neill "dreamed of bringing my own people—and *all* Americans who weren't born to wealth or advantage—into the great tent of opportunity."[83]

O'Neill's "epic" began with the Irish-Americans of North Cambridge, among his "own people." His father told him "all politics is local," advice he never forgot. O'Neill's early life revolved around a block in North Cambridge, Barry's Corner, as much as Studs Lonigan's life centered upon his block in Chicago. However, O'Neill was not consumed by parochial values as was Studs, James T. Farrell's brutish model of the Irish-American. O'Neill went far beyond the block or Barry's Corner. In time, O'Neill would lead his conservative constituency in opposition to the Vietnam War, in pursuit of Richard Nixon during the Watergate scandal, and against Ronald Reagan's economic policies at the height of Reagan's popularity. "Maybe it all boils down to the fact that one of us lost track of his roots while the other didn't," writes O'Neill of Reagan, an Irish-American who never even read *The Last Hurrah*.[84]

Man of the House might well be a "last hurrah" for the kind of political values Tip O'Neill embodied: local, Irish, New Deal, based upon talk rather than television imagery. However, it is a story of triumph, not defeat, as was O'Connor's version of the Curley legend. While remaining local in his concerns and his character, Tip O'Neill transcended Boston Irish provincialism; he became a national presence, a model of wider cultural assimilation. *He* had read Edwin O'Connor's novel and he took its lessons to heart.

IN *The Last Hurrah* Frank Skeffington takes Adam Caulfield under his wing because "I think you ought to know something about this city." He then goes on to describe his red brick city as "a grand freak."

> It changed overnight, you know. A hundred years ago the loyal sons and daughters of the first white inhabitants went to bed one lovely evening, and by the time they woke up and rubbed their eyes, their charming old city was swollen to three times its size. The savages had arrived. Not the Indians; far worse. It was the Irish. They had arrived and they wanted in. Even worse than that, they got in. The story of how they did may not be a particularly pretty one on either side, but I doubt if anyone would deny that it was exciting and, as I say, unique. Moreover, it's not quite over yet, though we're in its last stages now.[85]

That story, the story of O'Connor's Boston, is still not over, in fact or in fiction. In the works of Edwin O'Connor Irish-Americans take their proper place in Boston's religious and political history, though his heroes, in the characteristic Boston mode of spiritual quest, search for an even better world, above and beyond their red brick city upon a hill. At the end of his days with the mayor, Adam saw that Frank Skeffington, his people's "chieftain," had been on a quest. Adam, too, had been on a quest to know himself by better understanding his people's history and the city they remade in their own image. "The pilgrimage, and with it, a part of his life, was over: he was going home."[86]

5

Black Boston's Books:

PHILLIS WHEATLEY, W. E. B. DU BOIS, DOROTHY WEST, MALCOLM X, WILLIAM STANLEY BRAITHWAITE, AND OTHERS

H ENRY JAMES thought it "a complex fate, being an American," a proposition he illustrated in *The Bostonians*.[1] Being Irish-American in Boston compounded the complexities; however, being black in Boston, as in the rest of America, could fairly be described as a tragic fate. Boston's blacks arrived as slaves; they have endured as servants, served as soldiers and sailors, survived economic discrimination, struggled for educational opportunity and political recognition—battles far from resolved in a city which affirms its commitment to liberty and justice. Yet Boston's blacks, judging from their worthy but under-appreciated literary record, found compensation and self-justification in the city upon a hill.

Boston's blacks not only have helped shape its history; they have seen the city, examined its emblems and weighed its myths from their own informing perspective.

IN 1638 the first black slave arrived aboard a trading vessel, *Desire*, as cargo from Providence, in the Bahamas. Such allegorical states of place and emotion, Providence and Desire, define the black experience in Boston. Boston merchants shipped slaves from the West Indies, the Guinea coast, and Madagascar, thus tainting the fortunes of the city's first families.[2] Relatively few blacks arrived in Boston; their number did not rise past 10 percent of the city's population until after the Civil War. They served largely as house-servants and thus were accorded greater liberties than Southern slaves, but their presence pricked the conscience of Boston's best. In 1700 Samuel Sewall, diarist and recanting witch-trial judge, wrote "The Selling of Joseph," an antislavery tract. "These *Ethiopians*," wrote Sewall, "as black as they are; seeing they are the Sons and Daughters of the First *Adam*, the Brethren and Sisters of the Last Adam, and the Offspring of GOD; They ought to be treated with a Respect agreeable."[3] In *The Negro Christianized* (1706) Cotton Mather argued that each slave-owner had a responsibility to Christianize his slaves.

However, several generations of slaves silently disappeared, serving the colonial mission, until their presence was registered and their voices heard, during the era of the Revolution. In 1770 runaway slave Crispus Attucks, along with three white fellow demonstrators, was killed when a British squadron opened fire on Boston citizens, resulting in the Boston Massacre, an event which sublimated Boston's antiblack prejudices under the cause of national freedom. Attucks's blood sacrifice forced Boston to pay attention to the presence of its black citizens, though some Bostonians, like John Adams, tried to dismiss those who attacked the British troops as "a mob," or "a motley rabble of saucy boys, negroes and molattoes, Irish teagues and outlandish jack tarrs."[4] Out of just such class and racial outcasts Boston would find volunteers to fight its good fights and, eventually, transform its citizenry.

The painful condition of blacks in Boston was eloquently registered in a series of petitions written before the Revolution. In 1773, for example, four slaves petitioned the House of Representatives to allow the "*Africans* . . . one day in a week to work for themselves, to enable them to earn money." These petitioners tried to touch a nerve in Boston's conscience by appealing to its claimed affirmation of liberty. "We expect great things from men who have made such a noble stand against the designs of their *fellow-men* to enslave them." In 1774 Governor Thomas Gage and the general court were petitioned by "a Grate Number of blackes of the Province . . . held in a state of Slavery within a free and christian Country." This lament reveals that no amount of kindly treatment by well-intentioned Bostonians could mitigate the pains of slavery. Slaves' lives were made intolerable because "the endearing ties" between husband and wife were broken. Their children were "taken from us by force" and sold. "Thus our Lives are imbittered." Boston had betrayed, and would continue to betray its claimed values—liberty and Christianity—in its treatment of blacks. This was clear to Abigail Adams, who educated her husband, John, on this point: "I wish most sincerely there was not a slave in the province; it always appeared a most iniquitous scheme to me to fight ourselves for what we are daily robbing and plundering from those who have as good a right to freedom as we do."[5] Attucks's sacrifice and Boston blacks' continued support of the fight for liberty during the Revolution and the Civil War demonstrated to America how fully these people had absorbed Boston's highest values and, in turn, showed Bostonians how much they had to learn from their black citizens.

IN 1770, nine years after Phillis Wheatley arrived in Boston, the sixteen-year-old slave lived with her owners on King Street, where she might have heard sounds from the Boston Massacre. While Crispus Attucks died on Boston's streets, fighting for liberty, Phillis Wheatley conducted a more oblique and subtle campaign, through poetry rather than protest, for just recognition.

Little beyond the emblems and values of Anglo-American Boston was available to Boston's first black poet. Born around 1753, perhaps in Senegal, and bought "for a trifle" when she was seven by John Wheatley, a respected tailor, her African identity was nearly obliterated in the middle passage to America, though she did recall that her mother "poured out water before the sun at his rising."[6] Her past must have seemed an empty vessel which she could only fill with the cultural wines of the country in which she found herself.

Apparently she was named after the ship which carried her to Boston, the *Phillis*.[7] Thus she was renamed by slavery and baptized into Boston Christianity. Mrs. Susanna Wheatley oversaw Phillis's education, stressing religious training and readings in the classics. By age fourteen she was publishing poetic tributes and elegies. Rufus Griswold noted in *The Female Poets of America* (1877) that this slave girl was trained better, her curiosity more encouraged, than most white children in Boston.[8] Certainly Phillis Wheatley strained to succeed in Boston's cultural terms: through personal piety and devotional poetry. In 1771 Wheatley was formally baptized in the Old South Meeting House. Throughout her late teens she wrote most of the poetry for which she is remembered—a poetry intended for a white audience, a poetry in praise of Boston worthies and values.

In 1772 Wheatley was examined by groups of distinguished Bostonians who quizzed her to determine whether she indeed wrote the poems she claimed. Rev. Charles Chauncey, pastor of the Tenth Congregational Church, John Hancock, Thomas Hutchinson, the Governor, and others then signed and certified in their "Attestation" to the authenticity of the volume, though no Boston publisher was brave enough to issue her work.[9] However, *Poems on Various Subjects, Religious and Moral* was published in London, in 1773. In that year Wheatley went to England, where she was celebrated as a colonial oddity, but accepted as an authentic American poet.

Wheatley's poems are shaped more by her piety, particularly in her lyrical elegies, than by her sense of place or race. Having been wrenched from her original, earthly, African home, she prepared herself in Boston for a new home in heaven by writing poems on the Christian afterlife.[10] In her most famous poem, "On Being Brought from Africa to America," she created a myth to rationalize her fragmented life into a parable of salvation.

> 'Twas mercy brought me from my *Pagan* land,
> Taught my benighted soul to understand
> That there's a God, that there's a *Saviour* too:
> Once I redemption neither sought nor knew.
> Some view our sable race with scornful eye,
> "Their colour is a diabolic die,"
> Remember, *Chieftians*, *Negros*, black as *Cain*,
> May be refin'd and join th' angelic train.[11]

Here Wheatley subtly used the religious values which Boston gave her to confront Boston prejudices: "Remember," she enjoined forgetful Boston, all men and women have an equal opportunity for salvation! Her unqualified Christian faith granted her sufficient resonance and status to preach to anyone. Though Hester Prynne, after her public rebuke, became a secret rebel by allowing herself free speculations that challenged the authority of the Boston theocracy which judged her, Phillis Wheatley affirmed the Boston establishment's religious values. But, Wheatley matched Hester's subversiveness by illustrating Boston's racial prejudices. Both Hester Prynne and Phillis Wheatley invoked an ideal of freedom and justice, divine and earthly, first stated as Boston's mission by John Winthrop; her words stuck in the throat of pious, patriarchal, practical Boston.

Though her references were muffled, indications of racial pride and devotion to the Boston area, a sense of American place, can be detected in Wheatley's works. On 30 October 1774, for example, she wrote a revealing reply to a letter from John Thornton, a wealthy British merchant who financed "Evangicals" in Africa, a man who presumed to serve as Wheatley's religious guide. Her sly letter affirmed Wheatley's independence, insisted upon her American identity and detached her from his mission to Christianize Africa. Thornton had proposed that she return to Africa with two black Evangicals to aid in converting the heathen, but she gracefully declined his invitation, saying she was unsuited to talk to the Anamaboe, or Africans of the current Ghana region. "Upon my arrival, how like a Barbarian shou'd I look to the Natives; I can promise that my tongue shall be quiet / for a strong reason indeed / being an utter stranger to the language of Anamaboe."[12] She was, in short, too much a Bostonian to be mistaken, despite her color, for an African. With rare eloquence, Phillis Wheatley wrote in the language of Boston, which ranged from piety to political purpose, tinged by irony. Bostonians took her in captivity then taught her how to speak their language. They filled the vessel of her being with their cultural and religious values; Phillis Wheatley, however, eloquently turned her powerful voice upon Bostonians, urging them to *remember* their unfulfilled promises.

THE black experience in Boston has been marked by irony, drama, and, despite oppression, extraordinary achievement. Boston's black writers have composed their own resolutions of Boston's racial tensions. Many of Boston's black citizens have believed in Boston's promises—freedom, justice, culture, economic opportunity— more seriously than have most white Bostonians.

From their arrival as slaves, Boston's blacks have had a tense, paradoxical relationship with Yankee Boston. Slavery, on one hand, succeeded by social prejudice and economic discrimination, held black citizens apart from their equal share in the community. On the other hand, the promise of freedom and equality, intrinsic to the self-definition of the Boston colony, encouraged blacks to seek their full covenant in the culture. In *Freedom's Birthplace* (1914) John Daniels underscored this lasting Bostonian contradiction between the city's devotion to "spiritual freedom" and its tolerance of slavery. "It was a contradiction, moreover, which in modified degree and form has survived to the present, and which still troubles the Boston community."[13] The aptness of Daniels' assessment has been further illustrated by the tensions surrounding school integration in Boston in the mid-1970s. In "liberty's chosen home," blacks and whites still battle on "common ground."[14]

Unlike the hot, fertile American South, a rigid local climate and poor soil determined that New England would not sustain a vast number of slaves and dictated close relations between the races.[15] However, it was the special promise of American life, as it was articulated in Boston, that held out hope for the slaves of New England, those who were caught in the crossfire of conflicting regional values. Boston's blacks supported two traditions, white and black, which merged during the abolitionist period, though racial division reemerged and persisted long after the Civil War.[16] Boston would infuse its black citizens with religious and political ideals; in turn Boston's blacks would bear witness to their pains, inspiring and educating Boston to live up to its own compromised moral mission. Thus Boston's blacks became, says William D. Piersen, "black Yankees—a very special breed of Afro-American New Englander."[17]

BLACKS have long contributed to Boston's struggle for liberty. Monuments and occasional verses remind Bostonians of black sacrifices for Bostonian ideals. On 8 March 1770 Boston held a public funeral and made common burial of those killed in the Boston Massacre. Their burial site is located in the cemetery next to Park Street Church, near the grave of Samuel Adams. The inscription on the stone reads:

> Long as in Freedom's cause the wise contend,
> Dear to your country shall your fame extend,
> While to the world the lettered stone shall tell,
> Where Caldwell, Attucks, Gray and Maverick fell.[18]

A monument was erected in 1888 on Boston Common, with inscribed tributes from Daniel Webster and John Adams. The monument portrays Freedom, treading upon the British Crown; Attucks, ironically enough, lies at Freedom's feet.[19]

The Civil War inspired even more memorable verse and monuments in tribute to black heroism. In September 1862, President Lincoln issued his Emancipation Proclamation. On 1 January 1863 Boston celebrated: in Tremont Temple the Proclamation was read aloud to a black audience and Frederick Douglass led the singing of an old hymn, "Blow ye the trumpet, blow!"[20] For the occasion Emerson composed his "Boston Hymn," a poem which embodies the high moral purpose of the Boston voice. Emerson even presumed to speak in God's voice to the issue of ransom payments for freed slaves:

> Pay ransom to the owner
> And fill the bag to the brim.
> Who is the owner? The slave is the owner,
> And ever was. Pay him.[21]

During the Civil War the Fifty-fourth Massachusetts Infantry, composed of black soldiers who were led by Robert Gould Shaw, flower of Brahmin culture, *embodied* the union between two peoples who were joined by moral and political purpose, though separation of races and class stations were preserved in the army's ranks. In May 1863 the Massachusetts Fifty-fourth marched through Boston to the Common where ceremonies marked their departure for action in South Carolina, a disastrous military engagement which all but wiped out the regiment. Shaw, two officers, and thirty-one soldiers were killed at Fort Wagner in July 1863, a blood sacrifice which became a central occasion in the definition of Boston's identity, an epiphany which would be reshaped by monument makers, memorialists, and poets during the next century.

Dedicated in 1897, the memorial to Shaw and his troops, a bronze bas-relief created by Augustus Saint-Gaudens, faces the

Massachusetts State House in constant reminder of Boston's double myth of Brahmin nobility and black sacrifice.[22] Boston's "black Yankees" learned well the lessons and values of Boston culture; in turn, they offered Boston a reason to practice the idealism it preached. Boston's blacks humanized and politicized the city's Puritan heritage.[23]

MANY escaped slaves sought freedom and protection in Boston; some found their voices in Boston. William Wells Brown, who escaped from Lexington, Kentucky, made his way to Boston and there wrote his *Narrative of W. W. Brown, a Fugitive Slave* (1847) and a novel, *Clotelle* (1853). Frederick Douglass, a recently escaped slave, shaped his postslavery self and defined his mission by listening to a Boston abolitionist, William Lloyd Garrison, who spoke at a gathering Douglass attended in Nantucket in 1841. Douglass soon became a public witness against the slave system. His classic testimony, *Narrative of the Life of Frederick Douglass*, "Written by Himself," was published in 1845 under the imprint of the Boston Anti-Slavery Office, with endorsements by Garrison and Phillips included. Douglass's autobiographical tract climaxes in his evocation of the moment when he realized his identity and purpose: when he first read Garrison's *Liberator*. "The paper became my meat and my drink. My soul was set all on fire."[24] The Boston abolitionist community had discovered its greatest voice.

Yet, Douglass would not subordinate himself to the policies of Boston's radical abolitionists. They split over Douglass's plan to found another antislavery paper. In *Frederick Douglass' Paper* Douglass won away an audience which took possession of the issue of freedom, even if that meant separating themselves from their Brahmin allies.[25] That is, a primary black voice, authenticated and authorized by Boston's abolitionists, learned to speak for itself.

WILLIAM WELLS BROWN and Frederick Douglass were not the only escaped slaves who found their voices and visions in Massa-

chusetts under the tutelage of Boston abolitionists. Writings by
three former slave women exemplify Boston's role in spreading
awareness of black life under slavery. In journals and in autobiographical fictions, these women bore eloquent witness to the pains
of slavery and challenged white readers' prejudices in narratives
designed to induce outrage and sympathy. Each of these black
women writers unconsciously echoed in her prose narrative aspects
of Hester Prynne's story, the quintessential Boston myth: the tale
of a woman who rebels against and then redeems the society whose
hypocritical and harsh values had made her an outcast.

Charlotte L. Forten, from Philadelphia, was schooled in Salem,
where she learned strict abolitionist values. For Forten Boston
culture meant literature, particularly writings with a social and
moral purpose. She was inspired by the example, personal and
poetic, of Phillis Wheatley. "She was a wonderfully gifted woman,
and many of her poems are very beautiful," wrote Forten in an
1854 journal entry on Wheatley. "Her character and genius afford
a striking proof of the falseness of the assertion made by some that
hers is an inferior race."[26] Forten also appreciated Henry Ward
Beecher's lecture, "Patriotism" of January 1855, both for its beauty
and for its denunciation of "the wicked and unjust laws of our land."
Emerson and Theodore Parker became her heroes. But Charles
Sumner, whom she heard praise the Constitution in 1855, dissatisfied her by tempering his political passions.[27] Garrison, however,
fulfilled her desire to hear unqualified denunciation of slavery.
Forten's journal records her own radicalization in abolitionist Boston and her consequent devotion to liberty and education.

Harriet E. Wilson's novel, *Our Nig*, printed in Boston in 1859,
ennobled an escaped slave and satirized bourgeois racism in the
North.[28] A disturbing novel, *Our Nig* offers few myths of reassurance for either escaped slave or abolitionist. Instead, it presents a
compelling heroine, Frado, who seeks a new life on her own terms.
Near the end of this novel Frado is left homeless with a newborn
child, abandoned by her husband. Frado then leaves her profession
as a milliner to write her story. That is, she moves from the household art of Hester Prynne to the public art of the writer to support

herself, to make known her tale, to shape a redemptive parable of her reimagined life. Though repudiated by a repressive society, Frado, artist of the needle and the word, became an independent woman, a woman of mind and purpose, a model for other women, and a redeemer of her culture—a black Hester Prynne.

Harriet A. Jacobs's *Incidents in the Life of a Slave Girl* (1861) also registered the escaped slave woman's point of view and endowed Boston with special significance.[29] The narrative presents Linda Brent, the narrative persona, the story of her resistance to her master's effort to seduce her, and shows how she arranged her children's escape to freedom. As in *Our Nig*, *Incidents* presents the heroine's fall, for Linda Brent became pregnant outside marriage. Again Hester Prynne, cultural rebel and struggling parent, serves as a mythic archetype for another of Boston's literary heroines, another woman who was caught in a crisis of cultural values.

In 1842 Jacobs escaped from slavery to New York; then, fleeing a designing white man, she came to Boston in 1844. In 1860 Lydia Maria Child, noted journalist and abolitionist, negotiated a contract for Jacobs with the Boston publishers, Thayer and Eldridge. Arrangements were later made to buy plates from the Boston Stereotype Foundry and to publish her book "for the author." It was long thought that Child actually wrote *Incidents* under Jacobs's name—a charge which echoes white Boston's nervous need to authenticate Wheatley's poetry and Douglass's narrative—but recent scholarship has refuted this accusation, crediting Jacobs with authorship and Child only with the editorial work she claimed.[30] Harriet A. Jacobs's *Incidents* holds its proper place in the literature of Boston's blacks because its author there found safety and artistic encouragement, from both blacks and whites—freedom and culture.

RACE and class, prejudice and promise, vied in the drama of W. E. B. Du Bois's fine mind, just as these tensions reverberated in the consciousness of all black Bostonians. In his recollections of his years at Harvard, Du Bois tells a revealing incident which combines all of these conflicts. While he was a Harvard undergraduate Du Bois felt most at home within the black community; there members of Boston's black bourgeoisie instructed him in class and racial pride.

> Mrs. Ruffin of Charles Street, Boston, and her daughter, Birdie, were often hostesses to this colored group . . . of professional men, students, white-collar workers, and upper servants, whose common bond was color of skin. . . . She was the widow of the first colored judge appointed in Massachusetts, an aristocratic lady, with olive skin and high-piled masses of white hair. Once a Boston white lady said to Mrs. Ruffin ingratiatingly: "I have always been interested in your race." Mrs. Ruffin flared: "Which race?" She began a national organization of colored women and published the *Courant*, a type of small colored weekly paper which was then spreading over the nation. In this I published many of my Harvard daily themes.[31]

As in a parable, incident illustrates purpose. Du Bois was here granted a lesson in self-assertion by an assured, black Boston woman who also assisted him in bringing his novice writings to notice. Social and intellectual pride here subverted racial prejudice. Boston provided Du Bois with a nurturing context for his aspirations. Social activist, editor, writer of sociological analysis, fiction, and polemics, Du Bois found his voice in Boston, in both the black community and at Harvard.

In his graduate year at Harvard, 1890–91, Du Bois worked on his prose in English 12 under the instruction of Barrett Wendell, and came to a sense of himself and his mission, as a surviving essay from that course indicates.

> For the usual purposes of identification I have been labeled in this life: William Edward Burghardt Du Bois, born in Great Barrington, Massachusetts, on the day after Washington's birthday, 1868. . . . My boyhood seems, if memory serves me rightly, to have been filled with incidents of surprisingly little importance, such as brooks with stones across, grass, and gate-posts. In early youth a great bitterness entered my life and kindled a great ambition. I wanted

to go to college because others did. I came and graduated and am now in search of a Ph.D. and bread. I believe, foolishly perhaps but sincerely, that I have something to say to the world and I have taken English twelve in order to say it well.[32]

In his *Autobiography* Du Bois recalled with satisfaction that Wendell praised that final sentence and chose his essay, from compositions submitted by a class of fifty, to read aloud.[33] From the black bourgeoisie of Beacon Hill to the white professor in English 12, Boston and Harvard shaped Du Bois's values, raised his social and political consciousness, buoyed his self-esteem, prodded his ambition, and fired his rhetoric.

Great Barrington, a small town along the Housatonic River, deep in the rural fastness of western Massachusetts, was a childhood idyll, a place of innocence and a myth of Eden for Du Bois: a secure place, where his family had been established since colonial days. In Great Barrington, it seemed, God was in His heaven, and all was right with the world, because its citizens were distributed according to a benevolent, if stratified, design. That, at least, is the myth of innocence evoked in his remembrance of things past, a narrative which muffles pains.

> My town was shut in by its mountains and provincialism; but it was a beautiful place, a little New England town nestled shyly in its valley with something of Dutch cleanness and English reticence. The Housatonic, yellowed by the paper mills, rolled slowly through its center; while Green River, clear and beautiful, joined in to the south. Main Street was lined with ancient elms; the hills held white pines and orchards and then faded up to magnificent rocks and caves which shut out the neighboring world. The people were mainly of English descent with much Dutch blood and with a large migration of Irish and German workers to the mills as laborers.[34]

Yet, Du Bois hints at a "great bitterness," which entered his young life when his father abandoned his family and his mother was compelled to take on domestic work. However, in Du Bois's memories—memories which may exaggerate his innocence for dramatic contrast with the awareness, particularly the racism he would encounter outside Great Barrington—the pastoral town of his boyhood was nearly all idyll, a happy valley of skating by moonlight, coasting, playing Indian, watching the brook flow past his front door, admiring the lovely niece of the landlady, a girl in possession of what Du Bois's biographer calls "sweet eyes and filmy dresses."[35]

In Great Barrington Du Bois recalled little overt racial prejudice. Indeed the few blacks who lived there were preferred to the Irish and German (and Catholic) newcomers who worked in the mills. Du Bois was the only black to graduate in his high school class of thirteen in 1884; he delivered a class oration on Wendell Phillips, who had died the previous February. "I was born in a community which conceived itself as having helped out down a wicked rebellion for the purpose of freeing four million slaves."[36] Thus Boston's heroes, institutions and values, from Phillips to Harvard, were vivid in Du Bois's mind long before he saw Boston.

Great Barrington's townspeople even contributed to the college education of their chosen son.[37] However, he would be the beneficiary of the kind of higher education *they* deemed fitting for a gifted black boy. Though "his heart was set on Harvard," the scholarship Du Bois won sent him to Fisk University, in Nashville, Tennessee, where he spent three years (1885–88) before he finally fulfilled his original plan and transferred to Harvard as a junior in 1888. Du Bois's years at Fisk developed his racial consciousness and intensified his anger at the color barriers he saw all around him in the deep South. There he discovered his mission, though he lacked the training to carry it forward. "I was determined to make a scientific conquest of my environment, which would render the emancipation of the Negro race easier and quicker. The persistence which I had learned in New England stood me now in good stead."[38] Du Bois, then, beyond the womb of Great Barrington, his character toughened by New England, was educated in two Americas: black and white, impoverished and cultured.

At Harvard, while eager to learn from great models—Charles W. Eliot was president; William James, Josiah Royce, George Santayana, Charles Eliot Norton, and George Lyman Kitteridge were on the faculty—Du Bois did not forget the lessons of Fisk, though he learned to sing Harvard's songs. "I had my own 'island within' and it was a fair country. . . . I was in Harvard but not of it and realized all the irony of 'Fair Harvard.' I sang it because I like the music."[39]

Du Bois felt fully at ease only in the company of blacks at Harvard and in Boston. For four years he rented a humble room in a "colored home," at 20 Flagg Street, owned by a woman who descended from Jamaican slaves. From there, as we have seen, he made his way into Boston's black bourgeoisie and he learned about Boston's black politics. However, Du Bois also made the most of his stay at white Harvard. "Harvard of this day was a great opportunity for a young man and a young American Negro and I realized it." He was the frequent guest of William James; he became a member of the Philosophical Club and he discussed Kant with Santayana; Du Bois absorbed enough of what Harvard had to offer to become a *cum laude* graduate in 1890. At commencement he brought his knowledge of the South to Harvard Yard in an address portraying Jefferson Davis as an embodiment of a civilization which combined manhood, heroism, "moral obtuseness and refined brutality."[40] Then Du Bois stayed on at Harvard until 1892 to study for his M.A. in history.

If Great Barrington represented innocence in the symbolism of Du Bois's life, Fisk and the South stood for experience, the bitter awareness of racial repression, while Harvard embodied enlightenment, the best of white culture, with residual strains of class and racial prejudices. Harvard and black Boston, then, shaped the synthesis to the dialectical forces of W. E. B. Du Bois's struggle of values. Harvard prepared him for a great career by grounding in him the intellectual assurance and literary skills which, combined with his racial awareness and moral passion, benefited him when he returned to the South and wrote *The Souls of Black Folk*.[41]

IN *Contending Forces*, a novel published in 1900, Pauline E. Hopkins modeled two of her characters on Du Bois and Booker T.

Washington. Will Smith, the novel's romantic hero, goes from Harvard to the study of philosophy in Germany, as did Du Bois. Dr. Arthur Lewis, president of a black industrial school in Louisiana, represents Washington. Indeed the novel not only incorporates the debate over black identity between Du Bois and Washington, it also, as it has been said, embodies Hopkins's own "elitist views," stressing "the self-sufficient Afro-American community."[42]

Hopkins was born in Maine, perhaps in 1859, and educated in Boston's public schools, where she won an essay contest on the evils of intemperance sponsored by William Wells Brown, whose fiction would serve as her model and inspiration. Like Brown, Hopkins came to believe that fiction was a proper form to preserve the history and to enforce a sense of identity among black people. "Fiction," she wrote, "is of great value to any people as a preserver of manners and customs—religious, political and social. It is a record of growth and development from generation to generation. No one will do this for us."[43]

Hopkins joined the staff of Colored American Magazine at its beginning in 1900 and stayed on until 1904; she may have been dismissed for her black militancy. This magazine published her novel under the Colored Co-operative Publishing Company of Boston. Contending Forces is an appeal to white readers for understanding, using the props of romantic fiction. Here we discover female virtue under siege, after the model in Brown's Clotelle.

Contending Forces focuses upon the "number of well-to-do families of color whose tax-bills show a most comfortable return each year to the city treasury."[44] Through the American Colored League her characters appeal to the conscience of Boston, but, as it had been for slave petitioners in the early 1770s, irony is embedded in their solicitation.

> Massachusetts is noted for being willing to see fair play: she hears the complaints of the Negro, and listens with attention to the accusations of the Southern whites [over lynchings], weighs the one against the other, and, naturally enough, the scales tip in favor of the white brother.[45]

Hopkins's black Bostonians finally must depend upon themselves; their church, and their political leaders. Yet they are also inspired by the example of moral and political rectitude offered by Boston's white moral leaders. The novel's epigraph is taken from Emerson: "The civility of no race can be perfect whilst another race is degraded."[46] *Contending Forces*, then, shows white Boston's problems with its black citizens to be a crisis in Boston's culture and conscience.

NO work better embodies the post-1895 tensions within Boston—increasing white indifference to blacks, the growing number of southern blacks, and the worsening tensions within the black community over economic and cultural status—than Dorothy West's novel, *The Living Is Easy*. Though published in 1948, it is set in the Boston of World War I and after.

Dorothy West was born in 1910 and educated in Boston, at Girls' Latin School and Boston University, before she went to New York in 1926 to become part of the Harlem Renaissance. There she felt out of her league, a Boston innocent. "I was just a little girl from Boston, a place of dull people with funny accents."[47] Paradoxically, in New York City she found her artistic voice and her subject: nuances of class and race among Boston's blacks.

The Living Is Easy centers on the quest of Cleo Judson, a fictional version of West's mother, for respectability in Boston. For Cleo, married to a successful black businessman and mother of Judy (Dorothy), respectability meant the repudiation of her black heritage and the emulation of white, ascendancy ways. The novel is driven by West's anger at having been swept along in her mother's futile quest, but it concludes on a note of reconciliation.[48]

This is a novel in which fine discriminations of place register an active, symbolic presence. In a telling scene, Cleo and Judy ride on a Huntington Avenue trolley, passing from black to white worlds, moving from Boston's South End to Brookline. They wait to change for the Brookline Village trolley.

Cleo saw with satisfaction that she was already in another world, though a scant fifteen-minute ride away from the mean streets of the Negro neighborhood. There were white people everywhere with sallow-skinned, thin, austere Yankee faces. They had the look that Cleo coveted for her dimpled daughter. She was dismayed by Judy's tendency to be a happy-faced child, and hoped it was merely a phase of growth. A proper Bostonian never showed any emotion but hauteur.[49]

Cleo is a divided woman; while part of her wants to emulate the style of proper Bostonians, another part of her wants to assert her own demonstrative self. In short, she tries to thwart her own ir-repressible black spirit in futile imitation of haughty, repressive, white Bostonians.[50]

Cleo and Judy travel from the black South End to white Brook-line to rent a house from a Brahmin, Mr. Van Ryper, a man who has no prejudice against blacks because his hostilities are reserved for the new Irish immigrants in Boston. "The Irish present a threat to us entrenched Bostonians. They did not come here in chains or by special invitation. So I disclaim any responsibility for them, and reserve the right to reject them." But he *will* rent to the "colored."[51]

West here judges the Bostonian habit of invidious distinctions: racial, ethnic, and class. The final irony, West's last turn of the screw in this scene, reveals that Cleo's new house is actually *not* in Brookline, "a private world," but is located instead across the boundary line in Roxbury, "which that thundering herd of Irish immigrants have overrun." Van Ryper *is* moving to Brookline, "the last stronghold of my generation."[52] The symbolic passage of Cleo Judson, then, is incomplete. Indeed, soon the Irish would move out and Roxbury would replace the South End as Boston's principle black ghetto.

Dorothy West describes a world in which blacks are divided by the expectations of class and race. A repressed minority in Boston, they alternate between imitation and condemnation of Boston's white culture. Simeon Binney, a black Boston publisher—based upon William Munroe Trotter, Harvard classmate of Du Bois and publisher of the *Guardian,* a polemical newspaper supportive of black causes—takes the Boston ideals of liberty and justice most seriously, but he lacks courage in times of crisis. Cleo Judson incorporates Boston's prejudices: she not only does not want to live in the black sections of Boston, she also does not want to be identified with blacker-skinned Bostonians, those who had newly arrived from the South; she adopts Boston's symbols of culture as a way to separate herself from her people. Yet, in time of crisis she has the moral courage to stand up for her family and her race. When a black man is facing a white jury in the South, Binney says nothing, out of fear of condemnation by Boston's black bourgeoisie. However, when it is discovered that the victim is her sister's husband, Cleo becomes mobilized. She raises money to hire a lawyer to free her brother-in-law. The point of the parable is clear: family ties hold firm against class intimidation, while high-minded liberal dedication fails. In her own way, personal and familial, Cleo Judson affirms black power, setting herself against the grain of Boston's prejudiced ways—including her own.

MALCOLM X, advocate of a far more aggressive version of black power in the 1960s, came to full racial consciousness and learned lessons in pride and prejudice during his Boston years. Born in Omaha, Nebraska in 1925 of mixed racial heritage, young Malcolm Little was at first proud of his white skin, though later he would "hate every drop of that white rapist's blood that is mine."[53] In Lansing, Michigan, his father, a Baptist minister, was killed by whites. After his mother had a breakdown in 1937, the eight Little children became state wards.

In the summer of 1940 young Malcolm came by bus, sitting in the back, to Boston. He had relatives in the Sugar Hill section of Roxbury, "the Harlem of Boston."[54] Although by the 1980s Sugar Hill, near Franklin Park, had declined to an area notorious for drugs and violence, in Malcolm's day this was a proud, middle-class area.[55] There Malcolm had an epiphany of what it meant to be black.

> I didn't know the world contained as many Negroes as I saw throng-
> ing down town Roxbury at night, especially on Saturdays. Neon
> lights, nightclubs, poolhalls, bars, the cars they drove! Restaurants
> made the streets smell—rich, greasy, down-home black cooking!
> Jukeboxes blared Erskine Hawkins, Duke Ellington, Cootie Wil-
> liams, dozens of others. If somebody had told me then that some
> day I'd know them all personally, I'd have found it hard to believe.
> The biggest bands, like these, played at the Roseland State Ball-
> room, on Boston's Massachusetts Avenue—one night for Negroes,
> the next night for whites.[56]

Jazz represented the achievement of black culture for Malcolm and Boston meant jazz.

Malcolm Little also witnessed examples of integration for the first time: interracial couples walked the city streets, blacks and whites worshiped together at church. Boston still stirred his imagination when he returned home for the eighth grade. Indeed, Boston showed Malcolm his destiny. "All praise is due to Allah that I went to Boston when I did," he would write later. "If I hadn't, I'd probably still be a brainwashed black Christian."[57]

Back in Boston, Malcolm learned further lessons. After his half-sister, Ella, told him to "get the feel of Boston," he discovered the Waumbeck and Humboldt Avenue Hill sections of Roxbury, where the black Four Hundred lived and looked down from their heights upon those in the "town" of Roxbury. Malcolm came to see them as "brainwashed" in their attempt to imitate white society.[58] Black Boston, he saw, was as divided by class distinctions as white Boston.

On the other hand, in Boston Malcolm was astonished to find a statue to Crispus Attucks. But Malcolm was drawn less to Boston's past lives than he was to Roxbury's lowlife. "Not only was this part of Roxbury much more exciting, but I felt more relaxed among Negroes who were being their natural selves and not putting on airs."[59] He was impressed by the sharp "cats" around pool halls.

Shorty, who racked balls, instructed him in street lore. Malcolm took a job as a shoeshine boy at Roseland Ballroom, where Benny Goodman played. Soon he wore zoot suits, smoked, and drank. He even had his hair straightened with a conk. In time he quit shining shoes and became a regular at the Roseland dances. Boston, then, formed the political and cultural consciousness of this man who would become a black Muslim spokesman and a major force in the black power movement of the 1960s.

The mature Malcolm X makes the point that he repudiated pretentious blacks: "people like the sleep-in maid for Beacon Hill white folks who used to come in with her 'ooh, my deah' manners and order corn plasters in the Jew's drugstore for black folks." By contrast, he ate soulfood, wore jazzy suits, danced the lindy-hop, got high or did "something, for relief from those Hill clowns."[60]

However, Malcolm's Boston world grew small and harsh. He was drawn to Laura—a girl who read books but who had "no airs like the others, no black Bostonese"—whom he took to Roseland to see the Count Basie band. But Malcolm dropped her for a white woman, and Laura became a drug addict. Economic opportunities in Boston were severely limited. He was working as a mere bus boy at the Parker House at the time of Japan's attack on Pearl Harbor. Finally, a railroad job took him away to New York. Small's Paradise, a Harlem bar, represented another world to Malcolm. "Within the first five minutes in Small's, I had left Boston and Roxbury forever."[61]

In fact, Malcolm returned. After World War II, back in Boston and addicted to cocaine, he ran a burglary operation out of his Harvard Square apartment, near the Law School. Arrested for passing stolen goods, he was sentenced to eight to ten years in 1946, at age twenty-one. He served a total of seven years, starting in Charlestown State Prison. In 1948 he was transferred to Concord Prison, then to Norfolk Prison Colony, where he began to read of Allah and encountered the teachings of Elijah Muhammad. Back in Charlestown, Malcolm became a Muslim. Released in 1952, he moved to Detroit. His Boston education was complete.

In his *Autobiography,* Malcolm notes a final symbolic visit to Boston, when transformed as Malcolm X, he spoke at Harvard Law School:

> I was invited to speak at the Harvard Law School Forum. I happened to glance through a window. Abruptly, I realized that I was looking in the direction of the apartment house that was my old burglary gang's hideout. It rocked me like a tidal wave. Scenes from my once depraved life lashed through my mind. *Living* like an animal; *thinking* like an animal![62]

Having arrived within the circle of privilege which Harvard represents, where Du Bois had learned articulation and gained stature, Malcolm could see the "depraved" world of his youth beyond its high windows. For Malcolm Little, who became Malcolm X, Boston remained, as it had been for so many other black Bostonians, an allegorical landscape on which they quested to discover their personal and racial identities, where they renamed themselves and reshaped their voices.

It should be added that Boston educated *both* Malcolm X and Martin Luther King, Jr., who studied at Boston University's School of Divinity (1951–54). "Both men," writes Marilyn Richardson, "went on to place their spiritual commitments at the service of the struggle to change secular history; like [Crispus] Attucks and [David] Walker, [publisher of *Walker's Appeal* (1829), which called for black action against slavery], they paid with their lives."[63]

SOME blacks blended into Boston's culture more smoothly than Malcolm X. The strategy established by Phillis Wheatley—to praise Boston's culture, but to accompany that praise with reminders that Boston had betrayed its values through its mistreatment of its black citizens—was carried forward by William Stanley Braithwaite: Boston poet, critic, and anthologist.

Boston's emblems of culture and civility have long been converted into poetic imagery. A familiar iconic site served Braithwaite—reviewer for the prestigious Boston *Evening Transcript* and
developing poet—in his 1904 poem, "In the Public Garden."

> The illumined fountain flashed in the pond,
> It was purple, and green, and white,—
> You and I in the crowd, and beyond,
> The shining stars and night.
> Beyond were the shining stars and the night,—
> And near was the fountain at play.
> —But ah, the dreams that have taken flight,
> And never come home to stay.[64]

Braithwaite's Public Garden holds beauty, the suggestion of
transcendence, and nostalgia for lost certainties—literary themes
characteristically Bostonian. It may come as a surprise to learn
that Braithwaite was a black Bostonian, for nothing in this poem's
romantic spectrum of colors suggests the stark, black-and-white
realities of Boston life: economic caste, social class, and racial
antagonism, topics he dealt with vividly in other writings. Above
all, William Stanley Braithwaite, born in 1878, was a cultural syn-
thesizer; his urbane voice simultaneously celebrated Boston's black
presence and the city's Brahmin literary inheritance.

In this poem, and in his long, productive literary life, Braithwaite
transcended the limitations imposed upon him by racial prejudices,
but he never forgot who he was or where he came from. His well-
educated father, a native of British Guiana, died in 1886, so the
boy had to find his own route to culture through the streets of
Boston. Indeed, he first worked as an errand boy who prided
himself on knowing his way around Boston's circuitous streets,
though he also enjoyed leaving these streets to play hockey on
Boston Common. In time he became a noted man of letters who
advanced the careers of Robert Frost, Edward Arlington Robinson
and others, as well as his own.

Braithwaite mounted an assault upon the citadel of Boston's
Brahmin culture; not to undermine it, like Malcolm, but to take

his place inside its walls. In *The House under Arcturus: An Autobiography* (1941–42) he remembered the day in September, 1890 when he set out in search of work in Boston; his personal quest was amplified and made significant by his ability to transcend his personal problems and identify with the symbols of Boston. His language took on a loft and pitch requisite for entry into that shining city on a hill.

> Crossing the harbor on the ferry-boat I beheld the huddled city in the autumnal morning sunlight; the gray shaft of the Ames Building towering beside the gilded dome of the State House on Beacon Hill, a symbol, I imagined it, of my spirit, lofty in its direction and reach, but unable in its repulsing granite surface to absorb and effulge the radiance of the morning sun. There was my native city, the city that I loved, veined with memories, though shadowed as they were with the sorrows of death and the shadows dissolving in the illuminated activities of play and school; and now I was to ask, nay, not ask, but demand of it, the right to labor in a man's world.[65]

As he labored in this world, Braithwaite retained that wistful note of lyric self-consciousness about Boston, the psychic center of his universe. As Braithwaite had to leave the Common hockey field to work, so too did he leave "the fountain of play"—his youth of economic security and protection from racial injustice—with regret, but also with determination to succeed.

Braithwaite flew past the nets of oppression on the wings of poetry. His life changed when he took a position as typesetter for Ginn and Company, in their Cambridge building, from which he looked across the Charles River to the fine homes on Beacon Hill. There, as he set type for Keats's "On a Grecian Urn," he experienced an "annunciation." Receiving his calling as an artist, Braithwaite soon was composing and publishing his own verse.

Boston simultaneously held him at arm's length and beckoned him into its literary sanctuaries. When in 1904 he published *Lyrics of Life and Love* at his own expense, Braithwaite sought a subscription from Colonel Thomas Wentworth Higginson. The colonel embodied both Civil War heroism—he had led black soldiers, as he recalled in *Army Life in a Black Regiment*—and Brahmin literary values, for Higginson "discovered" Emily Dickinson. Higginson not only endorsed Braithwaite's efforts, but he also recommended the work to his friends. Braithwaite visited Higginson's Cambridge home, which the black poet saw as a shrine where he could imagine "the faint, subtle echoes of the mighty spirits that had glorified the environs of Cambridge and Concord in the nineteenth century." Braithwaite gained subscriptions from many prominent literary Bostonians: Julia Ward Howe, Arlo Bates (who wrote Boston novels, *The Pagans* and *The Puritans*), Mark De Wolfe Howe, and others. When he visited Edward Everett Hale (author of *The Man without a Country* and *James Russell Lowell and His Friends*), Hale signed the subscription and—alluding to the then current Du Bois–Washington controversy—said "Young man, it is no disgrace to hoe potatoes."[66] But Braithwaite had a mind to harvest other crops.

Though many in his day considered this an unlikely role for a black Bostonian, Braithwaite, the former errand boy, became a principal arbiter of taste and talent in the Boston literary community and beyond. Braithwaite set out to define the state of the art of poetry in his time by writing criticism and poetry, by editing anthologies; and he also set out to record what it meant to be black in white Boston. As a result, he was celebrated by both black and white literary figures. W. E. B. Du Bois called Braithwaite "the most prominent critic of poetry in America" and William Dean Howells praised him as "the most intelligent historian of contemporary poetry I know."[67] In a long career as an author and editor, Braithwaite published more than thirty volumes of poetry, stories, autobiography, and criticism. As his letters show, he knew the best minds of several generations—Howells, Higginson, Amy Lowell, Carl Sandburg, Du Bois, Frost, and others—and he gained entry into all levels of American literary culture.

Braithwaite always looked back on Boston with wonder. He was aware of the political idealism and literary heritage associated with the city. When he honored William Wells Brown, the "First Negro Novelist," for the *Pittsburgh Courier* in 1953, Braithwaite described Brown's journey—from slavery in Kentucky, via Canada, to freedom and fame in Boston—as a more heroic version of his own quest. "In Boston, with access to books, and the association of eminently cultured friends, his own proficiency in knowledge and culture broadened and deepened, and he became an effective lecturer in the crusade against slavery."[68]

In 1919 Braithwaite praised Du Bois's *Souls of Black Folk* for beginning a poetic tradition for black writers—"a quivering rhapsody of wrongs endured and hopes to be fulfilled"—but Braithwaite did not develop a separatist philosophy for black Americans; he believed that "all great artists are interracial and international in rendering in the medium of any particular art the fundamental passions and the primary instincts of humanity."[69]

Braithwaite's most eloquent writings draw upon personal, racial, and regional memories in Boston. In his autobiography he recalls hearing Frederick Douglass lecture at the Park Street Church in 1888. Though then a boy, Braithwaite had a sharp ear and eye for cultural associations. I "heard his thunderous voice go echoing upwards to vanish through the delicately beautiful Christopher Wren steeple on the church that pointed to heaven above the Old Granary Burial Ground where slept in eternal peace the parents of Benjamin Franklin."[70] After Douglass's inspiring lecture, Braithwaite and his great-grandmother's husband, a former slave, left the church and crossed the gas-lit Common on their way home, a walk which stirred a memorable meditation on the black experience in Boston. Both young Braithwaite and his Boston, then, were buoyed by a detectable air of idealism, youth and high ambition. Braithwaite saw himself enlarged by the city; he felt the city embedded itself in his being.

> The Common was silent and spectre-like, and the surrounding streets, Boylston, Tremont, Park, and Beacon, yet untouched with the modernity that has since altered their aspects. Up the sloping mall on the northern side where hilly Beacon Street rose to its crest, stood the State House with its famous Bullfinch front and golden dome. And opposite, on the Common side of the street, was the

site where ten years later they were to place the great St. Gaudens monument which in bas-relief immortalized Col. Robert Gould Shaw leading his Negro troops (the 54th Massachusetts Regiment, which Frederick Douglass had been instrumental in organizing) against the ramparts of Fort Wagner. Its beauty and historical significance could not exist without a related tribute to the historic memory and figure of Frederick Douglass, whose living greatness I had that night of my boyhood seen and heard.[71]

Braithwaite composed his character out of inspirations drawn from Boston's black heritage: Brown's literary achievement and Douglass's dedication to social justice.

Throughout his writing career Braithwaite seized every opportunity to celebrate his black heritage in Boston's history and culture. In the final year of his life, 1962, Braithwaite wrote an essay about a former slave, Mrs. Washburn, whom he had known when he was a boy growing up in Boston. Mrs. Washburn had come to Boston, as had so many former slaves who sought freedom in the city of abolitionism, after the Civil War. When Braithwaite was a boy she had lived on Buckingham Street, near the tracks of the Boston and Albany Railroad which separated Boston's black and white communities. There, amid the din of railroad cars, Mrs. Washburn recounted to young Braithwaite the bombardment of Richmond and the fall of the South. Caught up again in her memories of threat and emancipation, she swabbed her gums with a snuff stick, which she chewed upon like a cigar, and she grew excited. From the trains, smoke and flames, sound and fury, blended with her vivid tale of guns and drums. After her saga of peril, she sent young Braithwaite home to his mother, his imagination still reeling. On the dim, lamplighted streets he relived her past. "Those intervals of menacing blackness were filled in my boyish imagination with all the terror that Mister Grant had rained on Richmond."

His reminiscence, written more than six decades later, was Braithwaite's celebration of the birth of his historical and racial consciousness. "The past is with me today, the last phase of the

Civil War. Mrs. Washburn's dramatic recital of the capture of Richmond, her barometric snuff-stick, and the lamplighted streets through which I walked home."[72]

Braithwaite's Boston would lose some of the wonder it held for him as a boy. He left Boston to teach at Atlanta University (1935–45), then he lived in Harlem; but he preserved the memory of the city which had inspired him into racial and cultural consciousness. William Stanley Braithwaite went far in retrieving and preserving the dreams of black Bostonians by placing their experience at the center of Boston's imagination, within its Brahmin emblems. Distant from his Boston youth by years and geography, Braithwaite's recollections are tinged in sentiment, masking the pains and anxieties he must have felt as a young black man in Boston. Perhaps his recollections are rhetorical resolutions of problems never resolved on the streets of the city. Beneath the placid, refracted image of the fountain in his poem, "In the Public Garden"—purple, green, and white in reflection—lay stark, black-and-white images of the racial nightmare from which he was trying to awake. He would as well have Boston, his city, wake to its collective past.

BOSTON has provided a double, often divided identity for its black citizens. While practicing systematic discrimination and reneging upon its frequent and eloquently stated promises, Boston has also offered former slaves and their descendants a heritage which values freedom, justice, and education; Boston appointed itself the center of antislavery passions and political idealism, values incorporated by Boston blacks. Slave importation to Boston ended by 1790. Public monuments to Crispus Attucks, Robert Gould Shaw, and the Fifty-fourth Massachusetts Regiment testify to the city's appreciation of black sacrifice to its ideals. The African Meeting House was founded on Beacon Hill in 1805 and became the center of a number of associations that formed a web of black culture in Boston. There troops were recruited for Civil War combat. There Boston's black culture heritage is preserved today. Boston's black population thus formed a self-protective cultural haven in a hostile environment. In turn, as William D. Piersen says, "their choices influenced the lives of white Yankees as well, helping to mellow those rather puritanical people."[73]

Further, Boston offered limited literary and cultural opportunities for blacks. Harvard in particular educated, certified, and celebrated black leaders, from Du Bois to Malcolm X. Boston University educated Dr. King and houses his papers. In Boston some black writers received assistance in telling their stories, particularly during the abolitionist period, or they were supplied with an audience for those stories, tales which bore witness to racism and sought promise of release from bondage. In Boston many black writers, from Wheatley to Braithwaite, learned to express themselves in finished literary forms; many stayed to celebrate both black and Yankee cultures. Boston provided black writers with compelling literary models, not all black, ranging from the brave Attucks, who died fighting for a political principle of justice which excluded him, to Hester Prynne, the archetypal enemy within the gates of the repressive, hypocritical Boston community. The examples of Wheatley, Brown, Douglass, Du Bois, and others provided a coherent black literary tradition in Boston for those who, like Braithwaite and West, came later.

Despite the city's unresolved patterns of racial discrimination, Boston's blacks have made the most of their limited chances to leave a compelling record of their experiences. Boston has proved as flexible a region in the imaginations of its black citizens as it has for Brahmin and ethnic Bostonians. Boston has been designed in the mind as much as it has been found in the streets. Each of these black writers has composed his or her sense of special place from the variety of possibilities offered by the city. For Wheatley, Boston was a place of transit, where she paused to learn poetry and prayer, on her way to a better place in another world. For Douglass and many other escaped slaves, Boston stood for political principle and support in their effort to bear witness to slavery's injustices. For Du Bois, Boston meant the black bourgeoisie, Beacon Hill respectability, and Harvard's promise of possibility. For Braithwaite,

Boston was a divided land: in its center city Brahmin culture flowed like the fountain in the Common, but across the railroad tracks an escaped slave woman told him another story. The trick was in the reconciliation. Dorothy West's characters told us more about the passage from black to white Boston; Malcolm X repudiated downtown Boston culture, both Brahmin and black bourgeoisie, preferring the energetic, dangerous underlife of black ghetto culture. While constantly disappointing the aspirations of its black citizens, Boston has provided its black writers, as it offered it immigrants, a model of America, an emblem available for their recasting, a symbolic landscape of the imagination.

IN early 1988, the Boston Athenaeum acknowledged the centrality of the black presence to Boston culture in "Two Hundred Years of Community and Culture: An Exhibition of Books, Painting, and Sculpture by and about Blacks in Boston." Finally, within the central institutional symbol of Boston culture, black Bostonians took their proper place and achieved overdue recognition for all they contributed to Boston in life and art.

The exhibition served as testimony of the central places blacks have held, for more than two hundred years, in Boston history and culture. In 1773 slaves from Boston petitioned officials for their liberty. "We have no property! We have no wives! No children! We have no city! No country!"[74] The Athenaeum exhibition demonstrated that Boston blacks *have* won a home for themselves in Boston and they have, in the process, helped shape the mind of the city.

AS Boston has its Freedom Trail, marked by a red line on the sidewalks, a route which guides us to significant sites, largely from the city's white history, so too does Boston have its Black Heritage Trail, an unmarked route through the center of the city which takes us to memorable sites from the history of black Boston. The Black Heritage Trail begins at the African Meeting House on Beacon Hill, the oldest black church building still standing in the nation, and winds through the North side of Beacon Hill, where blacks settled in great number in the nineteenth century. Boston's Freedom Trail and Black Heritage Trail intersect, fittingly enough, at the Shaw Memorial, which commemorates that moment when black and white joined to affirm a principle of justice and to fight and die for the freedom of the slave. It was Boston's best moment, memorialized in its finest monument, an emblem of the ideals for which the city has, at its best, stood.[75]

6

Boston Manners and Morals:
HENRY ADAMS, GEORGE SANTAYANA, JOHN P. MARQUAND, JOHN CHEEVER, AND JOHN UPDIKE

I N THE MONOMYTH composed by Greater Boston's autobiographers and novelists of manners, the region possesses a resonant sense of the past which defines, confines, and inspires its inhabitants. A symbolic landscape is marked by moral and social divisions; class tensions draw its citizenry into ancient and depleting battles, conflicts which leave them with an abiding sense of loss. Life does not measure up to their preconceptions. Reality does not match their vision. In compensation, Greater Boston is a region that stirs intensities of thought and feeling, inspires heroic efforts either to recompose a fixed social order or to transcend it to new frontiers of imagination. Consciousness of *place*—social, moral, spiritual—and *past* characterizes the representative men and women of Greater Boston in these writers' works.

In literature, Boston is better known for its commitment to the romance than to the novel of manners. Hawthorne veered toward the romance, a mode, as Richard Chase notes, that exploited the picturesque, moved toward melodrama and idyll, plunged beyond morality to the dark recesses of consciousness, muted concern for the hero's relation to society, and "assumed freedom from the ordinary novelistic requirements of verisimilitude, development and continuity."[1] William Dean Howells saw the romance as the characteristic Boston form. However, Boston novelists have written successful novels of manners, beginning with those social satires of the mid-1880s by James and Howells: *The Bostonians* and *The Rise of Silas Lapham*. More forcefully than any other city, Boston, that stratified "common ground," has maintained its class distinctions and has respected its territorial differentiations. As a result, its writers have been obliged to describe, in informing myths, its manners and morals. If, as one critic of the form notes, "writing an American novel of manners has never been easy"—because class nuances are hard to detect in a nation that claims to be democratic— the novel of manners has been a required form for the proper portrayal of Boston and its surrounding communities.[2]

After James and Howells, the region's other notable novels of manners—written by George Santayana, John P. Marquand, John Cheever, and John Updike—fulfill the requirements of the form. They give primary attention to manners as "signals of value," with particular emphasis upon class distinctions, during volatile periods of Boston's past.[3] Manners, and all that they imply in these works, make the man and the woman, determine relations, and define social values. Yet these writers also retain elements of the romance, with its magical and moral emphases, in their novels of manners, just as Hawthorne included selective realistic characteristics, common to what he called "the novel," in his romances. In these novels of manners, melodrama and idyll surround the heroes, characters who live in society's midst, as formally required, though they yearn for worlds elsewhere. They quest. Reluctant or tentative voyagers, they present impeccable exteriors, but they choose to live their most passionate lives within their own psyches, after the fashion of Hester Prynne, the ambiguous saint of Boston letters. These local novelists and certain autobiographers of manners dramatize moral imperatives which challenge the prevailing social codes. Though these writers respect "the ordinary novelistic requirements of verisimilitude, development and continuity," their heroes, psychic voyagers of the near-at-hand, undermine the serene surfaces of their lives with remembrances of things past and dreams of transcendence. Such are the general characteristics of the rich memoirs and novels of manners written by Henry Adams, George Santayana, John P. Marquand, John Cheever, and John Updike, writers who develop a formal tradition established by Howells and James. Works by these writers define the region in a network of invidious class distinctions which try the souls of promising young men and women.

These writers present Boston as class-fractured, past-haunted, fearful of the future, and smug. But within this smothering context, we discover plausible fictional and autobiographical heroes who seek a true education and try to reshape their lives. Henry Adams, who learned his manners and morals in Boston, serves as a model in art and life for later novelists of manners. Born in the shadow of a daunting public and private history, in a city of waning influence and waxing class division, shaped by a Puritan vision in which Boston was the allegorical site of contending moral forces, miseducated by Harvard, Adams nevertheless shaped an original relationship with the universe. Adams's Boston is a lesser place: decline and fall were, for him, the Boston way. Henry Adams began with the surface of Boston's manners and penetrated to the substance of its many meanings. Like Adams, Greater Boston's autobiographers and novelists of manners would reimagine what Boston means.

IN 1838 Henry Adams was born, as he put it in the opening sentence of *The Education of Henry Adams*, "under the shadow of

Boston State House."[4] Seventy-nine years later, Robert Lowell, as he put it in "Antebellum Boston," also "was born under the shadow of the Boston State House, high on Beacon Hill."[5] Boston's long shadows colored the lives of these writers, both born to an elevated and privileged perspective on the city. Though each tried to remove himself from its influence, its manners and morals, Boston shaped their characters and destinies—along with the fates of many fictional characters.

In Henry Adams's informative myth of place, Boston had dealt him a fortunate hand, but he chose not to play its game. His world was defined by his father's second-floor library, in Charles Francis Adams's Mount Vernon Street house, high on Beacon Hill. There eighteen thousand volumes surrounded and reassured the Adams vision of the world. There the Conscience Whigs articulated a world that was slipping away from them.[6] Henry insists he was miseducated to take his place within a patrician world of waning influence in post-Jacksonian America, so he became first an observer, a spectatorial eye, then an exile from his native grounds.

When he was only six, in May of 1844, the city was transformed by a series of symbolic events. The Boston and Albany Railroad opened, Cunard steamers appeared in the harbor, and the telegraph informed Bostonians that Clay and Polk were nominated for the presidency. Insular, isolated Boston, where generations of Adamses were nurtured, was threatened on all sides. Henceforth Boston would be more intimately linked to the rest of America by rail and its shores would be assaulted by Irish immigrants, brought by Cunard ships; meanwhile the news from Washington, now telegraphed, was clear: no Adams need apply![7]

Still, Henry Adams was reared to resist: reform was bred in the blood of this great-grandson and grandson of presidents. Politics, the family business, was, in the Adams vision, "the systematic organization of hatreds," a crusade against evil. Family heritage was reinforced by the lessons of nature and geography which, read in proper typological fashion, taught him that life, inner and outer, was a struggle of contending forces represented by the contrasting but equally symbolic landscapes of Quincy and Boston.

The chief charm of New England was harshness of contrasts and extremes of sensibility—a cold that froze the blood, and a heat that boiled it—so that the pleasure of hating—one's self if no better victim offered—was not its rarest amusement; but the charm was a true and natural child of the soil, not a cultivated weed of the ancients. The violence of the contrast was real and made the strongest motive of education. The double exterior nature gave life its relative values. Winter and summer, cold and heat, town and country, force and freedom, marked two modes of life and thought, balanced like lobes of the brain. . . . Town was restraint, law, unity. Country, only seven miles away, was liberty, diversity, outlawry, the endless delight of mere sense impressions given by nature for nothing, and breathed by boys without knowing it.[8]

Geographical distance—the family home in Quincy was only seven miles away from Boston—is intensified by Adams's empowering imagination. Nature's stark alternatives symbolized Adams's divided mind. Above all, Boston taught Henry Adams to see the world as a series of conflicting emblems. Families, seasons, and sites stood as animate embodiments of ideas. Boston winters and Quincy summers fought over his nature as though they were God and Death and he were Everyman in the medieval morality play. "With such standards, the Bostonian could not but develop a double nature. Life was a double thing."[9]

Henry Adams's Boston affirmed a confident vision of the universe, based upon old money and Puritan values. "Boston had solved the universe; or had offered and realized the best solution yet tried."[10] Of course, as Adams's irony suggests, Boston's solutions were found wanting, particularly by those newcomers, the Irish, who were hostile to the Brahmin class and their worldview. Adams called those outcasts *blackguards*, thus translating their social status into terms of moral opprobrium. For Adams, as for Thoreau, the invading Irishman was an antitype whose misguided values helped to define the correctness of the Brahmin or Yankee visions.

Yet Henry Adams, like Robert Lowell after him, was also intrigued by raffish Boston as an exciting and dangerous alternative to his confining class and ideological world. "The puritan city had always hidden a darker side. Blackguard Boston was only too educational, and to most boys much more interesting." A snowball fight on the Boston Common in 1850 is transformed in Adams's memory into a parable of contending classes and values, a foreshadowing of more serious divisions and violence. On the day of the great snowball battle between Boston boys, his Latin School crowd met and at first repelled an attack from West End outlanders. However, as it grew dark, many of his classmates drifted off. Henry Higginson, Adams's peer, was struck with a stone inside a snowball, then led away, bleeding. The Latin School lads were driven back to the Beacon Street Mall by "a swarm of blackguards from the slums, led by a grisly terror called Conky Daniels," who, it was rumored, "with a club and a hideous reputation, was going to put an end to the Beacon Street cowards forever." Only the resolute defense of their turf by classmates Savage and Martin turned away Daniels's rowdy crowd and saved the day for the boy Brahmins. Characteristically, Adams sought for "the obvious moral" in this parable: "that blackguards were not so black as they were painted."

When Savage and Martin were killed in the Civil War, Adams wondered whether they had discovered their own bravery, had learned how to die, on Boston Common.[11] Adams, however, forgot about Conky Daniels, the blackguard with a club from the slums, who was just as likely to have been prepared on Boston Common for death in the Civil War. Daniels and his followers were part of an immigrant influx which drove middle-class Boston families into the Back Bay area by the late 1850s.[12] Class tension in Boston, as Adams hints, became more open and cruel—rocks inside snowballs—despite the common fate that awaited so many Boston young men during the Civil War.

Adams fought against his circumscribed Boston fate by taking his education into his own hands. Harvard may have failed to provide him with an education which would prepare him for the strange new world of the twentieth century, but it did offer him a way out of Boston. James Russell Lowell, who succeeded Long-fellow as professor of belles-lettres, had brought a love of German culture back to Harvard, where he invited his students to follow his intellectual passion. Adams followed Lowell's example and went to Germany for two years. The best that Boston and Harvard could offer Henry Adams, then, was exile. When, after serving with his father, minister to England during the Civil War, Henry returned to Harvard to teach history (1870–77), he judged himself a failure, but he came to think more kindly of Harvard and what it represents in America. "Harvard College might have its faults, but at least it redeemed America, since it was true to its own."[13]

For all that, Henry Adams's Boston, particularly after the Civil War, was a social model of devolution. He made this clear in *The Life of George Cabot Lodge* (1911). Lodge, born in 1873, faced a Boston made even more crass by commerce than the pre–Civil War Boston of Adams's youth. Lodge was the son of Henry Cabot Lodge, a former student of Adams who went on to become an isolationist Republican Senator. George Cabot Lodge, in turn, became a writer of sonnets. In Adams's view, twentieth century Boston would heed neither high-minded politics from the Adamses nor poetry from the Lodges. Since Emerson's youth, wrote Adams, "the sense of poetry had weakened like the sense of religion." Adams seized upon the example of Lodge to show how all had devolved. "The Boston of 1900 differed from his parents and grand-parents of 1850, in owning nothing the value of which, in the market, could be affected by the poet."[14]

America might be finished with Adamses, but Henry Adams was not finished reimagining America, in history and fiction, when he left Boston for Washington. Though he would recall his Boston youth indirectly in *George Cabot Lodge* and directly in *Education*, Adams would not remain long enough to tell the story of post–Civil War Boston, an ethnic passion play. His novels of manners, *Democracy* and *Esther*, are set in Washington and New York. However, others devoted themselves to the manners mode in order to record the shifting social surface of Boston in and beyond the era when it was transformed by immigrant arrivals.

BOSTON "was a moral and intellectual nursery, always busy applying first principles to trifles," wrote George Santayana in his autobiography, in a dismissive tone and reductive imagery which recalls Henry Adams and anticipates Robert Lowell: three privileged Bostonians who saw Boston as a confining kindergarten.[15] These writers would spend their lives coming to terms with their Boston heritages. They fled its influence while carrying its values, in various literary forms, into other countries.

But George Santayana was no Boston Brahmin; he was not even one of their blood relations. His mother was a Catalonian, born in Glasgow, who met George Sturgis, of the Boston Sturgises, in Manila. They had three children who survived infancy. After Sturgis died, she married Augustin Santayana, George's Spanish father. Born in Madrid in 1863, George did not arrive in Boston until 1872, when his mother, as she had promised Sturgis, brought their children there to be educated. At eight George was sufficiently worldly to see the city, as he ever would, from an outsider's point of view.

Boston was Santayana's "reversible accident." Nevertheless, Boston and Cambridge educated Santayana: he attended Miss Welchman's kindergarten on Chestnut Street, then the Brimmer School in the South End. He studied at Boston Latin School on West Street for eight years; finally he graduated *summa cum laude* from Harvard College in 1886. He would always associate education with the frigid winters of Boston and Cambridge. Though a successful student, Santayana, as he said of his Latin School years, "remained there, as I remained later at Harvard for twenty-five years, a stranger at heart."[16]

As had Henry Adams, after graduating from Harvard, Santayana went to Germany to study; then he too returned to teach at Harvard (in 1894). Always the tourist in Boston-Cambridge, Santayana believed that Europe was his true home; during his American years he crossed the Atlantic thirty-eight times. After teaching philosophy for twenty-three years at Harvard, where he had felt a prisoner of claustrophobic Boston and Cambridge culture, in 1912 the forty-eight-year-old Santayana resigned his teaching position and returned to Europe, reversing the course which had been chosen for him as a boy. Though he would never return, he would (like Isak Dinesen, who reinvented Africa after she had left it forever) set his mind's eye on Boston in two memorable works: *Persons and Places*, his autobiography, and *The Last Puritan*, his novel of manners, a fictional evocation of proper Boston, its achievements, and its costs.

The three parts of Santayana's autobiography, which he began in 1920, were published between 1944 and 1953, the year after his death. Evocative, satiric, and gossipy, the luminous prose of his memoirs shows that some of those who remember the past are doomed to repeat it.

Living again in Europe, distant in time and space from his Boston-Cambridge years, Santayana looked back upon his youth with amused wonder. In such a tone, having developed a detached persona that echoes Adams's cool narrative voice, Santayana evoked the Boston of 1856, whose emblems were the State House and a theater called the Museum, where Emerson and Fuller went to the ballet. "Emerson is said to have exclaimed, 'This is art!' To which Margaret Fuller replied with added rapture, 'Ah, Mr. Emerson, this is religion!' "[17] Santayana's aestheticism makes Boston into a theater of the imagination, reducing its luminaries, as had Emerson and Hawthorne before him, to actors in a farce.

Yet Santayana was not happy during the nine years he lived at a house on the waterside of Beacon Street. There, as he later recalled, romance and realism—art and commerce, beauty and truth—vied for his attention, in a moral psychodrama. For example, the waterview was arresting, particularly when the day's late light glazed the Boston background into an art object, "especially when the summer sunset lit up the scene, and darkness added to distance made the shabby bank opposite more inoffensive." However, such beauty for Santayana, as it also was for Henry James, was modified by the "counter-effects" of mean backyards in the foreground, as though Boston were an ineptly executed painting. "The stench from the mudflats" was a constant reminder that Boston was insistently real: a world of conflict, divided between imaginary beauty and "dull routine," like the symbolically separated Charles River Basin.[18]

Boston was an insufficient world for Santayana. Perhaps any earthly place would have failed him. His "metanoia," or philosophic insights into ideal states, and his Catholicism taught him to seek higher worlds, beyond Boston. In his Catholic renunciation of Boston's offerings, Santayana, though hostile to Irish immigrants, curiously anticipates Edwin O'Connor. Indeed, while he was trapped in Boston Santayana took telling pleasure in the music he heard at the Church of the Immaculate Conception, at Boston College. Through religion or art, "the end is to escape to another world, to live freely for a while in a medium made by us and fit for us to live in. . . . Only the artificial can be good expressly."[19] Boston was worthy, for Santayana, to the extent that it supplied occasion for good artifice, for imaginative release.

The Last Puritan: A Memoir in the Form of a Novel is an exercise in artifice, a useful fiction through which Santayana delineated a stark, simplified myth of Boston's persons and places. Completed in 1935, it took him forty-five years to write, from his Harvard days to his period of exile, when Boston was much on his mind. Curiously, Oliver Alden, Santayana's tragic anti-hero, spent little time in Boston. Still, Alden carried Boston embedded within him, as determining as a genetic code. Though physically removed—he was reared in Connecticut, attended Williams College, spent only a year at Harvard, and lived his last years abroad—Alden was marked by one side of the Boston Idea, a form of Puritanism which has declined into a repressive gentility, as though he too had been reared under the shadow of the State House.

Nathaniel Alden, Oliver's uncle, embodies, in Santayana's spiteful satire, a pure version of the desiccation of Puritan vision and values. At the novel's opening, set in 1870, we witness Alden in an informing gesture. He emerges from his home at the top of Beacon Street, as he does every Tuesday and Friday, and turns left, setting forth for King's Chapel. "He always turned to the left, for never, except to funerals, did Mr. Nathaniel Alden walk *down* Beacon Hill."[20]

Down Beacon Hill, where Beacon Street is crossed by Charles Street, across from the Boston Garden and Common, he might encounter alien voices and habits which could challenge the serene, monied sanctuary within which Alden encased himself. Cosmic election and class prejudices are evident in geography:

> The corner of Beacon and Charles Streets was central and respectable. Indeed it formed a sort of isthmus, leaving the flood of niggerdom to the north and of paddydom to the south, and connecting Beacon Hill with the Back Bay—the two islands of respectability composing socially habitable Boston.[21]

Far safer, then, to turn left, toward the center of Boston. There Hawthorne had already set his myth of Puritanism, the myth Santayana appropriates, though his latter-day Puritans seek safety and propriety—not salvation, which they already presume is assured—above all else. King's Chapel, which had become the sanctuary of high Unitarianism, would affirm the social and moral identities of its parishioners, who found safety and certainty within the closed doors of its pews.

Such was the background, such were the values, which shaped the son of Nathaniel's wayward brother. Oliver Alden was a man weighed by duty, with little sense of imagination. In the words of the novel's narrator, the "life" of Oliver illustrated an example of "Puritanism Self-condemned. Oliver was THE LAST PURITAN."[22] Perhaps, as John McCormick suggests, "he is defeated and doomed, not so much a last as a lost puritan."[23]

Oliver Alden, never his own man, was the product of the forces that made him. When Oliver briefly attends Harvard he meets his fate. To emphasize the grip of New England upon Oliver's consciousness, Santayana has Oliver choose uncomfortable lodgings in Divinity Hall, digs once occupied by Emerson. "What was good enough for Emerson is good enough for me."[24] Indeed the meanness and discomfort of received ideas is Oliver Alden's special providence.

Never at ease in the world, rejected by those whom he loves, Oliver seeks transcendence or obliteration. He enlists in the army, determined to die in France in the Great War. However, even that is denied Oliver Alden, who is killed after the armistice in a motorcycle accident, an absurdist's death. His valediction is nothing less than a suicide note (Oliver's father, a dour model, had already committed suicide) for the Puritan tradition.

> I was born a moral aristocrat, able to obey only the voice of God, which means that of my own heart. My people first went to America as exiles into a stark wilderness to lead a life apart, purer and soberer than the carnival life of Christendom. . . . We are not wanted. . . . I shan't shut myself up in Beacon Street or mince my steps or wear black gloves. But I can keep my thoughts inviolate, like Uncle Nathaniel, and not allow the world to override me. We will not accept anything cheaper or cruder than our own conscience. We have dedicated ourselves to the truth, to living in the presence of the noblest things we can conceive. If we can't live so, we won't live at all. [25]

The Last Puritan is George Santayana's long farewell to the city of his youth and middle years; it is his divorce decree from Boston, his city of self-destructive self-consciousness, the city which indirectly made and broke Oliver Alden, its representative man. "A moral nature burdened and over-strung," concludes the narrator of Oliver's sad life, "and a critical faculty fearless but helplessly subjective—isn't that the true tragedy of your ultimate Puritan?" [26]

JOHN P. MARQUAND'S *Late George Apley* (1937) might well have been titled *The Last Brahmin.* As in the Boston fictions of George Santayana and Edwin O'Connor, Marquand articulates the quintessential Boston myth of loss. Marquand too composes a satiric yet loving portrait of a dying figure who represents a fading tradition. Satire fades into sentiment as readers become reconciled to such a figure, who no longer wields power over the community, a figure whose archaic or morally suspect values held an honorable core. [27]

"Boston is the only city in America you could satirize," said Marquand, ambiguously.[28] Though they shared satiric perspectives on Boston, Santayana was not enthusiastic about Marquand's work. "Mr. Marquand's hero seems to me not so much Bostonian as provincial."[29] Of course, that is just Marquand's point: Boston *is* provincial. That is why Marquand chose a Boston stuffed-shirt, Horatio Willing, as his narrator.

When Marquand moved to Beacon Hill in 1927, he joined the Tavern Club and the Athenaeum, vantage points from which he could observe Boston aristocracy. His investigation was aided by acquaintance with fellow club and library member, Mark A. De Wolfe Howe, author of *Barrett Wendell and His Letters* and other flattering biographies of Boston Brahmins. Howe's reverent portraits inspired Marquand's gentle satire. In her memoir of her father, Helen Howe made the line of influence clear. "It would be absurd to pretend that Father's style of writing—florid in manner, kindly in comment, often tepid in subject matter—did not serve as the model for Horatio Willing, Mr. Apley's biographer." (*Time* magazine was sufficiently confused on this point to print a picture of Mark De Wolfe Howe with the caption "The Late George Apley . . . ?")[30]

Like Howells before him, Howe was an outsider—born in Bristol, Rhode Island, in 1864—who came to Boston, saw it with smiling eyes and seduced the city with his gentle pen; he was no repressed Brahmin, like Apley, timidly yearning for a world elsewhere. Indeed, Boston was Howe's heavenly city. *Time* was true to the spirit of Howe, who composed for himself a perfect persona of the solid man of Boston, surrounding himself with its literary institutions and emblems: Beacon Hill homes, membership on Harvard's Board of Overseers. Further, he became one of the directors of the Atlantic Monthly Company, a trustee of the Boston Symphony Orchestra, a member of the library committee of the Boston Athenaeum and the vestry of Trinity Church; he was, as well, a member in good standing of the Tavern Club and the Examiner Club. Howe perfectly registers his tone and attitude toward revered Boston cultural sites in one of his book titles: *A Partial (And Not Impartial) Semi-Centennial History of the Tavern Club 1884–1934*.[31]

On all of these Boston institutions Mark De Wolfe Howe cast his kindly eye. He became, as would Marquand's Willing, a tribal memorialist and protector. When Mrs. Annie Fields, widow of the publisher James T. Fields, planned to bring out a volume of her letters, Howe advised her to mute her sentimental nicknames ("Pinny," "Fuff") for Sarah Orne Jewett. "I doubt . . . whether you will like to have all sorts of people reading them wrong," Howe told Mrs. Fields.[32] Just such a "Boston marriage," its psychological complexities and social symbolism, had fascinated Henry James in *The Bostonians*, but Howe drew the veil. When Howe composed *Memoirs of a Hostess*, based on Mrs. Fields's diaries, he treated the relationship in most high-minded terms, as a joining of "true *aristophiles*."[33] Howe saw Mrs. Fields, who died in 1915, as Willing would see Apley—an emblem of a finer age. His memoirs, then, are reminders to the citizens of twentieth century Boston to live up to the tarnished ideals—"those lasting 'things that are more excellent'—of the true *aristophiles*, dead and gone."[34]

Howe's *Barrett Wendell and His Letters*, the principal model for Marquand's *Apley*, is a defense of Wendell's caste values. Wendell taught at Harvard (1880–1917), wrote a biography of Cotton Mather and *A Literary History of America;* Wendell was open about his bias for Americans of "the better sort," adopting the term "gentleman" as an unambiguous designation of praise.[35] Howe approved. Howe, as his daughter noted, became the happy insider in Boston's world of gentlemanly culture, while Marquand never did. "Father, in short, took to Boston and all its ways like a duck to water—as he took to life itself. . . . John, on the other hand, carried within the seeds of discord with himself as well as his environment."[36]

Marquand claimed *Apley* was accurate. "Every incident has repeated itself with small variations in Boston. . . . I have a good deal of respect for Boston and a reluctant respect for George Apley. I have a good deal of Apley in myself."[37] Marquand's defensiveness suggests his sensitivity to criticism that he had gone too far in his send-up of proper Bostonians.

The Late George Apley is "a novel in the form of a memoir." After his death, Apley's son, John, enlists Horatio Willing, "Boston's Dean of Letters," a "compiler of distinguished pasts" in John's fine phrase, to "take in hand my father's notes and letters." Willing does so with a reverent hand, willing to ignore compromising evidence, insisting upon the significance of George Apley, whose writings reveal, says Willing, "the true spirit of our city and of our time, since Apley was so essentially a part of both."[38] Marquand too suggests that Apley was what Emerson called a representative man—not a hero, but a man whose life illustrates the values of his time. This then is a novel of Boston, with George Apley as its emblem. Apley, for Willing and for Marquand, "is" Boston in the same way Thoreau was Concord; both were men who embody the spirit of a place, men whose lives are parables of defining purpose, men through whom we may understand what a place means.

However, Marquand's novel is more than a flattering portrayal of "a true son of Boston"; it is also a fascinating study of Boston's contending voices, for John Apley's loving but far more realistic point of view is registered in counterpoint to Willing's puffery.[39] John comes to honor but not to flatter the memory of his father. With tact and irony, John urges Willing to do the same. As a result, Willing's record of Apley's life contains a range of evidence sufficient to make him a rounded character, not a caricature like Santayana's Nathaniel Alden. John's realization of his father's unfulfilled life gradually asserts itself. "Father was a frustrated man, but then I could see that he had been trying all his life to get through the meshes of a net, a net which he could never break, and in a sense it was a net of his own contriving." John Apley, then, embodies the center of consciousness in this novel whose hero, his father, devoted his life to rationalizations—occasionally relieved by epiphanies of realization—supported by his ever-willing biographer.

"I am the sort of man I am, because environment prevented me from being anything else," said George Apley in a sad, candid moment.[40] Indeed, the sense of a shaping heritage lays like a heavy hand on Apley's life. The first Apley arrived in 1636; successive Apleys took up slave trading, then more legitimate seafaring activities. Thomas Apley, George's father, and his uncle, William Apley, built textile mills at Apley Falls. In describing Apley's background, Marquand clearly alludes to the success of the Lowell, Jackson, and Appleton families, the Boston Associates who developed an industrial system for Waltham and Lowell, Massachusetts. Writing of these "enterprising elite," Robert F. Dalzell, Jr. underscores their ability to combine technologically innovative and socially regressive goals. "As businessmen they were innovators operating on a scale unparalleled in America at the time, yet ultimately they hoped to check the thrust of change—to alter the world they knew only enough to make it secure for people like themselves." Their Boston—composed largely of State Street, Beacon Hill, Back Bay and Harvard—became a class and cultural preserve against immigrant encroachment. Its stability was financed by out-of-town mills, whose employees were drawn from the rural poor and recent immigrants. For example, the financing and establishment of the Boston Athenaeum by these "friends of improvement" stood as their emblem of Boston as a cultural preserve, "ornamental to the metropolis," an institution whose holdings would provide "a source of rational enjoyment" to its citizenry.[41] George Apley, too, stands for "rational" enjoyments, stifling his feelings.

The "friends of improvement" help to explain the sense of enclosure inherited by George Apley. A lineage of strong men had, through acts of wickedness, bravura, and brilliance built up fortunes for their descendants to maintain, though these fortunes were often tied up in protective, inhibiting trusts. As a result, resolute Apleys were replaced by cautious Apleys and the authority of Apley women increased in George's generation. George lacks the ruth-lessness that characterized his father's generation and all those American Apleys before him. "I move along a narrow groove," George admits to a friend, at age thirty-two.[42]

George's early youth was spent in the opulent, if narrow, groove of a life, like Henry Adams's youth, divided between two places, country and city. Hillcrest, the Apley family home in Milton, em-bodied the gentility of his mother, who was the author of a poem published in *The Atlantic Monthly*, "Blue Hill at Eventide"; she was also a watercolorist, a pianist and, of course, a Unitarian. His father spoke for the commercial values of State Street, values which permeated the Beacon Street home of the Apleys. George shuttled between these two symbolic sites, which framed and limited his life's story.

By the time he attended Harvard, in the class of 1887, George Apley, to the satisfaction of his pious biographer, "was emerging as a type, perhaps, but a type of which Harvard may be definitely proud." For all that, Willing had to admit to a certain "instability" in young George, a passing impulse to break away from his class's less-than-great expectations. Willing, prodded by John, reluctantly allows into the record George's brief passion for Mary Monahan, his "SWEET WILD ROSE," as George called her. George loved her because, as he wrote to her, "you took me away, just as I hope you will take me away forever from everything which binds and ties me."[43] When George's parents heard about this dalliance they *sent* him away, to Europe to forget this Irish-Catholic girl; there he experienced a revelation of his native identity and his inescap-able fate. In a letter to a classmate, George explained, in an apt, if bizarre, image that he finally knew who he was.

> It seems to me that all this time a part of Boston has been with me. I am a raisin in a slice of pie which has been conveyed from one plate to another. I have moved; I have seen plate after plate; but all the other raisins have been around me in the same relation to me as they were when we were all baked.[44]

Thereafter George, a baked and sliced raisin, sees the world inescapably "through a local haze."[45] Such is the power of definition imposed upon him by his family, his city.

Predictably, George Apley marries within his tribe: to Catherine Bosworth, of the estimable Boston-Concord Bosworths, in 1890. Thereafter he becomes the captive of *two* families' expectations of probity and propriety. George, a Harvard Law School graduate, finds his inevitable place in a proper firm which manages real estate and searches titles. He becomes a dutiful, public man of Boston. In a late letter to his son, Apley worries that John might neglect such obligations, the heart of what it means to be a Bostonian. "You can go to the uttermost ends of the earth but, in a sense, you will still be in Boston; and this is not true alone with you and me; it has been the same with others." John, too, comes to agree that his Boston identity is an inescapable fate.[46]

At the end of his days, George Apley admits his life has been too full of talk, too empty of purposeful action, but in another letter to his son he also affirms, with Marquand's obvious sympathy, his values: "I have stood for many things which I hope will not vanish from the earth."[47] Though George Apley's values have been narrow, class-ridden, parochial, pretentious, and patrician, they have also been honorable and, for the most part, unselfish. He remained loyal to his family and he put the best face upon the code of his clan. The novel which began in satire ends in tribute. Finally the voices of Marquand and Willing merge. As in the cases of Santayana's elegy to the "last Puritan" or O'Connor's "last hurrah" for a dying Irish politician, we are told that we shall not look again on the like of the late George Apley, the end of the Brahmin line.

Marquand's novel allows us entry into a private world of privilege and possession, the Boston ascendancy's sanctuary. He invites us to smile at their archaic and provincial values, to scorn their snobbery and bigotry. Yet, in the end Marquand restores approval to this world. George, if not representative of all Brahmins, is a worthy man. While the models for such a man fade away, fiction grants George Apley a perpetual place in our imaginations.

Marquand's Greater Boston was "a double thing," divided, as it also was for T. S. Eliot, between the city and the seacoast, north of Boston. For Marquand, Curzon's Mill in particular and Newburyport in general stood as an alternative world to Boston, as Quincy stood for Henry Adams. Curzon's Mill had been built by John's great-grandfather, Samuel Curzon, in 1820. In John's day its forty-seven acres of countryside and farmland between the Merrimack and Artichoke Rivers were a very heaven from which he was removed by his improvident father.[48] Marquand felt something of an outsider in both places, country and city. Boston was a sanctum of privilege which he could not quite penetrate. Curzon's Mill was the Eden young John visited each summer, the paradise from which he was banished each fall—the rightful inheritance, as he saw it, which he never received.[49]

Marquand settled for two years at Curzon's Mill with his first wife, Christina Sedgwick, after their marriage in 1922; they lived in the family "Brick House," then owned by the Brill family, but they found little happiness there. Marquand again returned in 1937, with his second wife, Adelaide Hooker, this time to a large house on Kent's Island, outside Newburyport, to find his place in the town where he had felt so displaced as a boy. There he wrote novels which removed him from this haunted, coastal place, settling his score with social Boston. In *Wickford Point* (1937), for example, Marquand's alter ego, Jim Calder, tries to go home again, yet he finds Wickford Point, Marquand's fictional version of Curzon's Mill, beautiful but paralyzing.[50]

H. M. Pulham, Esquire (1941) is a novel about an alter ego, Pulham, a man who was divided between Boston and New York. After serving in the Great War, Pulham, who had been born and bred in Boston, finds New York—its bustle, energy, sexuality—liberating and exhilarating. Boston, in contrast, is timeless, unchanged. New York means opportunity; Boston means responsibility. Typically, Marquand's hero has his New York dalliances, then he settles, as Apley had, for his Boston fate. Though Pulham never did what he wanted to do, his life was not driven by any selfishness, any self-seeking which made him turn his back on all he held dear. "I stayed because I was meant to stay," he explains.[51] H. M. Pulham's Boston meant the recognition of life's limits, maturity, a sense of loss, the satisfaction at having done one's duty. Pulham becomes another Apley.

Both Charles Gray, in *Point of No Return* (1961), and Willis Wayde, in *Sincerely, Willis Wayde* (1955), repudiate their home place of Clyde, Massachusetts (Marquand's fictional version of Newburyport), so that they might succeed in modern America. Gray is sympathetic; Wayde isn't. Both young men "wanted to get on," as John Gray said of his son, but both were prevented from doing so by their attachments to Clyde.[52] Not until each makes his break with Clyde can he truly "get on." Both men free themselves from the felicities, the illusions, the innocence and the circumscribing certainties of Clyde, to fulfill their dreams of success. In each novel, the hero, having cut the bonds of home and having made a tentative success for himself in New York, returns to Clyde so that he may repudiate it, again and forever. He validates his success in the world east of Eden, beyond Clyde, in Manhattan and its suburbs.

Marquand complained about being read as a regionalist. "It seems since Pulham that no matter what my efforts may be I am always writing about Boston."[53] Of course, for all of his travels and his various fictions, Marquand was essentially just that, a regionalist whose most carefully staked-out fictional field was bounded by Boston and those communities along its radial lines of class ascendancy: Cambridge, Concord, Curzon's Mill (Wickford Point, Harcourt Mill), and Newburyport (Clyde). His male protagonists are either born and bred in Boston (George Apley, H. M. Pulham) or they are shaped by a North Shore community (Jim Calder, Charles Gray, Willis Wayde) which appears idyllic, particularly in retrospect. But such communities reveal the fatal seed of class distinction: some of Marquand's bright young men are locked forever on the outside of grand houses, behind whose doors disappear unattainable golden girls. Others, like Apley and Pulham, are drawn to vigorous women outside their class, but these tribal men settle for unhappy marriages to Brahmin women. Calder, Gray, and Wayde are drawn to beautiful, haughty young women who will not, despite their own counterattractions, lower themselves to the level of these ambitious upstarts.

Marquand's Bostonians lack will and imagination; they cannot break out of the bell jars of their caste and class worldviews. In important ways they do not want to leave Boston, despite their yen for worlds unknown, for Boston has defined as well as confined them. Place is fate. They choose to remain within the psychic confines of Brahmin Boston, believing there is good in the old ways, embodying waning values of loyalty and honor. On the other hand, Marquand's North Shore heroes, men of lesser class standing, have little trouble breaking away because they are sent packing by the grand house world, particularly its golden girls. These young men grow up to be successful in business or finance but they settle for middling marriages. Each of them returns to the community of his youth and early promise only to learn that he was right to have left, that there is greater good in the *new* ways.

John P. Marquand's profound ambivalence toward the places of his youth and maturity resulted in the ironies and complexities of his best fiction. His North Shore was a site of innocent dreams, pastoral beauty, and young love, an Atlantis of the imagination; yet it was also a static world—timeless, dominated by calculating women, repressive of male sexuality, thwarting of ambition, reactionary in its values, and fixed in its class structure. His Boston was even more rigid, but, since it was portrayed from the inside, it appears more attractive. Though it is stuffy, petty, bigoted, and lacking in what Teddy Roosevelt called masculine traits, it is a world which stands for selfless values; Apley and Pulham, men who have missed the flower of life, know that there are things more important than happiness. Marquand's Greater Boston, then, is a complex world of invidious class distinctions and affirming values of morality and character.

IN *The Wapshot Chronicle* (1957) and *The Wapshot Scandal* (1963), John Cheever's fictional St. Botolphs, south of Boston, bears a striking resemblance to John P. Marquand's imaginary Clyde, Massachusetts, north of Boston. Cheever's West Farm, home of the Wapshots, is another Wickford Point, home of the Brills: both places are cultural and psychic havens against a changing America.[54] Both Marquand and Cheever were reared in idyllic surroundings, in small-town Massachusetts, though Cheever, born in 1912, was nearly two decades younger than Marquand. Each boy was infused with great expectations which were dashed when his businessman father suffered reverses through stock market gambling. Each young man then chose a career which repudiated business, though each would become a commercial and critical success. Each writer focused his best artistic energies on coming to terms with the constricting world of his youth. For Cheever, as for Marquand, character is developed through a combination of heritage and environment. Place is destiny: either it will tether you or, if you break the bond and escape, it will haunt you in your exile.

Indeed, so similar are their representative families and settings—though Cheever converts both into elements of the romance, while Marquand is a dedicated moral realist—that Cheever includes a demur in his Wapshot family saga. After describing the Wapshot family, "spread out in their rose garden above the river, listening to the parrot and feeling the balm of those evening winds that, in New England, smell so of maidenly things," he adds that "it would be wrong to say as an architectural photographer once did, after photographing the side door, 'It's just like a scene from J. P. Marquand.' They are not like this—these are country people." Yet the same might accurately be said of Marquand's more genteel country people, who are also shocked by new worlds located in Boston and New York.[55] Marquand and Cheever, then, are novelists of manners, allied in their efforts to reshape the Greater Boston landscape into coherent myths which they can contain in their novels.

John Cheever told his children that the first Cheever to arrive in America, Ezekiel, came aboard the *Arbella* in 1630. John admired this ancestor for his name, his status, and his accomplishments, for Ezekiel Cheever became a schoolmaster at Boston Latin School. "A rare incidence of Piety, Strength, Health and Ableness," said Judge Samuel Sewall, after the death of Ezekiel Cheever. "The Welfare of the province was much upon his spirit. He abominated periwigs." In *Home before Dark*, a memoir of her father, Susan Cheever remembers his delight in quoting that passage. John Cheever too abominated emblems of pretension and brooded upon the welfare of his home province, Boston and surrounding towns.[56]

John Cheever also told his children of a schism in the Cheever family, beginning with his grandfather Cheever who had shipped out of Newburyport, on Boston's North Shore, spent too long in the South Sea Islands, and made love to so many island girls that he was banished by his family to Boston's South Shore. In *The Wapshot Chronicle* he is called Benjamin Wapshot, whose son, Lorenzo, in his journal, describes the confrontation between the widely traveled captain and the good women of St. Botolphs when Benjamin finally returned home. "Aunt Ruth raised her umbrella high in the air and brought it down most savagely upon the back of his head. Aunt Hope beat him angrily on the port side and Mother charged him from the bow."[57]

There were, then, two family strains: rakish and staid Cheevers, those who were banished and those who remained within their tribal boundaries. Susan Cheever received this myth, elaborated by her father in family stories and his fiction. "We exiles knew the power of the past, but we also understood the transience of worldly circumstances. They could have their humorless Boston respectability with its piss-pot social rules and regulations and its dumpy Richardsonian architecture."[58]

However, John Cheever's children, Susan and Federico, eventually discovered that the ironic reality of Cheever family history was more ambiguous than their father's jaunty, dichotomized myth. Ezekiel Cheever arrived not in 1630, aboard Winthrop's *Arbella*, but in 1637, aboard the *Hector*. Furthermore, Ezekiel Cheever, they discovered, was not even a direct ancestor, though he was a distant relation; Ezekiel's first cousin, Daniel Cheever, their direct ancestor, emigrated from Canterbury to Boston in 1640 and became a prison-keeper in Cambridge![59] Apparently there had been *no*

Cheever schism, Susan Cheever learned from a direct descendant of Ezekiel, David Cheever, who had established the family genealogy. "As I spoke to David Cheever, I began to understand my father's sense of being an exile. Like many of my father's stories, his version of the schism has an inherent truth, outside of the facts."[60] John Cheever recomposed his Greater Boston heritage into useful fictions.

The facts of John Cheever's childhood, in Wollaston and Quincy, just south of Boston, were not idyllic. His father, Frederick Lincoln Cheever—a shoe salesman, though his son later described him as a shoe factory owner—sold his interests in Whitteridge and Cheever, a shoe factory, to play the stock market. He lost so much that John's mother, much to his embarrassment, opened the Mary Cheever Gift Shoppe in Quincy and his father moved out, events echoed in *The Wapshot Chronicle*. By 1928 John had to drop out of Thayer Academy and attend Quincy High School, though he later returned to Thayer—only to be expelled for smoking, an event he shaped into a story, "Expelled," his first publication. After the crash of 1929 resulted in more losses, John's father borrowed on the family home in Wollaston, eventually losing it in a bank foreclosure in 1932.

Loss, separation, and bitterness were facts of John Cheever's young life.[61] Small wonder, then, that Cheever's fiction is characterized by a yearning for a lost home. His Wapshot novels restore Cheever's rightful inheritance by recreating a myth of the Wapshots so that he might become reconciled with the loss of this illusory world, just as Marquand invoked the Newburyport of his youth, where he had felt rejected, so that he might have his alter ego characters repudiate it for him.

In Cheever's novels and stories, his most sympathetic characters often lapse into eloquent meditations on personal and national depletion of purpose and energy. Like a weary advertising man in "The Death of Justina," they often sense in their American landscape "the absence of that inner dynamism we respond to in some European landscapes"; they too wonder what to make of a diminished thing. "There are some Americans who, although their fathers emigrated from the Old World three centuries ago, never seem to have quite completed the voyage and I am one of these."[62]

Like Henry Adams, Cheever's characters have been expelled from their proper place in America. Raised on "the boarding school virtues: courage, good sportsmanship, chastity, and honor," they end up, as Michiko Kakutani put it, "succumbing to such suburban sins as alcoholism or adultery."[63] John Cheever casts a judgmental New England eye, conditioned by a Puritan conscience and its fondness for allegory, upon such behavior patterns: "the constants that I look for are a love of light and a determination to trace some moral chain of being." Nostalgia mixes with moral exemplum in *The Wapshot Chronicle*, which Cheever admitted was "a posthumous attempt to make peace with my father's ghost."[64] This novel, along with sections of *The Wapshot Scandal*, demonstrates John Cheever's best effort to rid himself of the New England mind and spirit which formed his character and created his sad temperament.

Speaking of St. Botolphs, Cheever said, "The impulse to construct such a village came to me late one night in a third-string hotel on the Hollywood Strip where the world from my window seemed so dangerously barbaric and nomadic that the attractions of a provincial and a traditional way of life were irresistible."[65] St. Botolphs has a prelapsarian innocence in its airs and graces, despite the failures of Leander, an eccentric ferryboat captain, his disappointed wife, and the eccentric and ancient Honora, who controls the family money.[66] St. Botolphs is the Wapshots' paradise lost. This New England village provided the Wapshot boys, Moses and Coverly, a place as certain, as sustaining, as confining as a womb. But each leaves home and loses his soul in a faceless, placeless, modern America. By the end of *The Wapshot Scandal*, all is lost; the Wapshot boys' parents are dead or fled, their marriages have disintegrated, their dreams of success have soured. Cheever takes over the narrative to elegize: "I will never come back, and if I do there will be nothing left, there will be nothing left but the headstones to record what has happened; there will really be nothing at all."[67]

John Cheever left the Boston area, in his life and his fiction; Manhattan, its suburbs and upper-state New York became his adopted, imaginative landscape. But he was to make a final symbolic visit to Boston, in the 1974–75 academic year, to teach two writing courses at Boston University. It was a difficult year for him, for he was deep in the grip of alcoholism. His Boston friends worried about him, but nothing would deter his drinking. One of his colleagues in Boston, Anne Sexton—"I'm not the living Sylvia Plath"—committed suicide in October, an event that sent Cheever into deep depression.[68] John Updike, then living in Boston, tried to watch over Cheever, as did others in the Boston literary "family": particularly Robert Manning, editor of *The Atlantic*, and Margaret Manning, book editor of the *Boston Globe*. Despite their efforts, Cheever's condition declined to the point where he could not go on teaching. After his resignation in March 1975, John Updike took over his classes.

Things got worse for Cheever before they got better, but after Boston he recovered. After a period in Smithers Alcoholic Rehabilitation Center in New York he joined Alcoholics Anonymous and went on to write some fine fiction. After Cheever's death in June 1982, Updike spoke at the memorial service, held in Norwell, Massachusetts, of Cheever's "willed act of rebirth" which gave him seven sober and productive years.[69] His bottoming-out and his turnabout, fittingly enough, began in Boston, the general territory of his own tentative beginnings. Greater Boston was Cheever's first and his near-final territory, the place in which he discovered, lost and rediscovered his identity, vocation, and spiritual direction.

WRITING about Cheever's late novel, *Oh What a Paradise It Seems* (1982), John Updike argued that Cheever's dismay at contemporary America "is redeemed by the generosity with which Cheever feels, like an American of a century and a half ago, the wonder of this land of promise." In particular Cheever enforced Updike's sense of the New England place. "Were Cheever less a

New Englander than he is, with the breath of Thoreau and Emily Dickinson in his own lovely quick light phrasing, he might fail to convince us that a real glory shines through his transparent inventions."[70] The same might fairly be said of Cheever's successor in the genre of manners fiction, John Updike, a self-declared, adopted New Englander.

John Updike was born and reared in Shillington, Pennsylvania. His primal landscape appears as his destiny in his early fiction. However, the Greater Boston region—beginning at Cambridge with Harvard at its center, extending to selected sites in Boston, then reaching north to the Massachusetts–New Hampshire border—holds resonant symbolic significance for Updike. In a memoir on his struggles with psoriasis, Updike explains that he was originally drawn to Ipswich, Massachusetts, "this ancient Puritan town," because there he could "bake and cure myself" on its beaches. "If Shillington gave me my life, Ipswich was where I took possession of it, the place where in my own sense of myself I ceased to be a radically defective person."[71] Updike's New England: a land and seascape of personal and moral struggle, a social system of subtle discriminations and passions, a semiallegorical territory where a man may find or lose his identity and his control over life, where he may suffer illnesses and seek cures, where he may lose or find his soul.

Boston appears frequently, if peripherally, in Updike's fiction. Only one novel, *Roger's Version*, of his trilogy of fictions based upon *The Scarlet Letter*, is set in the Boston-Cambridge region, though *A Month of Sundays* and *S.* contain Updike's oblique reflections on these ancient Puritan towns. Other Updike works also touch, glancingly, upon Boston proper.

Couples (1968), Updike's most Cheeverish novel of manners, a work which examines the sexual and status anxieties of the region, is also a parable of Updike's generation. Born in the economically depressed early 1930s and coming of age in the cautious 1950s, no longer young during the sexual revolution, this newly emboldened generation sought renewed youth, a new life, through extramarital love, their mode of immoral quest during the Kennedy era. "The men had stopped having careers and the women had stopped having babies. Liquor and love were left." More like frightened children than responsible adults, they gathered for sports or parties and then they broke off in new pairings. Updike catches the note of pathos in the circumspect, protected lives of American suburbanites. So frightened are they of isolation that on the night of John Kennedy's assassination they even decide to go ahead with their planned party. The hostess decides "it would be a wake, an Irish wake, and a formal dinner-dance was very fitting for the dead man, who had such style."[72]

Couples is deeply embedded in the New England of Updike's imagination, a novel set in one of those Puritan towns. Tellingly named Tarbox, located twenty-seven miles south of Boston, the town bears a striking resemblance to Ipswich, which lies as many miles north of Boston, as though Updike wished to generalize the significance of Tarbox as a representative American place of that era. Tarbox, "this sexpot," says Piet Hanema, the novel's central character, in the middle of a tense exchange with his wife. "A sexpot is a person, not a place," replies Angela, his wife. "This one's a place," insists Piet. "Don't be silly. The town is like every other town in the country."[73] Exactly.

However, Tarbox also has particular regional traits and emblems which place its affluent residents in a New England moral context. "A golden rooster turned high above Tarbox," atop the Congregational church, a local landmark. "If God were physically present in Tarbox, it was in the form of this unreachable weathercock."[74] The God of Tarbox supervises their sad lives and futile quests.

Late in the novel, after much coupling, conspiracy, and consequence among the couples, "the supernatural proclaimed itself" in a sudden storm.[75] Lightning strikes and burns the Congregational church. The cock is felled; their God is removed. Fire reaches up to the rains, warring elements in nature, as Piet picks up a soaked pamphlet, dated 1795, which says that all nations must

> know that the LORD is God, and to offer unto him sincere and devout thanksgiving and praise. But if there is any nation under heaven, which hath more peculiar and forcible reasons than others,

for joining with one heart and voice in offering up to him these
grateful sacrifices, the United States of America are that nation.[76]

For Piet, as for Hawthorne's Rev. Dimmesdale, God reveals Himself to his town in judgment against those who offend Him through adultery and those who betray the national mission.

In an essay on New England churches, Updike recalls learning something about "New England fair-mindedness" in Harvard's Memorial Chapel, because there were displayed plaques commemorating Harvard's dead, both American *and* German soldiers, from the Great War. Updike also recalls the Congregational church in Ipswich, where he once worshiped. On some winter mornings only a dozen would attend, while the minister shouted over the groaning furnace. "I have never felt closer to the bare bones of Christianity than on those bleak and drafty Sunday mornings, with the ghosts of frock-coated worshippers and patient carpenters making up for our sparse attendance."[77] Lightning struck and burned down this church in 1965, offering Updike a model for *Couples*, providing him another opportunity to reflect upon the nature of the regional character and divine judgment.

Updike's most admired essay on Boston, "HUB FANS BID KID ADIEU," from *Assorted Prose* (1965), a lyrical account of the career and final game of Red Sox hero Ted Williams, shows that his Boston can provide playgrounds for adults. "Fenway Park, in Boston, is a lyric little bandbox of a ballpark. Everything is painted green and seems in curiously sharp focus, like the inside of an old-fashioned peeping-type Easter egg." For all that, Fenway Park is a site where judgments occur between absolutes and deviations. "It was built in 1912 and rebuilt in 1934, and offers, as do most Boston artifacts, a compromise between Man's Euclidean determinations and Nature's beguiling irregularities."[78]

As a boy in Shillington, Updike "didn't know Beacon Hill from Bunker Hill or Fenway Park from the Public Garden." But as he notes elsewhere, he was drawn to the Red Sox because of Ted Williams, particularly in 1946, when the team won the American League pennant. Four hundred miles from Boston, fourteen-year-old Updike listened to the final game of the World Series that year, between the Red Sox and the Saint Louis Cardinals, on his father's car radio in the Shillington High School parking lot. When the Red Sox lost he was stunned. "Dazed and with something lost forever, I emerged into the golden September afternoon, where my class-mates were jostling and yelling, nuzzling their steadies, sneaking smokes and shooting baskets in a blissful animal innocence I could no longer share."[79] The Boston lesson of loss was his, long before Updike became a Greater Bostonian.

Updike even offers the presence of the Red Sox as one of his reasons for moving to Massachusetts in 1957. "I wanted to keep Ted Williams company while I could."[80] So it was no surprise that John Updike was part of the small crowd that went to Fenway Park to see Ted Williams end his career on 28 September 1960, a char-acteristically chill, overcast Boston afternoon.

Updike sets his saga deep into the character of the city which Williams had represented since 1939. "In the two decades since Williams had come to Boston, his status had imperceptibly shifted from that of a naughty prodigy to that of a municipal monument."[81] Williams, long bitter about his treatment by the Boston press, told the crowd during the brief ceremonies honoring him, "I want to say that my years in Boston have been the greatest thing in my life."[82] Williams's home run during his final time at bat was, for Updike, a moral triumph of art and character over circumstances of adversity. Though Williams's career was a tale of mythic pro-portions—paralleling the sagas of Jason, Achilles, and Nestor—it was, as well, a particularly Bostonian tale of the willful hero first condemned for his ego but finally winning the respect of the com-munity through courage and art. Ted Williams: a latter-day Hester Prynne!

Attending an opening-day game at Fenway Park in 1979, Updike wondered whether Bostonians, with their tradition of Puritan hu-bris, expected too much from their team and their city.[83]

What makes Boston—little old Boston up here among the rocky fields and empty mills—think it deserves championship teams all

the time? . . . The founding Puritans left behind a lingering conviction, I fear, that earthly success reflects divine election, and that
this city built upon a hill is anciently entitled to a prime share.[84]

If, for Updike, Ted Williams is a representative Boston hero, the
Red Sox embody a paradigm of purpose. They raise Bostonians'
hopes each spring, return their sense of lost youth, flirt with victory, then they fail, again and again, each fall, confirming their
regionally conditioned belief that true happiness in this world cannot last.

In *Roger's Version,* a more complex myth of post-Puritan Boston,
John Updike rewrites *The Scarlet Letter* from the perspective of
Roger Chillingworth, Hester's eerie husband, in the persona of
Roger Lambert, divinity school professor; Cambridge-Boston in
the mid-1980s serves as his model community.[85] Updike's Roger
tries to deny the presence of God in his life but, through sin, he
comes to acknowledge His guiding hand in all things. Hawthorne
cleared the ground of the fictional landscape which Updike has
appropriated: both *The Scarlet Letter* and *Roger's Version* are parables of middle-class infidelity; both writers set their lovers against
a censorious community; both writers seek evidence of God's presence in the fallen ways of men and women; both writers see a
universe of implications in Boston and its adjacent towns.

Roger's Version is a novel of crossings, spiritual and physical, in
the contemporary urban landscapes of Cambridge and Boston, a
realistic but also a symbolic topography. "Our city, it should be
explained, is two cities, or more—an urban mass or congeries
divided by the [Charles] river whose dirty waters disembogue into
the harbor that gave the colonial settlement its *raison d'être.*"[86]
The colonial settlers may have been attracted to Boston's fine harbor, but their justifications for their existences transcended commerce; their Boston served as an allegorical landscape, full of
perilous slides to perdition and marvelous ascents to salvation. So
it remains for Updike's Bostonians and Cantabridgians.

Roger Lambert, well past the middle of his life, enters no dark
woods, but he does drive his impeccable Audi down Sumner Bou-

levard (Cambridge's Massachusetts Avenue) into marginal sections
of town. Outside his Edenic garden near Harvard, Lambert delights in common pursuits. His is a spiritual quest through profane
realms. Roger enters into a brief affair with his half-sister's daughter, trying to substitute sex for God.

Finally, Updike's hero decides the world, with its messy passions, is too much with him. He bends to God's will. In a Boston
restaurant at the top of a hotel, where he says goodbye to his young
lover, Roger renounces, like Christ tempted by Satan, all that world
beyond and beneath him. Boston again is exposed as an allegorical
plain on which its citizens are tested. "This city spread so wide
and multiform around and beneath us: it was more than the mind
could encompass, it overbrimmed the eye; but was it all? Was it
enough? It did not appear to be."[87] As it was for Hawthorne,
Updike's Boston is an "ordinary" world which holds transcendent
truths. For Updike, Boston remains a site of personal and cultural
conflict, a city still in the making, a place whose rich images can
be recalled and reshaped to artistic ends. Beneath its high-tech
prosperity, its high-style glitz and its political clout, lie anxieties
over the separations between the people we once thought we were
and those we have become, or those we might yet imagine ourselves to be.

As Updike increasingly identified himself with the region, so did
he, in his critical essays, develop his ideas on his territorial predecessors, including Hawthorne, Emerson, and Howells. In particular "the theme of religious belief" emerges, "like a gravestone
rubbing," in his reflections.[88] In "Hawthorne's Creed" Updike's
Hawthorne struggles under the weight of his family and regional
history, a struggle which resulted in the Salem romancer's dour
view of his native grounds. Hester Prynne represents his efforts
to transcend that oppressive atmosphere, just as she urged Rev.
Dimmesdale to reject Puritan Boston. In *S.* (1988) Updike allows
Sarah Worth, his latter-day version of Hester, to escape her Puritan
heritage, to transcend New England's sexual and ideological inhibitions.[89] Hawthorne's legacy to Updike was a capacity for faith
in a life of the mind and spirit.

He believed, with his Puritan ancestors, that man's spirit matters; that the soul can be distorted, stained, and lost; that the impalpable exerts force against the material. Our dreams move us: this is a psychological rather than a religious truth, but in a land where, as Emerson said, "things are in the saddle," it gives the artist his vote.[90]

Updike demurs from Emerson's radical idealism and blind faith in the goodness of man, but he discovers that Emerson has renewed his faith.

It was Emerson's revelation that God and the self are of the same substance. He may have been wrong, too blithe on Mankind's behalf, to think that nature—what he called the *"other me"*—is possessed of optimism and always answers to our soul; but he was immensely right in implying that the prime *me*, the ego, is perforce optimistic.[91]

For Updike, Greater Boston—extending from mannerly Boston through academic Cambridge to the well-to-do communities of Ipswich and Beverly Farms, places central to his fiction—was where he came of age as a man and an artist. Its landscape is resonant with associations, from Harvard and the Red Sox to *The Scarlet Letter,* which he has appropriated to his artistic purposes. Above all it is a territory which suggests, through its history and literature, spiritual struggle. The moral romancer, Hawthorne, became his principal regional literary model, though the moral realist, Howells, another outsider who made himself into a New England writer, left his mark as well on Updike's art. And Emerson became his spiritual guide, renewing his faith in life and God.

IN *The Hero with a Thousand Faces*, Joseph Campbell argues that the true hero is "the man or woman who has been able to battle past his personal and local historical limitations to the generally valid, normally human forms." He must, finally, return, "transfigured, and teach the lesson he has learned of life renewed."[92] The equivocating heroes of these autobiographical and fictional narratives of manners and morals in Greater Boston engage in tentative but informing battles against their local historical limitations, their complex fates. If they do not always battle past their limitations or teach us larger lessons of life beyond Boston, their authors do. Boston and surrounding communities within its sphere of influence are seen and reseen in these novels of manners as socially complex, historically rooted places which circumscribe the lives of their troubled residents. These writers thus revise and revive the region's identity, its sense of itself as a significant place.

7

Boston's Sphere of Influence:
NORTH, SOUTH, AND WEST

I F BOSTON is not the hub of the universe, it has been the center of radial lines of influence which spread in three directions. The local literary imagination has created three territories which define the outer edge of the Boston Idea: north to New Hampshire, south to Cape Cod, and west to Amherst, the Connecticut Valley and the Berkshires. These grooves of influence, like long-laid railway tracks, are still open for reciprocal exchange between Boston and those New England places encompassed within its arc. "I like to see it lap the Miles— / And lick the Valleys up," wrote Emily Dickinson of trains which ran on a railway built by her grandfather, trains which led from Amherst to Belchertown and beyond, toward Boston's beacons.[1]

North of Boston

HENRY DAVID THOREAU

Unlike the placid Concord River, the Merrimack, formed in New Hampshire's White Mountains, runs rapidly east through Lowell, past Newburyport and Plum Island to the sea. In *A Week on the Concord and Merrimack Rivers*, Henry David Thoreau recalled his 1839 trip with his brother John, up the Concord River to the Pawtucket Falls, where they encountered the mighty Merrimack. "We now felt as if we were fairly launched on the ocean-stream of our voyage, and were pleased to find that our boat would float on Merrimack water." The fast-flowing waters of this region, against which the Thoreau brothers rowed, stirred literary associations for Henry.

> As we glided over the broad bosom of the Merrimack, between Chelmsford and Dracut, at noon, here a quarter of a mile wide, the rattling of our oars was echoed over the water to those villages, and their slight sounds to us. Their harbors lay as smooth and fairy-like as the Lido, or Syracuse, or Rhodes, in our imagination, while, like some strange roving craft, we flitted past what seemed the dwellings of noble home-staying men, seemingly as conspicuous as if on an eminence, or floating upon a tide which came to those villagers' breasts.[2]

For Thoreau the intersection of the Concord and Merrimack rivers brought a realization of contending energies, nature and civilization, and provided his own passage to wider waters, past these noble villages of men and women, citizens who were content and well-placed. The Merrimack carried Thoreau, both missionary and explorer, into a landscape of imaginative extravagance and teeming significance.

THOUGH Thoreau ignored Lowell's factories, which he and his brother paddled past, these mills also represented a dream of liberation for Boston merchants seeking investments and for factory "operatives," farm girls who sought temporary release from their rural labors and immigrants seeking labor. In the half-century before the Civil War, Lowell, Massachusetts was the center of a vast experiment in industrialization, principally in cotton textiles. The Waltham-Lowell system, as it was called after the cities in which it was established, was a product of the Boston Brahmin mind. Francis Cabot Lowell and Nathan Appleton, showing the way of investment to other Boston merchants, set up the Boston Company, which built a factory system in Waltham and then established America's first industrial center in the Merrimack Valley. The Boston Manufacturing Company, under the direction of Patrick Tracy Jackson, the brother-in-law of Francis Cabot Lowell, was formed in 1822; it established the factory system of Lowell. In 1826 Lowell became a township; then in 1847 Lawrence, site of the Essex Company, was incorporated, expanding the mill system and Boston's influence.

Though primarily interested in returns on their investments, these Boston Brahmins were also concerned with the social and cultural effects of their commerce. Profits from the Waltham-Lowell system served to underwrite many of Boston's finest institutions: the Boston Athenaeum, Massachusetts General Hospital, Harvard University, and many other jewels in Boston's cultural crown. As Robert F. Dalzell, Jr. notes in his study of the Boston Associates, Longfellow came into ownership of the gracious and historic Craige House in Cambridge, a house which now bears Longfellow's name, with financial support from his wealthy father-in-law, Nathan Appleton; here Boston Brahmins fused art and commerce, poetry and power.[3]

However, these businessmen did not wish to exploit the region north of Boston merely to build up their own financial and cultural accounts. Wishing to avoid the degradation of Manchester and other English factory towns, the Boston Company set up its workers—young, unmarried farm girls who put in a period of factory labor before they returned to farm life—in company-owned boarding houses, where the company took responsibility for their physical well-being and moral character. The investors' motives were not purely philanthropic, but they did wish to create a exemplary work force—moral, unrebellious, and punctual, a new model army—to operate their industrial machine. These Brahmin investors wished to return value to the New England rivers and countryside, from which they extracted profit.[4]

LUCY LARCOM

Lowell, because of its mills and its mill workers, became one of the wonders of America for literary pilgrims from England. In 1842 Charles Dickens toured America and wrote *American Notes*. Dickens saw Lowell as an embodiment of the new and the good, a fusion of the industrial and the pastoral.

> The very river that moves the machinery in the mills (for they are all worked by water power), seems to acquire a new character from the fresh buildings of bright red brick and painted wood among which it takes its course; and to be as light-headed, thoughtless, and brisk a young river, in its murmurings and tumblings, as one would desire to see.[5]

Dickens was also impressed by the cleanliness and decorum of the young women who labored in the mills. He was particularly charmed by *The Lowell Offering*, a publication which described itself as "a repository of original articles, written exclusively by females actively employed in the mills." Dickens found it pleasant to read tales which "inculcate habits of self-denial and contentment, and teach good doctrines of enlarged benevolence," tales which also expressed "a strong feeling for the beauties of nature." Dickens compared British and American mills, contrasting "Good and Evil, the living light and deepest shadow."[6] Lowell, like the Boston of its founders, was an allegorical plain on which moral forces struggled for innocents' souls.

WHEN Dickens visited the Lowell mills, an eighteen-year-old mill "operative," Lucy Larcom, could not leave her work to meet him. Had she, Dickens would have seen her as she saw herself, as a successful embodiment of the Lowell mission to combine labor, morality, and culture. "The young women who worked at Lowell had the advantage of living in a community where character alone commanded respect," wrote Lucy Larcom near the end of her life, in her memoir of place, her spiritual autobiography, *A New England Girlhood*.[7]

Lucy Larcom was born in 1824, in the idyllic and pastoral surroundings of Beverly, Massachusetts, along the same Cape Ann which would later grip the imagination of T. S. Eliot. She was shaped by a restrictive but supportive religious training, which she incorporated into pastoral imagery. The New England Puritan heritage was "a mighty tree against the trunk of which we rested, while we looked up in wonder through the great boughs that half hid and half revealed the sky." Her favorite book was *Pilgrim's Progress*. "Oh, how I used to wish that I too could start off on a pilgrimage!"[8] In *A New England Girlhood* that is just how she construes her life, as a pilgrim's quest through a symbolic landscape, surrounded by romantic symbols, for revelation of purpose.

When she was ten years old, Lucy's father, a ship captain, died. Driven by economic necessity, Lucy's mother then moved her family of eight children to Lowell, where she became a housekeeper for a corporation boarding house and Lucy went to work in a textile mill. This setting, however, was no Dickensian horror of bottling-factory victimization, for the Larcoms believed in the *idea* of Lowell, which they incorporated into the value structure of the New England mind. "From the beginning, Lowell had a high reputation for good order, morality, piety, and all that was dear to the old-fashioned New Englander's heart." Lucy went to work as a bobbin-changer with a light heart and found her labors untaxing, though the noise of the machines always bothered her. The great water-wheel which powered the mill machines awed her, reminding her of "the great Power which keeps the mechanism of the universe in motion."[9]

Nor did the mills separate Lucy from nature. She delighted in living in view of the Merrimack, where Penobscot Indians glided past in canoes. She might even have seen the Thoreau brothers paddle past. Nature and industry were equal wonders to young Lucy. "We made a point of spending [holiday time] out of doors, making excursions down the river to watch the meeting of the slow Concord and the swift Merrimack."[10]

Further, Lucy Larcom came to realize that she was part of a larger movement of women into the mainstream of American life. The mill experience made her feel that she "belonged to the world, that there was something for me to do in it, though I had not yet found out what." Feminism—"the mutual bond of universal wom-anhood"—was thus fostered by the mills and incorporated into pastoral imagery. "The girls who toiled together at Lowell were clearing away a few weeds from the overgrown track of independent labor for other women."[11]

In what she called her "poemlets," Lucy Larcom celebrated New England nature: "I chanted the praises of Winter, of snow-storms, and of March winds . . . with hearty delight."[12] Her first works had appeared in the *Operatives' Magazine*, published by "mill-girls" in the First Congregationalist Church. *The Lowell Offering*, first produced by the Universalist Church, combined with the *Operatives' Magazine* to form the publication which gave Lucy Larcom her public voice, the kind of voice which caught Dickens's atten-tion. Her writings would also impress John Greenleaf Whittier, who advanced her career. Religion, commerce, feminism, nature, and literature combined in her Lowell.

Lucy Larcom, who went on to become a popular poet of the day and an influential teacher at Wheaton Seminary, illustrates the limited success of the Lowell experiment. She embodied the New England transition from shipping to manufacturing in her family history and she made the symbolic move from village to factory town. On balance this was a success, for in the Lowell mills she gained authority, formed lasting bonds with other women—*A New England Girlhood* is dedicated, in part, "To My Girl-Friends In General"—and she found her literary voice. However, after a decade Lucy Larcom could no longer successfully detach herself from the harsh sounds of the mill machines. The great waterwheel— that Dynamo, as Henry Adams would call it—ground her down. "Vanquished," she left in 1845.[13] Blending commerce and culture, nature and civilization, so too would the dream of Lowell be sacrificed to the exacting demands of American capitalism.

ANTHONY TROLLOPE

For Anthony Trollope, who visited in 1861, Lowell was a far more prosaic though not less promising place than it had been for Dickens, as Trollope reported in *North America* (1862). Trollope also noted the workers' cleanliness and culture, and praised *The Lowell Offering*. Trollope approvingly cited a handbook to Lowell which described twelve-hour-day factory work in the most idyllic terms: "girls from the country, with a true Yankee spirit of independence, and confident in their own powers, pass a few years here, and then return to get married with a dower secured by their exertions." Trollope, like Dickens before him, could only wonder at this miracle of commerce and culture, seeing in Lowell "the realization of a commercial Utopia."[14]

However, Trollope saw Lowell in contrast to sordid English factory towns and, no doubt, through his reading of Dickens on America, for Trollope did not notice that the utopian factory system of Lowell was already in decline. The farm girls in the mills were then being driven for greater productivity by a new generation of managers who showed diminishing concern for their cultural and moral condition. Immigrant laborers increasingly worked the mills of "Spindle City." The ideal of a pastoral, moral work force was gradually abandoned; working conditions declined to the point that a strike in Lawrence in 1912, backed by the IWW, resulted in open warfare between militia and strikers.

JOHN GREENLEAF WHITTIER

Thoreau, Dickens, and Trollope had just been passing through the Merrimack Valley, voyagers seeking renewal in a new land or investigating a brave new world of technology. Like Lucy Larcom, John Greenleaf Whittier, the "wood-thrush of Essex County" (a territory encompassing twenty-six towns north of Boston), knew the region from the inside; he created a compelling myth of regional decline, the evidence of which English visitors missed.

Whittier incorporated two of the great themes of Boston literature, nostalgia and moral purpose, into his most famous writings. From *Legends of New England* (1831), poems and prose, to *Leaves from Margaret Smith's Journal* (1849), a prose reconstruction of colonial life, to *Snow-Bound* (1866) and *The Tent on the Beach* (1867), his most popular poetry collections, Whittier was a poet of place: the fast-disappearing rural territories of the Merrimack Valley.

"Whittier was a shoot of the oldest New England," wrote Van Wyck Brooks.[15] He was born in the Haverhill farmhouse which his ancestors had built in the seventeenth century. Coming to poetry after six generations of farming, steeped in the folklore of his region, Whittier was a peasant poet who was inspired by Robert Burns; in turn, Whittier influenced Robert Frost, a poet who adopted New England farming. Poetry became Whittier's means of escape from a life of rural labors.

> And must I always swing the flail,
> And help to fill the milking pail?
> I wish to go away to school;
> I do not wish to be a fool.[16]

Discovered and encouraged by William Lloyd Garrison, then a twenty-one-year-old editor of the *Free Press* of Newburyport,

Whittier seized his chance to flee the farm, though he paid the debt to his past by composing a poetry of nostalgia which idealized his childhood and sentimentalized rural life. In 1836 he sold the Haverhill farm, which he could not manage, and bought a cottage in Amesbury, where he lived with his mother. There, after renovations enlarged the house to include his famous Garden Room, he wrote the political and nostalgic poems which won him a national audience.[17]

The Quaker abolitionist side of Whittier made claims for his Commonwealth's moral idealism in "Massachusetts to Virginia" (1843). "The voice of Massachusetts" insists "No slave upon her land!"[18] Whittier, like Emerson, also excoriated Daniel Webster for moral compromise in 1850, when Webster supported the Fugitive Slave Bill, in "Ichabod": "When faith is lost, when honor dies, / The man is dead!"[19]

Snow-Bound appeared in 1866, when the abolitionists' cause was finally won, when America began its turn toward modernity: to western expansion, to industrialization, to urban concentration. So Whittier's most famous poem struck a national nerve of fond memory for a way of life which many Americans, like Whittier, actually wished to abandon. More specifically, *Snow-Bound* articulated a personal and regional nostalgia for a life fading into extended economic decline—into the sere pastoral of Robert Frost—and transformed by the immigrant-driven mills and factories of Lawrence and Lowell, the later literary landscape of young Jack Kerouac.

Whittier stressed the powers of the snowstorm to transform all into a world of wonder, as though enclosure by snow had released his imagination: "strange domes and towers," Chinese roofs, even "Pisa's leaning miracle" appeared before him. The storm meant protection, not confinement, though Whittier admits that "Time and Change" have ravaged the Eden he recalls. "How strange it seems, with so much gone / Of life and love, to still live on!"[20] Poetry was his act of devotion to a lost world. Post–Civil War America passed by Whittier, who wanted to forget that he had felt himself a fool doing farm labors, who wanted to remember himself and be remembered as a "barefoot boy, with cheeks of tan," ever young and innocent, walking the woods, tenting out near the ocean.[21]

Donald Hall, a twentieth century poet who also records his life north of Boston in poetry and prose, notes that the youthful outing Whittier described in *The Tent on the Beach* occurred at Hampton Beach, New Hampshire. Just across the Massachusetts border; the site "has become a row of ugly cottages, hot dog stands, bars, roller skating rinks, and beer halls. . . . The industries of New England are going the way of the farms, but they leave behind them not cellar holes but slums."[22] Whittier's poems record pre–Civil War America, creating a preindustrial and precommercial myth of lost innocence, a myth central to American literature and particularly appropriate to the morally driven and nostalgic literature of Greater Boston.

ROBERT FROST

Robert Frost incorporated the landscape of southern New Hampshire into Boston's sphere of influence. In England in 1912, Frost culled a body of lyrics he had written during his period of farming in Derry, New Hampshire. The two volumes, which appeared in England in 1913, the lyrics in *A Boy's Will*, and the dramatic monologues in *North of Boston*, established his career and announced his themes: a realization of loss and a compelling sense of New England place.

New England was Frost's, in imagination, before he was New England's, in fact. The title of Frost's first volume came from Longfellow's "My Lost Youth," establishing Frost's continuity with the New England fireside poets, poets read aloud to him by his mother during his first decade of life in San Francisco. Longfellow recalled the "dear old town" of his youth and remembered a Lapland song which evidently suited Frost's own mood of reverie for Derry: "A boy's will is the wind's will, / And the thoughts of youth are long, long thoughts."[23] Lawrence, Massachusetts, where he went to school, and the farmlands of southern New Hampshire became his New England. While he was in England, Frost's thoughts were stirred by nostalgia for Derry. Years later, Frost told an audience "I wrote the poem 'Mending Wall' thinking of the old wall that I hadn't mended in several years and which must be in terrible condition. I wrote that poem in England when I was very homesick for my old wall in New England."[24] Frost's poems of New England, then, may be seen as New England wall-building with words.

The title of Frost's second volume was harder to come by; he considered *Farm Servants, New England Eclogues, New Englanders,* and *New England Hill Folk* before he decided on *North of Boston.*[25] In 1949 Frost explained his choice of title. "It gathered itself together in retrospect and found a name for itself in the real estate advertising of the Boston Globe. . . . I like its being locative."[26] "Locative" for Frost, then, was that cheap, hard to cultivate but symbolically resonant real estate north of Boston.

Robert Frost portrays a sere, autumnal New England, a landscape of depletion, a people of limited options who live in a cashless and rocky terrain, a world where final things are implied within the commonplace. In the opening poem of *A Boy's Will,* "Into My Own," Frost interprets trees as "the merest mask of gloom," wishes they "stretched away unto the edge of doom" and yearns for escape.[27] In his post-Puritan pastoral, nature has not ceased to mean. The idea of home and human obligation are discussed by a farmer and his wife in another poem when an unreliable hired man comes back to their farm, seeking a haven in his sickness. "Home is the place where, when you have to go there, / They have to take you in," says the farmer, but his wife has more mercy: "I should have called it / Something you somehow haven't to deserve."[28] Thus do Frost's wry and canny New England people bring "the sound of sense," a rhetorical and philosophical principle derived from Emerson, to their lives, interpreting their place, defining their quest.[29]

Perhaps Frost was recalling and repaying his debt to Boston, staking out his own geographical map of spiritual and artistic growth, in the title of his second volume. He believed his decision in 1897 to become a special student at Harvard was a turning point in his life. Frost, a Dartmouth College dropout, had intended to perfect his Latin and Greek at Harvard so he might become a high-school teacher and support his young family, but he found more. He was also drawn to William James, who had just published *The Will to Believe*. At Harvard Frost discovered Virgil's eclogues, works which would inspire his own pastoral lyrics in Derry. Though William James was away from the campus, Frost was influenced by his encounter with James's *Psychology* in "General Introduction to Philosophy," under Hugo Munsterberg. James provided justification for the exertion of a boy's will to shape his life. George Santayana's aestheticism shocked Frost, but he listened to the philosopher, as he did to George Lyman Kitteredge on Milton and Nathaniel Southgate Shaler on historical geology. Without a degree, but with renewed purpose and persona, Frost left Harvard in March 1899, ready to resume his effort to harvest a living and to shape a writing career from farming.[30]

Frost and his wife, Elinor, returned to Lawrence, Massachusetts, where they had met in high school, but he soon looked some twelve miles north of Lawrence to make a new life. Frost, who feared tuberculosis and suffered from severe hay fever, was advised to get out of the mill town by his doctor. With the help of his grandfather, Frost and his growing family settled on a farm with thirty acres, a house and a barn, in Derry, not far from Salem, New Hampshire, in 1900. There he remained, failing at farming but succeeding at forming an original poetic voice, until 1909 when he moved his family to Derry Village, so he could be near Pinkerton Academy, where he taught. The sale of the Derry farm in 1912 provided funds for Frost and his family to go to England and begin his career as a poet, a career rooted in observations and recollections of farm life in Derry.[31] Today, amid the commercial drek and housing developments of southern New Hampshire, Frost's restored farm, maintained by the New Hampshire Division of Parks and Recreation, stands as a model of an extinct way of life and illustrates his living body of poetry. Frost, like Whittier, reminds New Englanders where they came from, who they are.

This is not to suggest that Frost was the ever-happy bard in his pastoral retreat. Not long after he settled in Derry, Frost composed a poem titled "Despair," narrated from the point of view of a man who is glad that he has drowned himself.[32] At first Frost was so weighed down by the burdens of family obligation and farm labor that he considered suicide. Frost, like Whittier, suffered the life of the rural poor, broke away from its grip, then memorialized it in verse. But Frost saw greater ironies and complexities in his translations of rural facts into poetic images.

Between 1902 and 1906 Frost made the most of his hard life in Derry. Thoreau's *Walden* and Emerson's essays taught him how to love nature. His neighbors taught him to see the world with a wry eye. His competence as a poultry-farmer grew. His children gave him joy.[33] His love for Elinor, an increasingly lonely and desperate woman, remained, as he shows in lyrics like "The Pasture," which celebrate his pleasure in nature and his link to her.

> I'm going out to clean the pasture spring;
> I'll only stop to rake the leaves away
> (And wait to watch the water clear, I may):
> I shan't be gone long. —You come too.
> I'm going out to fetch the little calf
> That's standing by the mother. It's so young
> It totters when she licks it with her tongue.
> I shan't be gone long. —you come too.[34]

Frost's invitation to Elinor to share his work and his wonder at nature's ways serves as well as his injunction to us to journey beyond our limits, into a transformed world. Frost's pasture—like Thoreau's Merrimack and Whittier's snowstorm—is a path to transcendence. The poet's epiphany in a regional scene hints at universal design. "If design govern in a thing so small," Frost would add, with up-country irony.[35]

Frost's process of reconciliation with rural life is evident in "Mowing," a poem which concludes with an injunction which he was willing himself to believe: "The fact is the sweetest dream that labor knows. / My long scythe whispered and left the hay to make."[36] Like Thoreau at Walden, Frost learned to harvest tropes and metaphors from the sweet and sour facts of his adopted native ground. Frost discovered himself, man and poet, in his landscape. In England Frost could reshape the Derry experience to the requirements of his poetic imagination. "Places are more to me in thought than in reality," he would admit.[37]

The poems in *A Boy's Will* are characterized by subjectivity and focus on first youth, but in *North of Boston* his poems are more dramatic translations of landscape into imaginative designs. In Derry, he found a west-running brook, a mending wall, and many arched birches; there too lay the intersecting paths, challenging him to decide which road to take in life and art. There grew the apple trees that required picking, trees that yielded Frost a harvest of more than apples. In "After Apple-Picking," the poet, on his two-pointed ladder, "sticking through a tree / Toward heaven still," picks his load of apples and seeks what exceeds his grasp.

> For I have had too much
> Of apple-picking: I am overtired
> Of the great harvest I myself desired.[38]

As Thoreau went to the woods to confront life, Frost went to the farm to seek a cure from the psychic illness induced by urban life. So he noted in 1952. "I might say the core of all my writing was probably the five free years I had on the farm down the road from Derry Village toward Lawrence. . . . It turned out right as a doctor's prescription."[39]

Frost defended and defined his New England heritage, with Boston at its center, in a 1937 commencement address at Oberlin College. He was pained, he said, that *North of Boston* had been "described as a book about a decadent, lost society." Though he admired *The Flowering of New England*, Frost resisted Van Wyck Brook's "slight suggestion of Spenglerian history,—indication of decline." Frost saw no sign of decline or degradation in the New England character. Boston, for all that had been said against the Puritans, represented to him a living tradition of culture and freedom. Indeed the New England tradition for Frost had shaped the nation. "And the thing New England gave most to America was the thing I am talking about: a stubborn clinging to meaning,—to purify words until they meant again what they should mean."[40]

This, too, was the message of Frost's "The Gift Outright," the poem he read at John F. Kennedy's inaugural in January 1961. "The land was ours before we were the land's."[41] Frost's America was a land of opportunity for those who sought the significance of their quests in Massachusetts and Virginia. That territory, north of Boston, became Frost country: staked out in his life, reimagined in his art. Reflecting upon two aspects of the Boston heritage on the occasion of the election of this Boston president, Frost told Kennedy, "Be more Irish than Harvard."[42] Robert Frost, who struck his own balance with regional ways, who reshaped our sense of New England place, died in Boston on January 29, 1963.

ANDRE DUBUS

The region stretching from the Merrimack Valley to Frost's southern New Hampshire has long been transformed from a pastoral retreat into a region of industrialization, immigration, and economic depravation. John Updike knows it well, for he has lived his adult life along its edge, in wealthy communities of northeastern Massachusetts, from Ipswich to the Beverly coastline. In a tribute to the fiction of Andre Dubus, a contemporary tale-teller of grim, local lives, Updike catches the spirit of this depleted place. "The Merrimack Valley was the New World's first real industrial belt, and has been economically disconsolate for decades; the textile mills moved south, and then foreign imports undermined the leather and shoe factories. But life goes on. . . ."[43] Andre Dubus broods upon life's qualified on-goingness in an enclosing, withered landscape.

The characters who appear in the dour world of Dubus's fiction live along the Merrimack River, a century and a half after Thoreau launched his canoe upon it, but Dubus's characters know no passage route from their place of stasis to any ocean of opportunity. They are landlocked, place-bound down-and-outers whose American dreams have turned to nightmares, though many of them conduct their desperate lives with dignity.

Dubus is a prose poet of an American place in decline. In "Townies," a character reflects upon regional decay.

> He had lived all his life in this town, a small city in northeastern Massachusetts; once there had been a shoe industry. Now that was over, only three factories were open, and the others sat empty along the bank of the Merrimack. Their closed windows and the dark empty rooms beyond them stared at the street, like the faces of the old and poor who on summer Sundays sat on the stoops of the old houses farther upriver and stared at the street, the river, the air before their eyes.[44]

Dubus's people sit, stunned by a world that has passed them by. Ground down by the low expectations of their class, surrounded by urban blight, circumscribed by a dour Catholicism which reenforces their sense of sin and shame, often leashed by some addiction (food, alcohol, love), Dubus's characters need absolution, a sudden infusion of grace. But his people can imagine no other place.

In "The Pretty Girl," Polly, a young woman who is fearful of being assaulted by her estranged husband, thinks of moving away from tatty Haverhill to nearby Amesbury or Newburyport, upscale seaside towns. "Maybe even to Boston," Polly tells a friend. "I don't know why I said Boston. Isn't it funny it's right there and nobody ever goes to live there?"[45] Boston, that world elsewhere. Instead of leaving, however, she stays and confronts her husband, who again returns to rape her, but this time she stops him with a bullet. This story stands, as do so many of Dubus's pointed tales, as testimony to Merrimack Valley residents' constriction of imagination and their courage to tough-out their hard lives.

The fiction of Andre Dubus contains his artful rendition of characters for whom no sin or good deed goes unpunished; characters who are caught in briar patches or lost in the woods; characters, in Dubus's eyes, who should, nevertheless, be grateful for the qualified blessings of their not-so-wonderful lives. Thoreau's "noble home-staying men" have become an underclass of shut-ins in these end-of-the-century stories of depletion by Andre Dubus.

MAXINE KUMIN

Despite such regional transformations, the pastoral wonders of the Merrimack Valley—articulated by Thoreau, Whittier, and Frost— remain, though they are diminished and threatened by ominous industrial parks, proliferating shopping malls, urban sprawl, pollution, spreading suburbs, and condo developments. As Dubus reveals the inner life of latter-day "operatives," other writers remind us of the primal life of nature. Maxine Kumin's *Up Country: Poems of New England,* as its title indicates, shows that the influence of Robert Frost is still strong in the last years of the twentieth century, north of Boston. In her poetry, fiction, essays, and journals, Kumin immerses herself in the landscape and imagination of southern New Hampshire, and becomes well-versed in country things.

Born in Germantown in Philadelphia in 1925, Kumin first translated herself into a suburban housewife in Newton, Massachusetts; then into a poet, along with her friend, Anne Sexton; finally into a "hermit," as she describes herself, a woman who tends her keep of horses, garden, and poetry in Bradford, New Hampshire. Now "provincially a New Englander, a Yankee, with the extra-deep taproot of a transplant," Kumin has completed a quest, realized herself northward, up along Thoreau's Merrimack, into Frost's "clearing."[46]

Kumin celebrates her debt to Thoreau and Frost in "A Sense of Place," an essay in which she admits "I cannot imagine myself living, as a writer, outside New England." This may be another way of saying that New England, as it first appeared for her in the works of Thoreau and Frost, fired her imagination. Frost defined the New England character which has shaped her being. "Best of all the New England poets, Robert Frost captured this mixed essence of Samaritan and curmudgeon."[47]

Frost opens "Mending Wall" with his famous aphorism, "Something there is that doesn't love a wall," suggesting an invisible, shaping presence beneath the ordinary appearance of country scenes.[48] In "Stones," from *Up Country,* Kumin evokes the same transcendent mystery.

> The doors of my house are held open by stones
> and to see the tame herd of them hump their backbones
> as cumbrous as bears across the pasture in
> an allday rain is to believe for an afternoon
> of objects that waver and blur
> in some dark obedient order.[49]

As Frost defined the New England voice and vision for her, Thoreau guided Kumin into its rocky landscape. "The landscape I walk is his. I visit his trees, inspect his snowstorms, seek out his moose."[50] Like Thoreau, Kumin works her fields—one of her essay collections is titled *To Make a Prairie*—and harvests her poems.[51] "In a poem one can use the sense of place as an anchor for larger concerns, as a link between narrow details and global realities."[52]

Much of Kumin's poetry, then, derives from her quests through New England poets and places. "These New England upland pastures are like a secret garden, like the impulse toward a poem."[53] Out riding one of her horses, she looks at overgrown paths through Frost's metaphors, as roads not taken, routes which might lead her to the "other side." In the high New England way, then, Kumin's life and art reflect her search for meaning: "the quest is real. To get there you have to go in deep."[54] Kumin learns to make all she can of a declining, traditional way of life in the New England hills. "Increasingly I think we are transients here," writes Kumin.

> What will become of that not-quite-vanished system of values that lingers in the New England countryside, abetted by the harshness of the climate and the exigencies imposed by isolation? I don't want to write elegies to vanishing virtues, nor do I want to mythologize the remaining stalwarts. But I cannot be blind to the miniature fortitude of humans pitted against the vagaries of weather.[55]

In the tradition that derives from Thoreau and Frost, Maxine Kumin writes poetry and prose which celebrates the sanctification of her place, "my hardscrabble kingdom on a hill." As well, she explores a woman's interior landscape, and she laments an age in which the world around her is becoming increasingly commercial and suburban; she regrets the loss of a traditional, New England world in which "human beings still felt some connection to and responsibility for the animal lives and the land in their keeping."[56] Maxine Kumin tends her keep, renewing New England's natural and poetic resources, north of Boston.

JACK KEROUAC

When Jack Kerouac came off the road in the early 1960s to revisit Lowell, Massachusetts, he talked with a friend about the mill city where he was born in 1922, the city he described in five novels. "Some day this city will put up a statue of me. And I'll even pose naked for it if they want."[57] Such a commemorative statue must have seemed wildly improbable for this beat generation writer, particularly when he came home again in 1967, hobbled by phlebitis and the alcoholism which would kill him in two years. Lowell, it seemed, was no place for a footloose writer who celebrated subversive lives and ideas. As Ann Charters, Kerouac's first biographer, noted, Lowell was "poor, dirty and rundown, both working class and obstinately bourgeois, belligerently provincial."[58] However, such comments underestimated Lowell's capacities for transformation and its will for reconciliation with its famed, wayward son.

In June 1988, the Lowell Historic Preservation Commission sponsored a week-long series of events marking the dedication of the Jack Kerouac Commemorative: eight massive blocks of granite, on which passages from Kerouac's works are sandblasted into panels, a sculpture set in Eastern Canal Park, a one-acre plaza near the Merrimack River. The pavement is patterned in a cross-and-circle design which reflects both Kerouac's youthful Catholicism and his adult mysticism.[59] Jack Kerouac, then, has truly come home; he has finally been accepted into the larger pattern of economic and cultural revival of Lowell.

The Lowell Public Art Collection celebrates Lowell's past in the same terms that Dickens and Trollope, nearly 150 years earlier, saw its future: a Lowell in which nature, labor, and art are one. Unlikely as it once might have seemed, Jack Kerouac—French-Canadian descendant of mill-workers, local sports hero, celebrity, lover, drinker, prose-poet of the Merrimack region and bizarre worlds beyond—speaks for the New Lowell.

The commemorative contains passages from Kerouac's "Lowell books": *The Town and the City* (1950), *Doctor Sax* (1959), *Maggie Cassidy* (1959), *Visions of Gerard* (1963), and *Vanity of Duluoz* (1968); also inscribed are passages from his books of geographic and spiritual travels: *On the Road* (1957), *Mexico City Blues* (1959), *The Scriptures of the Golden Eternity* (1960), and *Book of Dreams* (1960). Kerouac's self-portrait, from *Lonesome Traveler* (1960), is included:

> Had beautiful childhood, my father a printer in Lowell, Mass., roamed fields and riverbanks day and night, wrote little novels in my room, first novel written at age 11, also kept extensive diaries and "newspapers" covering my own-invented horseracing and baseball and football worlds—Had good early education from Jesuit brothers at St. Joseph's Parochial School. Took long walks under old trees of New England at night with my mother and aunt. Listened to their gossip attentively. . . . Final plans: hermitage in the woods, quiet writing of old age, mellow hopes of Paradise (which comes to everyone anyway) . . .[60]

There is little evidence that Paradise ever came to Jack Kerouac, except in transient moments of stimulation, in or out of Lowell. But it is revealing to see that this rhapsodist of apparently aimless movement through American cities saw himself as a pastoral poet: reared in nature like Whittier, roaming fields and streams like Thoreau, his heart set on a hermitage. Jack Kerouac recomposed Lowell and himself to the salvific myth of his imagination.

The first significant "road" which Kerouac set out "on" was the one which took him away from a series of humble residences north of the Merrimack, across the Moody Street Bridge into downtown Lowell. His Lowell novels portray young men, alter egos all, on quests for recognition and self-realization. Across the bridge, in Lowell's inner-city, Kerouac, reared in French-Canadian Catholic culture, learned to speak American English, and then he made himself over into a legendary local football hero.

In *The Town and the City* Lowell is called "Galloway"—an echo of Galway, in recognition of Lowell's Irish-American character— and he is Peter Martin. Galloway is set deep into the New England landscape, the shaping grounds of primal home. The novel's opening echoes Thoreau's epiphany of place.

> The town is Galloway. The Merrimack River, broad and placid, flows down to it from the New Hampshire hills, broken at the falls to make frothy havoc on the rocks, foaming on over ancient stone towards a place where the river suddenly swings about in a wide and peaceful basin, moving on now around the flank of the town, on to places known as Lawrence and Haverhill, through a wooded valley, and on to the sea at Plum Island, where the river enters an infinity of water and is gone. Somewhere far north of Galloway, in headwaters close to Canada, the river is continually fed and made to brim out of endless sources and unfathomable springs.[61]

Though *The Town and the City* is a realistic novel, it reveals Kerouac's near mystic identification with the Merrimack, whose origins, like his own, reached toward Canada; its route coursed through Lowell's turbulence, its goal was "an infinity of waters" beyond Lowell. In *Maggie Cassidy* Kerouac's fictional persona, Jack Duluoz, is torn between two young women, as was Kerouac in high school. Maggie is a "townie" who wanted to hold Jack back, while Pauline is worldly, promising exotic and erotic release. Duluoz, like his author, "vacillated between the known and the new world," then chose to go on the road, away from the home he left but never forgot.[62]

Kerouac chose to accept a football scholarship to Columbia University rather than go to Boston College, where he was also courted, because he wanted to escape the provincial, to meet his fate in the wider world of New York City. Kerouac was born again as a latter-day wandering bard whose prose-poems were based upon the epic tales of his home ground. Renewed Lowell, in turn, has reinvented Jack Kerouac, whose life had troubled many local residents, not in a naked statue, but in an artful grouping of granite blocks, into which are inserted marble panels, on which are preserved his words of tribute to his home town.

OUT of a vision of commerce, culture, nature, and moral purpose, Bostonians might be said to have dreamed up Lowell, Lawrence, and the mills of the Merrimack Valley. In turn these industrial cities transformed the countryside and its people. The City upon a Hill became Spindle City along a river. Good country people lost their old place in the pastoral order, then found their new, less certain place in urban industry. The literary record presents the story, from many compelling angles, of this dream: found, lost, and remembered. The mighty Merrimack, by route of the sluggish Concord River, links Boston, like a blood line, to the landscape, fact and image, north of Boston.

South of Boston—Cape Cod Writers

WILLIAM BRADFORD

> Being thus arrived in a good harbor, and brought safe to land, they fell upon their knees and blessed the God of Heaven who had brought them over the vast and furious ocean, and delivered them from all the perils and miseries thereof, again to set their feet on the firm and stable earth, their proper element.[63]

227

So wrote William Bradford of the safe arrival of the *Mayflower* pilgrims, after some 65 days at sea, at Provincetown Harbor on 21 November 1620. On the previous day, in the midst of a storm, they had sighted the highlands of Cape Cod, but they could not transit the "dangerous shoals and roaring breakers," so they rode out the storm and landed later, in calmer waters.[64] Their arrival, then, was the completion of a dangerous physical passage and the climax of a spiritual quest.

Yet the stark Cape landscape appeared less a promised land and more a threatening waste land to Bradford's voyagers, who felt hemmed in by the turbid ocean on one side and hostile Indians on the other.

> Besides, what could they see but a hideous and desolate wilderness, full of wild beasts and wild men—and what multitudes there might be of them they knew not. Neither could they, as it were, go up to the top of Pisgah to view from this wilderness a more godly country to feed their hopes; for which way soever they turned their eyes (save upward to the heavens) they could have little solace or content in respect of any outward objects.[65]

In his account of their brief stay on land that is now called Provincetown, before they settled in the more commodious region of Plymouth, Bradford began to shape a vision of Cape Cod as a testing ground. He saw it as a place to which one travels to escape civilization's corruptions, a place where one could learn, as Thoreau said on going to Walden Pond, "to live deliberately, to front only the essential facts of life," to discover what life *means*.[66] Cape Cod, then, is another country, to which the desperate, the driven, and the visionary take passage—those who sense mystery and seek revelation. However, Bradford and his followers found no Pisgah, no mount of sufficient height from which to survey the new world. The elemental Cape—ocean, sand, sky—offered itself as an allegorical landscape, a site of trial where God tested the voyager's character and faith, a place which held lessons in beauty and truth. "The good God," wrote Cotton Mather, taking a more benign view of the region, "gives this people to suck of the abundance of the seas."[67] For all its shifting implications, these English pilgrims explored the Cape from its tip to the mainland (now the Cape Cod Canal): that is, they moved from the "lower" Cape, around Provincetown, to the "upper" Cape, as though they were in ascent, in quest of the City upon the Hill. Cape Cod literature, like the literature of Boston, is characterized by quests, described in a series of spiritual autobiographies.

Symbolic Landscape

Today Provincetown's Pilgrim Monument—a 252-foot granite tower built on a hundred-foot hill, dedicated in 1910—provides a perspective which was unavailable to Bradford; on a clear day we now can see the whole arc of the land which forms Cape Cod Bay. So, too, have our writers built verbal structures to provide original view points from which we can imagine the Cape and understand its meaning. Indeed Provincetown has long been seen as a visionary landscape. It became, for example, the "first art colony in America" in 1899, when Charles W. Hawthorne established the Cape Cod School of Art. Provincetown remains a painters' haven.[68] Cape Cod, however, has been better represented in words than in visual images.

Cape Cod: sixty-five miles of curving land, a glacial deposit built up, composed and recomposed by wind and sea, by shifting sand deposits over thirty thousand years. These arresting facts, though, do not do justice to Cape Cod's power over our imaginations, its metaphorical implications.

For Robert Finch, a contemporary naturalist, the Cape is "a rising horizontal Matterhorn, a flattened precipice projecting outward rather than upward, but an imposing eminence nonetheless, full of isolated grandeur."[69] Here Finch frames an image of quest and ascent which builds upon Bradford's desire to locate Pisgah. Indeed Finch recalls his own youthful quest for height and biblical resonance. In the early 1960s Finch wandered out into the "outback," the vast dunes between Route 6 and the Atlantic Ocean, in

search of Mount Gilboa and Mount Ararat, two of Provincetown's
largest dunes.

> The impression of the dune landscape was immediately biblical,
> reminiscent of those valleys and desert wildernesses I had always
> imagined the tribes of Israel wandering through. There is something
> fundamentally allegorical about the dune country: each feature—
> every bush, bog, ridge and buried tree trunk—stands out from its
> background with a kind of concentrated suggestiveness. The scale
> is small and uncluttered, an expressionist landscape that seems cre-
> ated for parables and myths.[70]

Later Finch recalled the lessons of the great storm of February
1978 which swept Henry Beston's hut, celebrated in Beston's book,
The Outermost House, out to sea. Finch thinks Beston would have
approved. "He knew where it was he lived. The house had been
but the shell for the book, which he established on imperishable
foundations." Finch was aware of the truth of Beston's vision that
"creation is here and now."[71] Cape Cod teaches transcendence,
reminds us that we must put aside childish and earthly things.
Cape storms transform ordinary landscapes, cleanse ephemera from
beaches and souls, expose us to spiritual realms.

THERE are, of course, many sides to Cape Cod. The Kennedy
compound at Hyannisport symbolizes entrenched wealth, the political and social status of the upper Cape, while the memory of
the cultural revival during and just after World War I, centered
around the Provincetown Players, represents Cape Cod's long literary tradition. Today most of the Cape is encroached upon by
unchecked development: condos and malls crowd the landscape
and the Cape's water supply is threatened. So Cape Cod offers
many models, teaches many lessons. However, the essential
Cape—beyond politics, social status, land development, and even
art—is that territory encompassed by the Cape Cod National Sea-

shore, established in 1961. It includes twenty-seven thousand acres in six towns: Chatham, Orleans, Eastham, Wellfleet, Truro, Provincetown. There, on the outer beach of the lower Cape, one still can encounter in nature, in one's self, the essential. Those who go there—particularly along the high beach dunes of Wellfleet or the vast dunes of Provincetown, patrolled by vigilant flocks of birds—respond in awe, a wonder not unmixed with fear, an exhilaration at confronting a rare and compelling expanse. There one is detached from mainland life and placed into a primal conjunction of land, sea, and sky. Here is how Clare Leighton, a contemporary chronicler, puts it:

> When we think of the beach on Cape Cod, we mean the vast expanse of the back shore—the back side, as they call it here—facing the Atlantic. The gentler side, nestled in the curve of the aroma of the Cape, is never the beach; it is always the bay. And, though both are built of sand and both are subject to the rhythm of the tides, yet they are utterly different. Even the life upon their shores is different; horseshoe crabs and scallops, oysters and clams cannot be found along the Atlantic at low water; they require the shelter of the bay. This, fringing the Atlantic, is an austere, wild world.[72]

It is that Cape, austere and wild, amplified by haunting literary presences, which Bradford first encountered, which endures in our imaginations.

HENRY DAVID THOREAU

Henry David Thoreau imagined Cape Cod into being more powerfully than anyone. To seek "another world," Thoreau took his trip so that he might learn more than Concord had to teach. "I have been accustomed to make excursions to the ponds within ten miles of Concord, but latterly I have extended my excursions to the seashore."[73] Thoreau, however, saw Cape Cod not as a separate place, not as an island, but as part of the main, a territory within the body politic of Massachusetts. The Cape serves as a protective arm for the Commonwealth:

Cape Cod is the bared and bended arm of Massachusetts: the shoulder is at Buzzard's Bay; the elbow, or crazy-bone, at Cape Mallebarre; the wrist at Truro; and the sandy fist at Provincetown,—behind which the State stands on her guard, with her back to the Green Mountains, and her feet planted on the floor of the ocean, like an athlete protecting her Bay,—boxing with northeast storms, and, ever and anon, heaving up her Atlantic adversary from the lap of the earth,—ready to thrust forward her other fist, which keeps guard the while upon her breast at Cape Ann.[74]

Thoreau's powerful and reassuring metaphor—an arm which encircles, not a mountain to climb—has endured. Henry Beston, for example, accepted Thoreau's organic metaphor as a given, "both exact and inescapable," with Truro the "wrist" of the "forearm" that drew Beston's attention.[75]

Thoreau's *Cape Cod*, based on three visits between 1849 and 1851, is a meditation which was motivated by his intense personal need to know his place in the universe, to account for death within a system of transcendental affirmation. Thoreau may have been on a quest for purification of guilt he felt over living on after the sudden death of his beloved brother, John, in 1842; Thoreau also included reflections on the death of Margaret Fuller, who was drowned off Fire Island in July 1850. He even incorporated into his narrative a premonition of his own early death.[76] *Cape Cod*, edited after his death by Sophia, his sister, and Ellery Channing, his hiking companion, was published posthumously in 1865. His week's tour, begun in October 1849 with Channing at his side, was also, it has been argued, a confrontation with "New England and its Calvinism," an ideological inquiry into revealing places and symbols.[77]

In Boston, en route to Cape Cod, Thoreau and Channing learned of the wreck of the *St. John* (a ship from Galway which had been carrying Irish immigrants at the height of the Great Famine) from a handbill: "Death! one hundred and forty-five lives lost at Cohasset." So "we decided to go by way of Cohasset." These pilgrims, Thoreau and Channing, sought "another world" in the evidence of a shipwreck. Ellen Sewall Osgood, whom Thoreau's brother had courted and who remained Henry's unrequited love, escorted Thoreau and Channing along the beach in Cohasset, where more than two dozen corpses were recovered while the winds still blew from the storm which sunk the *St. John*. Thoreau's clinical description was observant and detached; then he "turned from this and walked along the rocky shore."[78] Perhaps he was trying to distance himself from the shocking scene. Perhaps, too, because these were Irish immigrants, pilgrims with whom he showed little sympathy, his detachment was sincere. These voyagers, for Thoreau, may have been better off dead on Cape Cod than they would have been alive in Boston.

Death vied with beauty throughout Thoreau's walk from Orleans to Provincetown. Today the beach has been eroded by some hundred yards, so that the actual track of Thoreau's journey is now covered by the Atlantic. Thoreau was particularly delighted by the Cape's fresh air, as though he had left a cigar-smelling, closed room in Concord. "The towns need to be ventilated. The gods would be pleased to see some pure flames from their altars. They are not to be appeased with cigar-smoke."[79] Odors of death and beauty contend in stark psychodrama in Thoreau's *Cape Cod*.

In Truro Thoreau enjoyed the smell of bayberry bushes along his walk, but he turned somber upon again encountering evidence of the *St. John* wreck. In composing this moment he was reminded of Margaret Fuller's death, which occurred two years after the *St. John* went down, as though all deaths merged into Death. The stark seashore was full of lessons for Thoreau. "There is naked Nature—inhumanly sincere, wasting no thought on man, nibbling at the cliffy shore where gulls wheel amid the spray."[80]

In Truro Thoreau also contemplated the prospect of Provincetown. He took satisfaction in belonging to two worlds: Thoreau felt both enclosed within the arm of Massachusetts, his earthly realm, and open to an ocean of spiritual transcendence. "The inhabitants of all the lower Cape towns enjoy thus the prospect of two seas."[81]

As in his trip up the Merrimack, Thoreau's Cape Cod quest was an extension of inquiry beyond his Concord world, though Walden Pond had prepared him for the Atlantic. "The ocean is but a larger lake."[82] In the value-laden geography of Thoreau's imagination, Boston stood as a daunting middle ground of commercial degradation, between the opportunities for spiritual transcendence in Concord or on Cape Cod. This symbolism of place became evident to Thoreau when he took a steamboat from Provincetown to Boston in 1850. Boston, he thought, was a mere port, measured by barrels of imports.

> The more barrels, the more Boston. The museums and scientific societies and libraries are accidental. They gather around the sands to save carting. The wharf-rats and custom-house officers, and broken-down poets, seeking a fortune amid the barrels. Their better or worse lyceums, and preachings, and doctorings, these, too, are accidental, and the malls of commons are always small potatoes. When I go to Boston, I naturally go straight through the city (taking the Market in my way), down to the end of Long Wharf, and look off, for I have no cousins in the back alleys,—and there I see a great many countrymen in their shirt-sleeves from Maine, and Pennsylvania, and all along the shore and in shore, and some foreigners beside, loading and unloading and steering their teams about, as at a country fair. When I reached Boston that October, I had a gill of Provincetown sand in my shoes, and at Concord there was still enough left to sand my pages for many a day; and I seemed to hear the sea roar, as if I lived in a shell, for a week afterward.[83]

That gill of sand served Thoreau not only as a symbol of the Cape's actual presence, more than one hundred miles from Concord. It also aided Thoreau in his translation of the Cape experience into an act of the imagination, his extended account and meditation, his *Cape Cod*, a book in which we can still hear the sea roar against the shore with his invested significance. Thoreau's *Cape Cod* is an encounter with death, an exploration of a stark and beautiful landscape where death's presence is inescapable. His journey, then, is a crossing to another realm of mystery and a carrying back of the news. Unlike the Irish immigrants aboard the ill-fated *St. John*, Thoreau is better off for having made his trip. Like Ishmael, who floats away from the wrecked *Pequod* on a coffin at the end of

Moby-Dick, Thoreau survives his dangerous journey and returns with an amazing and revealing story to tell. He passes quickly through corrupt Boston to placid Concord, with Cape Cod sand in his shoes, sand ready to dry his words on the pages of *Cape Cod*.

HENRY JAMES

In Henry James's *The Bostonians,* Cape Cod—actually a fictional version of Marion at the southern end of the Cape on Buzzard Bay, where James had spent a weekend in 1883—appears languid and lulling, but it turns out to be a place which allows passions to erupt and revelations to be known. On a long train ride from Boston, through "slanting light [which] gilded the straggling, shabby woods, and painted the ponds and marshes with yellow gleams," the novel's hero, Basil Ransom, pursues Verena Tarrant, whose feminism he has vowed to silence in marriage, to "Marmion." There Verena is summering with Olive Chancellor, her loving benefactor; Miss Birdseye, the last leaf of an age in which New England bloomed with idealism; and other Boston feminists who were seeking rest from their labors. "Ransom had heard that the Cape was the drowsy Cape, the languid Cape, the Cape not of storms, but of eternal peace."[84]

However, human nature, red in tooth and claw, soon expresses itself in gender conflict. Ransom renews his sexual grip on Verena, while Olive fights him off so that she might hold onto the girl: "it was war to the knife." When Miss Birdseye dies during a languid Cape evening, it is as though all that was noble, selfless, innocent, and naive in the New England character died with her.[85] When Ransom entices the reluctant Verena out boating on the bay, renewing his spell of passion over her will, his triumph over Boston feminism is all but complete. Cape Cod in *The Bostonians* is another country, where Ransom, an unreconstructed Southerner, and Olive, a principled Bostonian, can do battle on common ground. Cape Cod serves as a landscape of pastoral passions.

In *The American Scene*, James pursued the "supreme queerness" of Cape Cod. Following the route of Ransom, James traveled south from Boston by train in the summer of 1904, journeying back in his own memories to a territory where distinctions blurred. "I already knew I must fall back on old props of association, some revival of the process of seeing the land grow mild and vague and interchangeably familiar with the sea, all under the spell of the reported 'gulf-stream,' those mystic words that breathe a softness wherever they sound." This journey of fact and imagination yields one of the oddest and most arresting images in which Cape Cod has been caught. "Cape Cod, on this showing, was exactly a pendent, pictured Japanese screen or banner; a delightful little triumph of 'impressionism,' which, during my short visit at least, never departed, under any provocation, from its type."[86]

Henry James's Cape Cod, an object of art, is a world away from either Bradford's threatening, stern, and moral landscape or from Thoreau's morally testing plain. For all that, as we have seen in *The Bostonians*, dark and passionate forces lurk beneath the placid and deceiving surface of the Cape. James may have treated the Cape as though it were an aesthetic object of contemplation, seeking out the proper angle of perspective for conversion into verbal designs, but he, like Bradford and Thoreau before him, saw it as a landscape on which one should properly conduct a quest for "the shy spectre of a revelation." Yet in this sparsely populated territory, James, the novelist of manners, the aesthete, could discover no final meaning. "I had again to take it for a mystery." Perhaps "the constituted blankness was the whole business, and one's opportunity was all, thereby, for a study of exquisite emptiness."[87] Cape Cod, in short, is James's unmarked canvas, open to receive impressions, waiting to discover what more might be made of it.

In stressing the Cape's "blankness," James was, perhaps unconsciously, echoing William Bradford, who imagined (before his arrival) that the presence of absence was America's greatest attraction. "The place they had thought on," wrote Bradford of the Pilgrims' deliberations in Holland, "was some of those vast and unpeopled countries of America, which are fruitful and fit for habitation, being devoid of all civil inhabitants, where there are only savage and brutish men which range up and down, little otherwise than the wild beasts of the same."[88] For James, the Cape retained much of its mystery, even elements of its brutishness.

EUGENE O'NEILL

Many other American writers have been inspired by Cape Cod, its mystery and its multiple meanings, to fill in its exquisite emptiness. Eugene O'Neill is forever associated with Cape Cod because of his brief involvement with the Provincetown Players in 1916. O'Neill was drawn to the Cape by John Reed—the former Harvard cheerleader who would write *Ten Days That Shook the World,* a record of the 1917 Russian Revolution—and other Greenwich Village theater people, particularly George Cram "Jig" Cook. They sought to discover and display, *far* off-Broadway, a native American drama through their productions of one-act plays in a deserted Provincetown fish house. Drawn to their vision, O'Neill came to the Cape, first to Truro—where he and his lover, Terry Carlin, lived on the beach in the rotting hull of a ship—then to a shack in Provincetown, across from Reed and his lover, Louisa Bryant. When the group held a reading of O'Neill's *Bound East for Cardiff*—the monologue of a dying sailor who speaks longingly of the land life he missed—they knew they had discovered an authentic and original American dramatic talent. The play was mounted in the Wharf Theater, a loosely boarded shell of a building, set well out onto a pier in Provincetown harbor, through which the audience could see water, watch fog rise, and hear foghorns—the perfect naturalistic and symbolic setting for O'Neill's plays.[89] Soon O'Neill not only had a new mistress, the mesmerized Louisa Bryant, but also a new career. The Provincetown Players, soon relocated back in Greenwich Village, achieved an identity and established Provincetown's reputation as an artistic community.

Bound East for Cardiff was based upon O'Neill's sea experiences, which began in 1910 when he sailed out of Boston Harbor for Buenos Aires. The play was written in 1914–15 for George Pierce Baker's famous Harvard English 47 class in playwrighting, a class which O'Neill, then twenty-six, attended as a special student. Baker rejected the play, considering it insufficiently dramatic, but the Harvard experience established O'Neill's enduring relationship with Boston. O'Neill's first book, *"Thirst" and Other One Act Plays*, underwritten by his father, was published by Boston's Gorham Press while he was at Harvard. Throughout his life O'Neill would return to the region. In 1948 he and his wife Carlotta lived in Marblehead, just north of Boston. His last years were spent in the Shelton Hotel in Boston's Kenmore Square, where he died in 1953. O'Neill was buried in Forest Hills Cemetery, Jamaica Plain.[90]

O'Neill, of course, was no local colorist. Boston and Provincetown do not figure into his dramatic works as significant settings. On the other hand, O'Neill *was* at times a New England writer. In *Desire under the Elms* (1924) O'Neill dramatized the fall of an aged Puritan farmer, Ephriam Cabot, who tried to impose his will on his sons and his young wife. In his New London, Connecticut dramas (a comedy, *Ah, Wilderness* [1933], and two tragedies, *Long Day's Journey into Night* [1941] and *A Moon for the Misbegotten* [1943]), O'Neill pursued what he called in *Moon*, "a New England Irish Catholic Puritan[ism], Grade B," a fusion of Irish-Catholic guilt and fustian with regional righteousness and repression.[91] These New England tragedies deal with an Irish-American family much like his own. The Tyrones are isolated in a disapproving community, a family thus thrown back upon its own diseased relations. Here, at the outer edge of Boston's influence, O'Neill made his most compelling record of New England's cultural isolation.

EDMUND WILSON

The Cape proved a haven for many other writers as well. In 1924 Eugene O'Neill persuaded the Provincetown Players to produce Edmund Wilson's first play, *The Crime in the Whistler Room*. Wilson married Mary Blair, an actress in O'Neill's plays. During the summer of 1927, Edmund Wilson lived in Provincetown, first on Commercial Street, then in Eugene O'Neill's house on Peaked Hill, a bluff overlooking the sea. Harry Kemp, who had recently built his shack nearby, was then writing a novel, *Love among the Cape-Enders* (1931), which satirized in florid style the Province-town Players group. In 1930 Wilson took over O'Neill's converted Coast Guard station again, during the first summer of his second marriage, to Margaret Canby. John Dos Passos and his wife lived in Truro. E. E. Cummings and Conrad Aiken visited. The lower Cape, from Provincetown to Wellfleet, took on literary resonance.

Wilson recalls his first visit to Truro in 1920, to stay with Edna St. Vincent Millay, whom he had been seeing in Greenwich Village. In those days the train went through to Provincetown; Wilson was carried from there to Truro by cart, where he got lost. Finally he found the Millay family, staying at a house lent to them by "Jig" Cook. Wilson remembers seeking privacy with Millay outside the packed house; sitting outside, in mosquito-infested night air, he proposed marriage. She replied, "that might be the solution." Marriage turned out not to be the solution for Millay, but Cape Cod remained a useful option for Edmund Wilson throughout his long life.[92]

Wilson's journal entries on Cape Cod range from the erotic to the rhapsodic. In 1930 he walked with his bare-breasted wife along the Provincetown dunes; there they made love, confirming the liberating powers of the pastoral. "Love in mid-afternoon in the remote crater of a sand dune—her solid soft human body after the hard rough grainy sand.—Limitations of nocturnal city love, love confined to beds and couches, I realized for the first time."[93] The Cape held possibilities for aesthetic *and* erotic release.

In 1941 Wilson bought a house in Wellfleet, where he took refuge from World War II. There in 1945, at a party which he and Mary McCarthy, his third wife, hosted, Wilson met Elena Mumm Thornton, who would become his fourth wife.

Mary McCarthy retaliated against Wilson and satirized the Cape art community in her 1955 novel, *A Charmed Life*. There Wellfleet became New Leeds, a town to which members of the "artistic community" moved "to make a better life." This was a place of exaggeration, celebrating among its residents twenty-one chronic drunkards, three village idiots, and random "beached failures and second-raters." "New Leeds was, literally, the seacoast of Bohemia."[94]

As McCarthy's title implies, New Leeds tried to transcend, through sexual and artistic license combined with moral indifference, the regional heritage of Puritan consequence. In the novel, Martha Sinnott, romantic heroine and playwright, returns to New Leeds with her second husband, though the village had been the site of her painful divorce from her first husband, Miles Murphy, an unscrupulous writer and psychologist: McCarthy's parody of Wilson. Martha and Miles have sex after a party. As a result, Martha becomes pregnant and struggles with the question of abortion. But Martha dies before the novel ends; she is killed in a car accident by a female alter ego, who is driving on the wrong side of the road. That is, Martha dies accidentally at her own hand, another heroine deluded by "Arcadian affectation." Beneath the Cape's natural beauties lie undeniable moral consequences.[95]

Long after Mary McCarthy left Wellfleet, Cape Cod still served as a refuge of reflection for Edmund Wilson, a quiet place far from Manhattan's crowds, though his late years were spent in two country houses: one in Wellfleet and the other in his Talcotville family home in the lower Adirondacks. Edmund Wilson's Cape Cod began in rapture and ended in domesticity; throughout his life it was a place of beauty and inspiration, a solution to many of his personal and professional problems.

NORMAN MAILER

The Cape Cod portrayed by Norman Mailer, long a part-time Provincetown resident, in his 1984 novel *Tough Guys Don't Dance,* offers little solace, beauty, or refuge. Indeed, its vision is a return to Bradford's "hideous and desolate wilderness, full of wild beasts and wild men." The novel's hero, Tim Madden, depressed over abandonment by his wife, gets drunk on a bleak November night, during which extraordinary things occur, as in a romance; the next morning he wakes hung-over, amazed to see a tattoo on his arm, blood in his Porsche and the severed head of a young woman in the place where he usually kept his marijuana stash; however, he has no memory of what transpired.

Cape Cod serves as Mailer's bleak setting for these lurid events: land's end as the waste land. Provincetown is deserted and grey, a chill November in its soul, not the lively summer place of the tourist season—a proper site for strong analogies.

> Back in summer, the population had been thirty thousand and doubled on weekends. It seemed as if every vehicle on Cape Cod chose to drive down the four-lane state highway that ended at our beach. Provincetown was as colorful then as St. Tropez, and as dirty by Sunday evening as Coney Island. In the fall, however, with everyone gone, the town revealed its other presence.[96]

Provincetown's population then dropped from near sixty thousand to some three thousand people, most of whom were wary shut-ins, in retreat from oncoming winter weather and lurking dangers.

Mailer's Provincetown, echoing Bradford's symbolic landscape, is a battleground of contending moral forces, differing visions of the universe. Tim Madden, before calamitous events enmesh him, walks to the end of town, "out to where the last house meets the place on the beach where the Pilgrims first landed in America," and speaks for Mailer when he reflects upon the history of the Cape. "It is not the rocks but the shifting sands that sink you off Cape Cod. What fear those pilgrims must have known on hearing the dull eternal boom of the surf. Who would dare come near that shore with boats such as theirs?" They sailed north, west, then south; mystified by these turns in the coastline, they turned back and finally encountered a natural harbor.

Today, across from a large motel, a plaque commemorates the Pilgrims' landing. There, for Mailer, is where you come to the heart of the American matter, the center of yourself.

> There is where you come to the end of the road, to the farthest place a tourist can ride toward the tip of Cape Cod and encounter the landing place of the Pilgrims. It was only weeks later, after much

bad weather and the recognition that there was little game to hunt and few fields to till in these sandy lands, that the Pilgrims sailed west across the bay to Plymouth.[97]

Poets of Place

Norman Mailer's terminal vision of a society without resources, a land with lurking terrors, should not be the final word on Cape Cod. In Bradford's day the sparsely populated Cape threatened his band of pilgrims. In Mailer's day, the over-populated Cape threatens the life-support system of all residents and visitors. However, there is still game to hunt on Cape Cod, if you look; there are still fields to till, particularly if you wish to harvest, as did Thoreau in *Walden*, tropes and metaphors. Cape Cod still offers informing and affirming parables for those who seek meaning and value in its landscape—particularly for those who begin their hunt early in the day.

Melissa Green, in *Squanicook Eclogues* (1987), brings a Puritan sense of amazement and purpose to her evocation of the local landscape, even while she debates her father's interpretation of its significance.

> My father solemnly believed a God could live
> Articulate in sumac and arbutus leaves;
> That daily-witnessed death could be outrun
> If once observed and written down. In sun, in rain,
> I learned that duty and devotion are the same
> When love and terror walked together. As the stream
> Diverged, we stood on separate banks. He tried to show
> Me where a red-eyed vireo might nest, the shy
> Elusive whippoorwill might hide, but I could not
> Distinguish anything except the wildest note
> Of pity in their singing.[98]

Melissa Green reinterprets her father's reading of the landscape as text. Separated by a diverging stream, a physical emblem of their differing visions, she subtracts his quest for God through the observation of natural things, and adds her feelings to nature—her identification with the implications of the song a bird sings. However, father and daughter stand together on the grounds of a common assumption: that nature is a source of mystery and meaning.

In *American Primitive* (1983) Mary Oliver, who was reared in southern Ohio, also refocuses her poetic eye on the symbolically teeming territory of Wellfleet, a town that spans from the Cape's Outer Beach to the Bay. There even snow falls like probing questions.

> . . . its white
> rhetoric everywhere
> calling us back to *why, how,*
> *whence,* such beauty and *what*
> the meaning; such
> an oracular fever! . . .[99]

Oliver finds no answers, but she feels a sense of union with nature. In "Morning at Great Pond" Oliver experiences a post-Puritan epiphany of faith. At dawn over the pond "forks of light" dissolve night's ". . . craven doubt." Great blue herons and wood ducks appear on the water and a deer drinks, ". . . knee-deep / in the purple shallows. . . ."

> as she turns
> the silver water
> crushes like silk,
> shaking the sky,
> and you're healed then
> from the night, your heart
> wants more, you're ready
> to rise and look!
> to hurry anywhere!
> to believe in everything.[100]

For Oliver the questions posed by the season's first snow are answered by the symbols of day's first light.

Robert Finch, another early riser, also notices the many small birds and animals which take over Cape Cod while people are not looking. In *Common Ground* Finch goes out before dawn to listen to the sequence of bird songs: first a whippoorwill, then a wood-thrush. "In the deep unity of dawn and its connected lives, the aberration of man on the landscape seemed even more glaring than usual. . . . In such a time and setting the very homes of my neighbors looked strange, unfamiliar, unreal."[101] The essential Cape is still available to early risers, those seekers who are sensitive to the nuances of sound and sight.

HENRY BESTON

It is just this unfamiliarity that pilgrims to Cape Cod have long sought. Thoreau quested for "another world" in *Cape Cod*, the narrative of his reflective walks along the outer beach. In *The Outermost House,* the record of his year of semi-isolation in a hut along the Atlantic beach in Eastham, Henry Beston sought a way to live within that other world. *The Outermost House* is, then, Beston's *Walden*. Beston built his two-room hut, with windows on all sides, the "Fo'castle," on a Nauset Beach dune in 1927. "I went there to spend a fortnight in September. The fortnight ending, I lingered on, and as the year lengthened into autumn, the beauty and mystery of this earth and outer sea so possessed and held me that I could not go." However, unlike Thoreau, that tourist, Beston was not interested in making invidious distinctions between the Cape and Boston. Beston sought a rhythm beyond the beat of cities. Beston's Cape is a self-contained wonder; his nature is "a place of the instancy and eternity of creation and the noble ritual of the burning year." Such are the assumptions behind Henry Beston's theme and method.[102]

As Thoreau drew inward and visionary during the winters he spent on the shore of Walden Pond, so too does Beston discover himself and his mission during the worst winter on the Cape for fifty years. The storms of late February 1928 resulted in many wrecks and drownings. The *Montclair* went down, killing a crew of five. A body from the wreck was found, buried in sand, a week later, in Orleans. Beston, like Thoreau before him, found all this exhilarating, revealing. "To understand this great outer beach, to appreciate its atmosphere, its 'feel,' one must have a sense of it as a scene of wreck and elemental drama." Beston became another Crusoe during that winter, living, he said, like a migratory bird, enjoying his separation from man and the corruptions of civilization. "No one came to kill, no one came to explore, no one even came to see. Earth, ocean, and sky, the triune unity of this coast, pursued each one their vast and mingled purposes as untroubled by man as a planet on its course about the sun."[103] On the Cape, man dissolves into the elements.

During his year on Nauset Beach, Henry Beston abandoned civilization so that he might better come to terms with nature, learn and transmit its lesson: "Live in Nature, and you will soon see that for all its non-human rhythm, it is no cave of pain."[104]

CLARE LEIGHTON

Clare Leighton, an adopted resident of Cape Cod, also admires the Cape for its storms and lessons. Indeed, the storms *are* lessons, occasions of epiphany.

> Cape Cod storms—tempests, as the people call them when they include thunder and lightning—hold a special quality of drama. Here, where the land is flat and low, it is like being at sea. The heavens are open to view. We can see them in their majesty, the horizon a complete circle around us.[105]

Leighton's Cape provides a mystic revelation of cosmic design. The rhythm of life, so hidden in our cities, is evident and reassuring on the Cape. "Watching the discipline of the tides, with their evident rhythm, we can surrender our fears, reminded that we are part of the universe and live within the pattern of order that is beyond our control."[106]

ROBERT FINCH

Robert Finch's Cape Cod is an even more compelling and complex landscape of discovery, "an unknown coast. For each individual arriving new on its shores, it offers a place to begin, to stumble, to leave and return to, and finally, perhaps, to stay." More eloquently than anyone since Thoreau, Finch appreciates the significant symbolic place Cape Cod holds in the American imagination, "a figure at once microscopic and unique, representative and individual." Indeed, Robert Finch, as he acknowledges, is as indebted to his literary predecessors—he cites Thoreau, Beston, John Hay, author of *The Great Beach*, and Conrad Aiken, poet—as he is to his experience as a Cape Cod resident. Finch recognizes that those things which we seek on Cape Cod (escape from civilization, transcendence into nature, insight into a sense of moral purpose and cosmic design) are threatened by regional overdevelopment, but he remains optimistic that a purposeful quest will still be rewarded on Cape Cod, particularly along its outer beach. "Greatly altered in appearances—in places to the point of unrecognizability—Cape Cod nonetheless remains as fundamental, challenging and unexhausted a departure point for discovery and self-discovery as it ever was."[107]

Each of Finch's rhapsodic books on the Cape describes a physical and moral journey, a passage from the ordinary and confusing world of experience to some transcendent realm of beauty and awareness. His titles reveal his thematic intent and hint at his visionary purpose: *Common Ground: A Naturalist's Cape Cod* (1981), *The Primal Place* (1983), and *Outlands: Journeys to the Outer Edge of Cape Cod* (1986). *The Primal Place*, for example, takes its title from Conrad Aiken, who saw himself as a voyager who discovers the wonder of the near-at-hand. "I feel like Ulysses," wrote Aiken. "And so far west. Brewster begins to seem more than ever like the Primal Place—We shall see!"[108] Though Finch does not travel far, restricting his search in this book to his West Brewster neighborhood, he too seeks sight and insight into the nature of Nature. "I bear witness and recognize myself for what I so manifestly am: a part of what I behold." Paradoxically, Finch here has transcended his given grounds, only to be enclosed by the larger vision of wholeness in Thoreau's image, "the broad, sweeping arm of the Cape [which] curves round to the east, swinging north and peeling down to nothing on the horizon, gathering us all in."[109] Where one stands is, then, the primal place, a fact made particularly evident on the symbolic landscape of Cape Cod.

A dead whale, washed up on the Dennis shore, teaches Finch to review our myths of Cape Cod.

> We substitute human myth for natural reality and wonder why we starve for nourishment. 'Your Cape' becomes 'your Mall,' as the local radio jingle has it. Thoreau's 'huge and real Cape Cod . . . a wild rank place with no flattery in it,' becomes the Chamber of Commerce's 'Rural Seaside Charm'—until forty tons of dead flesh wash ashore and give the lie to such thin, flattering conceptions, flesh whose stench is still the stench of life that stirs us to reaction and response.[110]

Like Thoreau and so many others who are drawn to the Cape, Finch loves storms both for their fierce beauty and for what they uncover. "For sheer power and visual spectacle, Nauset in a northeaster is better than a thousand Niagaras." The blizzard of February 1978 which destroyed Henry Beston's outermost house reminded Finch of the merely "cosmetic changes" made in the landscape by man. Cape Cod, with its shipwrecks and its stark landscape, exhilarated Thoreau, but challenged his transcendental optimism. In *Walden* he spoke of the pond's waters flowing into the Ganges, an emblem of spiritual communion, but on the Cape Thoreau faced isolation and emblems of death. When Finch, however, writes of the tides along the outer beach—so powerful, unrelenting, and cleansing—he returns to the symbolic waters of *Walden*. Even tiny tide-fingers bear blessings for Finch. "It is the moving finger of universal forces, that writes, here on these shallow summer sands—inspired, passionate holy water."[111]

CAPE Cod, that strange, glacial outcropping which extends into the Atlantic and encloses the waters around the Massachusetts coastline with its protective arm, is a symbolic landscape, a semi-allegorical plain on which seekers and seers have found transcendence and revelation. They have left us the records of their quests, from Bradford's perilous landing to Mailer's horrific discoveries. Many writers have traveled from Boston and elsewhere to remote places on the Cape in order to confront life in nature, to observe its motions and to delineate its meanings. Cape Cod, writes Finch, forces "us to reevaluate our ideas about who we are and where we live, to revise and perhaps reverse our perspectives on ourselves and the earth."[112] Cape Cod, then, stands well within the larger territory of literary Boston, a landscape of moral implications. On its outer beach pilgrims still quest and reflect, in spiritual autobiographies, on matter and meaning south of Boston.

Walking Westward

EMILY DICKINSON

Emily Dickinson, like Thoreau, had little use for Boston. While he scorned the city's soulless commercialism, she dismissed Boston's culture. In four visits Emily Dickinson spent nearly a year in and around Boston, but she always missed Amherst, her home, more than a hundred miles to the west.[113] As her biographer, Richard B. Sewall, points out, the Dickinsons "did not transplant easily."[114] Emily Dickinson, an exotic flower, rooted and flourished in Amherst.

Amherst's history has been marked by religious fervor, poetic expression, and ideological tensions. Settled in the mid-eighteenth century, Amherst derived its early character from Thomas Hooker and his followers, dissenters from Boston's version of the covenanted community. Amherst became a model of Connecticut Valley orthodoxy, though it was also marked by large, individual landholders, so private property and public polity were sometimes at odds. First the colonial rebellion against England, then Shay's Rebellion and finally separation between the First and Second churches were issues which divided Amherst in the eighteenth century, but by Emily Dickinson's day Amherst had reverted to its earlier religious and political conservatism. The town was controlled by prominent and pious elders like Edward Dickinson, Emily's father. With Amherst College, founded to train missionaries, at one end of town and an agricultural college, which would become the University of Massachusetts, at the other end, Amherst clung to Federalist party values and Congregationalist principles, placing itself in opposition to the increasingly democratic and Unitarian ways of Boston and Cambridge.[115] Set on a plateau with fair prospect in all directions, Amherst deemed itself a city upon a hill, custodian of the Puritan errand into the wilderness, responsible for the moral mission which Boston had abandoned.

Isolation has also marked Amherst's history. As recently as 1962 Amherst was satirized for its chill inner and outer weather in Alison Lurie's novel, *Love and Friendship*. There Amherst, only slightly disguised as "Convers," is the despair of a Convers [Amherst] College teacher who sends this note to his friend in New York.

> We are all frozen in together here, between the ice mountains. North road blocked by ten-foot glacier. West road impassable since Christmas. South road hazardous, unsanded, three cars wrecked trying to escape. No east road. . . . No sun. No mail. Forecast: cloudy and colder. Help help help help.[116]

Emily Dickinson would have understood this lonely cry, though she never wanted to live anywhere else.

IN the summer of 1846, her sixteenth year, Emily Dickinson visited Boston, where she was briefly happy—"No not happy, but contented," she revised—because she had seen Mount Auburn Cemetery ("city of the dead"), Bunker Hill, the Horticultural Exhibit, attended two concerts and the Chinese Museum; however, even this account of her visit, written in a letter to a school friend, concludes in an expression of her desire to be again among her family and friends in Amherst. Before she and her sister, Vinnie, left to visit their brother, Austin, in Boston in 1851, Emily made it clear to him that they had no interest in Boston culture. "We don't care a fig for the *museums*, the stillness, or Jennie Lind."[117] When they returned to Amherst, her anti-urban prejudices confirmed, Emily wrote to Austin that they were "rich in disdain for Bostonians and Boston, and a coffer fuller of *scorn, pity, commiseration*, a miser hardly had."[118] In Boston again in 1864 to consult an eye doctor, Emily felt she had been made a prisoner, trapped in a Cambridgeport rooming house for some seven months. "The Physician has taken away my Pen," she reports.[119] Emily Dickinson's Boston, then, was at best all show and sham; at worst it threatened to "silence" her poetic voice. Perhaps that is what she meant by Boston's "stillness."

Safely home in Amherst, but culturally isolated, Dickinson sought some saving grace in Boston culture. In early 1862 Thomas Wentworth Higginson published an *Atlantic* essay, "Letter to a Young Contributor," which invited unpublished writings. In response she sent Higginson four poems and a letter:

> Mr. Higginson. Are you too deeply occupied to say if my verse is alive? The mind is so near itself—it cannot see, distinctly—and I have none to ask—Should you think it breathed—and had you the leisure to tell me, I should feel quick gratitude—If I make the mistake—that you dared to tell me—would give me sincerer honor—toward you—I enclose my name—asking you, if you please—Sir—to tell me what is true? That you will not betray me— it is needless to ask—since Honor is its own pawn—[120]

This touching letter reveals her cultural isolation even among her friends and family in Amherst, and her trust that a Boston man of letters might (if not too deeply occupied) be able to provide not just a true judgment of her work. He might also rescue her, a doubting poet in a land of true believers.

Dickinson could not have chosen a more representative voice of Boston culture than Higginson. Unitarian pastor, Emersonian, abolitionist, women's rights advocate, and Civil War hero, Higginson was also an author: his works ranged from reminiscence (*Cheerful Yesterdays*) to biographies of literary lights (Margaret Fuller, Longfellow, Whittier and more), to history (*Army Life in a Black Regiment*). Higginson spoke in the measured, assured tones of the high-minded, rationalist-reformist Unitarian culture of Boston.

Higginson's Boston voice offered an alternative to the equally assured Amherst voice of Edward Dickinson, who defined the limits of Emily's outer life. Her esteemed father also embodied the staunch Congregationalism of Amherst, which prided itself on sustaining Puritan standards in the face of that Cambridge apostasy, Unitarianism. Edward Dickinson was an exemplary if stern man. Long-time treasurer of Amherst College, which his own father had helped to found, successful lawyer, elected representative in both the Massachusetts General Court and United States Congress, Edward Dickinson personified Amherst's righteous piety and purpose. He supported his daughter's education at Amherst Academy and Mount Holyoke Female Seminary, but he discouraged her from "excessive" reading, though he did not spend enough time at home to enforce his wishes. A man of little warmth or imagination, he would not have approved of her quirky, passionate poems. Perhaps Higginson, who invited young poets to submit their work, would.

As it turned out, her faith in Higginson was misplaced, for he understood her rare and eccentric gift little better than did her father or most of Amherst's citizenry. Higginson did not think her poems—irregular in rhyme and rhythm, odd in formal arrangement, irreverent or cryptic in matter—fit for publication. Indeed, he saw her as his "partially cracked poetess of Amherst."[121] Higginson preferred the predictable poetry and popular prose of Helen Hunt Jackson. Jackson, Dickinson's age, had known the poet since their childhood in Amherst. However, Jackson left Amherst to become twice a wife, a mother, and a popular author, roles remote from Dickinson's experience. Jackson visited her and encouraged publication of her poems. Two of Jackson's novels, *Mercy Phil-*

brick's Choice and *Esther Wynn's Love-Letters*, are loosely based upon Dickinson's life.[122]

It took Mabel Loomis Todd, Austin's mistress, to persuade Higginson to publish Dickinson's poems after her death, in three series in the early 1890s. The poems in these editions were "sicklied o'er with T. W. Higginson," just as Alice James, another New England recluse, feared they might be.[123] Higginson regularized Dickinson's punctuation and muffled her colloquialisms: "heft" was altered to "weight," for example, in "There's a certain Slant of light. . . ."[124]

Higginson brought all his Boston cultural baggage with him when he visited Emily in the Dickinson home, the Homestead, on Main Street in Amherst in 1870. He could no more puzzle out her person than he could comprehend her poetry. After the visit, Higginson wrote to his wife, "I never was with any one who drained my nerve power so much. Without touching her she drew from me. I am glad not to live near her."[125] Higginson's Boston and Dickinson's Amherst were separate worlds. "My Business is Circumference," is how she explained her oblique art to Higginson, that literal and centered man.[126]

At their second meeting in late 1873, Dickinson cultivated her eccentricity, presenting herself to Higginson in an angular, airy, enigmatic fashion, just the way he saw her poetry. Higginson reported, in a letter to his sister, that she "glided in, in white, bearing a *Daphne odora* for me, and said, under her breath, 'How long are you going to stay?' "[127] No doubt by then Dickinson had seen the limited usefulness of Higginson as a mentor. As Sewall notes, she sought his advice, but she never followed it.[128]

Dickinson's letters to Higginson were declarations of her determined isolation, her tentative and futile efforts to reach beyond the pieties of her community and family.

> They shut me up in Prose—
> As when a little Girl
> They put me in a Closet—
> Because they liked me "still"—[129]

In her poetry, her spiritual autobiography, she named her isolation and spoke to imaginary readers who might understand her strange language. In her Main Street home, she told Higginson, "they are all religious—except me—and address an Eclipse, every morning—whom they call their 'Father.' "[130] But Emily Dickinson characteristically was betwixt and between, for she resisted the Congregational belief in original sin, and removed herself from the emotional currents of revivalism that still washed through the Connecticut Valley, a region haunted by Jonathan Edward's righteous spirit.

A century before Dickinson's day, from his Northampton pulpit Edwards stirred the soul of the valley into a Great Awakening. There was a streak of Edwards which stuck in Dickinson: his passion for the meaning-laden world and the informing word. Edwards's rhapsodic responses to nature anticipated Emerson's pantheism. "The beauty of the world consists wholly of sweet mutual consents, either within itself or with the supreme being," wrote Edwards. "As to the corporeal world, though there are many other sorts of consents, yet the sweetest and most charming beauty of it is its resemblance of spiritual beauties."[131] Edwards's words also anticipate Dickinson's passionately interpretative response to nature, though she repudiated Edwards's stern God.[132] Like Edward Taylor, the seventeenth-century Puritan preacher and secret poet of nearby Westfield, Dickinson kept her rhapsodies (and her heresies) to herself.

There was something dark, wild, possessed about Emily Dickinson—the *heft* of her language, the slash and dash of her punctuation—that shocked Higginson and mystified other more cautious and rational Bostonians who wished to leave behind these echoes of darker Puritanism. Yet Howells understood when he reviewed her poetry in 1891. Dickinson's isolation, he said, was a "natural evolution, or involution, from tendencies inherent in the New England, or the Puritan, spirit."[133]

Dickinson, in the manner of Puritan New England, dwelt in "possibilities," amid the mysteries and meanings of nature. She has been compared to Anne Bradstreet, but she is closer in spirit to those emotional rebels against Puritan paternalism, those real and imaginary women, Anne Hutchinson and Hester Prynne.[134] Alan Tate might have been right: "Cotton Mather would have burned [Emily Dickinson] for a witch."[135]

Like Frost's oven bird, Emily Dickinson learned "in singing not to sing," and "knew what to make of a diminished thing"—to make a muffled song of her New England.[136] More cheerily, Dickinson claims "The Robin's my Criterion for Tune."[137] More gloomily, she sees landscape and weather as metaphors for inner and outer states.

> There's a certain Slant of light,
> Winter Afternoons—
> That oppresses, like the Heft
> Of Cathedral Tunes.[138]

Cheery or gloomy, true to Puritan principles, the natural world remains a configuration of mystery through which she quested for meaning.

Dickinson traveled even less than did Thoreau; she mostly stayed in Amherst, near the Dickinson Homestead: walking within the garden and apple orchard in two acres around her house, or the eleven acres of fields across the street, leading to Amherst College. In time she further circumscribed this narrow orbit. In 1879 she wrote to Higginson: "I do not cross my father's ground to any house or town."[139] Finally, she sentenced herself to the solitary confinement of her corner bedroom, removed from Amherst's comings and goings.

> Sweet hours have perished here,
> This is a timid room—
> Within its precincts hopes have played
> Now fallow in the tomb.[140]

Dickinson's spiritual journey crossed the more expansive and dangerous landscape of the mind. She mapped "internal differences / Where the Meanings, are."[141] In doing so, she set herself deep in, and defined herself sharply against, the American Puritan tradition which began in Boston and, to paraphrase Frost, realized itself vaguely westward.

ROBERT FROST

In 1916 Robert Frost told an interviewer that his literary theory was based upon New England Puritanism. The root source of the term "Puritan" implied, as Lawrance Thompson put it, "purification from unscriptural and corrupt forms of ceremonies, renewal of original meanings in words, disciplined simplification of human responses." Perhaps, then, it is no surprise that Robert Frost found his way in 1916 to Amherst, the Puritan town which became his adopted home. At his eightieth birthday party in 1954, held in Amherst's Lord Jeffery Inn, it was noted that Frost had spent twenty-three of his last thirty-eight years living in Amherst and teaching at Amherst College. "What begins in delight ends in wisdom," Frost told his admiring audience, applying his definition of poetry to his Amherst experience.[142]

However, Frost left evidence of few poetic delights in Amherst. No body of Frost poetry represents his long stays in this town; instead, his association with Amherst is illustrated by conflicting convictions. Amherst College's new president, Alexander Meiklejohn, first invited Frost to teach there in 1917. Frost's seminars on poetry were then based on Emerson's assumption that form grew out of need; however, he soon became suspicious of Meiklejohn's liberalism, which allowed latitude for Amherst students to modify college traditions. By January 1919 Frost, tired of Meiklejohn's encouragement of student self-expression, resigned. In a letter to a friend, Frost explained:

> I discovered what the Amherst Idea was that is so much talked of, and got amicably out. The Amherst Idea as I had it in so many words from its high custodian is this: 'Freedom for taste and intellect.' Freedom from what? 'Freedom from every prejudice in favor of state home church morality, etc.' I am too much a creature of prejudice to stay . . . [and] listen to such stuff.[143]

For Frost, the new Amherst Idea of Meiklejohn lacked the Puritan rigor of the old Amherst Idea. Even Emily Dickinson, the "belle of Amherst," was suspect. Frost spoke of his admiration for Dickinson, but he wondered if "she gave up the technical struggle too easily."[144] Despite his reservations, however, in 1922, after Meiklejohn had been fired, Frost returned to Amherst to teach and to resume his struggle, in the old high way of Amherst Puritanism, against modernist heresies. Along with a course in American literary rebels, he taught a course called "Judgments," in opposition to "Meiklejaundice."[145]

In 1948 a Doctor of Letters was awarded Frost by Amherst College and he was appointed Simpson Lecturer in Literature, a position he held for the rest of his life. In October 1963, after Frost's death, groundbreaking ceremonies for the Robert Frost Library at Amherst College were held. President Kennedy, at whose inauguration Frost had read in 1960, spoke of poetry and power. "Because of Mr. Frost's life and work . . . our hold on this planet has increased."[146] What began in debate ended in Amherst's wise adoption of Robert Frost as one of its own. The town's holding of major poets had been increased by one.

ROBERT FRANCIS

When Frost bought his first house in Amherst in 1932, a fellow poet and Amherst resident, Robert Francis, who had not yet met Frost, rejoiced in light verse.

> Robert Frost is here in town again . . .
> Best of all—you've heard?—he comes to stay.
> This is his home now. He is here for good.
> To leave us now would be running away.
> (I too would stay forever if I could.)[147]

Francis once described Frost as "America's greatest living poet." Frost in turn graciously saw Francis as "the best neglected poet."[148]

Humble Francis, however, did not claim even this much for himself. "I am a poet, minor. Or I try."[149]

Unlike Frost, Francis did claim Amherst as his poetic territory; there he set his verse; there he remained, "forever." He became a "local poet" with a defiance, for his "local" did not mean provincial. The term "could mean that his poems have roots as well as blossoms."[150] In eight volumes of poetry and four volumes of prose, Francis shaped a worthy poetry of place and claimed his own place in the tradition of Dickinson and Frost. Francis demonstrated that the values they embodied, poetic and philosophical, were still alive late in the twentieth century.

Amherst today—the center of a five-college network which includes Amherst College, the University of Massachusetts, Hampshire College, Mount Holyoke, and Smith College—remains a cultural center which partially defines itself by its self-conscious independence from Boston culture. Like Dickinson and Frost before him, Francis took what he needed from Boston and left the rest behind as he headed for the western Massachusetts hills to find himself and define his art.

Francis was born in 1901 in Pennsylvania, the son of a Baptist minister who moved from one church and state to another, but Francis was shaped by Boston and its surrounding towns. In 1910 he spent a year in Dorchester, then ten formative years in Medford, just outside the city. Boston and what it stood for would stay with Francis always. Emerson remained a model and guide for Francis, as had the Concord sage for Dickinson and Frost. "Emerson is my master," noted Francis in his journal, in 1936.[151] Emerson was more Concord than Boston for Francis, but his reading of Santayana's *The Last Puritan* in the early 1950s brought Boston proper back to him, as his journal entry indicates.

> Santayana himself as well as his people in the book touch me in all
> sorts of ways. Boston, Harvard, poetry, philosophy. The year that
> this great novel was published (1936) was the year of my first book
> of poems; and in reviewing it for the monitor someone said it was
> as if the Last Puritan had written it.[152]

However, Francis's Puritanism was less moral than aesthetic. He echoed Frost when he wrote, "It must be the puritan in me that responds to the challenge to purify the language of the tribe."[153]

Francis drew his Puritanism not only from his father—who would become pastor of the South Amherst Congregational Church, the center of Amherst's waning Puritanism—but also from Harvard. Francis attended Harvard as a day student; he graduated in 1923. In the tradition of Henry Adams, Francis claims to have learned nothing in his undergraduate years. "Harvard left me absolutely free to work out my own salvation, as work it out, slowly and gropingly, I would have to do if any salvation were to be mine."[154] This "negative" gift of freedom to search for personal "salvation" is, of course, the most valuable lesson Harvard *could* teach: Francis's life after Harvard became a serious but not unplayful quest for significance. In the tradition of Thoreau, another dissatisfied Harvard man, Francis set off in his own direction, turned his back on Boston's conventional patterns of success and marched to his own rhythms.

After a year abroad, Francis became a student at the Harvard School of Education, to prepare himself to become a high-school teacher. Upon graduation in 1926, he was advised by a woman in Harvard's placement bureau to accept a teaching job in Amherst. "Amherst was a good place to come from, she said. She meant, of course, that it was a good place to go to in order to come from. I was to find it a good place to go to stay."[155]

Francis's career as a teacher, like Thoreau's, was short-lived, but his commitment to Amherst was complete. In 1926 Amherst was full of poetic echoes and pastoral emblems for Francis. Everyone in town knew where "Emily" was buried. The Agricultural College sold fresh dairy products to residents. In Amherst, centered in poetry and pastoralism, Francis sought "nature," "leisure," and "solitude."

Francis modeled his life after Thoreau's; in 1940 Francis moved into a "small, one-man (but not one-room) house, . . . three and a half miles north-northwest of Amherst center." There, a withdrawn stoic, he devoted his life to writing, his holy calling. If

"Emily" had her oddities, so too did Francis become an Amherst poet-eccentric: the poet who dwelled in the woods, along with a hen named Gladys, who lived in his fireplace. With characteristic humility, Francis stated the goal of his quest. "Thoreau said he went to Walden to drive life into a corner. My motive was less ambitious: to drive only my life into a corner."[156]

Francis's poetry drew upon the plain speech, the careful observation of natural phenomena and the insistent moral interpretation he found in Thoreau, Dickinson, and Frost. In the lowly but tenacious juniper bush, for example, he saw a model for his own life. His house, named early in World War II, became "Fort Juniper," a symbol of retreat from the world's terrors.

> From where I live, from windows on four sides
> I see four common kinds of evergreen:
> White pine, pitch pine, cedar, and juniper.
> The last is less than tree. It hugs the ground.
> It would be last for any wind to break
> If wind could break the others. . . .
> Here is my faith, my vision, my burning bush.
> It will burn and never be consumed.
> It will be here long after I have gone,
> Long after the last farmer sleeps. And since
> I speak for it, its silence speaks for me.[157]

Robert Francis carried forward a poetic tradition inspired by the Puritan concern for salvation. He too saw his life as a quest for significance and his poetry as a spiritual autobiography. In the Puritan manner of self-examination, Francis kept an exacting journal, a record of his days and ways, a fluctuating chart of his chills and fevers. Francis also wrote an autobiography, *The Trouble With Francis*, which reveals his desperate loneliness and his undeterred mission in the face of unrelieved poverty. Balancing Francis's devotion to Amherst as a symbolic landscape is his sense of its repressive moral atmosphere. Francis tells us that he did not reveal or act upon his homosexual impulses because "I live in a New

England town," where such things were neither admitted nor allowed.[158]

Robert Francis assigned himself the role of custodian of Amherst's poetic tradition. He modeled much of his poetry after Robert Frost's work and he paid constant tribute to Emily Dickinson's personal and poetic examples. Near the end of Francis's *Collected Poems* he includes an imaginary dialogue between Dickinson and Frost. The poets are represented as trees, set between Dickinson's grave (with "Called Back" carved on her tombstone) and Amherst College's new Robert Frost Library ("a fort of learning"). Francis's poem, "Two Ghosts," articulates the persistence of the New England poetic tradition, for both Dickinson and Frost, in Francis's myth as in fact, wrote a poetry of calling, of nature, of divination, of pain and formal feeling.

Amherst. Dark hemlocks conspiring at the First Church midway between the Mansion on Main Street and the back entrance (the escape door) of the Lord Jeffery Inn. Between one and two after midnight

R   Someone is here. Angelic? Or demonic?

E   Someone less than someone.

R   Emily?

E   How could you divine me?

R   An easy guess, you who were ghost while living and haunting us ever since.

E   A ghost to catch a ghost?

R   A poet to catch a poet.

E   And you—you must be the Robert who said:
"The petal of the rose it was that stung."
Or did *I* say it?

R   We both have said it now.

E   Sweet the bee—but rose is sweeter—
Quick his sting—but rose stings deeper—
Bee will heel—rose petal—never

R   You talk of bees who were yourself white moth.

E   Seldom flitting so far from home.
Oftener the other way to touch my stone.
Have you seen it?

R   *Called Back?*

E   The stone keeps calling me back.

R   I would have cut a different epitaph.
    Called on. Called ahead.

E   But on and back are both one now, aren't they?

R   My stone is not a stone but a heap, a pile—

E   Why should immortality be so stony?

R   —a mass, a mausoleum, a mock mountain over there. Have you
    seen it?

E   Oh, I took *that* for a factory or fort.

R   Fort of learning, factory of scholars.
    And my name cut deep in granite. Have you seen?

E   I never dared to go so far—so near.

R   "Less than someone," you said. I say, "More than someone."
    You are a name now, Emily. . . .[159]

RICHARD WILBUR

Though both Frost and Francis perpetuated New England Puritanism in the purity of their language and the ideological structures of their verses, Francis, the "happy pessimist," was more consistently playful.[160] No one, however, could argue that Richard Wilbur's poetry has been characterized by imitation. Wilbur, too, found his own way into the New England Puritan poetic tradition, where he shaped his unique voice.

Born in New York in 1921 and reared in rural New Jersey, Wilbur first met his fated poetic landscape when he was an undergraduate at Amherst College. It took the disorders he encountered as a soldier in World War II, however, to hurt him into poetry. After war service, Wilbur went to Harvard for a master's degree and stayed to teach. He also became a part of a circle of poets—including John Ciardi, Richard Eberhart, and Archibald MacLeish—and a contributor to Cambridge's Poets' Theater of the 1950s.

Wilbur also distinguished himself in the company of the best poets of his generation: Robert Lowell, Theodore Roethke, and John Berryman. But while they were experimenting with formal dislocations in life and art, Wilbur sought, as the titles of his early volumes suggest, *Ceremony*, an ordered celebration of *Things of This World*. If Lowell could be seen to represent the strain of worldly repudiation in New England Puritanism, Wilbur embodies its prophetic exhilaration, its celebration of God's presence in nature's emblems.

A formalist like Frost, Wilbur found in poetic certainty and ceremony "a partial and provisional attempt to establish relations between things."[161] Eventually, after a career of teaching at Harvard, Wellesley, and Wesleyan, Wilbur discovered his fitting poetic emblems in Cummington, Massachusetts, a rural town west of Amherst. In the manner of Dickinson, Frost, or Francis, but in his own style, Wilbur there sought significance in "the beautiful changes" of every living thing. In "April 5, 1974," nature presents Wilbur, another New England poet who is questing for meanings while pretending to stroll, with a mystery to tease thought, a wonder to inspire revelation.

> The air was soft, the ground still cold.
> In the dull pasture where I strolled
> Was something I could not believe.
> Dead grass appeared to slide and heave,
> Though still too frozen-flat to stir,
> And rocks to twitch, and all to blur.
> What was this rippling of the land?
> Was matter getting out of hand
> And making free with natural law?
> I stopped and blinked, and then I saw
> A fact as eerie as a dream.
> There was a subtle flood of steam
> Moving upon the face of things.
> It came from standing pools and springs
> And what of snow was still around;
> It came from winter's giving ground
> So that the freeze was coming out,
> As when a set mind, blessed by doubt,
> Relaxes into mother-wit.
> Flowers, I said, will come out it.[162]

Such a poem—in which natural facts, eerie as a dream, reverberate with implications—could have been set outside New England, but Richard Wilbur insists his poetry should be seen within the New England poetic tradition. Wilbur's "fact" echoes Frost's "fact"— "the sweetest dream that labor knows."[163] Robert Frost, he has said, "staved off confusion by taking a stand inside a New England rural culture which . . . possessed a certain vitality." An outsider, like Frost, who made (or composed) New England into his home ground, Wilbur too is "a New Englander by choice. I've decided on a region which gives me a feeling of belonging somewhere."[164]

West of Boston, Richard Wilbur has found his humble place in the universe, as he playfully explains in "On Having Mis-Identified a Wild Flower."

> A thrush, because I'd heard wrong,
> Burst rightly into song
> In a world not vague, not lonely,
> Not governed by me only.[165]

THOREAU'S journeys from civilization into nature link these three places in New England, places which surround Boston and extend the city's sphere of influence. As a young man, Thoreau traveled north of Boston, seeking freedom and revelation by following the route of the Concord and Merrimack rivers. In *The Maine Woods* and in "Ktaadn," his essay on his climb up Maine's stark mountain, Thoreau arrived at an epiphany of indifferent nature, "nature primitive—powerful gigantic aweful and beautiful, Untamed forever."[166] Later, after several journeys south of Boston recorded in *Cape Cod*, Thoreau confronted the brutal exhilarations of a nature which tossed the drowned bodies of immigrants along its shores, then washed those shores clean. But Thoreau's true symbolic direction was westward, on his errand into the wilderness, following "the prevailing tendency of my countrymen," as he put it in "Walking."[167]

Santayana's Nathaniel Alden, emerging from his Beacon Street home in *The Last Puritan*, always turned left, or east, toward King's

Chapel and Boston's center city. Thoreau would have had no use for such a man, but he would have understood. "We go eastward to realize history and study the works of art and literature, retracing the steps of the race; we go westward as into the future, with a spirit of enterprise and adventure," wrote Thoreau.[168] Ironically, Nathaniel Alden might have been more at home than Thoreau west of Boston, in the conservative Amherst of his and Emily Dickinson's day. Thoreau's true west was more idea, his vision of transcendence, than actual place.

Of course Thoreau had to travel in both directions to establish his symbolic dialectic. "Eastward I go only by force; but westward I go free." The actual route of Thoreau's travels—"not a circle, but a parabola"—is less important than that these trips follow radial routes away from civilization: commercial Concord or Boston. On the other hand, Thoreau, no Lewis or Clark, circumscribed his journeys well within the confines of what might be called the Boston Idea. For Thoreau was no casual saunterer along New England's rivers, woods, and coastal beaches. He was on a quest for spiritual enlightenment, in the best Puritan tradition. "For every walk is a sort of crusade, preached by some Peter the Hermit in us, to go forth and reconquer this Holy Land from the hands of the Infidels." Thoreau, however, was on no heresy hunt; his God was diffused into all natural things. Yet his journeys were no less quests through symbolic landscapes. "The West of which I speak is but another name for the Wild; and what I have been preparing to say is, that in Wilderness is the preservation of the World."[169]

Reflecting on the American "spirit of place," D. H. Lawrence noted, "Men are free when they belong to a living, organic, *believing* community, active in fulfilling some unfulfilled, perhaps unrealized purpose."[170] Such was the purpose sought by the Puritan founders of *New* England. Their sense of mission configured the Boston Idea: the establishment of a city upon a hill whose beacon casts an exemplary, wide-reaching light. Though England's seventeenth-century political turmoils implied that old England was not guided by New England's higher lights, places nearer Boston would fall under its religious and cultural glare.

More parabola than circle, a symbolic landscape arcs around Boston from Frost's autumnal forests, north of Boston, to Henry Beston's storm-battered outermost beach on Cape Cod, south of Boston. Westward, into the Pioneer Valley and Berkshires, where Melville encountered in Hawthorne a "shock of recognition," lay the extension of the old Boston Idea of spiritual community and culture in Puritan Amherst and its subversion in the poetry of Emily Dickinson.

Contemporary writers in Greater Boston and beyond renew their covenants with such symbolic landscapes by describing, directly or obliquely, their spiritual quests. The increasingly crowded territory radiating from Boston—such areas were designated Metro North, Metro West, Metro South in the 1980s—still holds burning bushes, still yields sermons in stone, still flows with emblematic waters.

8

A New England Genius:
TRADITION AND REVISION IN
THE BOSTON OF T. S. ELIOT,
ROBERT LOWELL, AND OTHERS

In the autumnal blue of your church-hooded New England, the porcupine sharpens its golden needles against Bostonian bricks to a point of needless blinding shine.

—JOSEPH BRODSKY,
"Elegy: For Robert Lowell"

THE BOSTON IDEA—of polity, of moral mission, of spiritual quest—began in settlements along the Massachusetts coastline, from Cape Cod to Cape Ann, before it took root in Shawmut, which became Boston. Secure in its Boston-Cambridge base, from Beacon Hill to Harvard, it spread a hundred miles in all land directions, taking territories like an occupying army, infusing itself into the nation's notion of itself. Constantly questioned, amplified, and revised, the Boston Idea was further energized and revitalized by newcomers, native and immigrant. Multiple variations along its radial lines of influence were registered in generations of tales and poems. Perhaps its most eloquent documents, examples of Boston's

266

unflagging will to renew itself, have been produced by two descendants of its first settlers: T. S. Eliot and Robert Lowell. As in the case of Henry Adams, Eliot and Lowell were children of Boston's Puritan, patrician tradition; like Adams they rebelled against, but never abandoned the Boston Idea. In "Tradition and the Individual Talent," Eliot noted that "the historical sense . . . involves a perception, not only of the pastness of the past, but of its presence"—and he spoke of the writer's need to shape that tradition to his own imaginative needs.[1] Eliot and Lowell reexamined and renewed Boston's literary tradition with their considerable, individual talents.

On 5 December 1988, at Harvard's Sanders Theater, the literary community of Cambridge and Boston observed the centennial of T. S. Eliot's birth. It was something of a family gathering, a memorial for one of its own. Though Eliot was born outside Boston, stayed in the city briefly and became an exile, he was, beginning and end, a distinctly Boston writer.

Eliot entered Harvard in 1906, and he completed his baccalaureate requirements in three years, though his degree was granted in 1910. He was editor of the *Advocate,* member of the Signet Society, the Stylus, and the Southern Club; Eliot also wrote the Class Ode. He earned an M.A. in 1910 and, after a year in Europe, he worked for three years on a doctorate in philosophy. In 1914 a fellowship took him to Oxford. Eliot returned to Harvard in 1932–33 as the Norton Professor of Poetry. At Harvard's 1947 commencement, Eliot was awarded an L.L.D. In 1955 Eliot made his final public appearance at Harvard, a benefit reading for the *Advocate,* at Sanders.[2]

Thirty-three years later, friends, students, writers, and appreciative readers again came to Sanders to listen to his words. They celebrated him in poetry, song, reminiscences, and scenes from his plays. The evening concluded with a series of slides, images of Eliot, accompanied by his recorded voice reading the concluding section of "Little Gidding," from *Four Quartets:* "The end is where we start from."[3] The Boston-Cambridge literary community defines itself in such memorials, and the definition is particularly sharp when it honors those poets who find Boston, measured by Boston standards, wanting.

Eliot has said that the "emotional springs" of his poetry come from America.[4] Boston and Harvard, with their Puritan heritage, were central sources for Eliot's values and poetry. In turn, Boston, an early model for his waste land, is colored by the several shades of grey in Eliot's imagination.

NEAR the beginning of his career as a poet, T. S. Eliot acknowledged the shaping presence of the New England literary tradition. In a memorial essay on Henry James, published in *The Little Review* in 1918, two years after James's death, Eliot called attention to James's "Hawthorne Aspect."

> The point is that James is positively a continuator of the New England genius; that there is a New England genius, which has discovered itself in a very small number of people in the middle of the nineteenth century—and which is *not* significantly present in the writings of Miss Sara Orne Jewett, Miss Eliza White, or the Bard of Appledore, whose name I forget. I mean whatever we associate with certain purlieus of Boston, with Concord, with Salem, and Cambridge, Mass.: notably Emerson, Thoreau, Hawthorne and Lowell.[5]

Lowell, in this case, is James Russell Lowell, "the beloved Ambassador," but Eliot defines and sustains a regional heritage of literary achievement, a thread that runs from Hawthorne through James Russell Lowell and Henry Adams to Robert Lowell. Robert Lowell and Eliot, according to Lowell, set themselves against their stuffy ancestors. Lowell records a telling moment when they walked together through Harvard Yard; we hear Lowell say, wistful for a lost heritage, "Ah Tom, one muse, one music, had one the luck."[6]

T. S. Eliot and Robert Lowell were sons of fathers who, though moderately successful, had been overwhelmed by the greater success of their fathers; both poets felt themselves the end products of played-out lines of New England Brahmin achievement. Each was shaped by a strong mother who reared her son to the strict, high-minded religious and cultural standards of Boston. Thus, becoming a poet was a means of simultaneously embracing international literary culture and subverting parochial family expectations. Eliot and Lowell eventually rejected the religions of their mothers and the narrow proprieties of their fathers, opting for Anglo-Catholicism and Catholicism. Both became exiles from their families' native grounds, but both came home again to write poems which mocked provincial pretensions, poems which reminded Greater Bostonians that they had abandoned the high and holy purpose of the settlement. Though Eliot and Lowell set themselves against the grain of stone cold Boston, after the example of Emerson, they nevertheless wrote in the rigorously self-conscious, Puritan mode. Each composed his spiritual autobiography in oblique poems; each wrote parables of conversion, calls to a new life. Each revised the Boston literary tradition and reinvented Boston in his works.

A "halo of dignity" is bestowed by the Boston literary tradition which Eliot invokes in his tribute to James. It rests over "Longfellow, Margaret Fuller and her crew," those who, along with others, insisted on the "leisure" necessary for true culture. In distinguishing these writers from others who affirmed the strenuous life of culture and commerce, Eliot's Boston again served as a conscience—this time for the bustling, bullying America of Teddy Roosevelt.[7]

James, for Eliot, was part of a "literary aristocracy" which emerged from America's cultural center: Greater Boston. At the same time, these writers were alien from most of what Boston society represented, as Eliot makes clear in his withering assessment. "The society of Boston was and is quite uncivilized but refined beyond the point of civilization." In Eliot's myth of place, Boston culture nurtures with one hand and thwarts with the other. Hawthorne, for Eliot, as he was for James, was a representative man: "the soil which produced [Hawthorne] with his essential flavor is the soil which produced, just as inevitably, the environment which stunted him."⁸ Boston was characterized, Eliot might have said, by its negative capability.

Eliot was born in St. Louis in 1888. Though he became a British citizen in 1927, Eliot's commitments to Boston and its North Shore were deep, abiding, and determining. During his boyhood Eliot's family summered on Cape Ann, in a house in Gloucester built by his father in 1896.⁹ Eliot's paternal grandfather, William Greenleaf Eliot, called "the Saint of the West" by Emerson, spread Boston Unitarianism to the frontier. Eliot's protective mother, Charlotte Champe Eliot, who published a reverential biography of her father-in-law, imparted Boston Unitarianism, while his father, Henry Ware Eliot, Jr., imparted propriety. Eliot repudiated this heritage, as would Lowell; both poets rejected parents who, ignoring good and evil, instead revered, in Eliot's words, what was "done" and "not done." At the same time, again like Lowell, Eliot took pride in his family's deep American roots. Eliot once said he imagined himself at home in pre-1830 America, when the nation seemed "a family extension."¹⁰ Then—before the full impact of nineteenth century industrialization and immigration violated this "family" unity—Eliot believed Boston had been a homogeneous and coherent culture, untouched by the dislocations of the modern waste land. Boston, then, was at once Eliot's lost dream of cultural coherence and a daunting place of strict manners and social conformity.

When Eliot studied at Harvard, he came home again to Greater Boston, to the first place of the Eliots in America. His ancestor Andrew Eliot had moved from East Coker to Salem, then settled in Beverly, where he became town clerk in 1690. He may have been a judge at the Salem witch trials, tying Eliot and Hawthorne to the same grim strain of New England Puritanism.

In the established style of other writers whose families had Harvard "houses" named after them—Adams, Eliot, and Lowell—Eliot scorned Boston's claims for cultural ascendancy. Boston was still "a family extension," for his uncle, Christopher Rhodes Eliot, was a prominent Unitarian minister in the city and another cousin, Charles W. Eliot, was president of Harvard. But young

Tom Eliot's family feelings fluctuated in Boston's chill cultural climes.

Eliot alluded to James and mocked Boston in "Portrait of a Lady." In this early poem an assured Boston *grand dame,* at ease amid her bric-a-brac, gives advice to the poet who wonders, "should I have the right to smile?"[11] In another early poem, Eliot satirized the self-referential provinciality of Beacon Hill matrons who limited themselves to the Boston newspaper that flattered their class. "The readers of the *Boston Evening Transcript* / Sway in the wind like a field of ripe corn."[12] In "Cousin Nancy," Eliot burlesqued the alleged link between Boston society and the New England literary tradition. Miss Nancy Ellicott "Rode across the hills and broke them— / The barren New England hills— / Riding to hounds / Over the cow-pasture," while "upon the glazed shelves kept watch / Matthew and Waldo, guardians of the faith, / The army of unalterable law."[13]

These poems successfully distanced Eliot, Harvard student, from the grasp of his well-placed, extended Boston family. Given Eliot's sense of propriety, his reverence for the New England tradition, and his respect for Arnold and Emerson, those "guardians of the faith," however, it is clear that Eliot protested too much. Just as the poet was granted easy entry into Brahmin drawing rooms, so too was Eliot part of what he caricatured. Later, reviewing Henry Adams's *Education,* Eliot clearly identified with those who have been burdened by conscience and driven by self-improvement, those apprehensive creatures hobbled by what Eliot called "the Boston doubt."[14]

Eliot developed this figure of the timorous inquirer in "The Love Song of J. Alfred Prufrock," a poem which may satirize both Boston drawing rooms and himself.[15] There, Eliot's persona wanders "through certain half-deserted streets, . . . Streets that follow like a tedious argument / Of insidious intent / To lead you to an overwhelming question." The speaker lacks the courage to frame such a question, so he settles for the kind of mannered, pretentious chatter Eliot overheard in Beacon Hill drawing rooms. "In the room the women come and go / Talking of Michelangelo." Ever afraid "to force the moment to its crisis," the speaker realizes that the mermaids do not sing to him.[16]

This dramatic monologue derives from the same self-irony he expressed in being a Boston Eliot:

> How unpleasant to meet Mr. Eliot!
> With his features of clerical cut,
> And his brow so grim
> And his mouth so prim
> And his conversation, so nicely
> Restricted to What Precisely
> And If and Perhaps and But.[17]

However, Boston meant more than manners to T. S. Eliot.

Lyndall Gordon's biography of Eliot describes his 1914 spiritual crisis, when he had returned from Paris to Harvard to study philosophy. It was then that Eliot began writing religious poetry. Though cool to institutional Christianity, Eliot became something of a visionary in the New England tradition of literary mystics, of Emerson and Thoreau, whose writings subverted and transcended Boston's stiff manners and rationalist values. Certainly Eliot saw religion in what might be called a Boston dialectic as he moved toward his formal conversion to the Church of England in 1927. As he noted in the early 1920s, "There are only 2 things—Puritanism and Catholicism. You are one or the other."[18] Such a choice was particularly evident in Boston after 1830, when immigrants from Catholic Ireland, then from Italy, began to polarize the city into religious and ethnic enclaves. Eliot made his own synthesis of this cultural heritage by becoming a Puritan Anglo-Catholic. As a Harvard freshman in 1938, Robert Lowell, who would become a Puritan Roman Catholic, recognized the Boston basis of Eliot's Anglicanism. It looked to Lowell like harrying, New England Calvinism.[19]

By 1930 Eliot, who had fled the confines of Boston in 1914, began to acknowledge Massachusetts as his ancestral home, particularly Cape Ann, evoked in *Ash Wednesday*.[20] His long-standing Boston friend, Emily Hale, embodied Boston's intelligence and grace. In *The Dry Salvages* Eliot recalled Andrew Eliot's 1669 crossing to the New World. *East Coker* brought the poet back to that place in England from which the Eliots had sailed to America. Like Hawthorne before him, who made his pilgrimage to England's Boston, Eliot retraced his family's route to seek the source of his being. "Home is where one starts from."[21] Though St. Louis was Eliot's place of birth, his ancestral birthplace was East Coker. Eliot's cultural birthplace was Boston.

Following the examples of Hawthorne and James, Eliot made his journey to England in the persona of a New England Puritan, combining his grand tour with his spiritual pilgrimage.[22] In so doing, Eliot placed himself deep in the New England tradition. Like James, Eliot too has a "Hawthorne Aspect": a sense of history, an eye for buried sins, a sense of place, a feel for symbolic reverberations, a sense of family, an ear for the resonance of abandoned high purpose. He also shared Hawthorne's mystical and prophetic sense of the future, along with his need for expiation, for release from past and place, his desire to transcend family and home—his will to be born anew.

Eliot's *The Waste Land* is based upon an aesthetic theory of detachment which is articulated in his essay "Tradition and the Individual Talent." There, "the progress of an artist" is seen to depend on "a continual extinction of personality," his transcendence from biography, geography, and history.[23] Invoking the myth of the Fisher King's blighted land, in need of a Deliverer, *The Waste Land* moves toward depersonalization and abstraction. As Helen Gardner says, "there are no characters in the strict sense, no persons, and in the end the city itself dissolves."[24]

The city, of course, is London, the center of modern paralysis for Eliot; his "Unreal City" is a version of Augustine's Earthly City, far from the City of God.[25] However, *The Waste Land* also echoes Eliot's Boston, the city whose winding streets he wandered with spiritual intent. In 1914, in Boston at age twenty-six, Eliot wrote three visionary fragments, meditations emphasizing conversion experiences, which he drew upon in writing *The Waste Land*. Rather than accept this poem as mythic, abstract, and impersonal, it can be reread as an oblique autobiographical statement, one which places Eliot in the main line of New England visionaries, one which subsumes "Boston" into "London."[26] Tradition, then, for Eliot, is more than inheritance; it is an act of creation, a *personal* fusion of time past and time present. Tradition becomes art; "the historical sense involves not only the pastness of the past, but of its presence." Even when Boston was part of Eliot's past, it remained a living presence in his mind and poetry. Pious and proper Boston is reprocessed by his imagination into a modern landscape of anomie and anxiety.

ELIOT's relations with Boston-Cambridge were brief, tangential, and metaphoric, but Robert Lowell's mind and art were directly shaped by Boston culture. Like Eliot, Lowell valued Boston's negative capability, the city's passion for moral self-examination. We cannot walk its streets without recalling his poetry. For Helen Vendler, "the Boston State House, the Shaw Memorial, Beacon Street, the Boston Common, the Public Garden, the King's Chapel Burying Ground . . . are different now because they are wreathed, invisibly but powerfully, in Lowell's lines."[27] More than anyone in his time, Robert Lowell has given Boston a voice: at once evocative, angry, burdened, nostalgic, and moral. Lowell's Boston poetry constitutes his spiritual autobiography, his record of the growth of a poet's soul in relation to his shaping *place*. Lowell's Boston is distinguished by its resonant history, its moral idealism, and its failure to fulfill its high mission.

BEFORE he was anything else, Robert Trail Spence Lowell IV was a Lowell. He was born in 1917, behind the brownstone pillars of his grandfather Wilson's home at 18 Chestnut Street, "high on Beacon Hill," at the center of Brahmin Boston.[28] For Lowell, Boston meant family, tradition, and culture; these were the defining, enriching, and oppressive elements of his life. Lowell would often return to these significant places, the setting of his birth and the site of his early childhood, for they held the secrets to his identity. He identified with Henry Adams's ambivalence about the Brahmin heritage of great expectations.

I too was born under the shadow of the Boston State house, and under Pisces, the fish, on the first of March 1917. America was entering the First World War and was about to play her part in the downfall of four empires. At this moment, the sons of most of the old, aristocratic, Republican Boston families were waiting on their doorsteps like spent hounds. They were, these families and sons, waiting and hoping for a second wind. James Michael Curley was out of jail and waiting for a mandate from the people to begin the first of his many terms as Mayor of Boston. Nothing from now on was going to go quite as expected—even downhill.[29]

Here Lowell drew upon the example of *The Education of Henry Adams* to establish himself as a detached observer of the Yankee-Celt passion play, taking a neutral tone toward the Irish, but dismissing his own kind as "spent hounds," panting for an unlikely second wind in a race they had already lost to the immigrants.

For all that, being a Lowell gave Robert identity, authority, a tradition to articulate and repudiate, as other poets have noted. Elizabeth Bishop spoke openly of his privilege, once reminding Lowell, "All you have to do is put down the names! And the fact that it seems significant, illustrative, American, etc. gives you, I think, the confidence you display about tackling any idea or theme *seriously,* in both writing and conversation. In some ways you are the luckiest poet I know!"[30] Seamus Heaney, who knew Lowell in his last years, reflected upon the blending of public and private, personal and familial voices in Lowell's refusal of an invitation to the White House in 1965, in the midst of the Vietnam war.

He spoke at that time with a dynastic as well as an artistic voice, recalling how both sides of his family had a long history of service to the *rem publicam*, and this preoccupation with ancestry was a constant one. From beginning to end, his poems called up and made inquisition of those fathers who had shaped him and the world he inhabited. . . . [Lowell's voice conjured] an "unblemished Adam" from what he was later to call "the unforgivable landscape."[31]

Brahmin Boston was the cultural landscape against which Lowell rebelled, the territory which he exploited, the native ground of his poetic vision.

Lowell was the issue of two long lines of family privilege and power. A Wilson had arrived on the Mayflower. Another Wilson had married the daughter of John Stark, a general in the Revolutionary War. The Lowells, too, had had a guiding hand in New England since 1639. James Russell Lowell—poet, editor, minister—was his great-great-uncle. Amy Lowell, poet and eccentric, was his cousin, as was her brother, A. Lawrence Lowell, president of Harvard. Though the Lowell family had amassed a fortune in banking and industry, Robert's branch of that family was less affluent and influential.

Robert Lowell came to see his parents as icons of Boston in decline: his weak father stood for fading Brahmin values and his strong mother represented the feminization of Boston culture. His father, whose name he bore, was a passive figure who failed to establish his identity either in the United States Navy or as a businessman. He was a man reduced, in his son's eyes, to pathetic acts of self-affirmation; he even painted his name and rank on the garbage cans outside his 91 Revere Street home. Robert's mother, Charlotte Wilson Lowell, was determined to remind her husband and her only son of their aristocratic burdens and bearings. As her son put it, "the theme of her early married life was clear and constant and alarming: *I want to live in Boston,*" where her family could take its rightful place in the local firmament.[32]

Robert Lowell was late in realizing the implications of his name. "I never knew I was a Lowell till I was twenty."[33] When, at that age, he discovered James Russell Lowell, Robert felt "a blood-kinship" with his ancestor's opposition to the Mexican War and his pro-Union, Civil War poetry. Robert Lowell came into full consciousness of his family heritage when he saw in it elements of protest, when he found a secret escape passage behind the wall of family portraits.

Robert Lowell would also give his own stamp, rebellious and at times scandalous, to the family name and heritage. Where his mother was proud, he would mock her pretensions. Where his father was meek, he was bold, even to the point of thrashing his father, in the family's Marlborough Street home in 1936, when his father opposed Robert's engagement to a young lady considered by the Lowells to be unsuitable.[34] Robert redefined what it meant to be a Lowell, just as he reshaped our understanding of what it means to be a Bostonian.

For all of his complaints over the burdens of being a Lowell, however, Robert celebrated a model of rebelliousness *within* the family line. Raffish Amy Lowell—"big and a scandal, as if Mae West were a cousin"—served him better than dignified James Russell Lowell, for she offended his parents' sense of propriety.[35] "Amy Lowell was never a welcome subject in our household. Of course, no one spoke disrespectfully of Miss Lowell. She had been so plucky, so *formidable, so beautifully and unblushingly immense*, as Henry James might have said." Here Lowell has his fun with cousin Amy by devising a parody of a Jamesian appreciation, at the same time that he uses her example to mock the staid aesthetic and moral values of his parents. For them, Amy Lowell's poetry was too loose. They wondered, "was *poetry* what one could call Amy's loud, bossy, unladylike *chinoiserie*—her free verse!" They agreed with Robert Frost's strictures against such unkempt composition.[36] Robert Lowell emerges from this exchange with a Lowell-sanctioned, anti-Lowell artistic credo. His sense of ambivalence provided him a double perspective—at once insider and outsider—on Boston, the city which shaped him, the city which he reshaped in words.

James Russell Lowell and Amy Lowell celebrated their family name as much as they transcended its commercial associations. In the nineteenth century, the Lowells had enlarged their fortune through the introduction of the factory system in the cotton mills of Lawrence and Lowell, Massachusetts. Amy Lowell gained one version of her poetic licence—the economic freedom and the privilege of position which allowed her to become a poet—through her family name. When James Russell Lowell died in 1891, in Amy Lowell's sixteenth year, she attended his state funeral; she was impressed by his achievements as a poet and a diplomat. She too, she decided, would be "Somebody."[37] Conservative in her private life, she was a radical poet, identified with modern poetic styles—imagism and polyphonic prose. Biographer and essayist, she won the Pulitzer Prize posthumously in 1926.

In her own way, Amy Lowell passed along her determination to be somebody to Robert Lowell. In 1935, when he was a student at St. Mark's, a posh private school twenty-five miles west of Boston in Southborough, young Lowell wrote to his house Master, Richard Eberhart.

> I have been reading lately Wordsworth's "Prelude" and Amy Lowell's life of Keats. I have come across many magnificent passages in the "Prelude" and have found Amy Lowell invaluable as a critic. But what has impressed me most is the picture both give of the young poet forming into a genius, their energy, their rapid growth and above all their neverending determination to succeed.[38]

Later, Robert Lowell would register his reservations about the poetry of Amy Lowell, and he would distance himself from the poetry of James Russell Lowell. But he took what he needed from both family poets to compose himself into both a Boston Lowell and a poet, on his own terms.

JAMES Russell Lowell's life centered around the family residence, Elmwood, in Cambridge; there he was born and there he died. Lowell's Cambridge home served as a reassuring base for his sense of proper place in the world and the universe. William Dean Howells portrayed Elmwood as an emblem of civility, as Lowell's haven of culture in the pastoral mode. "He dwelt in the embowering leafage, amid the quiet of lawns and garden plots broken by few noises ruder than those from the elms and the syringas where 'The oriole clattered and the cat-bird sang.' "[39]

Elmwood, a three-story Georgian structure, built in 1767 for the last Lieutenant-Governor of the Royal Province of Massachusetts, was acquired by the Lowells in 1818; it later became the residence of the President of Harvard University. Longfellow wrote of its pastoral quiet in "The Herons of Elmwood."[40] Yet there were seldom times quiet enough to appreciate the herons in James Russell Lowell's busy and productive life. James Russell Lowell was a celebrated poet, a scholar and an editor; in 1857 he assumed Longfellow's role as professor of modern languages at Harvard and became editor of *The Atlantic Monthly*. For five years he coedited, with Charles Eliot Norton, *North American Review*. In 1877 Lowell was appointed to the American mission in Spain by President Hayes. In 1880 he became minister to England.

A man of range, vitality, and commitment, Lowell was a spokesman for the values of his class, high-minded Cambridge-Boston Brahmins. He became a propagandist of place, as his jaunty provincialism makes clear in his celebration of Massachusetts for its poetry rather than its commerce in *A Fable for Critics*. Yet, Lowell also praised the industries which were transforming Massachusetts; he even found evidence of provincial poetic beauty in "the cataract throb of her mill hearts," the trip hammers, sledges, saws, and the shuttles; such were the instruments which played his "Dear Baystate's song!"

> What though those horn hands have as yet found small time
> For painting and sculpture and music and rhyme?
> These will come in due order. . . .
> Thy songs are right epic, they tell how this rude
> Rock rib of our earth here was tamed and subdued.[41]

This style of open chauvinism—strained by allusion, bombast, and unlikely conceits—marked his poetry. Yet, as Martin Duberman points out, Lowell's strong character and estimable values emerge, even when his verses fail. It is this will to use his poetry in the service of a social ideal—Lowell saw poets as "messengers of heaven"—that gave his poetry its contemporary power and its lasting interest. Lowell was not, as he saw Thoreau, a reclusive writer who sentimentalized nature. Lowell was a man fully engaged in the society of his day.[42] He wrote against slavery—risking his writing career by taking strong abolitionist stands—and opposed the Mexican War in *The Bigelow Papers;* later he wrote in support of Lincoln's Civil War policies in *North American Review*. When he was minister to England in the 1870s, he even went against Brahmin values by supporting Charles Stewart Parnell's efforts to gain home rule for Ireland.

After Colonel Robert Gould Shaw was killed, Lowell wrote to Shaw's mother to say that he would rather that his name be known and blessed, like Shaw's, "through all the hovels of an outcast race, than blaring from all the trumpets of repute." In his "Ode Recited at the Harvard Commemoration" of Civil War dead, Lowell also reassured a nation, in inflated rhetoric addressed to "Country," personified as a weary woman:

> What words divine of lover or of poet
> Could tell our love and make thee know it,
> Among the Nations bright beyond compare?[43]

In the more subtle "Memoriae Postum," Lowell portrayed Shaw as a fallen figure of moral purity, but Lowell also expressed fear that Americans would be "heedless" of Shaw's example—the same tack Robert Lowell would later take.[44]

James Russell Lowell established a compelling voice of duty and idealism in his celebration of local values; that voice can still be detected in Robert Lowell's poetry, particularly in "For the Union Dead," a poem which also holds up the fallen soldier as an embodiment of commitment, in order to challenge the heedless living. Robert Lowell too would write in the prophetic, public tradition of Puritan Boston.[45] Though Robert Lowell had to shape authenticity from his own far less happy experience of local place, he learned a public responsibility for his poetry from his family mentor, James Russell Lowell.

AMY LOWELL was no provincial, though she too developed a deep commitment to her family and her regional place. For her, as for James Russell Lowell and Robert Lowell, family tradition was embodied in a particular place, in her case Sevenels, the family home in Brookline, Massachusetts, so named because it contained seven "L's," seven Lowells, her parents and their five children.[46] At age twenty-six, after her father's death, Amy became the mistress of Sevenels. Always the point of return from her many travels, Sevenels served as her haven for the rest of her life, "her citadel" against the assaults of a changing world that threatened her class and her chosen profession with indifference or derision.[47]

Yet she set herself against the values of her class and family by choosing to become a slightly Bohemian poet. "I belonged to the class which is not supposed to be able to produce good creative work," she said, celebrating both her class allegiance and her deviation from her class's image.[48] For all that, Amy Lowell took her family's civic responsibilities as seriously as had James Russell and, though more obliquely, as would Robert. Among other civic crusades, she led the battle to keep her beloved Boston Athenaeum from being moved from its proper perch atop Beacon Hill.[49] Amy Lowell's tribute to the Boston Athenaeum sums up her pride in her family tradition and Boston culture. For her it is a place which provides transport to other worlds of imagination, a refuge where she has passed

> Long, peaceful hours seated on the floor
> Of some retired nook, all lined with books,
> Where reverie and quiet reign supreme!

All the more reason, then, why the Athenaeum should stay where it was put in 1847.

And must they take away this treasure house,
To us so full of thoughts and memories;
To all the world beside a dismal place
Lacking in all this modern age requires
To tempt along the unfamiliar paths
And leafy lanes of old time literature?[50]

Since the Athenaeum, she insists, is "our birthright," it should remain a haven against crass modernity. For Amy Lowell, Boston's significant places, its homes and cultural emblems, must remain intact, paradoxically so that they might always provide places for imaginative escape for the city's hemmed-in sons and daughters. All the Lowell poets can be seen as preservers of sacred Boston sites—family residences, public institutions, and monuments—which resonate with symbolic significance. All the Lowell poets brought such significant places to the attention of "heedless" Bostonians.

"91 Revere Street," from Robert Lowell's *Life Studies*, is one of the great embodiments of Boston as an emblematic place, an essay which evokes, articulates, and exorcises through art a world which weighed upon him throughout his life.[51] Here Lowell begins with a place, an address, and ends with a compelling vision of the city's significance.

When the Lowells moved into their unadorned Beacon Hill townhouse, Boston was a fixed city, conscious of its cultural divisions.

In 1924 people still lived in cities. Late that summer, we bought the 91 Revere Street house, looking out on an unbuttoned part of Beacon Hill bounded by the North End slums, though reassuringly only a few blocks away from my Grandfather Wilson's brown pillared house at 18 Chestnut Street.[52]

Lowell grew up intrigued by these clashing classes and styles. His mother, however, was appalled.

My mother felt a horrified giddiness about the adventure of our address. She once said, "We are barely perched on the outer rim of the hub of decency." We were less than fifty yards from Louisburg Square, the cynosure of old historic Boston's plain-spoken, cold-roast elite—the Hub of the Hub of the Universe. Fifty yards![53]

Those fifty yards measured the gap which separated Robert Lowell from full absorption into Brahmin culture. Too far for his mother, too close for him, those fifty yards quantified his psychic and aesthetic distance from the heart of the Boston matter.

The Lowell house was dark and stiff, resounding with echoes of his mother's recriminations over his father's failures and haunted by his imperious ancestors, whose portraits gazed down from its walls. Robert was particularly fascinated by the portrait of his great-great grandfather, Mordecai Myers, resplendent in "his sanguine War of 1812 Uniform with epaulets, white breeches, and a scarlet frogged waistcoat." He held a sword. Young Robert needed to believe that this ancestor, his grandmother Lowell's grandfather, had been a romantic and daring figure. "Great-great-grandfather Mordecai! Poor sheepdog in wolf's clothing! In the anarchy of my adolescent war on my parents, I tried to make him a true wolf, the wandering Jew!" There was no ancestral or paternal sheepishness in him, the Lowell who willed himself into the persona of a wolf, a symbolic Jew, or a Catholic convert—that is, into any guise which would detach him from the flock of proper Bostonians. "Great-great-grandfather Myers had never frowned down in judgment on a Salem witch. There was no allegory in his eyes, no *Mayflower*."[54]

Robert Lowell, with allegory in *his* eyes, would discover, along with the "snobbery, fashion, habit, inertia" in the regional tradition, "maybe something nobler: a longing in New England so strong for what is not that what is not perhaps exists. Or maybe something still deeper, a peculiar strain or genius that is unkillable, inescapable."[55] In "91 Revere Street" Lowell describes how he learned to look upon Boston and the world through his own eyes, seeking a reality beyond Lowell family appearances. Lowell's search for a true father was his quest for a living heritage, a spiritual legacy. *He* supplied the terms which define his name. Out in the allegorically resonant streets and parks of Boston, Lowell learned who he was and where he lived.

As a young student in Brimmer School, Robert Lowell was surrounded by girls; he even wished to become one. Women, after all, were the source of authority and power in his own household. His mother's standards of propriety tyrannized the Lowell home. According to Jean Stafford, Lowell's first wife, his "mother put on white gloves and ran her fingers over the mantle and table tops to see if the maids had dusted properly."[56] In time Lowell came into his young manhood through an epiphany of identity, a scene in the Public Garden, that semi-private garden for Brahmin Beacon Hill and Back Bay, from which he sought release.

In his informing parable of place, "91 Revere Street," Lowell recalls his younger self, strolling with other Brimmer School students on a sunny spring afternoon, "on the polite, landscaped walks of the Public Garden." He broke away to loiter at the heavy iron fence which separates the Public Garden from Charles Street and, beyond, "the historic Boston Common, a now largely wrong-side-of-the-tracks park." Two worlds competed for the boy's attention: the polite, carefully landscaped terrain of his given ground and the raffish, exciting territory beyond the confining fence, a world which stirred his imagination.

On the Common there were mossy bronze reliefs of Union soldiers, and a captured German tank filled with smelly wads of newspapers. Everywhere there were grit, litter, gangs of Irish, Negroes, Latins. On Sunday afternoons orators harangued about Sacco and Vanzetti, while others stood about heckling and blocking the sidewalks. Keen young policemen, looking for trouble, lolled on the benches. At nightfall a police lieutenant on horseback inspected the Common. In the Garden, however, there was only Officer Lever, a single white-haired and mustached dignitary, who had once been the doorman at the Union Club. He now looked more like a member of the club.[57]

The contrast could not be more lucidly or dramatically drawn: the Common world embodied war echoes, ethnic and racial vitality, politics and latent dangers—unattainable wonders all—which beckoned across the impassable divide of Charles Street. On the other side, where he was fenced in like a statue, flourished the rigid, repressive Garden world, where even the policeman assumed the guise of a Brahmin club employee, a figure doubly empowered as a spy on wayward boys. Young Lowell struck a blow for personal liberty, literally and symbolically, against his own class. As he would later knock down his own father to detach himself from the demands of family, here the frustrated boy thrashed his peers, to detach himself from the rules and regulations of the Garden.

> One day when the saucer magnolias were in bloom, I bloodied Bulldog Binney's nose against the pedestal of George Washington's statue in full view of Commonwealth Avenue; then I bloodied Dopey Dan Parker's nose; then I stood in the center of a sundial tulip bed and pelted a little enemy ring of third-graders with wet fertilizer. Officer Lever was telephoned. Officer Lever telephoned my mother. In the presence of my mother and some thirty nurses and children, I was expelled from the Public Garden. I had been such a bad boy, I was told, "that *even* Officer Lever had been forced to put his foot down."[58]

It is really, of course, young Robert Lowell who here put his foot down, in a tulip bed, his first step away from the restraints represented by the Garden's formal enclosure, his first step toward the open world which was represented by the Common. Banished, east of Eden!

Before Lowell read "For the Union Dead" in the Public Garden at the Arts Festival in June, 1960, he told an appreciative audience of 4,000 that he had been once ejected from the Garden for misbehavior, but that "tonight partly makes up for it."[59] Finally the Garden included art and welcomed the whole range of the Boston community—proper emblems and listeners for his poem about Boston's mislaid heritage.

In "The Public Garden," a poem also from *Life Studies*, the Garden, seen from an adult perspective, becomes a waste land, a "burnished, burned-out" place where shedding mallards dive, "searching for something hidden in the muck."[60] His family's arid Brahmin world would have had Robert remain silent if his writing meant the expression of revealing, embarrassing, unrhymed or unstructured thoughts, in the manner of Amy Lowell. So writing for Lowell served as his dismissal of a Brahmin world of repression and decorum, his dive into Boston's muck, a metaphor for its repressed underlife. Lowell's later public explosions—as a conscientious objector during World War II, as a frequent mental patient, as a demonstrative husband, as an anti-Vietnam war protester— were larger reenactments of this childhood epiphany.

In "At the Indian Killer's Grave," from *Lord Weary's Castle*, Lowell set his complaint against Brahmin Boston in historical and Hawthornian contexts. The poem's epigraph, from Hawthorne, allows Lowell license to judge his ancestors, buried behind King's Chapel, as Hawthorne had judged his: guilty of a savagery which had been empowered by their excessive, self-righteous piety. "Here, also, are the veterans of King Philip's War, who burned villages and slaughtered young and old, with pious fierceness, while the godly souls throughout the land were helping with prayer." Lowell's Boston has inherited a sense of original sin from its forefathers, who lost command of the city to "strangers." Thus clouds

> Weep on the just and unjust as they will—
> For the poor dead cannot see Easter crowds
> On Boston Common or the Beacon Hill
> Where strangers hold the golden Statehouse dome
> For good and always.[61]

Lowell also found in the Puritan-Indian material of Hawthorne a fitting emblem for America's involvement in Vietnam. In his play *Endecott and the Red Cross*, Governor Endecott explains to Thomas Morton of Merry Mount that the Puritan settlers "have come here to make a new world for ourselves. / I might almost say, / we have painfully cleared the path to heaven."[62] In *My Kinsman, Major Molineux*, a dramatic version of another Hawthorne tale, Lowell shows how Boston corrupts a rural innocent.[63]

However, it was another Boston public monument—Augustus Saint-Gaudens's work honoring Colonel Robert Gould Shaw and the black soldiers of his Fifty-fourth Massachusetts Regiment, dedicated in 1897—which drew Lowell's most eloquent embodiment of Boston as image and idea. The monument commemorates the occasion when Shaw and his forces paraded past the Statehouse, in July of 1863. At that time Governor John Andrew, codifying Boston's tradition of moral idealism, told Shaw "I know not, Mr. Commander, where in all human history to any given thousand men in arms there has been committed a work at once so proud, so precious, so full of hope and glory, as the work committed to you."[64] Less than two months later Shaw and most of his men were killed in an attack on Fort Wagner, South Carolina. At that moment, Shaw was transformed into an enduring Boston myth of noble sacrifice. In the words of Peter Burchard,

> To New Englanders of his own time, Shaw, in his youthful Victorian innocence, seemed a kind of saint. In the last few months of his life, in his latter days and final hours, he had drawn on his forefathers' deep convictions and sense of duty and his own devotion to the cause which had rekindled the imaginations of New England's poets and scholars, preachers and teachers and practical men.[65]

Shaw, high-minded son of the Beacon Hill Brahmins, was singled out for honor more than his men, though Sergeant William Carney's bravery won him the Congressional Medal of Honor, the first time a black man was so honored.[66] Shaw and his men took permanent place in Boston's historical and artistic imagination with the unveiling of the memorial. William James spoke to its achievement: "after the great generals have had their monuments and long after the abstract soldiers' monuments have been reared on every village green," Saint-Gaudens's tribute to Shaw and his men would live on.[67] (Robert Lowell would pick up "abstract soldiers" in his poem on Shaw.) On Memorial Day of 1989, the remains of some soldiers from the Fifty-fifth Massachusetts Volunteer Regiment—which had lain in a ditch on Folly Island, South Carolina, for 126 years—were ceremonially reburied in Beaufort National Cemetery. Massachusetts Governor Michael Dukakis was present to restate the moral of their sacrifice. "These black soldiers of the Massachusetts Fifty-fourth and Fifty-fifth regiments fought for their own freedom: and to ensure it both for others and for their own race."[68]

The memory of this sacrifice was preserved in language as well as bronze. The Shaw Memorial is a representation of Boston's idealized image of itself: righteous, brave and reverent. Shaw embodied patrician conscience and honor. Emerson, James Russell Lowell, and others had commemorated the Massachusetts soldiers' sacrifice. On Decoration Day of 1897, Booker T. Washington praised Sergeant Carney, who was present, wearing his medal. In 1900 William Vaughn Moody used the memorial to Shaw, "this delicate and proud New England soul," to denounce imperialist annexation in the Philippines, in "Ode in a Time of Hesitation."[69] Paul Lawrence Dunbar, in "We Wear the Mask," claimed, during a period of frequent lynching of black men, that Shaw's sacrifice was wasted. In 1941 John Berryman, Robert Lowell's friend, composed "Boston Common: A Meditation upon the Hero," a poem which contrasts the noble portrayals of Shaw and his troops with a contemporary Boston street-person found sleeping under Shaw's bronze charger. For Berryman, as for others, the Shaw memorial stood as a "paradigm, pitching imagination," inspiring poetry, teasing interpretation.[70]

Lowell's poetic meditation on the Shaw memorial, "For the Union Dead," took shape in early 1960. He composed a public poem in the manner of James Russell Lowell, who, as we have seen, had in 1865 recited his own ode to the Union dead at the Harvard Commencement ceremony. J. R. Lowell:

> We welcome back our bravest and our best,—
> Ah me! not all! some come not with the rest . . .[71]

Robert Lowell also echoes the 1928 poem by Allen Tate, Lowell's former teacher, "Ode to the Confederate Dead." Tate:

> Row after row with strict impunity
> The headstones yield their names to the elements,
> The wind whirrs without recollection . . .[72]

But Robert Lowell's poem transcends James Russell Lowell's pieties and Alan Tate's concerns with Southern honor. At the time of composition, Robert Lowell had also been reading Justice Oliver Wendell Holmes's "Harvard College in the War" and William James's dedication address.[73] Lowell's poem, then, fuses literary and regional cultures with autobiography as the poet attests to the moral leveling of his city upon a hill.

Extending the imagery of "The Public Garden," Lowell finds all of Boston arid and hollow in "For the Union Dead." His childhood delight, the old South Boston Aquarium, stands in "a Sahara of snow," its "airy tanks" dry. Again Lowell yearns for the past, but now for something deeper than the recovery of an idealized childhood. "I often sigh still / for the dark downward and vegetating kingdom / of the fish and reptile." Like the mallards of "The Public Garden," Lowell searches beneath Boston's mucky surface for hidden emblems of significance. Lowell is drawn to the Boston Common, no longer a vital alternative to the Public Garden, as a place transformed into a fenced construction site, raw and gouged, open for the hollowing-out of an underground parking garage. "A girdle of orange, Puritan-pumpkin colored girders / braces the tingling Statehouse"; the repudiated old values of Massachusetts clash with the commercial spirit of what was called the "New Boston."

Shaw is "out of bounds now" because he died for values symbolized by his erect statue: "he cannot bend his back," though those who walk the streets of contemporary Boston apparently can. As Lowell had identified with Hawthorne, Lowell also identifies with Shaw; anti-Puritan romancer, soldier, and poet hold the line in backsliding Boston.

EIGHT

Shaw represents a New England heritage of honor, lost to greed.

> On a thousand small town New England greens,
> the old white churches hold their air
> of sparse, sincere rebellion; frayed flags
> quilt the graveyards of the Grand Army of the Republic.[74]

Shaw and his troops embody a call to self-sacrifice which nags and mocks selfish, contemporary Bostonians, who are willing to rip open the city's surface—indeed, to tear out its soul—in the name of commerce and progress. The epigraph to this poem—*"Relinquunt Omnia Servare Rem Publicam"* (They gave up everything to serve the Republic)—shows how far Boston has slid, into a hollow hole, since Shaw's day.[75] Now, everywhere,

> giant finned cars nose forward like fish;
> a savage servility
> slides by on grease.[76]

In this powerful, summary image, Lowell repudiates contemporary Boston with all of the righteous indignation of one who speaks from and for a set of uncompromising family and regional values. Like a lay preacher, Lowell brings to mind a long-denied old faith. As he puts it in "New England and Further,"

> The old Faith was something of the mind. Intensely of the mind,
> the naked ideal hidden in vestments of a life-denying drabness,
> opposed to display and yet expensive, sensual, baroque disclosures
> of the flesh. Such the fable.[77]

Lowell's "For the Union Dead" is this "fable" renewed in words.

In "91 Revere Street" Lowell portrays Boston's old families and values as desiccated, trapped in an artificial garden, while he posits contemporary Boston as an open common, resonant with vitality. "For the Union Dead," on the other hand, plays off a fallen, contemporary Boston against an erect but shaken image of rectitude. But there is little contradiction. In both cases Lowell repudiates the given world which enclosed him and imagines a world elsewhere, either beyond confines, or, more convincingly, in the past, where Boston's first families, his own and Eliot's included, stood for more than propriety or personal gain.

A Lowell biographer calls "For the Union Dead" the poet's "sour final truce with Boston," citing, from a letter, one of Lowell's typical denunciations of the city: "We are awfully sick of Boston. The only unconventional people here are charming screwballs, who never finish a picture or publish a line. Then there are Cousins and Harvard professors. All very pleasant, but. . . ."[78] "We" included Elizabeth Hardwick, to whom Lowell was married from 1949 to 1972. Born in Kentucky, Hardwick was a writer of fiction—*The Ghostly Lover* was published in 1945—when they met at Yaddo in 1949. Though at that time Lowell was in the midst of one of his periodic breakdowns, Hardwick found Lowell "a very gripping sort of character."[79] Subsequently, Boston's character gripped her as well.

After a series of breakdowns, Lowell decided to return to Boston for a fresh start; by 1953 he thought, with guarded confidence, that he could both maintain a proper "garden" exterior and sustain a looser "common" interior. "That is I think I am now adult enough to be fairly conventional if not 'proper' outwardly, and not shock (or be shocked by) people. One doesn't want to change too much though."[80] Proper Boston could not change, or even long contain, Robert Lowell.

In 1955 they purchased a house at 239 Marlborough Street, "just exactly a block from the one I grew up in," commented Lowell, with his eye for fearful symmetry. Though house-proud—feeling "very lordly and pretentious in our new Boston house"—he was wary from the first, as he told William Carlos Williams, that "we might even become Boston worthies, if it weren't for the worm of life in us."[81]

Though Lowell successfully taught at Boston University, wrote *Life Studies,* and established something of a literary center at their home during these years, his return to Boston was not tranquil. In early 1958, after a stormy period, he was admitted to McLean Hospital in Belmont. There he wrote some of his most accomplished confessional poetry, works which further defined his relations to the city. "Waking in Blue" converts the experience of a psychiatric patient into another ironic turn against conventional Boston. He befriended his "Roman Catholic attendants," for example, because "there are no Mayflower / screwballs in the Catholic Church."[82] In "Home after Three Months Away" he portrays himself as spent, only able to gaze through his window, down to where "a choreman tends our coffin length of soil," on Marlborough Street.[83] In "Memories of West Street and Lepke," Lowell turns savagely upon himself, aristocratic and detached, and patronizingly mocks the pretensions of lesser Bostonians.

> Only teaching on Tuesdays, book-worming
> in pajamas fresh from the washer each morning,
> I hog a whole house on Boston's
> "hardly passionate Marlborough Street,"
> where even the man
> scavenging filth in the back alley trash cans,
> has two children, a beach wagon, a helpmate,
> and is "a young Republican."[84]

He and Boston, each an emblem for the other, were contemptuous, pretentious things.

HIS wife, long wary of Lowell's mother and the values she embodied, enforced his argument against Boston in her own writings. In a 1959 essay, "Boston: The Lost Ideal," Elizabeth Hardwick published her farewell words to Lowell's city.

> Boston—wrinkled, spindly-legged, depleted of nearly all her spiritual and cutaneous oils, provincial, self-esteeming—has gone on spending and spending her inflated bills of pure reputation decade after decade. Now, one supposes it is over at last.[85]

Hers is a curiously spiteful reflection, which takes little account of the pleasures Hardwick and Lowell had found in Boston. Record of those transient pleasures is evident in Hardwick's autobiographical novel, *Sleepless Nights,* published in 1979, a work in which she looks back in brief appreciation at her early days in Boston, through a citation from a letter.

> Here I am in Boston, on Marlborough Street, number 239. I am looking out on a snowstorm. It fell like a great armistice, bringing all simple struggles to an end. In the extraordinary snow, people are walking about in wonderful costumes—old coats with fur collars, woolen caps, scarves, boots, leather hiking shoes that shine like copper. Under the yellow glow of the streetlights you begin to imagine what it was like forty or fifty years ago. The stillness, the open whiteness—nostalgia and romance in the clear, quiet air. . . . More or less settled in this handsome house.[86]

Though evocative—a prose version of Childe Hassam's misty, idyllic *Boston Common at Twilight,* a painting of the urban pastoral glazed in slanting winter light that turns common Boston to gold— Hardwick's letter portrays Boston as a place where one is tempted to cease striving, where one might yield to nostalgia and romance, grow settled and senescent. It is not difficult to see why such a mood would quickly pass in a restless, ambitious woman who sought to be tested, who yearned for the energies associated with New York.

Elizabeth Hardwick, like other writers before her, got what she could from the ambience of Boston's cultural tradition; then she, with Lowell, moved on to Manhattan. In an essay on Margaret Fuller, Hardwick saw this as a proper pattern of self-development. Fuller, Hardwick decides,

> was born in the wrong place, the place thought to be the only right one for an American intellectual in the nineteenth century. That is, she was born in Cambridgeport, Massachusetts, around Harvard, Boston, Concord, and all the rest. She sprang out of the head of all the Zeuses about: her father Timothy Fuller, Emerson, Goethe.[87]

Yet, admitting the justice of Hardwick's point, that the patriarchal intellectual community of New England worthies circumscribed Fuller's growth, it is also fair to ask where else in nineteenth-century America Fuller could have received such special attention. Finally Hardwick grudgingly grants the value of Fuller's regional training: "what the whole span of her life shows is that she got all from being around Boston at the transfiguring moment, and would have lost all had she not escaped." Fuller, argues Hardwick, "was a sort of stepchild, formed and deformed by Concord, by the universalism and provincialism."[88]

Hardwick, too, would take Boston by storm, then leave it. For Hardwick, as for Lowell, Boston had a way of making the writer feel like a helpless child, nurtured but coddled. If it was only right and proper that Margaret Fuller grew up and moved from Boston on to New York in 1844, so too would it be the correct move for Elizabeth Hardwick in 1960.

Before she left, Hardwick said her unfond farewells in "Boston: The Lost Ideal." Her Boston, like Lowell's city, was an act of mind; yet, while Lowell stressed lost faith and honor, Hardwick emphasized misleading myths. "There has never been anything quite like Boston as a creation of the American imagination, or perhaps one should say as a creation of the American scene. Some of the legend was once real, surely." However, this local image of "grand, old families still existing as grand old families" is no longer true. Though Hardwick may have spoken from her painful experience with the Lowell family, she supplied different terms to explain the reality beneath the false image of Boston. "*Actual* Boston, the living city, is governed largely by people of Irish descent and more and more, recently, by men of Italian descent." While Hardwick mocked the first-family pretensions of Boston, she shared their scorn for the (vulgar?) children of immigrants who ruled the city. But these newcomers, with their vigorous styles, their new visions of what the city might become, their challenge to stuffy Brahmin ways, were, as she was, revisionists of the Boston myth, for all her inability to see the kinship.

The only saving grace in the city, for Hardwick, is found in those writers who were critical of Boston: Henry James, Henry Adams, and George Santayana in particular. Thus, as Marquand's George Apley illustrates for her, Boston culture has continued to decline into a tepid caution which muffles such articulate complaints. However, it should be stressed that it is just those writers who portray Boston's "decline," Robert Lowell included, who preserve Boston's soul, who *are* Boston.

For all of Hardwick's passionate denunciations, there is an attraction to Boston which even she must admit, an inwardness which characterizes the city, far from New York's neon and taxis: a Bostonian courtliness, a satisfying domesticity which she must have recollected from their best days on Marlborough Street, where "setting is serious."[89]

At the conclusion of "Boston: The Lost Ideal," Hardwick tries to balance her books on her husband's city. "Boston is defective, out-of-date, vain, and lazy, but if you're not in a hurry it has a deep, secret appeal." Clearly she *is* in a hurry, though her final paragraph dissolves into a semifictional evocation of place which shows Hardwick's ambivalence toward enclosed Boston. "Outside it is winter, dark. The curtains are drawn, the wood is on the fire, the table has been checked, and in the stillness one waits for the guests who come stamping in out of the snow." A narrow but felicitous life, one which might inspire literary reflections, such as those evocations of Boston in her own essay and fictions. But Hardwick's Boston, her version of Joyce's Dublin, is the center of paralysis, symbolized by its winter snow, its darkness, its yearning for lost glories, its suppressed passions, its eloquent remembrances of things past, its exquisite sense of *loss*.[90]

ELIZABETH HARDWICK was not the first of Robert Lowell's wives to move from anticipation to denunciation of Boston. Jean Stafford, married to Lowell from 1940 to 1948, set the pattern of responses that Hardwick would follow, each non-Bostonian wife fated to incorporate in her writings Robert Lowell's contradictory feelings about Boston. Jean Stafford made her contribution to this subgenre of literature in her 1944 novel on Boston snobbery, *Boston Adventure*.

Born in California and reared in Colorado, Stafford never felt properly placed, anywhere. Her father was an unsuccessful writer of western tales and her mother ran a boarding house in Boulder. Like a Howells heroine, she grew up with distant, idealized visions of Boston, a city of stability, tradition, and culture. Lowell embodied the cultural virtues of Boston in her eyes when they met in 1937, during a writers' conference at the University of Colorado. These fairy-tale dreams quickly turned into nightmares of pain and recrimination on her first visit to the Boston Lowells in 1938. When Lowell, who was driving drunk, crashed his car into a wall in Cambridge, she suffered massive head injuries. For Stafford, this act of violence came to typify Boston's hostility to outsiders, particularly when she was forced to sue Lowell, to the outrage of his family, in order to receive compensation for her medical expenses. Her beautiful face marred by a twisted nose, Stafford was transformed by Boston not into a lovely swan, as she had dreamed, but into an ugly duckling.

Though Lowell's parents did everything they could to prevent it, Stafford and Lowell were married in April 1940. In 1941, after his conversion to Catholicism, they married again in the Catholic church, removing themselves even further from ascendancy values.

Jean Stafford's *Boston Adventure* satirizes the piety and propriety of old Boston families, but it also recognizes their hypnotic powers. After the critical and commercial success of this novel, Stafford was further scorned by the Boston Lowells. In August 1945 she purchased a home in Maine, at Damariscotta Mills, which she hoped would serve as their haven from Boston's condemnation.

Lowell was drawn to the Damariscotta Mills house in part because it stood a few hundred yards from beautiful, tiny St. Patrick's Church, the oldest Catholic church in New England. Lowell became a daily communicant. Across from their house stood the grand mansion of the Kavanaughs, built by an Irish lumberman, James Kavanaugh, who had brought a colony of Irish-Catholics to Maine in the late eighteenth century. Inspired by this setting, Lowell wrote *The Mills of the Kavanaughs*, a strange, difficult and haunting poem, narrated from the point of view of Anne Kavanaugh, adopted daughter and widow, who addresses her dead husband.[91] In Damariscotta Mills, Lowell discovered the perfect anti-Boston: a pastoral place with remnants of an Irish-Catholic big house tradition.

However, the harsh facts of life in Maine—the house lacked insulation and they had no car to carry them away from it—qualified the purity of their idyll, particularly when their enforced isolation was assaulted by what Stafford would call, in the title of one of her bitter stories of Damariscotta Mills, "An Influx of Poets," during the summer of 1946. The strain of this effort—along with their alcoholism and his infidelity—ended their dream of a pastoral literary life in Maine; their marriage over, they closed the house in the fall of 1946. Damariscotta Mills represented a "failed escape" from Boston for Robert Lowell and Jean Stafford.[92]

Stafford's *Boston Adventure*, which financed the passing delusion of Damariscotta Mills, holds the shape of a fairy tale in reverse: a young woman is taken out of her lowly world and carried into the land of her dreams; transformed, she enters a beautiful house but soon she discovers that it is a prison from which she cannot escape. The story is Stafford's turn on Lowell's Garden and Common myth. Stafford's heroine is born into the Common world; then she gains entry into the lovely Garden, and lives unhappily there, ever after.

The novel focuses upon Sonia Marburg, the daughter of Russian and German immigrants; ten years old in 1925, she yearns for rescue from her humble origins, a fishing village in Chichester, just north of Boston. Sonia sleeps on a pallet in her mother's hovel and dreams of the elegant rooms of one Miss Pride, a Bostonian who vacations at the Hotel Barstow, where Sonia's mother serves as a chambermaid. Rather than accept the terrors of her actual world—poverty, ignorance, her father's drunkenness—Sonia "lives" with Miss Pride of Beacon Hill in her imagination. When asked what she wants to do when she grows up, Sonia replies, "I guess I want to live in Boston."[93] Her goal, then, is not to *do*, but to *be*, in Boston, the Byzantium of her dreams.

Sonia's dream comes true; she visits the city with Miss Pride, who calls herself "the most old-fashioned woman in Boston." They enter the city through its slums and then they come to the site that is, for Miss Pride, the heart of Boston: the Old Granary Burying Ground. Lowell, of course, had brought Stafford to the Indian Killer's grave of his ancestors as part of his grim tour of Boston. Sonia immediately understands its symbolic attractions: "the sparse and lowly graves of the harsh garden testified to the city's conviction of its rightness and its adamant resistance to change."[94] Miss Pride's home provides an apparently more benign illustration of the same point: Boston is a place of fixity, high purpose, and privilege.

> Her house was not far; its front windows faced Louisburg Square and here, as if it were an oasis chosen to delight the eyes of some favored heavenly power, the sun, hidden elsewhere by the city's smoke, shone brilliantly on white doorways and their brass trimmings.[95]

After Sonia is granted her dream to live in Boston as Miss Pride's protege, she becomes disturbed "by the strange feeling that I was not myself, or rather, that this was a phantom of myself, projected into Boston by my real being, still in Chichester."[96] She is left suspended between worlds. Soon Sonia discovers that Miss Pride is a narrow-minded bigot, nearly inarticulate with a pen, a hypocrite, and a secret tippler. Miss Pride's stylish niece, Hopestill Mather, is revealed as a moral monster. Yet, so strong is Sonia's need to believe, so unwilling is she to go home again, that even when she knows better, Sonia cannot shake herself free from her original illusion of beneficent Boston. Just as Hawthorne's Robin could not leave a cruel but exciting Boston in "My Kinsman, Major Molineux," Sonia cannot break the psychic grip of Miss Pride and the city she represents in *Boston Adventure*. At the conclusion of the novel, Sonia resumes her place in Miss Pride's third-floor loft, her room with a limited view. Sonia becomes the prisoner of a powerful image of place. In *Boston Adventure*, Jean Stafford created a useful fiction out of her own Boston misadventure.

IN "Boston: The Lost Ideal," Elizabeth Hardwick called *Boston Adventure* an "admirable novel."[97] As we have seen, Hardwick complained about the depletion of creative energies in Boston, though her husband and his first wife had considerably enriched its literature, as would Hardwick. Other, younger writers came of age in Boston, under Lowell's influence. In September 1958 Robert Lowell taught a striking group of young poets in his graduate writing seminar at Boston University. Anne Sexton, an unpublished housewife from nearby Newton, and George Starbuck, an editor at a Boston publishing house, enrolled. In 1959, Sylvia Plath joined them to hear Lowell discuss their poems. During the spring of 1959, Lowell, Sexton, Starbuck, and Plath would, after Lowell's classes, often go to Boston's Ritz bar, across from the Garden, where they drank, talked about poetry and suicide.[98] Robert Lowell cultivated those, like himself, who were hurt into poetry by living in or near Boston.

Sylvia Plath was then living in Boston, on Willow Street at the back of Beacon Hill, where she had come to introduce her husband, Ted Hughes, to the American literary world. For Plath—who was born in Boston, grew up in Winthrop and Wellesley, had been a patient at McLean Hospital after her suicide attempt, and had graduated from Smith College—the American literary world *meant* Boston. Boston, as Adrienne Rich has said, is where "the world of literary celebrity and success was deeply meshed with that other world of Boston, old money and Harvard."[99] Small wonder, then, that Plath was drawn to Lowell. She and Hughes had already met Lowell in 1958 in Northampton, after one of his releases from McLean, while she was teaching at Smith. Plath was then as fascinated by Lowell's pedigree as his poetry. They drove around Northampton, as she wrote, "looking for relics of his ancestors, and to the Historical Society and the graveyard."[100]

Though Sylvia Plath had reservations about Lowell as a teacher, she was clear about her debt to Lowell's writing. In a 1962 interview, she recalled her excited response to *Life Studies*, "this intense breakthrough into very serious, very personal emotional experience which I feel has been partly taboo. Robert Lowell's poems about his experience in a mental hospital, for example, interested me very much."[101] Yet Boston, as image and idea, remained faint in Plath's interior poems.

Robert Lowell gave Anne Sexton the encouragement that she needed to make a name for herself, along with the model of his confessional poetry. "I think he may like my work," noted Sexton, "because it is all a little crazy or about being crazy and it may be that he relates to me and my 'bedlam poetry'."[102] Lowell endorsed Sexton's first book, *To Bedlam and Part Way Back*, a work strongly influenced by his *Life Studies*. However, Sexton's poems, like Plath's, lack Lowell's rich, local, specific density—his familial and historical frames of reference. There is little physical sense of Boston in Sexton's poems, though her spiritual sense of the region is strong in those strange, late poems in *An Awful Rowing Toward God*. Only rarely does she place her poems outside the psyche or beyond the complexities of family or love relations. Yet in the climactic poem of *To Bedlam and Part Way Back*, "A Story for Rose, on the Midnight Flight to Boston," Sexton brings to a close the journey indicated in her title by coming home to Boston, a haven for a poet in a stormy world. "We bank over Boston. I am safe. I put on my hat. / I am almost someone going home. The story has / ended."[103]

FOR Robert Lowell the story of Boston never ended. Near the close of his life, he was still brooding about the New England literary heritage, still converting it into a paradox which would match his own life and letters, a tradition of rebellion against established Boston values, a negative capability.

> The myth of New England really comes into being in the nineteenth century. It was then that the great imaginative minds first clearly saw their heritage as something both to admire and to fear. There's nothing course, fleshy, or Rabelaisian about those opposed spirits, Hawthorne and Emerson. Both were anti-Puritans, conscious and deliberate about it, yet sure they had inherited the essence.[104]

Even when he and Hardwick settled in New York in the early 1960s, Lowell kept his tentative relations with Boston and Cambridge alive through a part-time teaching position at Harvard. In the fall of 1963, Hardwick was saying that the move from Boston "saved my life, although I did not know it at the time," but Lowell was then commuting to Cambridge for a two-day per week teaching schedule, handling his "odd split week between Cambridge and New York," moving between different worlds and conflicting sides of his own psyche.[105] This time, however, Lowell did not live in a symbolic site, Revere Street or Marlborough Street, which reverberated with his family's history. Rather, living in Cambridge, he became a transient, something of a camera eye, a detached observer. Characteristically, he was ambivalent. Yet his tentative relations with his home place—ever arriving, ever leaving—contributed to the energy and candor of his sonnet sequence. Through *Notebooks* and its successive revisions, Lowell reimagined his home ground.

A lunch date at a typical Cambridge restaurant, "an oldtime sweatshop remodeled, purple brick," brought the mature Lowell into sad confrontation with his own lost, younger selves; but Cambridge also had its redemptive side. "Say the worst of it, Cambridge speaks English, words are given a fighting chance to speak."[106] There, memories of dead literary greats stirred him into poetry: particularly Margaret Fuller, "Henry and Waldo."[107] Cambridge, too, linked him to living literary greats; these encounters were shaped into his loose sonnet form, as in the poem where he records an epiphany of New England family history, a moment which bonded poets against Boston Brahmins. Lowell walked through Harvard Yard, talking with T. S. Eliot.

> Caught between two streams of traffic, in the gloom
> of Memorial Hall and Harvard's war-dead. . . . And he:
> 'Don't you loathe to be compared with your relatives?
> I do. I've just found two of mine reviewed by Poe.
> He wiped the floor with them . . . and I was
>   delighted.'[108]

Here setting impinges and impedes—caught, as they are, in traffic and the shadows of Harvard's history—until Eliot releases Lowell from the weight of their first-family heritage.

In "Dawn," a poem based on a brief affair with a young student in 1969, Lowell managed to break the terms of gloom and paralysis in which he had long portrayed Boston.

> I'm through with looking steadily at the worst—
> Chaucer's old January made hay with May.
> In this ever more enlightening room,
> I wake beside the early rising sun,
> sex indelible on the flowering air—
> shouldn't I pray for us to hold forever,
> body of dolphin, breast of cloud?[109]

Finally, the enclosures of 91 Revere Street and the iron fence of Boston Garden open for the aging poet into the common freedoms of this "ever more enlightening room" in Cambridge, across the river from Boston.[110]

THOUGH Robert Lowell's life passed through what Helen Vendler calls one or another "emblematic location," Lowell's first and most important symbolic site was Boston.[111] In Joseph Brodsky's image, Lowell remains the porcupine who "sharpens its golden needles / against the Boston bricks." But that resultant "blinding shine" is not, for Lowell, "needless." He inherited a distinguished Boston name and he was shaped by Boston values. Lowell *placed* Boston at the center of his poetic imagination and endowed the city with the clarity and force of his vision. His best poems, particularly "For the Union Dead," honor Boston by holding the city to its ideals, spiritual and artistic.

While T. S. Eliot encountered family history, suffered religious crisis and found his images and inspiration for *The Waste Land* in Boston, Robert Lowell revealed the divided soul of the city—the

Shaw Memorial *versus* the Underground Garage; the Garden *versus* the Common—in more direct poetic designs. What Lowell said of Hawthorne and Emerson applies as well to Eliot and Lowell: both Boston-shaped poets were anti-Puritans, conscious and deliberate about it, yet sure they had inherited the essence.

9

Boston, City of Spirit and Flesh

However, as for the New England Conscience still persisting with enough vitality to stand up against a sinful world, as for its not being intimidated by the rapaciousness of our century, we have constantly fresh examples.

         —PERRY MILLER,
         "The New England Conscience"

N EW ENGLAND was founded consciously, and in no fit of absence of mind."[1] Samuel Eliot Morison's memorable observation applies not only to the founding of the Bay Colony, but to its shaping, expansion, and transformation, to the reinvention of its self-image and the reexamination of its covenant, all of which has been taking place over three and a half centuries. Mark De Wolfe Howe speaks of Boston as "a state of mind rather than a city."[2] That mind has long been self-directed to the measurement of personal character and community mission. Austin Warren argues "that the early Puritans had suffered *for* conscience; that the later New Englanders, especially those of the nineteenth century, suffered *from* conscience."[3] Either way, Puritan self-consciousness and conscience have not disappeared from the region, though Puritanism has long been disbursed into moral awareness and political passion. For those writers who were drawn to or shaped by the Boston Idea—the search for personal salvation and public mission in the new world—many values associated with the seventeenth-century settlers still grip the New England mind.

The journal, the autobiography, and the biography—as well as their poetic and fictional variations—have remained the most characteristic literary modes of the region. Self-examination helps measure a person's or a society's days and ways against an ideal standard of the Father's Word or the forefathers' original mission. Self-examination helps to renew covenants and promises redemption, particularly in the slough of despond or the throes of personal or communal deviation. Self-examination is also a means of self-dramatization, an assertion that individual and community matter in the eyes of God.

Though such self-examination exists in painting, particularly in a significant series of works which depict New England worthies, it is primarily a literary mode: record-keeping in words, a means by which enterprises may be weighed.[4] The journal constitutes an epic poem of the self, a social history of a people, a mode of moral measure. Samuel Sewall's *Diary*, which spans the late seventeenth to the early eighteenth century, shows the range of the form, for Sewall recorded his responses to widows he courted, witches he judged (and then repented for judging) in Salem, even acts of God, like the hailstones which broke windows in Boston's new meetinghouse. Though a worldly man, Sewall believed that the apocalypse was at hand and that New England represented the New Jerusalem, man's best and last chance for redemption. "So long as Plum Island shall faithfully keep the command post, notwithstanding all the hectoring words and hard blows of the proud and boisterous ocean; as long as any salmon or sturgeon shall swim in the stream of Merrimack, . . . so long as Christians be born there," then all will be well in the new world.[5]

The diary remains an instinctive and addictive form for regional writers. As Perry Miller and Thomas H. Johnson note,

> the habit became so thoroughly ingrained in the New England character that it remained a practice with various Yankees long after they had ceased to be Puritans, to the great enrichment of our political and literary history, as witness the diaries of John Quincy Adams and Gideon Wells, or the journals of Emerson, Thoreau and Hawthorne. Henry Adams, dissecting his career in the search for "education," is writing in the true New England tradition, and undertakes no more than countless Puritans had done when they submitted their lives to microscopic examination to discover if they had at any time found that vision of the unity and meaning of the universe which they called regeneration and for which he endeavored to substitute a dynamic theory of history.[6]

In confirmation of the Miller-Johnson thesis, Robert Lowell's *Notebook* (1970), an extended sonnet set, presents the poet as a flawed character who witnesses disruptions in his personal life that parallel derangements in the public realm. Lowell is only one example of the persistent attractions this form of self-examination holds for the post-Puritan, New England writer. John Updike fittingly titles his collection of autobiographical essays *Self-Consciousness*. "Nothing can bring you peace but yourself," wrote Emerson, in "Self-Reliance."[7] The quest for peace, then, is through the self. For modern New England writers, self-examination is a way to affirm one's central place in this world and the next.

Even when the Greater Boston writer cares nothing for peace and seeks to repudiate the world, he tellingly turns to the diary. Beginning in 1919 and carrying on his entries until his death in 1963, Arthur Crews Inman—a wealthy and neurotic recluse, semi-invalid, bigot, and misanthrope—compiled 155 volumes of diaries, amounting to seventeen million words. This hero of his own imaginings solicited marginal Bostonians through newspaper ads to come to his rooms, where he would bribe them to confess to their often sordid secrets and, frequently, to submit to his fumbling advances. He toured the city in his chauffeured Pierce-Arrow or Cadillac, searching for "diary fodder"; he sent his wife and members of his "staff" out onto the streets of Boston to recruit stories or "talkers."[8] Inman then scrupulously recorded his devious days and dark reflections on the American character—denouncing Jews, Irish, and blacks—and he mocked those he saw passing beneath the windows of his rooms in Garrison Hall, a run-down apartment hotel in the Back Bay.

Daniel Aaron, who edited these diaries, makes a case for Inman as an object of historical and literary curiosity. It is true that "Boston figures primarily as a backdrop for the Diary's 'plot,' " but Inman's Boston is a perverse metropolis, a projection of his obsessions. Aaron argues that "the Diary itself is an act of self-exculpation and a bid for the reader's 'understanding smiles.' "[9] But Inman inspires few smiles. The self that Inman reveals is truly a sick soul, an artless and actual version of Dostoevsky's fictional madman in *Notes from the Underground*. The Inman *Diary* is a perversion of the Puritan form of self-examination—an antiquest by an ingrown Bostonian who vaunted his spiritual degradation.

For other New England writers life remains a more exalted quest, through a symbolic terrain where God's text was read for meanings. Puritan settlers sought evidence of God's intent in the language of landscape and weather, and in their relations with Indians—both were symbolic encounters, as well as actual trials, in the new world. This typologic imagination diffused over time into a concern for national mission, but New England writers never lost sight of the original founders' goal: personal and communal salvation.

When a snake appeared in the midst of a sermon at the Cambridge synod in 1648, several elders shied away, but Mr. Thompson, "a man of much faith," trod upon its head until it was dead, reported John Winthrop, who knew that "nothing [falls] out but by divine providence." So Winthrop could supply the gloss on this parable. "The serpent is the devil; the synod, representative of the churches of Christ in New England. The devil had formerly and lately attempted their disturbance and dissolution; but their faith in the seed of the woman overcame him and crushed his head."[10] No leaf falls and no snake crawls without design.

New England, in the words of that Puritan visionary Edward Johnson, is a "place where the Lord will create a new Heaven, and a new Earth in, new Churches, and a new Common-wealth together," a *Wonder-Working Providence of Sions Savior*.[11] New England places, particularly those sites set within the region's original Puritan claims, still retain their symbolic significance. Greater Boston's writers still seek meanings in that resonant topology.

From the beginning of the settlement, there were those who would reawaken their spirit and renew their colony's fading mission through direct contact with nature, searching there for emblems of God's presence, embodiments of God's mystery, evidence of God's grace. John Cotton wanted his parishioners to *feel* the presence of God in the new world. But when in 1637 his disciple, Anne Hutchinson, heard God's voice, her testimony was judged heretical. This is the moment, argues Andrew Delbanco, when "the idea of a suprarational spirit was beginning to be beaten down in New England."[12] The antinomian line held faith in the ability of the self to create itself anew, apart from history and tradition. Arminianism, a parallel heresy, rejected divine decree and inspiration, making free will central to the moral and religious life. Both separatist impulses, antinomianism and Arminianism led to the celebration of the self, the invention of the American Adam or Eve.[13]

Though Hutchinson was banished, her faith was eventually vindicated by those who took up the celebration of the self—mystic, rapturous, American—in opposition to the Puritan rule of law and congregation. "The Emersonian, or antinomian, critique of rationalized Puritanism is everywhere in our literature, though it has naturally been especially acute within the New England tradition itself," writes Delbanco. New England, as its name indicates, was then at the center of tension between worlds, between the settlers' conflicting identities as English or American. The American celebration of self, which denies history, and the related faith that life can be radically renewed, have their sources within the dialectical debate among early Puritans in Boston.[14]

AS construed by Greater Boston's writers, a person's life is an *exemplum*, a struggle of values in a gradually unfolding design. Literature in New England still assumes the responsibility of combining art with instruction, beauty with truth. From Anne Bradstreet's "To My Dear Children" through John Berryman's *Homage to Mistress Bradstreet* to Anne Sexton's *The Death Notebooks,* the characteristic product of the New England mind (or the more intensely localized Greater Boston consciousness) remains the spiritual autobiography. In this form the writer or the writer's surrogate stands as witness, as one who holds out the vision of a new life in a lay sermon. Personal and community histories are conflated, each serving as an emblem for the other in a literature which shapes a myth of our past and defines a mission for our future.[15]

Throughout much of its history, the Greater Boston writer has been something of a cleric.[16] Many authors have summoned us to spiritual consciousness and castigated us for lapses from the ideal in works which have been called "jeremiads." As Sacvan Bercovitch explains,

> The Puritans' concept of errand entailed a fusion of secular and sacred history. The purpose of their jeremiads was to direct an imperiled people of God toward the fulfillment of their destiny, to guide them individually toward salvation, and collectively toward the American city of God.[17]

Character and community combine, religious and political missions merge, history and prophecy fuse in the New England mind. Alexis de Tocqueville concluded that "the whole destiny of America [is] contained in the first Puritan who landed on these shores, as that of the whole human race is in the first man."[18] The voice of that first Puritan still echoes in and around Boston.

AMONG the first women to land on these shores was Anne Bradstreet, who arrived in 1630 aboard the *Arbella.* Reared in aristocratic ease, only eighteen at the time and two years married, she was stunned by her encounter with America. She lived first in Charlestown and then in Newtowne, which came to be called Cambridge, where the Bradstreet house faced the common ground which would become Harvard Yard. When she "came into this country, . . . [she] found a new world, and new manners, at which [her] heart rose," testified Bradstreet near the end of her life. In fact, her heart sank at the prospect. Though she wanted to return to England, Bradstreet quickly determined that she was fulfilling God's design in America. "But after I was convinced it was the way of God, I submitted to it and joined to the church at Boston."[19]

Bradstreet wrote this important passage, in which realization of mission transforms a reluctant immigrant into an American, in "To My Dear Children," a brief work which established the importance of the spiritual autobiography in America. Like other, similar Puritan works—by Thomas Shepard or the Mathers, for example— her self-inquiry was directed to her children; her life should serve as a model from which they could learn to endure similar trials. Her life, she would have them know, was "a pilgrimage" in this world and a preparation for the next. Replicating her epiphany of conversion upon her arrival, she saw her life as a trial of her faith.

Bradstreet was reassured of God's overarching purpose and her place in the scheme of things by her observations of nature. In nature, for Bradstreet as for so many later American writers, she discovered God's presence, though she was no radical separatist from the church like her contemporary, Anne Hutchinson, who was banished and then murdered by Indians. Still, Bradstreet's errand into the wilderness provided her, as she told her children, with evidence of God's presence in

> the wondrous works that I see, the vast frame of the heaven and the earth, the order of all things, night and day, summer and winter, spring and autumn, the daily providing for this great household upon the earth, the preserving and directing of all to its proper end.[20]

In this passage, her life merges with her family's hopes and her community's promise in America; all dissolves into a cosmic vision of order. As Morison notes, "it was New England that furnished her material. The primeval forest beside her later home in North Andover, and the yet untamed Merrimack near by, inspired . . . her 'Contemplations.' "[21] In "Contemplations," Bradstreet saw the figure of God's purpose in the river's run.

> While on the stealing stream I fixt mine eye,
> Which to the longed-for ocean held its course,
> I marked, nor crooks, nor rubs that there did lie
> Could hinder ought, but still augment its force.
> "O happy flood," quoth I, "that holds thy race
> Till thou arrive at thy beloved place, . . .
> So may we press to that vast mansion, ever blest."[22]

For Anne Bradstreet, America, indeed life itself, was but a station stop for the pilgrim who sought God's presence; she made this clear in one of her "Meditations Divine and Moral": "We must, therefore, be here as strangers and pilgrims, that we may plainly declare that we seek a city above and wait all the days of our appointed time till our change shall come."[23] Shaped into poems, meditations, and letters, Bradstreet's spiritual autobiography helped define a literary mode which would persist, with telling variations and revisions, for three centuries: a personal testimony which exemplifies community mission, a retrospective self-inquiry in the service of prophecy, and a quest for grace and salvation. She would ascend from the city upon a hill to "the city above."

In 1964 John Berryman claimed particular place in the lineage of American poets in *Homage to Mistress Bradstreet*, which he describes as "an essentially seventeenth-century poem with twentieth-century implications."[24] In making himself over into a descendant of Bradstreet, Berryman also made her over in *his* image. Berryman's Bradstreet is a rebel, a woman who is closer to the passions of the Indians than she is to the pieties of the colonists. She says,

> I revolt from, I am like, these savage foresters
> whose passionless dicker in the shade, whose glance
> impassive & scant, belie their murderous cries
> when quarry seems to show.[25]

In short, Berryman has made Mistress Bradstreet into a familiar figure in literary modernism—a passionate, rebellious, self-conscious, divided being. Despite such liberties, Berryman demonstrated Bradstreet's continuing relevance for those who would, in his words, tirelessly "phrase / anything past, dead, far, / sacred, for a barbarous place."[26] In her spiritual autobiography, Bradstreet held out a vision of a redemptive mission in America. In his version of her confession, Berryman looked back in wonder at her powers to articulate herself as a poet in opposition to American culture; he ascribed to her his own mission.

If John Berryman tried to take on the voice of Anne Bradstreet, Anne Sexton assumed much of her persona and poetic tasks. A lonely Massachusetts housewife, Sexton was sharply conscious of her psychic separation from the community. For her, as for Anne Bradstreet, poetry was a means to affirm her identity as a thinking woman. Sexton's poetry began, at the suggestion of her therapist, as a search for personal articulation, for healing. *To Bedlam and Part Way Back*, Sexton's first collection of poetry, inspired by the teaching of Robert Lowell and modeled after his confessional poetry, implies quest through the dark night of the soul, a trial of her faith in life.[27]

And death. *The Death Notebooks*, Sexton's final collection, describes a spiritual quest which Bradstreet would have understood. "Gods" opens the volume and defines the terms of Sexton's quest.

> Mrs. Sexton went out looking for the gods.
> She began looking in the sky—
> expecting a large white angel with a blue crotch.
> No one.[28]

Like Hawthorne's Ethan Brand, Sexton's poetic persona travels in search of a missing spiritual dimension, though Brand sought sin while Sexton seeks gods. As it had with him, her search took her home again.

> Then she journeyed back to her own house
> and the gods of the world were shut in the lavatory.

At last!
she cried out,
and locked the door.[29]

Sexton, of course, addresses the terms of her quest for gods with more irony and humor than Bradstreet allowed herself, but the drive to seek out transforming spiritual presences is evident in both women, despite their separation by three centuries.

The autobiographical impulses of New Englanders did not always maintain such an exalted level of selfless devotion as that of Anne Bradstreet. Benjamin Franklin's *Autobiography*, wrote Herman Melville, illustrated "a bookkeeper's mind" and D. H. Lawrence cursed Franklin for fencing off "my dark forest, my freedom." However, Max Weber saw Franklin's *Autobiography* as a lay sermon, his preaching of Puritan self-abnegation while he was in search of an earthly heaven: the fulfillment of the American dream.[30] Certainly Franklin, that Bostonian in exile, echoed the Puritan idea of fulfilling God's mission, though Franklin stressed worldly success by defining his literary purpose as an expression of gratitude to God and as a model for his posterity. One must seek to do and be good, because it pays off. "That it was therefore in every one's Interest to be virtuous, who wish'd to be happy even in this World."[31]

Seeing America in 1630, Anne Bradstreet was daunted; reassured by nature, she accepted the argument from design, believing that there was a divine purpose to which she should submit her will. In the America of the next century, Franklin saw more immediate rewards in the practice, even in the pretense, of virtue. Though one stressed heavenly, the other, earthly rewards; each autobiographer measured actions, personal and communal, against moral ideals; each prophesied a promising vision for posterity: family and community.

EVEN those autobiographies which emphasize caste and class, reflecting Boston's long-standing passion for invidious distinctions

313

among its citizens, hold spiritual dimensions. Samuel Eliot Morison, in *One Boy's Boston 1887–1901* (1962), attacked the popular myth that Boston Brahmins were bloodless snobs.[32] In contrast, Nat Hentoff in *Boston Boy* (1986) found Boston to be "the most anti-Semitic city in the nation."[33] However, common ground joins these conflicting perceptions. For both, the Brahmin from Beacon Hill and the Jew from Roxbury, Boston was a city symbolic of moral purpose. Their autobiographies exemplify, despite their conflicting perceptions, the characteristically Boston theme of spiritual quests.

Morison presents his family as men and women whose generosity of spirit and selflessness belied the conventional myth of the proper and pious Bostonians. Born in 1887 on Brimmer Street at the base of Beacon Hill, Morison recalls a lively, open childhood in a Boston in which, amazingly, "there were no distinctions of wealth" and ancestry did not count. Morison's Boston was not composed of "bigoted Protestants, nasty to the Irish." Rather, his Boston was open, democratic, idealistic. A "solid core of nobility and bourgeois" families endowed Harvard, the Museum of Fine Arts, the Opera House, Massachusetts General Hospital, and other Greater Boston institutions whose existence affirmed the collective faith in community. Morison describes a benevolent Boston, a city in which class distinctions are softened by respect and affection. The family's Irish maids, for example, were "girls of character, whom we loved and they us." His nurses showed Morison "how the poor lived" and "imparted folklore and wisdom that cannot be got from books." Order and justice reigned. For Morison, then, Boston remained a city upon a hill, a place of purpose and passion. "Despite all the sneers and jeers at 'Proper Bostonians,' 'Boston Brahmins' and the like, there was a remarkable pattern of living here that existed nowhere else in the United States."[34]

Morison, of course, saw Boston from the privileged vantage point of his kind, the Yankee-Brahmin class. As we have seen, writers from the black and Irish populations of Boston were less reassured by their experiences of the city. The Jews of Boston, who shaped the tradition which gave Nat Hentoff his voice in *Boston Boy*, have also left eloquent evidence of their struggle for recognition in the city, a largely autobiographical record of a far different Boston.

Mary Antin's *Promised Land* (1912) is a parable of purpose and new-found patriotism, a tale of a young woman from Poltz, Russia, who found a home and realized her promise in Boston. "In Poltz we had supposed that 'America' was practically synonymous with 'Boston.' "[35] And so it was, for when young Mary published a poem in praise of George Washington—just as had young Phyllis Wheatley—she won the city's approval. "It's so simple in Boston," she exulted. She found her voice and gained acceptance through both her testimony of hard times and her literary expressions of gratitude to Boston, *her* Promised Land.[36]

In the next generation, another Boston Jew, Isaac Goldberg, took a more ironic and resigned view of the city.

> And Boston itself? I am too used to it to dislike it. And why, for that matter, should I confuse its beauties with the arrant stupidities of its rulers? I like the tempo of its life; the easy accessibility of its suburbs; the sense of repose that need not be, for one who possesses no blue blood, a spiritual coma. The secret is that I am only geographically, and by virtue of birth and long residence, a Bostonian. I am too good an American to be a truly good Bostonian; too enamored of the American tradition to surrender to the administrative fervors of its political hetmen.[37]

Though a "good American," Goldberg saw Boston and the American promise of liberty as separate matters, and he sought "Bolsheviki" license for rebellion from the example of "the cradle of liberty," Faneuil Hall.[38]

Charles Angoff's *When I Was a Boy in Boston* (1947) celebrates the way in which the Angoffs "became Americanized in record time" during the first decades of the century, when they reveled in American symbols: ketchup, movies, and ice cream.[39] Mark Mirsky's novel, *Blue Hill Ave.* (1972), treats a lost way of life with parody. Mirsky satirizes Boston politics, for example, by having a Jewish state senator, Mayor "Curley's stooge in the Jewish district," intrude upon a Saint Patrick's Day parade in Irish South Boston and fake a heart attack to get attention and sympathy for his own run for mayor![40]

The most eloquent testimony to Jewish life in Boston was political reporter Theodore H. White's *In Search of History* (1981). In rich detail, White there evoked the two worlds that pulled at him when he lived on Eire Street in Dorchester, during and after World War I.

> Boston, Massachusetts, where little Jewish-American boys, pulled and tugged by stickball, hit-the-ball, baseball and jackknife, and by the movies, were forced to learn of nomads and peasants of three thousand years ago, forced to learn how shepherds watched their flocks at night, to learn of spotted lambs, of the searing summer and the saving rains, . . . without knowing that these rains were the monsoons of public-school geography.[41]

White's Boston constituted a new landscape and a new language. Mastering English and the circuitous streets of Boston's geography prepared him for his life's work as a traveling correspondent. As a boy White sometimes had to fight his way through the Irish streets of Dorchester to get to the Boston Public Library, forcing his own symbolic cultural passage. The politicians, police, and teachers— who taught him the fireside poets at the William E. Endicott School—were also Irish. White seized every opportunity Boston offered to transcend ethnic enclosure. Boston Public Latin School (to which he walked four miles a day, from Eire Street to the Fenway, during the Depression) and Harvard, where he was a day student, one of an outcast type called "meatballs," offered him the opportunity to become a "looter" of culture, a thief of the keys to new kingdoms. Harvard gave him identity and mission. A *summa cum laude* graduate in 1938, White won a fellowship from the Harvard-Yenching Institute, which bought him a ticket out of Boston. The Jewish boy from Dorchester had risen from street battles with the Irish to become "the creature of other people, of another past, beneficiary of all the Establishment had packed into the Har-

vard processing system."[42] Boston was a transforming and trans-
porting experience for Theodore H. White.

Unlike Morison, Nat Hentoff saw a Brahmin class, represented
by Henry Cabot Lodge, which wished to limit the entry of "inferior" immigrants into the city. Like Morison, Hentoff too wished
in his autobiography to counter a false myth which others held of
the city. But Boston was a city of multiple prejudices in Hentoff's
experiences. "It was in this city—so admired by many who have
never lived there—that I grew up," in the 1930s and 1940s.[43]
Hentoff is more bitter about Boston than was White, though their
experiences, a few years apart, were strikingly similar. As he
crossed the city between Roxbury and downtown, Hentoff was
regularly beaten up by Irish-Americans, who were emboldened by
Father Coughlin's anti-Semitic radio broadcasts. Thus, Hentoff developed the wary persona of the outcast, even distancing himself
from his own religious heritage.

Boston offered Hentoff both wound and anodyne. As a boy Hentoff sought out havens where he could escape Boston prejudices
and found them, like White, in the Boston Public Library and the
Boston Latin School. "I would be going to *their* school, in *their*
part of town, and so, I would be not only learning Latin and Greek
but learning about *them*."[44] Like Malcolm Little, Hentoff also found
his voice and ear in jazz. The Savoy, a nightclub in which he heard
jazz and drank with Ben Webster and other great black musicians,
became his "sanctuary" from a city filled with tensions. His route
through Boston was also a literal pilgrimage, through a landscape
of conflicting values, for personal salvation.

> Those of us who came out onto Massachusetts Avenue from the
> Savoy Cafe to find our various ways home occasionally walked in
> jazz time. But it was hard to sustain that pulse and good feeling in
> the heavy air of Boston, with its tribal hatreds, the anti-Catholics
> sometimes being almost as venomous as the anti-Semites, and all
> mocking the Negroes—which is why they loved listening to Amos
> and Andy on the radio. But behind the closed doors of the Savoy,
> I felt more at home than anywhere else I had ever been, including
> home.[45]

Yet Boston, as Hentoff admits, offered him much more than widely spaced sanctuaries from its heavy airs of prejudice. Boston offered him nothing less than the materials out of which he could compose a coherent self. He assembled his persona from proper Boston's marginal elements and energies, from Left-Jewish politics to black jazz. He learned lessons from those Boston Irish who fought for education and those who fought against their own church's indifference to anti-Semitism: people like Frances Sweeney, owner and editor of the *Boston City Reporter*, who exposed corrupt politicians, and George Frazier, columnist and man-about-town, a Boston Irishman who spoke boldly and wrote stylishly for the *Boston Globe*.[46] "Both those Boston Irish lit up the city as long as they were in it, and they put some of their fire in me. And some of their romanticism, too."[47]

Despite his problems with Irish toughs on the streets of Boston, Hentoff also learned from their clan leader, Mayor Curley, whose rhetorical denunciations of Yankees composed a verbal jazz which echoed the rhythms of musicians Hentoff loved. From all of those improper but influential Bostonians, Hentoff learned his profession: to be a troublemaker, a dissenter in the tradition that goes back to Anne Hutchinson. W. H. Auden said Ireland hurt Yeats into poetry; similarly, Boston hurt Hentoff into cultural appreciation, moving him from Boston Latin's high culture to jazz lowlife, to political advocacy, as his career as a critic and journalist indicates. This was his lasting lesson from Boston: "Frances Sweeney, shaking her long blond hair and showing us Boston boys the great fun of knowing that we didn't have to bow to anyone so long as we had our facts straight."[48] Nat Hentoff took on the burden of the jeremiad, becoming another in a long line of those who remind Boston of its failed mission, its fall from original grace, its need to measure up to its own moral standards.

A direct line of spiritual autobiography runs through Greater Boston's literature. Nathaniel Hawthorne's "The Custom-House" personalized *The Scarlet Letter* by identifying his quest for salvation through art with heroine Hester's spiritual crisis two centuries earlier. Ralph Waldo Emerson's essays and Henry David Thoreau's meditations were also personal testimonies—Thoreau insisted upon the upright *I* (the I as camera eye) in the opening paragraphs of *Walden*—which excoriated Boston for lapsing from its moral mission. They were prophecies of renewal: for the community in Thoreau's "Civil Disobedience," and for any "John or Jonathan" in *Walden*. "The sun is but a morning star," concluded Thoreau, his locally nourished ego finally disbursed into a universal vision.[49] George Santayana's *Persons and Places* traced an outsider's encounter with the Boston mission; Henry Adams's *Education* portrayed an insider's struggle with the same. Henry James's *American Scene* recorded the efforts of an exile to rediscover a lost America, documenting his own lost innocence in the midst of Boston's twentieth-century expansion and development. When James looked west from the top of Beacon Hill, he saw first the old Boston of his youth in the foreground, then the new land of Back Bay development, and finally an ominously transformed America stretching beyond Boston. Memoirs by these and other Boston writers fuse their discoveries of identities with their concepts of Boston and its abandoned mission. T. S. Eliot, another exile, whose contact with Boston was brief but intense, wrote disguised spiritual autobiographies in the form of cryptic, modernist, poetic parables. Robert Lowell's poems also showed the contingency of this once-Puritan form, for Lowell presented his life as an *exemplum*, a psychological and moral history of a Boston insider turned wayward, cautionary son. For contemporary Boston writers the spiritual autobiography continues to be a central mode of self-examination and prophecy.

CONCLUDING his 1912 study of the city's character, *Boston: The Place and the People*, Mark De Wolfe Howe wrote:

> The people of Boston are rich in their inheritances that are good to cultivate and or transmit. What shall be winnowed out of them all

for posterity, none may say. There is yet no reason to fear a discontinuance of that state of mind which is informed peculiarly with
the fruitful qualities of responsibility and rebellion.[50]

These seemingly conflicting traits indeed run deep in the grain of
Boston's history. So, too, does the even deeper impulse to testify
and to judge in spiritual records, in works which provide the moral
authority for responsibility and rebellion. All of this is clear in the
exemplary regional writings of May Sarton: novelist, poet, and
diarist.

Born in Belgium in 1912, Sarton has composed herself into an
authentic New Englander. The landscape of her imagination extends from Cambridge through New Hampshire to the Maine seacoast. Yet Sarton has, like many of Greater Boston's best writers,
a paradoxical relationship with the region. "May Sarton was born
an outsider and has remained one," writes Carolyn G. Heilbrun.
Though deeply rooted in New England places, Sarton "has sought
salvation in exile no less fervently because it was frequently of her
own choosing."[51] In nearly fifty-volumes of semi-autobiographical
fiction, in confessional poetry, and in searching autobiographies,
she has testified to what it means to be a woman in and beyond
Greater Boston in this century.

In *Faithful Are the Wounds,* a 1948 novel, Sarton portrayed
Harvard as an emblem of Cambridge-Boston values. It is the story
of the suicide of a Harvard professor, Edward Cavan, a character
modelled on F. O. Matthiessen, author of *American Renaissance,*
a Harvard professor who committed suicide in 1950. Drawing upon
her intimate knowledge of Cambridge, where she was reared, and
her family ties to Harvard, Sarton's novel evokes a world sustained
by intellectual energies but riven with moral strife. Cavan threw
himself under a train, leaving a note which expressed despair about
"the state of the world" during the McCarthy era.[52] His death
stirred the Cambridge-Boston community to moral reexamination,
recrimination and, finally, renewal. Cavan was disturbed by a
congressional witch hunt for Communists which threatened the
freedom of American academics. Sarton saw his concerns as just;

she shows that some of those who had failed to defend Cavan were stirred by his suicide to stand up to a congressional investigating committee. Her novel renewed the notion of Harvard as a center of moral leadership and Boston as a city of idealistic purpose.

In Sarton's vision, the buildings of Beacon Hill still stood for worthy values, however threatened: the repainted gold dome of the State House, the conjunction of the Athenaeum, the Civil Liberties Union, various Protestant church offices, Goodspeed's, the Bellevue Hotel. For Edward Cavan—as for Matthiessen, also a Beacon Hill resident—who contemplated Boston's emblems with a friend,

> its tradition was a living one, a tradition of reform, protest, fierce belief in general enlightenment and in the rights of minorities. Not for nothing was their final glance for the corner where Robert Gould Shaw stood in bas-relief leading his Negro regiment into battle.[53]

Thirty-four years after publishing *Faithful Are the Wounds*, Sarton, at age seventy-seven, was still writing fiction which held Greater Boston up to a mirror so that it might reexamine its personal and communal values. *The Education of Harriet Hatfield* (1989), a title which echoes Henry Adams's *Education*, tells the regional parable of a sixty-year-old woman who, after the death of her friend of thirty years—theirs was "what Henry James called a Boston Marriage"—opened a bookstore in Somerville, a working-class community next to Cambridge. "Hatfield House: A Bookstore for Women"—a place for reading, talk, and feminism, where women "come to some idea of who they really are"—recalls Elizabeth Peabody's bookshop on West Street, where Margaret Fuller led "conversations" more than a century before.[54]

Opportunities have, of course, opened for women in Greater Boston since Fuller's day, but there remain battles to be won, Sarton makes clear. Hettie receives a note threatening her if she will not close her "obscene bookstore." After being interviewed by a reporter, Hettie, who has always been private about her sexuality, is shocked to read a headline in the *Boston Globe:* "Lesbian Bookseller in Somerville Threatened." As *Wounds* took up the issue of leftist politics and academe in Cambridge in the 1950s, *Education* takes up feminism, lesbianism, and residual conservatism in the Greater Boston area in the 1980s. Curiously, Harriet realizes, "in Henry James' time what used to be called a Boston Marriage, two women living together, was taken pretty much for granted," but in modern Boston it is worthy of note and cause for alarm. Harriet Hatfield's unironic education is advanced when she decides that it is time, for herself and for her society, that "a whole submerged part of respectable society came out into the open."[55]

May Sarton writes fiction which records the social and political nuances of the Greater Boston region. In *The Small Room* (1961), about academic freedom; in *Mrs. Stevens Hears the Mermaids Singing* (1965), about a defiantly lonely elderly poet; in *A Reckoning* (1978), about a dying Boston woman's realizations; in *Anger* (1982), about a destructive heterosexual relationship; in *The Magnificent Spinster* (1985), about a Boston woman who settles in Maine, a woman who represents "the flowering of New England," and in other works of fiction and poetry, Sarton has placed her women both within and often against the masculine grain of the New England mind.[56]

In her journals—those records of her lonely, inward journeys in several New England places—May Sarton renews and extends the regional mode of spiritual autobiography. In *Plant Dreaming Deep* (1968) Sarton recounts her move to Nelson, New Hampshire at age fifty-four. There, alone, she rooted and realized her family lineage by digging deep in her gardens, actual and imaginary. Cambridge might serve "the hunger of the novelist," but it was in Nelson that Sarton realized that "the nourishment I craved was all the natural world can give—a garden, woods, fields, brooks, birds: the hunger of the poet." Sarton found, as Thoreau had found at Walden Pond, a place where she too could create new myths to live by: in her rocky New Hampshire outpost. There she discovered a plan which would sustain her writings for the rest of her life: "a project that will be accomplished here and have to do with the New England ethos."[57]

This plan is carried forward in *Journal of a Solitude* (1973), also set in Nelson, where place and person become metaphors for each other. "Now I hope to break through into the rocky depths, to the matrix itself."[58] But that breakthrough occurred in Maine, in a large house by the sea, where Sarton moved in 1973, after the love of her life died. A path led from the house to the sea, which Sarton saw as her muse. Along with her dog, she explored the beautiful and sere landscape of coastal Maine; alone at her writing desk, she came to terms with the death of loved ones and celebrated her sustaining need for solitude. "For growing into solitude is one way of growing to the end."[59] However, her record of her new life in Maine, *The House by the Sea* (1977), shows Sarton turning not to "the end," but to a new beginning, another novel: "my world . . . turns inward once more toward creation."[60] From Cambridge to inland New Hampshire to coastal Maine, May Sarton's life has been a quest for renewal, recorded in a series of spiritual autobiographies.

THREE works written in the late 1980s—a novel, an autobiography, and a collection of autobiographical essays—show that the spiritual autobiography remains a living form for Greater Boston's writers. These works confirm that there is yet "no reason to fear a discontinuance of that state of mind."

In *Vestments* (1988), a novel by Alfred Alcorn, set in Boston, a young man sacrifices his positions and his possessions to be free to search for God. In *Returning: A Spiritual Journey* (1988), a confession which climaxes in Boston, autobiographer Dan Wakefield achieves a willed act of rebirth. In *Self-Consciousness* (1989), autobiographical essays, John Updike shows that New England remains not only fertile territory for imagining fiction but also for furthering a spiritual quest.[61] It is Updike who cites Emerson—"We are natural believers"—but Alcorn and Wakefield would agree.[62] In each of these works a character quests for a coherent self in a culture too little conscious of its lost mission.

Boston and its surrounding towns serve as proper settings for these quests. In the places where the original errand into the wilderness was articulated, there still resonates the deepest sense of the past available to an American. There too is rooted the original promise of American life. Character and community are one in these contemporary spiritual autobiographies. Their protagonists have won their places in the world but find themselves lost in the wood; shedding their old lives, they transcend the world or return to it renewed.

In Alfred Alcorn's *Vestments* Sebastian (Bass) Taggert, a man in the midst of a life of loud desperation, tries to break his tawdry ties so he can find the Good. Sebastian is a dangling man, despite his flashy job as an editorial writer for a Boston television station, his classy girlfriend, and his smashing condo along Cambridge's Memorial Drive. "They were, he was loath to admit, the quintessential young urban professionals." She wanted marriage and a baby, but he could not commit. "Marriage. It would be like death, living death. He'd never be free again."[63] Instead, he seeks escape, transformation through simulated then actual faith in God. His quest begins in calculation—he dons a clerical collar to reassure his dying aunt, who, in her dotage, thinks he is a Catholic priest— but Sebastian ends in a sincere imitation of Christ. Alcorn writes a Jamesian novel of renunciation, setting it in the acquisitive Reagan era.

The world is too much with Sebastian, late and soon, though Alcorn firmly places his hero in contemporary Boston, where ordinary things have a nimbus of spiritual possibilities. Boston offers Bass a world of history (the Freedom Trail), wealth (a posh, downtown office), sex, and style, a consumer's paradise, though he sees it as a sterile trap. He even envies the freedom of the bums and panhandlers who lurk around the Old State House.[64]

Garbed as a priest, Bass discovers a transformed world. In the Museum of Fine Arts he views paintings with a fresh eye, as he looks for meaning and wonder. Gauguin's tapestry-like painting of pagan beauty speaks directly to his life: *Where do we come from? What are we? Where are we going?* Childe Hassam's *Boston Com-*

mon at Twilight "made him feel nostalgic for a Boston he had never known."[65] Bass seeks a transcendent world of wholeness, harmony, and radiance, beyond the boundaries of Boston or any actual place. In his persona as priest he is as possessed as any Puritan seeker.

Alcorn offers a plausible hero who wants to put the world—at least the world of achievements, possessions, and status—behind him. Though he might never make it, he hopes to emulate the mother superior of a nursing home, a model of selflessness, who told Bass, "I do what I do in the imitation of Christ and the worship of almighty God."[66] Other Greater Bostonians, who appear in purposeful prose narratives, have also heeded similar words.

Though autobiography rather than fiction, Dan Wakefield's *Returning* follows a similar pattern. (Wakefield had previously written three novels in which Greater Boston had been treated as moral ground, as his titles indicate: *Starting Over, Home Free,* and *Selling Out.*)[67] In *Returning* the central character learns by going where he has to go, sets forth on a quest to discover his purpose in God's design. Wakefield's confession originated in a course on "religious autobiography," in the King's Chapel parish house in Boston.

> It was there that for the first time I began to understand how my life could be viewed as a spiritual journey as well as a series of secular adventures of accomplishment and disappointment, personal and professional triumph and defeat. I started to see the deeper connections and more expansive framework offered by the sense of our small daily drama in relation to the higher meaning that many people call God.[68]

Wakefield's journey of consciousness took him back to the point of crisis, when all seemed lost. He was forty-eight in 1980, living in Hollywood, drinking heavily, stuck in a failed relationship, out of luck and low on hope. On an impulse of nostalgia for a place where he had once been happy, he returned to Boston. "Walking the brick streets of my old neighborhood on Beacon Hill, I felt in balance again with the universe, and a further pull to what seemed the center of it, the source of something I was searching for, something I couldn't name that went far beyond the satisfaction of scenery or local color."[69] In Boston Wakefield found sanctuary, home, even the presence of grace.

Wakefield's meditation tracks two time-lines. In the foreground we witness first his physical recovery—he exercises, diets, and swears off alcohol—and then his gradual involvement in King's Chapel's version of the transcendent life. (Alcorn's hero moves through a symbolically Catholic landscape, where the sins of the flesh, guilt, and atonement are well-marked. Wakefield's "road map" is marked by the signs of American Protestantism: baptism, loss of faith, false gods, and rebirth. The spiritual journey has many routes that lead to the same end, like Robert Frost's "roads that diverge in a yellow wood.")[70] In the background we witness Wakefield's picaresque life history from his youth in Indianapolis to his coming of age in New York, where he deserted religion and began to write. Sex, alcohol, and psychotherapy, a holy trinity for many of his generation, were then his sedatives for life's pains in Manhattan.

Though Wakefield was a successful writer of essays, novels, and screenplays, something was missing until he found his place: in Boston, in King's Chapel. He even discovered that one of his ancestors, John Wakefield, was buried in the nearby Old Granary Burial Ground, a sign that the author had arrived at his true home. "Knowing that the ancestors of my genealogical family were in the very ground of the place to which I had been so naturally drawn seemed part of the whole intricate pattern of my journey and return."[71] Boston became Dan Wakefield's symbolic and actual home ground.

John Updike claims no New England heritage. The region for him was an acquired taste. His early consciousness was formed in Shillington, Pennsylvania, a territory reinvented as "Olinger" in his early stories and in his series of novels about Rabbit Angstrom, the alter ego who stayed in his hometown while Updike went on to Harvard and literary recognition. Shillington represents family, Lutheranism, youth, self-discovery, and great expectations. "Shillington was my *here*."[72] New England, particularly the land- and seascapes north of Boston, became his adopted home, chosen rather than given, the place where image and experience modified each other into his mature prose.

Self-Consciousness shows Updike's investment in the symbolism of place, in the narrative of quest, and in the spiritual dimension of his life and work. Inspired by an Emersonian reverence for the developed self, *Self-Consciousness* is both a journal of self-consciousness—of shameful conditions and acts, afflictions and sins—and an account of the growth of a poet's soul, as Wordsworth called it, a record of the development of his conscious self. "A writer's self-consciousness, for which he is much scorned, is really a mode of interestedness, that inevitably turns outward."[73] *Self-Consciousness*, then, is John Updike's spiritual autobiography, evidence of his affinity with his elected home and its literary imagination.

As a boy in Shillington, Updike dreamed of Manhattan, as it was stylized in the pages of *The New Yorker*, a magazine for which he would work briefly and write for decades. However, it was Harvard in particular and New England in general which drew him away from Pennsylvania. New England, for Updike, represented a new world of possibilities and called up surprising dimensions of his own character.

> New England. I have been happy here. . . . I found, coming north to college, something flinty and dry, witty and reticent, complex and venerable, breathable and lucid that suited me. . . . I had not known the sea or the mountains until I came to New England. Lots of writers had been here of old, and had left their signatures on the air like those initials people with diamond rings used to carve on old window panes. There are distances in New England, hard to see on the map, that come from the variousness of regions set within a few miles of one another, and from a tact in the people which wordlessly acknowledges another's right to an inner life and private strangeness.[74]

Harvard was, for Updike (A.B., 1954), as it has been for so many, both a door into an even wider world and a place of permanence, resonant with regional and ideological symbolism, to which he would return.

After Harvard, Updike attended Oxford University, where he had been granted a fellowship to study painting. He returned to work at *The New Yorker* at the invitation of E. B. White, another self-elected New England writer. The New York of fact, however, did not match the New York of Updike's imagination. "New York was not going to help me unpack my shadowy message."[75] So Updike moved his family to Ipswich, Massachusetts—"a town much like Shillington in its blend of sweet and tough, only more spacious and historic and blessedly free from family ghosts"—where he remained for the next seventeen years, until the breakup of his marriage. Now remarried, he still lives nearby in Beverly on the Massachusetts North Shore. Ipswich and surrounding towns represented "actual life" in Updike's allegorical landscape. There he "felt well located artistically, in a place out of harm's . . . way," in touch with his subjects: middle-class Americans in crises of conscience.[76]

Living within the orbit of Boston-Cambridge, Updike has placed himself well within the tradition of New England literary concerns, particularly those centering upon spiritual quest. Here belief was in the air. "'Belief consists in accepting the affirmations of the soul; unbelief, in denying them.' Emerson's revelation that God and the self are of the same substance."[77] As did W. D. Howells a century earlier, John Updike came to Greater Boston from the American heartland, drawn by the region's literary and moral aura. Like Howells, Updike has claimed his place in several compelling fictions with New England settings and, as we have seen, in many critical appreciations of New England writers: Hawthorne, Emerson, Howells, and others. However, unlike Howells, who left Boston for New York in midcareer, Updike has remained on New England grounds in most of his writings and in his life.

Updike is "struggling to expose what should be—in decency, to conserve potency—*behind:* behind the facade, the human courtesies, my performance, my 'act.' " Behind his act—the act of making his life and the act of making fictions from his life—lies

Updike's truth: a vision of a beneficent America and a moral universe. "Wherever there is a self, it may be, whether on Earth or in the Andromeda Galaxy, the idea of God will arise."[78] John Winthrop would approve.

BOSTON lies far from the Andromeda Galaxy, but Boston writers have long sought metaphoric heights, in this city upon a hill, to give sufficient scope to their visions and to allow distant others to witness their errand into the wilderness. As it was in the beginning of the Boston mission, so has it, with modifications, remained: from Hawthorne, who reimagined the original Puritan world, to Updike, who recomposed Hawthorne's imaginings and renewed Greater Bostonians' sense of themselves. Boston writers have placed moral mission and spiritual quest at the center of their works, and at the center—indeed the Hub—of America's literary landscape, Boston.

Boston's prophetic books debate the city's future; Boston's historical meditations reexamine the city's mission. Edward Bellamy's *Looking Backward: 2000–1887*, a popular novel of 1888, looked forward to the brave new world of Boston's future, to the year 2000 when all would be ordered and serene in a benevolent dictatorship.[79] Like Michael Wigglesworth's *Day of Doom* (1662), *Looking Backward* held out a vision of salvation, a New Jerusalem or a Millennial City, though set in *this* world, within Suffolk County.

Bellamy used a future setting in his novel, as Hawthorne had used a past setting in *The Scarlet Letter*, as a strategy to dramatize the cultural failures of his own day. Hawthorne implicitly castigated lingering Puritan strains in pre–Civil War America, while Bellamy directly condemned economic inequities during the Gilded Age. Both *The Scarlet Letter* and *Looking Backward* are lovers' quarrels with Boston for not fulfilling its mission as an exemplary and worthy city upon a hill. Both novels call Boston back to its vision of a unified society, John Winthrop's place of "justice and mercy."[80]

A century after Bellamy's utopian novel predicted a bright, if repressive, future for Boston, Margaret Atwood imagines a horrific

future in her dystopia, *A Handmaid's Tale* (1986).[81] In the manner
of Orwell's *1984*, Atwood projects into the near future frightening
possibilities in contemporary America. Atwood's post-nuclear, poi-
soned America is a monotheocracy, where men rule every aspect
of women's lives from the cradle to the grave. Atwood sees Puritanism reborn in New England. Thus the novel is set in "Gilead,"
which once had been Cambridge. Harvard Yard becomes a place
of public punishments for rebels. For Atwood, Puritan settlers
"came to establish their own regime, where they could persecute
people to their heart's content just the way they themselves had
been persecuted."[82] As it was in the beginning of the Massachusetts
Bay Colony, so is it in the future: those who have the *word*, a
dedicated sense of righteousness with the power to make it prevail,
impose their wills upon those without language and power. Yet
Atwood allows her heroine's diary to survive, just as Hawthorne
claimed that documents containing Hester's story had survived.
Both anti-Puritan writers thus offer hopeful parables in which individual freedoms outlast theocratic tyranny. The word tyrannizes
and redeems, records and rescues—central beliefs of Boston's writers. For all of its writers, whatever their visions of the city's past,
present, or future, Greater Boston remains a place of significance
and consequence. These writers illustrate the wisdom in Eudora
Welty's insight on the relation between place and feeling: "Location
pertains to feeling: feeling profoundly pertains to place; place in
history partakes of feeling, as feeling about history partakes of
place."[83]

FROM Beacon Hill's heights we can still see Boston, however
transformed, spread around us. From this leveled peak we can
travel, overland or in our mind's eye, to those places which have
held significance for Bostonians and their writers: the Garden and
Common, Back Bay, the South End, all clustered in the city's
center. Beyond lie the hard edges of the city, where immigrant
energies, racial and ethnic identities have long been felt: the North

End, South Boston, Charlestown, and Dorchester. To the west lies Cambridge, central to Boston's self-definition from the beginning, and in particular Harvard, which embodies so much of the city's mind and soul.[84] We travel from Beacon Hill to Harvard to Concord, the pastoral and ideological counterpoint to pragmatic, commercial Boston. Farther west lie Amherst and the Berkshire Hills, Lenox, and other towns, at the outer edge of Boston's reach. This sphere of influence arcs north to include southern New Hampshire and south to encompass Cape Cod. All of these are sites which have been illuminated by the imaginations of Greater Boston's writers, writers who have infused such places with ideas, passions, and symbols. America's city upon a hill, though radically transformed, is still, as John Winthrop imagined it should be, a beacon—"the eyes of all people are upon us."

Notes

Preface

1. Henry James, *Hawthorne* (London: St. Martin's Press, 1967), 23; cited in Shaun O'Connell, "The Infrequent Family: In Search of Boston's Literary Community," *Boston Magazine* 67 (January 1975): 44–47, 64–68, 85–87.

2. Keith W. Stavely, *Puritan Legacies: Paradise Lost and the New England Tradition, 1630–1890* (Ithaca, N.Y.: Cornell University Press, 1987), 220–43.

3. Sam Bass Warner, Jr., *Province of Reason* (Cambridge, Mass.: Belknap Press, 1984), 122.

4. Stewart H. Holbrook, *The Old Post Road: The Story of the Boston Post Road* (New York: McGraw-Hill, 1962), 105–7.

5. Stavely, *Puritan Legacies*, 229–33.

6. Tracy Kidder, *The Soul of the New Machine* (New York: Avon, 1981), 8–9.

7. Sumner Chilton Powell, *Puritan Village: The Formation of a New England Town* (Middletown, Conn.: Wesleyan University Press, 1963), xix–xx, 116–32.

8. Holbrook, *The Old Post Road*, 100.

1. Approaching Boston

1. F. Scott Fitzgerald, *The Great Gatsby* (1925; New York: Charles Scribner's Sons, 1953), 182.

2. George W. Pierson, "A Study in Denudation," in C. Vann Woodward, *The Burden of Southern History* (New York: Vintage Books, 1961), 4.

3. Vann Woodward, *Burden*, 16.

4. Henry Wadsworth Longfellow, *Tales of a Wayside Inn* (New York: David McKay, 1970), 1–2.

5. Van Wyck Brooks, *The Flowering of New England* (New York: E. P. Dutton, 1952), 1–2.

6. Oliver Wendell Holmes, in John Freely, *Blue Guide: Boston and Cambridge* (New York: W. W. Norton, 1984), 10.

7. Walter Muir Whitehill, *Boston: A Topographical History*, 2d ed., enl. (Cambridge, Mass.: Belknap Press, 1968), 1.

8. "The landscape framed Boston's intimate dwellings and made its urban ways imperative." Jane Holtz Kay, *Lost Boston* (Boston: Houghton, Mifflin, 1980), 31.

9. J. Anthony Lukas, *Common Ground: A Turbulent Decade in the Lives of Three American Families* (New York: Alfred A. Knopf, 1985).

10. Thomas N. Brown, "Boston's Past: History as Common Ground," *Boston Sunday Globe*, 29 December 1985, A-13.

11. Trevor J. Fairbrother, ed., *The Bostonians: Painters of an Elegant Age, 1870–1930* (Boston: Museum of Fine Arts, 1986).

12. Trevor J. Fairbrother, "Painting in Boston, 1870–1930," in Fairbrother, ed., *The Bostonians: Painters of an Elegant Age, 1870–1930*, 38.

13. Ibid., 59.

14. John Winthrop, "A Model of Christian Charity," in Perry Miller, ed., *The American Puritans: Their Prose and Poetry* (New York: Anchor Books, 1956), 83.

15. Darrett B. Rutman, *Winthrop's Boston: A Portrait of a Puritan Town, 1630–1649* (New York: W. W. Norton, 1972), 7.

16. Ibid., 10.

17. Robert Frost, "The Gift Outright," Edward Connery Latham, ed., *The Poetry of Robert Frost: The Collected Poems, Complete and Unabridged* (New York: Holt, Rinehart and Winston, 1975), 368.

18. "John Winthrop's example," *The Boston Globe*, 12 January 1988; John F. Kennedy, "As a City upon a Hill," *Boston Globe*, 22 November 1988.

19. Perry Miller, "Individualism and the New England Tradition," in *The Responsibility of Mind in a Civilization of Machines*, ed. John Crowell and Stanford J. Searl, Jr. (Amherst: University of Massachusetts Press, 1979), 32.

20. Michael Zuckerman, *Peaceable Kingdoms: New England Towns in the Eighteenth Century* (New York: Alfred A. Knopf, 1970), 4–6.

21. Whitehill, *Boston: A Topographical History*, 7.

22. Walter Muir Whitehill, *Boston in the Age of John Fitzgerald Kennedy* (Norman: University of Oklahoma Press, 1966), 6.

23. Andrew Delbanco, *William Ellery Channing: An Essay on the Liberal Spirit in America* (Cambridge, Mass.: Harvard University Press, 1981).

24. Whitehill, *Boston in the Age of John Fitzgerald Kennedy*, 9–24.

25. Brooks, *The Flowering of New England*, 540.

26. Austin Warren, *The New England Conscience* (Ann Arbor: University of Michigan Press, 1967), 10.

27. P. Albert Duhamel, *After Strange Fruit: Changing Literary Taste in Post-World War II Boston* (Boston: Trustees of the Public Library of the City of Boston, 1980), 57.

28. Martin Green, *The Problem of Boston: Some Readings in Cultural History* (New York: W. W. Norton, 1966).

29. Ibid., 182.

30. Whitehill, *Boston in the Age of John Fitzgerald Kennedy*, 4.

31. F. O. Matthiessen, *American Renaissance: Art and Expression in the Age of Emerson and Whitman* (New York: Oxford University Press, 1941).

32. Alfred Kazin, *On Native Ground: An Interpretation of Modern American Prose Literature* (Garden City, New York: Doubleday, 1956), 1.

33. John Updike, *A Month of Sundays* (New York: Alfred A. Knopf, 1975); *Roger's Version* (New York: Alfred A. Knopf, 1986); *S.* (New York: Alfred A. Knopf, 1988).

34. Perry Miller, *Errand into the Wilderness* (Cambridge, Mass.: Belknap Press, 1956), 1–2.

35. William Faulkner, *Absalom, Absalom!* (New York: Modern Library, 1936), 261.

36. Henry James, *The American Scene* (Bloomington: Indiana University Press, 1968), 244.

37. Robert Lowell, "For the Union Dead," *"Life Studies" & "For the Union Dead"* (New York: Farrar, Straus and Giroux, 1964), 71.

2. Hawthorne's Boston and Other Imaginary Places

1. Samuel Eliot Morison, *Builders of the Bay Colony* (1930; Boston: Northeastern University Press, 1980), 135.

2. Nathaniel Hawthorne, *The Scarlet Letter* (1850; New York: Penguin Books, 1983), 76.

3. Ibid., 214–15.

4. Ibid., 273–74.

5. Ibid., 104.

6. Nathaniel Hawthorne, in Julian Hawthorne, *Nathaniel Hawthorne and His Wife: A Biography* (1884; USA: Archon Books, 1968), 94.

7. Hawthorne, *The Scarlet Letter*, 40.

8. Ibid., 41.

9. Ibid., 42, 43.

10. Nathaniel Hawthorne, "Preface," *Twice-Told Tales* (1851; Boston: Houghton, Mifflin, 1879), 1:v.

11. Hawthorne, in Philip Young, *Hawthorne's Secret: An Un-told Tale* (Boston: David R. Godine, 1984), 18. Julian Hawthorne, *Nathaniel Hawthorne and His Wife*, 96–97.

12. Hawthorne, in Mark Van Doren, *Nathaniel Hawthorne* (1949; New York: Viking Press, 1957), 7.

13. Ibid., 30.

14. Young, *Hawthorne's Secret*, 19.

15. Nathaniel Hawthorne, *The American Notebooks*, ed. Claude M. Simpson, Centenary Edition of the Works of Nathaniel Hawthorne (USA: Ohio State University Press, 1972), 8:20.

16. Ibid., 12.

17. Hawthorne, in Young, *Hawthorne's Secret*, 35.

18. Morton and Lucia White, *The Intellectual versus the City: From Thomas Jefferson to Frank Lloyd Wright* (Cambridge, Mass.: Harvard University Press and the M.I.T. Press, 1962), 41.

19. Walter Muir Whitehill, *Boston: A Topographical History*, 2d ed., enl. (Cambridge, Mass.: Belknap Press, 1968), 105–6.

20. Hawthorne, *Notebooks*, 7–8.

21. Leo McNamara describes the tale accurately as "Hawthorne's parable of misplaced assurance and rancorous discontent" which foreshadows post-revolutionary America. "Irish and American Politics in the 18th Century and Nathaniel Hawthorne's 'My Kinsman, Major Molineux,'" *Eire-Ireland* XXIV (Fall 1989): 20–32.

22. Nathaniel Hawthorne, "My Kinsman, Major Molineux," *"The Celestial Railroad" and Other Stories* (New York: New American Library, 1963), 41, 30, 48.

23. Nathaniel Hawthorne, "The New Adam and Eve," *Mosses from an Old Manse* (1854; Boston: Houghton, Mifflin, 1882), 2:10.

24. Nathaniel Hawthorne, "Sights from a Steeple," *Twice-Told Tales*.

25. Hawthorne, *Notebooks*, 496, 497.

26. Nathaniel Hawthorne, *The Blithedale Romance* (1852; New York: Penguin Books, 1983), 149, 159.

27. Hawthorne, in Julian Hawthorne, *Nathaniel Hawthorne and His Wife*, 227.

28. Hawthorne, *The Blithedale Romance*, 40.

29. Hawthorne, preface to *The Blithedale Romance*, 2.

30. Hawthorne, in Julian Hawthorne, *Nathaniel Hawthorne and His Wife*, 299–300.

31. Paul Brooks, *The Old Manse and the People Who Lived There* (n.p.: The Trustees of Reservations, 1983), 51–52.

32. Hawthorne, *Notebooks,* 315.

33. Julian Hawthorne, *Nathaniel Hawthorne and His Wife,* 245.

34. Hawthorne, *Mosses,* 9–10.

35. Ralph Waldo Emerson, "Nature," *Ralph Waldo Emerson: Selected Essays,* ed. Larzer Ziff (New York: Penguin Books, 1982), 64.

36. Ralph Waldo Emerson, "The Poet," *Selected Essays,* 281.

37. Ralph Waldo Emerson, "The American Scholar," *Selected Essays,* 105.

38. Gay Wilson Allen, *Waldo Emerson: A Biography* (New York: Viking Press, 1981), 10.

39. Emerson, in Brooks, *The Old Manse,* 19.

40. Joel Porte, *Representative Man: Ralph Waldo Emerson in His Time* (New York: Columbia University Press, 1988), 112–18.

41. Joel Porte, ed., *Emerson in His Journals* (Cambridge, Mass.: Belknap Press, 1982), 141.

42. Ralph Waldo Emerson, "Concord Hymn," *Selected Writings of Emerson,* ed. Donald McQuade (New York: Modern Library, 1981), 891.

43. Emerson, "Nature," *Selected Writings,* 5–6.

44. Alfred Kazin, *A Writer's America: Landscape and Literature* (New York: Alfred A. Knopf, 1988), 50.

45. Emerson, in *Emerson in His Journals,* 143, 567.

46. Allen, *Waldo Emerson,* 663–64.

47. Morton and Lucia White, *The Intellectual versus the City,* 26.

48. Emerson, in Allen, *Waldo Emerson,* 36.

49. Allen, *Waldo Emerson,* 36.

50. Ibid., 37.

51. Emerson, in Allen, *Waldo Emerson,* 299.

52. Emerson, *Selected Writings,* 6.

53. "The point is that Emerson delighted in the Common not because it was an artificial, cultivated, quasi-urban piece of ground but rather because he associated it with the country and the woods." Morton and Lucia White, *The Intellectual versus the City,* 28.

54. Thoreau, in William Howarth, *The Book of Concord: Thoreau's Life as a Writer* (New York: Penguin Books, 1982), 127.

55. Emerson, in Allen, *Waldo Emerson,* 344.

56. Ralph Waldo Emerson, "Boston Hymn," *Selected Writings,* 895.

57. Emerson, in Alfred Habegger, introduction to Henry James, *The Bostonians* (Indianapolis: Bobbs-Merrill, 1976), xii.

58. Emerson, in *Emerson in His Journals,* 420.

59. Morton and Lucia White, *The Intellectual versus the City,* 27.

60. Emerson, in *Emerson in His Journals,* 306.

61. Ibid., 269–70.

62. Ibid., 509–10.

63. Ralph Waldo Emerson, "Thoreau," *Selected Essays*, 394.

64. Henry David Thoreau, *Walden; or, Life in the Woods*, in *Henry David Thoreau: "A Week on the Concord and Merrimack Rivers," "Walden; or, Life in the Woods," "The Maine Woods," "Cape Cod"* (New York: Library of America, 1985), 407.

65. Thoreau, in Robert D. Richardson, Jr., *Henry Thoreau: A Life of the Mind* (Berkeley, Los Angeles, London: University of California Press, 1986), 170.

66. Emerson, "Thoreau," *Selected Essays*, 403.

67. Thoreau, in Richardson, *Henry Thoreau*, 78.

68. Thoreau, *Walden*, 326.

69. Channing, in Richard Lebeaux, *Young Man Thoreau* (Amherst, Mass.: University of Massachusetts Press, 1977), 45.

70. Emerson, "Thoreau," *Selected Essays*, 405.

71. Thoreau, in Howarth, *The Book of Concord*, 61.

72. Thoreau, in Richardson, *Henry Thoreau*, 389.

73. Howarth, *The Book of Concord*, ix.

74. Leo Marx, *The Machine in the Garden: Technology and the Pastoral Ideal in America* (New York: Oxford University Press, 1964), 245, 246.

75. Richardson, *Henry Thoreau*, 105.

76. Lebeaux, *Young Man Thoreau*, 212.

77. Richardson, *Henry Thoreau*, 147.

78. Richard Lebeaux, *Thoreau's Seasons* (Amherst, Mass.: University of Massachusetts Press, 1984), 34.

79. Thoreau, *Walden*, 361.

80. Ibid., 446.

81. Ibid., 336, 476–77.

82. Ibid., 586.

83. Hawthorne, in Julian Hawthorne, *Nathaniel Hawthorne and His Wife*, 292.

84. James R. Mallow, *Nathaniel Hawthorne in His Times* (Boston: Houghton, Mifflin, 1980), 264.

85. Henry James, *Hawthorne*, in Edmund Wilson, ed., *The Shock of Recognition* (New York: Farrar, Straus, and Cudahy, 1955), 519.

86. Nathaniel Hawthorne, preface to *The House of the Seven Gables* (1851; Boston: Houghton, Mifflin, 1964), 4.

87. Herman Melville, "Hawthorne and His Mosses," *The Portable Melville*, ed. Jay Leyda (New York: Viking Press, 1959), 406.

88. F. O. Matthiessen, *American Renaissance: Art and Expression in the Age of Emerson and Whitman* (New York: Oxford University Press, 1941), 322.

89. Hawthorne, *House*, 27.

90. Sophia Peabody Hawthorne, in Frederick C. Crews, *The Sins of the Fa-*

thers: *Hawthorne's Psychological Themes* (New York: Oxford University Press, 1966), 172.

91. Julian Hawthorne, *Hawthorne and His Wife*, 361, 366.

92. Melville, "Hawthorne and His Mosses," *Portable Melville*, 403.

93. Ibid., 400.

94. Ibid., 406, 415, 414.

95. Nathaniel Hawthorne, *A Wonder-Book for Girls and Boys* (Boston: Houghton, Mifflin, 1851), 11.

96. Ibid., 221–23.

97. Herman Melville, letter to Nathaniel Hawthorne, 16 April 1851; in Harrison Hayford and Hershel Parker, eds., *Moby-Dick* (New York: W. W. Norton, 1967), 555.

98. Herman Melville, dedication to *Moby-Dick: or, The White Whale*, ed. Luther S. Mansfield and Howard P. Vincent (New York: Hendricks House, 1962).

99. Herman Melville, "The Piazza," *Piazza Tales* (1856; New York: Hendricks House, 1962), 10–11, 15.

100. Edith Wharton, *A Backward Glance* (New York: Charles Scribner's Sons, 1964), 153–54.

101. Miriam Levine, *A Guide to Writers' Homes in New England* (Cambridge: Apple-wood Books, 1984), 46.

102. Wharton, *A Backward Glance*, 293.

103. Edith Wharton, introduction to *Ethan Frome* (1911; New York: Penguin Books, 1987).

104. Wharton, *A Backward Glance*, 294.

105. Cynthia Griffin Wolff notes the Hawthorne-Wharton link in *A Feast of Words* (New York: Oxford University Press, 1977), 163–64.

106. Wharton, introduction to *Ethan Frome*, xvii.

107. Wharton, *Ethan Frome*, 14.

108. Wharton, *A Backward Glance*, 294.

109. Wharton, introduction to *Ethan Frome*, xviii. Cynthia Griffin Wolff argues that "Ethan Frome is *no more than a figment of the narrator's imagination*" (*A Feast of Words*, 164).

110. Edith Wharton, *Summer: A Novel* (New York: Harper and Row, 1979).

111. Wharton admired *The Heart of Darkness* and Conrad admired *Summer*, notes R. W. B. Lewis in *Edith Wharton: A Biography* (New York: Harper and Row, 1975), 398.

112. Edith Wharton, *The Age of Innocence* (New York: Charles Scribner's Sons, 1968), 347.

113. Wharton, *A Backward Glance*, 296.

114. Abigail Adams to John Adams, in *The Feminist Papers: From Adams to de Beauvoir*, ed. Alice S. Rossi (New York: Columbia University Press, 1973), 10–11.

115. Helene G. Baer, *The Heart is Like Heaven: The Life of Lydia Maria Child* (Philadelphia: University of Pennsylvania Press, 1964), 15–18.

116. Baer, *Child*, 41. Lydia Maria Child, *Hobomok* (Boston: Cummings, Hilliard, 1824).

117. Josephine Donovan, *New England Local Color Literature: A Woman's Tradition* (New York: Continuum, 1988), 3.

118. Child, in William S. Osborne, *Lydia Maria Child* (Boston: Twayne Publishers, 1980), 121.

119. Lydia Maria Child to Margaret Fuller, in *Lydia Maria Child: Selected Letters, 1817–1880,* ed. Milton Meltzer and Patricia C. Holland (Amherst: University of Massachusetts Press, 1982), 10–11.

120. Lydia Maria Child, *An Appeal in Favor of That Class of Americans Called Africans* (Boston: Allen and Ticknor, 1833).

121. Baer, *Child*, 66.

122. Child, in Baer, *Child*, 65.

123. Lydia Maria Child to Charles Sumner, *Selected Letters*, 283.

124. Lawrence Buell notes the importance of the iconic New England village in Stowe's writings, from "A New England Sketch" to *Oldtown Folks*. "To study the cult of the New England village is to study the most distinctly New Englandish contribution to the American social ideal." *New England Literary Culture: From Revolution through Renaissance* (Cambridge: Cambridge University Press, 1986), 305.

125. Harriet Beecher Stowe, *Uncle Tom's Cabin: or, Life among the Lowly,* in *Three Novels* (New York: Library of America, 1982), 519.

126. Harriet Beecher Stowe, *The Minister's Wooing,* in *Three Novels;* Donovan, *Local Color Literature*, 62.

127. Harriet Beecher Stowe, *Oldtown Folks,* in *Three Novels*, 883.

128. Ibid., 885.

129. Donovan, *Local Color Literature*, 67.

130. Marjorie Pryse, introduction to Sarah Orne Jewett, *"The Country of the Pointed Firs" and Other Stories* (New York: W. W. Norton, 1981), ix.

131. Donovan, *Local Color Literature*, 3.

132. Bruce A. Ronda, introduction to *Letters of Elizabeth Palmer Peabody: American Renaissance Woman,* ed. Ronda (Middletown, Conn.: Wesleyan University Press, 1984).

133. Elizabeth Palmer Peabody, *Letters*, 49.

134. Megan Marshall, "Three Sisters Who Showed the Way," *American Heritage* (September/October 1987): 58–86.

135. Elizabeth Palmer Peabody, *Record of a School,* in *The Transcendentalists: An Anthology,* ed. Perry Miller (Cambridge, Mass.: Harvard University Press, 1960), 150.

136. Hawthorne, in Louise Hall Tharp, *The Peabody Sisters of Salem* (Boston: Little, Brown, 1950), 136.

137. Elizabeth Palmer Peabody, *Plan of the West Roxbury Community,* in *The Transcendentalists*, 466.

138. Margaret Fuller, in Paula Blanchard, *Margaret Fuller: From Transcen-*

dentalism to Revolution (Reading, Mass.: Addison-Wesley Publishing, 1987), 87.

139. Margaret Fuller, "The Great Lawsuit MAN versus MEN. WOMAN versus WOMEN," in *The Norton Anthology of American Literature*, ed. Nina Baym, Ronald Gottesman, Laurence B. Holland et al., 3d ed. (New York: W. W. Norton, 1979), 1:1521.

140. Fuller, in Blanchard, *Margaret Fuller*, 46.

141. Ibid., 133.

142. Julia Ward Howe, *Margaret Fuller* (1883; New York: Haskell House Publishers, 1968), 84.

143. Joel Myerson, *The New England Transcendentalists and the Dial: A History of the Magazine and Its Contributors* (London: Associated University Presses, 1980), 47.

144. Ralph Waldo Emerson, "The Editors to the Reader," in *The Transcendentalists*, 250.

145. Ralph Waldo Emerson, "Historic Notes of Life and Letters in New England," *Selected Writings*, 831.

146. Margaret Fuller, "The Great Lawsuit," *The Transcendentalists*, 458.

147. Ibid., 460.

148. Fuller, in Theodora Penny Martin, *The Sound of Our Own Voices: Women's Study Clubs 1860–1910* (Boston: Beacon Press, 1987), 99.

149. Blanchard, *Margaret Fuller*, 147.

150. Margaret Fuller, *Memoirs*, ed. Ralph Waldo Emerson, James Freeman Clarke and W. H. Channing, in *The Transcendentalists*, 333–34.

151. Miller, *The Transcendentalists*, 332.

152. Blanchard, *Margaret Fuller*, 186.

153. Margaret Fuller Ossoli, *Life without and Life within* (Upper Saddle River, N.J.: Literature House/Gregg Press, 1970), 193.

154. "Hester Prynne is not the antithesis but the fictional embodiment of a 'fictional' Anne Hutchinson." Hawthorne makes her repent to counter the antinomian implications of her story; see Amy Schrager Lang, *Prophetic Woman: Anne Hutchinson and the Problem of Dissent in the Literature of New England* (Berkeley and Los Angeles: University of California Press, 1987), 165.

155. Julia Ward Howe, *Reminiscences 1819–1899* (Boston: Houghton, Mifflin, 1988), 144.

156. Julia Ward Howe, "Margaret Fuller," *At Sunset* (Boston: Houghton, Mifflin, 1910), 67.

157. Howe, *Margaret Fuller*, 278.

158. Howe, *Reminiscences*, 144.

159. Howe, in Paul S. Boyer, "Julia Ward Howe," in *Notable American Women 1607–1950*, ed. Edward T. James, Janet Wilson James, and Paul S. Boyer (Cambridge, Mass.: Belknap Press, 1971), 2:226.

160. Edmund Wilson, *Patriotic Gore: Studies in the Literature of the American Civil War* (New York: Oxford University Press, 1962), 96.

161. Howe, in Martin, *The Sound of Our Own Voices*, 35.

162. Deborah Pickman Clifford, *Mine Eyes Have Seen the Glory: A Biography of Julia Ward Howe* (Boston: Little, Brown, 1979), 227–28.

163. Helen W. Wilson, *Literary Boston Today* (Boston: L. C. Page, 1902), 43.

164. Julia Ward Howe, "Old Home Week in Boston," *At Sunset*, 17.

165. Louisa May Alcott, in Madeleine B. Stern, introduction to *The Selected Letters of Louisa May Alcott,* ed. Joel Myerson and Daniel Shealy; assoc. ed. Madeleine B. Stern (Boston: Little, Brown, 1987), xxii. Louisa May Alcott, *Little Women* (1868; Boston: Little, Brown, 1968). See Sarah Elbert, *A Hunger for Home: Louisa May Alcott's Place in American Culture* (New Brunswick: Rutgers University Press, 1987), 2.

166. Amos Bronson Alcott, in Madelon Bedell, *The Alcotts: Biography of a Family* (New York: Clarkson N. Potter, 1980), 34–35.

167. Elizabeth Palmer Peabody, *Letters*, 27.

168. Louisa May Alcott, "Transcendental Wild Oats," *Alternative Alcott*, ed. Elaine Showalter (New Brunswick: Rutgers University Press, 1988), 364–79.

169. Alcott, "How I Went Out to Service," *Alternative Alcott*, 350–63.

170. Daniel Shealy, "Miss Alcott of Boston" (Paper delivered at the Northeast Modern Language Association Meeting, Boston, April 1987).

171. Louisa May Alcott, *Selected Letters*, 19.

172. Louisa May Alcott, *Work: A Story of Experience* (New York: Shocken Books, 1977).

173. Alcott, *Little Women*, preface.

174. Peabody, *Letters*, 225.

175. Nathaniel Hawthorne, *Tanglewood Tales* (1853; Boston: Houghton, Mifflin, 1881), 8.

176. Nathaniel Hawthorne, *Our Old Home: A Series of English Sketches* (Boston: Houghton, Mifflin, 1963), 176, 186.

177. Julian Hawthorne, *Nathaniel Hawthorne and His Wife*, 2:263.

178. Henry Wadsworth Longfellow, "Hawthorne," *Selected Poems*, ed. Lawrence Buell (New York: Penguin Books, 1988), 373–74.

179. Ibid.

180. Robert Lowell, *"Life Studies" & "For the Union Dead"* (New York: Farrar, Straus and Giroux, 1964), 38–39.

3. Boston, The Right American Stuff

1. Bartley Hubbard interviews Silas Lapham for the "Solid Men of Boston" series he writes for a Boston newspaper. William Dean Howells, *The Rise of Silas Lapham* (1885; New York: Penguin Books, 1985), 3.

2. Michael Anesko, "Notes to an Exhibition." *William Dean Howells 1837–1920: A Sesquicentennial Exhibition* (The Houghton Library, Harvard University, May 1987).

3. John Updike, "Address," Emerson Lecture Hall, Harvard University, 1 May 1987; "Howells as Anti-Novelist," *The New Yorker*, 13 July 1987, 78–88.

4. William Dean Howells, *Literary Friends and Acquaintance: A Personal Retrospect of American Authorship*, ed. David F. Hiatt and Edwin H. Cady, Selected Edition of W. D. Howells (1900; Bloomington and London: Indiana University Press, 1968), 49.

5. Howells, *Literary Friends*, 51.

6. Ibid., 54–55.

7. Ibid., 101.

8. Leon Edel, *Henry James: The Untried Years: 1843–1870* (London: Rupert Hart-Davis, 1953), 280–81.

9. Henry James, "The Art of Fiction," *Henry James: Literary Criticism: Essays on Literature, American Writers, English Writers* (New York: Library of America, 1984), 44–65. The James-Howells debate over the art of fiction and its proper setting is discussed in Kenneth S. Lynn, *William Dean Howells: An American Life* (New York: Harcourt Brace, Jovanovich, 1971).

10. James, in Edel, *Henry James: The Untried Years*, 205.

11. Edel, *Henry James: The Untried Years*, 281.

12. Howells, in Mildred Howells, ed., *Life in Letters of William Dean Howells*, 2 vols. (Garden City, N.Y.: Doubleday, Doran, 1928), 2:397.

13. James's tentative allegiance to the region of his youth has been noted by Morton and Lucia White. "[James] saw Boston bifocally as a rural center and as a town of history; a history, however, in which he showed no great interest. He loved neither the gentility of the Brahmins nor the frugality of Concord and could not abide New England's conception of culture as a matter of duty." We will see that James showed far more interest, even affection, than the Whites here allow. However, they capture Howells's complex attitude toward urban life in a sentence: "he was a theoretical anti-urbanist and a practical city-dweller, critical of the city's way of life but attached to urban people and places." Morton and Lucia White, *The Intellectual versus the City: From Thomas Jefferson to Frank Lloyd Wright* (Cambridge, Mass.: Harvard University and the M.I.T. Press, 1962), 78, 98.

14. Henry James, "William Dean Howells," in *The Shock of Recognition*, ed. Edmund Wilson (New York: Farrar, Straus and Cudahy, 1955), 507–8.

15. Howells, *Literary Friends*, 16, 14.

16. William Dean Howells, *A Chance Acquaintance*, Selected Edition of W. D. Howells (Bloomington and London: Indiana University Press, 1971), 36.

17. Ibid., 10.

18. Howells, in introduction to *Acquaintance*, xxvi.

19. Howells, *Acquaintance*, 36.

20. Ibid., 91.

21. Howells, *Literary Friends*, 127.

22. Ibid., 109.

23. Ibid., 153, 211.

24. Ibid., 164.

25. William Dean Howells, *Suburban Sketches* (1871; Freeport, N.Y.: Books for Libraries Press, 1898), 12, 61.

26. Ibid., 65–66.

27. Ibid., 67, 68.

28. Ibid., 72.

29. Howells, *Letters*, 1:141–42.

30. Oliver Wendell Holmes, in Howells, *Literary Friends*, 36.

31. William Dean Howells, *A Modern Instance*, ed. William M. Gibson (Boston: Houghton, Mifflin, 1957), 1.

32. Howells, *Letters*, 1:366.

33. Howells, *Literary Friends*, 138–39.

34. William Butler Yeats, "A Prayer for My Daughter," *W. B. Yeats: Selected Poetry*, ed. A. Norman Jeffares (London: Macmillan, 1974), 102.

35. Henry David Thoreau, *Walden*, in *"Walden" and "Civil Disobedience"* (1854; New York: Penguin Books, 1983), 73.

36. Howells, *Silas Lapham*, 145.

37. Ibid., 3.

38. Ibid., 315.

39. Ibid., 366; see also Kermit Vanderbilt, "Appendix: *Silas Lapham* and Anti-Semitism," in Howells, *Silas Lapham*.

40. Howells, *Silas Lapham*, 352.

41. Van Wyck Brooks, *Howells: His Life and World* (New York: E. P. Dutton, 1959), 165–66.

42. Howells, in Howard M. Munford, introduction to William Dean Howells, *The Minister's Charge; or, The Apprenticeship of Lemuel Barker*, Selected Edition of W. D. Howells (1886; Bloomington and London: Indiana University Press, 1978), xi, xvii, xxiv.

43. Howells, *Minister*, 68.

44. Howells, *Literary Friends*, 287, 280–81.

45. The incident is fully described in Justin Kaplan, *Mr. Clemens and Mark Twain* (New York: Simon and Schuster, 1966), 209–11.

46. Howells, *Literary Friends*, 293–97.

47. M. A. DeWolfe Howe, *The Atlantic Monthly and Its Makers* (Westport, Conn.: Greenwood Press, 1919), 60–76.

48. Howells, *Literary Friends*, 101–2.

49. Henry James, *Hawthorne* (1879; New York: St. Martin's Press, 1967), 119, 111.

50. Ibid., 24, 32.

51. Ibid., 55.

52. Ibid., 55–56, 34.

53. Ibid., 76–77, 109.

54. Henry James, *The Complete Notebooks of Henry James*, ed. Leon Edel and Lyall H. Powers (New York: Oxford University Press, 1987), 214.

55. Ibid., 217.

56. James, *Hawthorne*, 156.

57. Henry James, *Notes of a Son and Brother*, in *Henry James Autobiography*, ed. Frederick W. Dupee (Princeton, N.J.: Princeton University Press, 1983), 359, 444.

58. Ibid., 445–46.

59. Henry James, *The American* (New York: Charles Scribner's Sons, 1907), 41.

60. Henry James, *The Europeans*, in *The American Novels and Stories of Henry James*, ed. F. O. Matthiessen (New York: Alfred A. Knopf, 1947), 37–38.

61. Ibid., 160.

62. Henry James, "A New England Winter," in *American Novels and Stories*, 356.

63. James to Perry, in Alfred Habegger, appendix to Henry James, *The Bostonians* (Indianapolis: Bobbs-Merrill, 1976), 430.

64. James, *Notebooks*, 232.

65. Ibid., 20.

66. Jean Strouse, *Alice James: A Biography* (Boston: Houghton, Mifflin, 1980), 90.

67. Ibid., 200.

68. James, in ibid.

69. James, in Leon Edel, "Portrait of Alice James," *The Diary of Alice James*, (New York: Dodd, Mead, 1964), 12.

70. James, *Notebooks*, 19.

71. Henry James, *The Bostonians* (1886; Harmondsworth: Penguin Books, 1983), 15–16.

72. James, *The Bostonians*, 17, 70.

73. Madelon Bedell, *The Alcotts: Biography of a Family* (New York: Clarkson N. Potter, 1980), 91.

74. James, *The Bostonians*, 31.

75. James, *The Bostonians*, 189. Charles R. Anderson, in James, *The Bostonians* (Harmondsworth: Penguin Books, 1985), 436 n. 21.

76. *Henry James: Letters*, ed. Leon Edel (Cambridge, Mass.: Belknap Press, 1974), 3:106.

77. James, *The Bostonians*, 384–85.

78. Ibid., 117–18.

79. Ibid., 382, 389–90.

80. Henry James, *The American Scene* (1907; Bloomington and London: Indiana University Press, 1968), xxv, 1.

81. Ibid., 58, 69.

82. Ibid., 226.

83. Ibid., 228.

84. Ibid., 231.

85. Ibid., 232.

86. Ibid., 245.

87. Ibid., 256.

88. Ibid., 263.

89. Ibid., 265–66.

90. Ibid., 266–67, 268, 271.

91. Henry James, "Nathaniel Hawthorne," *The American Essays of Henry James*, ed. Leon Edel (Princeton, N.J.: Princeton University Press, 1989), 12–13.

4. Irish-America's Red Brick City

1. Robert Taylor, "A Labor of Love and Laughter," *Boston Globe*, 21 June 1989. Taylor, *Fred Allen: His Life and Wit* (Boston: Little, Brown, 1989).

2. Robert Manning, "Edwin O'Connor: 1918–1968," *The Atlantic* (May 1968): 55.

3. O'Connor, *The Best and the Last of Edwin O'Connor*, ed. Arthur Schlesinger, Jr. (Boston: Atlantic Monthly Press, 1970), 4.

4. Ibid., 9.

5. Edwin O'Connor, *The Last Hurrah* (New York: Bantam Books, 1967); *The Edge of Sadness* (New York: Bantam Books, 1967); *All in the Family* (New York: Bantam Books, 1970).

6. Edmund Wilson, " 'Baldini': A Memoir and a Collaboration," *The Best and the Last of Edwin O'Connor*, 344.

7. See Dennis P. Ryan, *Beyond the Ballot Box: A Social History of the Boston Irish, 1845–1917* (Amherst: University of Massachusetts Press, 1983), 71.

8. Thomas N. Brown, "Holding Boston Together," *Boston Globe*, 19 June 1989.

9. Patrick G. Russell, "Pope's Day Brawls in Early Boston," *Boston Globe*, 5 November 1989.

10. Thomas O'Connor, *Fitzpatrick's Boston 1846–1866* (Boston: Northeastern University Press, 1984), 11, 22.

11. Edward Everett Hale, in O'Connor, *Fitzpatrick's Boston*, 82.

12. Ralph Waldo Emerson, in O'Connor, *Fitzpatrick's Boston*, 90. Emerson, *Selections from Ralph Waldo Emerson*, ed. Stephen E. Whicher (Boston, 1957), 280.

13. Barret Wendell, in Thomas H. O'Connor, *Bibles, Brahmins and Bosses: A Short History of Boston* (Boston: Trustees of the Public Library of the City of Boston, 1976), 82.

14. Ryan, *Beyond the Ballot Box*, 64.

15. Henry Cabot Lodge, in Ryan, *Beyond the Ballot Box*, 75.

16. "But there is no point in using the term 'Boston' to include all the communities that then lived in the city; from our point of view, they never made one

community, because they never made one culture." Martin Green, *The Problem of Boston: Some Reading in Cultural History* (New York: W. W. Norton, 1966), 103.

17. Oscar Handlin, *Boston's Immigrants: 1790–1880* (1941; Cambridge, Mass.: Harvard University Press, 1969), 123.

18. Ryan, *Beyond the Ballot Box,* 63.

19. J. Anthony Lukas, *Common Ground: A Turbulent Decade in the Lives of Three American Families* (New York: Alfred A. Knopf, 1985), 246–47.

20. Matthew Arnold, "Discourses in America," in *Victorian Prose,* ed. Frederick William Roe (New York: Ronald Press, 1947), 410.

21. Hasia R. Diner, *Erin's Daughter in America: Irish Immigrant Women in the Nineteenth Century* (Baltimore: Johns Hopkins University Press, 1983), 70–105.

22. Ryan, *Beyond the Ballot Box,* 113–26.

23. Handlin, *Boston's Immigrants,* 142.

24. Doris Kearns Goodwin, *The Fitzgeralds and the Kennedys: An American Saga* (New York: Simon and Schuster, 1987), 6, 111, 318.

25. John Boyle O'Reilly, in William V. Shannon, *The American Irish: A Political and Social Portrait* (New York: Collier Books, 1966), 135.

26. Francis Russell, "A Forgotten Poet: John Boyle O'Reilly," *The Knave of Boston & Other Ambiguous Massachusetts Characters* (Boston: Quinlan Press, 1987), 170.

27. William A. Davis, "The Printing of the Green," *The Boston Globe Magazine* (4 June 1989): 71.

28. See George Potter, *To the Golden Door: The Study of the Irish in Ireland and America* (Boston: Little, Brown, 1960), 603.

29. Ryan, *Beyond the Ballot Box,* 103.

30. Oliver Wendell Holmes, in Shaun O'Connell, "Boggy Ways: Notes on Irish-American Culture," *The Massachusetts Review,* 26. (Summer-Autumn 1985): 386–87.

31. John Boyle O'Reilly, "The Exile of the Gael," in *Life of John Boyle O'Reilly, Together with His Complete Poems and Speeches,* ed. James Jeffrey Roche and Mrs. John Boyle O'Reilly (New York: Cassell, 1891), 414–18.

32. O'Reilly, in O'Connell, "Boggy Ways," 387.

33. Catherine Shannon, "John Boyle O'Reilly, Irish Prophet of Progressivism" (Paper delivered at the New England Regional American Committee for Irish Studies Conference, Salve Regina College, Newport, Rhode Island, 8 October 1988).

34. Marty Carlock, *A Guide to Public Art in Greater Boston: From Newburyport to Plymouth* (Harvard and Boston: Harvard Common Press, 1988), 48.

35. William Cardinal O'Connell, in Lukas, *Common Ground,* 378, 376.

36. Patrick A. Collins, in John T. Galvin, "Boston's Eminent Patrick from Ireland," *Boston Globe,* 17 March 1988.

37. Rose Kennedy, in Goodwin, *The Fitzgeralds and the Kennedys,* 144.

38. Rose Kennedy, in Garry Wills, *The Kennedy Imprisonment: A Meditation on Power* (Boston: Little, Brown, 1982), 63.

39. "The original Poets' Theater was founded in 1950 and flourished in Cambridge in the 50's and early 60's. A loose affiliation of some of America's finest poets, among them, Richard Eberhart, John Ashbery, Donald Hall, V. R. Lang, Alison Lurie, Frank O'Hara, Archibald MacLeish, and Edward Gorey, the Theater performed new works by poets for the stage. The Poets' Theater was the first to produce *Under Milk Wood* by Dylan Thomas, *All That Fall* by Samuel Beckett, William Alfred's *Hogan's Goat* and *Agamemnon* [directed by Mary Manning], and the first verse translations of Molière by Richard Wilbur." "About the Poets' Theater," notes to *The T. S. Eliot Centennial*, 5 December 1988.

40. Carol Flake, "Return of a Legend: Poets' Theater Will Be Revived for a Night," *Boston Globe*, 17 September 1987.

41. Mary Manning, "Go Lovely Rose," An Entertainment at the John F. Kennedy Library (unpublished), 20 September 1987.

42. James Michael Curley, *I'd Do It Again: A Record of All My Uproarious Years* (Englewood Cliffs, N.J.: Prentice-Hall, 1957), 61; Shannon, *The American Irish*, 231.

43. Margo Miller, "A Chance to Visit Curley's House," *Boston Globe*, 12 June 1989.

44. Thomas P. O'Neill, Jr. with William Novak, *Man of the House: The Life and Political Memoirs of Speaker Tip O'Neill* (New York: Random House, 1987), 27, 30, 29, 28.

45. Shannon, *The American Irish*, 204, 231.

46. James Carroll, *Mortal Friends* (Boston: Little, Brown, 1978), 244.

47. Joseph F. Dineen, *Ward Eight* (1936; New York: Arno Press, 1976).

48. Joseph F. Dineen, *The Purple Shamrock: The Hon. James Michael Curley of Boston* (New York: W. W. Norton, 1949), 322.

49. See Nat Hentoff, *Boston Boy* (New York: Alfred A. Knopf, 1986), 88–89.

50. Curley, *I'd Do It Again*, 359.

51. Curley, in Jack Thomas, "History for Sale: Curley's Storied Home Sits on Auction Block," *Boston Globe*, 2 February 1988.

52. Editorial, *Boston Globe*, 30 March 1988.

53. Nathan Glazer and Daniel Patrick Moynihan, *Beyond the Melting Pot* (Cambridge, Mass.: MIT. Press and Harvard University Press, 1963), 287.

54. Kerby A. Miller, *Emigrants and Exiles: Ireland and the Irish Exodus to North America* (New York: Oxford University Press, 1985), 8.

55. Ryan, *Beyond the Ballot Box*, 14.

56. O'Connor, *The Last Hurrah*, 352.

57. William L. Riordan, "Honest Graft and Dishonest Graft," *Plunkitt of Tammany Hall* (New York: E. P. Dutton, 1963), 3–7.

58. O'Connor, *The Last Hurrah*, 156.

59. Ibid., 340.

60. Ibid., 214.

61. Ibid., 54.

62. Maureen Dezell, "The Rise of the CWASP," *Boston Business* (Summer 1986): 34–60.

63. O'Connor, *The Last Hurrah*, 35.

64. Boston's old city hall, designed by Gridley J. F. Bryant and Arthur Gilman, was completed in 1865. In the style of the Second French Empire, "the building has few admirers among architectural historians, but it is not without its own decadent charm." *Blue Guide: Boston and Cambridge* (New York: W. W. Norton, 1984), 100–101.

65. O'Connor, *The Edge of Sadness*, 134, 22.

66. Ibid., 290.

67. Ibid., 375.

68. O'Connor, *All in the Family*, 108, 127.

69. Ibid., 220, 127.

70. Hugh Rank, *Edwin O'Connor* (Boston: Twayne Publishers, 1974), 171.

71. Wilson, " 'Baldini,' " *The Best and the Last of Edwin O'Connor*, 344.

72. O'Connor, *All in the Family*, 76–77.

73. Goodwin, *The Fitzgeralds and the Kennedys*, 366.

74. Joseph Kennedy, in ibid., 367.

75. Ibid., 503.

76. O'Connor, *All in the Family*, 353.

77. Patrick Kavanagh, "Epic," *Collected Poems* (London: Martin Brian & O'Keefe, 1964), 136.

78. Patrick Kavanagh, *Tarry Flynn* (Harmondsworth: Penguin Books, 1975); *The Great Hunger*, in *Collected Poems*, 34–35.

79. Daniel Aaron, in Rank, *Edwin O'Connor*, 192.

80. Edwin O'Connor, "The 'Cardinal' Fragment," *The Best and the Last of Edwin O'Connor*, 406.

81. Arthur Schlesinger, Jr., Introduction to *The Best and the Last of Edwin O'Connor*, 16.

82. O'Neill, *Man of the House*, 6.

83. Ibid., 378.

84. Ibid., 26, 330–31.

85. O'Connor, *The Last Hurrah*, 66.

86. Ibid., 427.

5. Black Boston's Books

1. Henry James to C. E. Norton (1872), in *Henry James: Letters*, ed. Leon Edel (Cambridge, Mass.: Belknap Press, 1974), 1:274.

2. John Daniels, *In Freedom's Birthplace: A Study of the Boston Negroes* (New York: Negro University Press, 1968), 2–8.

3. Samuel Sewall, *The Selling of Joseph*, in *Racial Thought in America: From the Puritans to Abraham Lincoln, A Documentary History*, ed. Louis Ruchames (Amherst, Mass.: University of Massachusetts Press, 1969), 1:51.

4. John Adams, cited in Sidney Kaplan and Emma Nogrady Kaplan, *The Black Presence in the Era of the American Revolution*, rev. ed. (Amherst, Mass.: University of Massachusetts Press, 1989), 8.

5. Kaplan and Kaplan, *Black Presence*, 11, 13, 15.

6. Phillis Wheatley, in Kaplan and Kaplan, *Black Presence*, 170.

7. "Chronology," *The Collected Works of Phillis Wheatley*, ed. John C. Shields (New York: Oxford University Press, 1988), 337.

8. Julian D. Mason, Jr., introduction to *The Poems of Phillis Wheatley* (Chapel Hill: University of Carolina Press), 30.

9. Henry Louis Gates, Jr., "In Her Own Write," foreword to *Collected Works of Phillis Wheatley*, vii–ix.

10. John C. Shields, "Phillis Wheatley's Struggle for Freedom in Her Prose and Poetry," *Collected Works of Phillis Wheatley*, 268.

11. Wheatley, *Collected Works*, 18.

12. Wheatley to John Thornton, 30 October 1774, *Collected Works*, 184.

13. Daniels, *In Freedom's Birthplace*, 2.

14. See Alan Lupo, *Liberty's Chosen Home: The Politics of Violence in Boston* (1977; Boston: Beacon Press, 1988); J. Anthony Lukas, *Common Ground: A Turbulent Decade in the Lives of Three American Families* (New York: Alfred A. Knopf, 1985).

15. William D. Piersen, *Black Yankees: The Development of an Afro-American Subculture in Eighteenth-century New England* (Amherst, Mass.: University of Massachusetts Press, 1988), 1.

16. James Oliver Horton and Lois E. Horton, *Black Bostonians: Family Life and Community in the Antebellum North* (New York: Holmes and Meier, 1979), viii.

17. Piersen, *Black Yankees*, 26.

18. See Daniels, *In Freedom's Birthplace*, 11.

19. Marty Carlock, *A Guide to Public Art in Greater Boston: From Newburyport to Plymouth* (Harvard and Boston: Harvard Common Press, 1988), 31.

20. Daniels, *In Freedom's Birthplace*, 71.

21. Ralph Waldo Emerson, "Boston Hymn," *Selected Writings of Emerson*, ed. Donald McQuade (New York: Modern Library, 1981), 895.

22. Carlock, *A Guide to Public Art*, 30–31.

23. Piersen, *Black Yankees*, 160.

24. Frederick Douglass, *Narrative of the Life of Frederick Douglass an American Slave, Written by Himself*, ed. Benjamin Quarles (Cambridge, Mass.: Belknap Press, 1960), 153.

25. Horton and Horton, *Black Bostonians*, 62–64.

26. Charlotte L. Forten, in Kaplan and Kaplan, *Black Presence*, 191.

27. Charlotte L. Forten, *The Journal of Charlotte L. Forten* (New York: Dryden Press, 1953), 57, 65.

28. Henry Louis Gates, Jr., introduction to Harriet E. Wilson, *Our Nig; or, Sketches from the Life of a Free Black, in a Two-Story White House, North. Showing That Slavery's Shadows Fall Even There* (New York: Vintage Books, 1983), xxvii.

29. Harriet A. Jacobs, *Incidents in the Life of a Slave Girl: Written by Herself,* ed. Maria Child (Cambridge, Mass.: Harvard University Press, 1987).

30. Jean Fagan Yellin, introduction to Jacobs, *Incidents,* xx–xxiv, xiv.

31. W. E. B. Du Bois, "A Negro Student at Harvard," in *Black and White in American Culture: An Anthology from the Massachusetts Review,* ed. Jules Chametzky and Sidney Kaplan (Amherst, Mass.: University of Massachusetts Press, 1969), 123.

32. W. E. B. Du Bois, "Something about Me (3 October 1890)," *Against Racism: Unpublished Essays, Papers, Addresses, 1887–1961 by W. E. B. Du Bois,* ed. Herbert Aptheker (Amherst, Mass.: University of Massachusetts Press, 1985), 16–17.

33. Du Bois, "A Negro Student at Harvard," 130.

34. W. E. Burghardt Du Bois, *Dusk of Dawn: An Essay toward an Autobiography of a Race Concept* (New York: Harcourt, Brace, 1940), 9.

35. Francis L. Broderick, *W. E. B. Du Bois: Negro Leader in a Time of Crisis* (Stanford, Calif.: Stanford University Press, 1959), 2.

36. Du Bois, *Dusk of Dawn,* 17.

37. Broderick, *W. E. B. Du Bois,* 6.

38. Du Bois, *Dusk of Dawn,* 20, 32.

39. Ibid., 37.

40. Du Bois, "A Negro Student at Harvard," 126, 131.

41. W. E. Burghardt Du Bois, *The Souls of Black Folk: Essays and Sketches* (Greenwich, Conn.: Fawcett, 1964).

42. Richard Yarborough, introduction to Pauline E. Hopkins, *Contending Forces: A Romance Illustrative of Negro Life North and South* (New York: Oxford University Press, 1988), xli–xlii.

43. Pauline E. Hopkins, in Marilyn Richardson with Edward Clark, *Black Bostonians: Two Hundred Years of Community and Culture: An Exhibition of Books, Paintings, and Sculpture by and about Blacks in Boston; Drawn Chiefly from the Collections of the Boston Athenaeum* (Boston: Atheneum, 1988), 23.

44. Hopkins, *Contending Forces,* 142.

45. Ibid., 224–25.

46. Ibid., epigraph.

47. Dorothy West, in Mary Helen Washington, *Invented Lives: Narratives of Black Women 1860–1960* (Garden City, N.Y.: Anchor Press, 1987), 344.

48. Dorothy West, "My Mother, Rachel West," in *Invented Lives,* 381–83.

49. Dorothy West, *The Living Is Easy* (1948; New York: Feminist Press, 1982), 39–40.

50. Ibid., 44.

51. Ibid., 47.

52. Ibid., 42, 48.

53. Alex Haley and Malcolm X, *The Autobiography of Malcolm X* (New York: Grove Press, 1966), 2.

54. Haley and Malcolm X, *Autobiography*, 34.

55. Daniel Golden, "The Souring of Sugar Hill," *The Boston Globe Magazine* (30 October 1988): 19–23, 61–65, 75–81.

56. Haley and Malcolm X, *Autobiography*, 34–35.

57. Ibid., 38.

58. Ibid., 40.

59. Ibid., 43.

60. Ibid., 60.

61. Ibid., 73.

62. Ibid., 287.

63. Richardson, "Community and Culture: A Dual Tradition," in Richardson with Clark, *Black Bostonians: Two Hundred Years*, 1.

64. William Stanley Braithwaite, "In the Public Garden," *The House of Falling Leaves: with Other Poems* (Boston: John W. Luce, 1908), 54.

65. *The William Stanley Braithwaite Reader*, ed. Philip Butcher (Ann Arbor: University of Michigan Press, 1972), 167.

66. Ibid., 184, 186.

67. W. E. B. Du Bois, in Butcher, introduction to *Braithwaite Reader*, 1.

68. *Braithwaite Reader*, 134.

69. Ibid., 53–54.

70. Ibid., 187–88.

71. Ibid., 191–92.

72. Ibid., 230–33.

73. Piersen, *Black Yankees*, 160.

74. See Richardson with Clark, *Black Bostonians: Two Hundred Years*, 5.

75. *Black Heritage Trail* (Boston: Museum of Afro-American History, n.d.); Charles Bahne, *The Complete Guide to Boston's Freedom Trail* (Cambridge, Mass.: Newtowne Publishing, 1985).

6. Boston Manners and Morals

1. Richard Chase, *The American Novel and Its Tradition* (Garden City, N.Y.: Doubleday Anchor Books, 1957), ix.

2. Jerome Klinkowitz, *The New American Novel of Manners: The Fiction of Richard Yates, Dan Wakefield, and Thomas McGuane* (Athens: University of Georgia Press, 1986), 1.

3. Klinkowitz, *Manners*, 2.

4. Henry Adams, *The Education of Henry Adams: An Autobiography* (Boston: Houghton, Mifflin, 1918), 3.

5. Robert Lowell, "Antebellum Boston," *Robert Lowell: Collected Prose*, ed. Robert Giroux (New York: Farrar, Straus and Giroux, 1987), 291.

6. Ernest Samuels, *Henry Adams* (Cambridge, Mass.: Belknap Press, 1989), 8.

7. Adams, *Education*, 5.

8. Ibid., 7–8.

9. Ibid., 9.

10. Ibid., 33–34.

11. Ibid., 41–42.

12. Oscar Handlin, *Boston's Immigrants: 1790–1880* (New York: Athenaeum, 1976), 96.

13. Adams, *Education*, 305.

14. Henry Adams, *The Life of George Cabot Lodge*, in *The Shock of Recognition*, ed. Edmund Wilson (New York: Farrar, Straus and Cudahy, 1955), 750, 755.

15. George Santayana, *Persons and Places: Fragments of Autobiography*, ed. William G. Holzberger and Herman J. Saatkamp, Jr., Critical Edition (Cambridge, Mass. and London: MIT Press, 1986), 49.

16. Ibid., xxv, 158.

17. Ibid., 45.

18. Ibid., 139, 161.

19. Ibid., 161.

20. George Santayana, *The Last Puritan: A Memoir in the Form of a Novel* (New York: Scribner's Sons, 1937), 16.

21. Ibid., 32.

22. Ibid., 6.

23. John McCormick, *George Santayana: A Biography*, (New York: Paragon House, 1988), 336.

24. Santayana, *The Last Puritan*, 416.

25. Ibid., 581–82.

26. Ibid., 602.

27. In Robert Grant's novel, *The Chippendales*, the Brahmins struggle harder to retain their hold on Boston, but Grant too portrays a class which has been brushed aside by Boston's new immigrant and commercial energies (New York: Charles Scribner's Sons, 1909). See too the telling discussion of Grant and his fiction in Sam Bass Warner, Jr., *Province of Reason* (Cambridge, Mass.: Belknap Press, 1984).

28. John P. Marquand, in Millicent Bell, *Marquand: An American Life* (Boston: Little, Brown, 1979), 252.

29. Santayana, in Bell, *Marquand*, 254.

30. Helen Howe, *The Gentle Americans 1864–1960: Biography of a Breed* (New York: Harper and Row, 1965), 321.

31. M. A. De Wolfe Howe, *A Partial (And Not Impartial) Semi-Centennial History of the Tavern Club 1884–1934* (Cambridge, Mass.: Riverside Press, 1934).

32. De Wolfe Howe, in Helen Howe, *Gentle Americans*, 84.

33. M. A. De Wolfe Howe, *Memoirs of a Hostess: A Chronicle of Eminent Friendships Drawn Chiefly from the Diaries of Mrs. James T. Fields* (Boston: Atlantic Monthly Press, 1922), 284.

34. M. A. De Wolfe Howe, *Hostess*, 305.

35. M. A. De Wolfe Howe, *Barrett Wendell and His Letters* (Boston: Atlantic Monthly Press, 1924), 6.

36. Helen Howe, *Gentle Americans*, 320.

37. Bell, *Marquand*, 251.

38. John P. Marquand, *The Late George Apley*, (1937; New York: Pocket Books, 1971), 3, 5.

39. Ibid., 196.

40. Ibid., 1.

41. Robert F. Dalzell, Jr., *Enterprising Elite: The Boston Associates and the World They Made* (Cambridge, Massachusetts: Harvard University Press, 1987), xii, 124.

42. Marquand, *Apley*, 21.

43. Ibid., 69, 71–74.

44. Ibid., 83.

45. Ibid., 84.

46. Ibid., 148–49.

47. Ibid., 286.

48. Stephen Birmingham, *The Late John Marquand: A Biography* (Philadelphia: J. B. Lippincott, 1972), 21.

49. Bell, *Marquand*, 24.

50. John P. Marquand, *Wickford Point* (1939; Alexandria, Va.: Time-Life Books, 1966).

51. John P. Marquand, *H. M. Pulham, Esquire* (1941; Chicago: Academy Chicago Publishers, 1986), 222.

52. John P. Marquand, *Point of No Return* (1949; New York: Bantam Books, 1961), 254; *Sincerely, Willis Wayde* (Boston: Little, Brown, 1955).

53. Marquand, in Bell, *Marquand*, 283.

54. John Cheever, *The Wapshot Chronicle* (1957; New York: Ballantine Books, 1986); *The Wapshot Scandal* (1963; New York: Harper and Row, 1964).

55. John Cheever, *The Wapshot Chronicle*, 24.

56. Susan Cheever, *Home before Dark: A Biographical Memoir of John Cheever by His Daughter* (New York: Pocket Books, 1985), 26.

57. John Cheever, *The Wapshot Chronicle*, 12.

58. Susan Cheever, *Home*, 28–29.

59. Scott Donaldson, *John Cheever: A Biography* (New York: Random House, 1988), 4–5.

60. Susan Cheever, *Home*, 31.

61. Ibid., 16–17. Michiko Kakutani, "John Cheever Is Dead at 70; Novelist Won Pulitzer Prize," *New York Times*, 19 June 1982.

62. John Cheever, "The Death of Justina," *The Stories of John Cheever* (New York: Alfred A. Knopf, 1987), 432.

63. Kakutani, "John Cheever Is Dead at 70."

64. John Cheever, in Kakutani, "John Cheever Is Dead at 70."

65. John Cheever, in Donaldson, *John Cheever*, 159.

66. Frederick R. Karl, *American Fictions 1940–1980: A Comprehensive History and Critical Evaluation* (New York: Harper and Row, 1983), 50.

67. Cheever, *The Wapshot Scandal*, 244.

68. Donaldson, *John Cheever*, 283.

69. Ibid., 357.

70. John Updike, "On Such a Beautiful Green Little Planet," *Hugging the Shore: Essays and Criticism* (New York: Alfred A. Knopf, 1983), 295.

71. John Updike, "Personal History: At War with My Skin," *The New Yorker* (2 September 1985): 44.

72. John Updike, *Couples* (1968; New York: Fawcett Crest, 1969), 17, 310.

73. Ibid., 222.

74. Ibid., 21.

75. Ibid., 460.

76. Ibid., 464.

77. John Updike, "New England Churches," *Hugging the Shore*, 66–67.

78. John Updike, "HUB FANS BID KID ADIEU," *Assorted Prose* (New York: Alfred A. Knopf, 1965), 127.

79. John Updike, "Rapt by the Radio," *Boston Globe*, 6 October 1986.

80. Updike, "Rapt by the Radio."

81. Updike, "HUB FANS BID KID ADIEU," 137.

82. Ted Williams, in Updike, "HUB FANS BID KID ADIEU," 142. In his autobiography, Williams amplifies his scorn for the Boston press and his love for the Boston fans, though he would not tip his cap to them after he hit his final home run. Ted Williams, with John Underwood, *My Turn at Bat: The Story of My Life* (New York: Simon and Schuster, 1969).

83. John Updike, "The First Kiss," *Hugging the Shore*, 56.

84. Updike, "Rapt by the Radio."

85. Indeed, *Roger's Version* (New York: Alfred A. Knopf, 1986) is not Updike's first work of fiction indebted to Hawthorne. *The Witches of Eastwick* (1984) is an Updike novel which indirectly draws upon the same heritage of local witchcraft

which Hawthorne made central to our understanding of the New England mind. More directly, *A Month of Sundays* (1975), the first novel in a planned trilogy of variant readings of Hawthorne's central text, takes up Hawthorne's theme of adultery in a portrayal of characters derived from *The Scarlet Letter*. "Adultery, my friends, is our inherent condition," writes Tom Marshfield, in a journal addressed to one Ms. Prynne. "Adultery is not a choice to be avoided; it is a circumstance to be embraced. Thus I construe these texts." Marshfield, a minister who has been rejected by his parishioners for seducing Alicia, his organist, has been ordered to a western resort, managed by Ms. Prynne, to deal with his problems. His journal is both an apologia and a mash note, for he ends up in Ms. Prynne's bed, forgiven for the act of adultery while he is, so to speak, in the midst of its enactment. *A Month of Sundays*, then, like *The Witches of Eastwick*, is something of a parody of Hawthorne's world of imagination, a curious entertainment. In *Roger's Version*, and in *S.*, the third novel of the trilogy, which centers on Hester, Updike treats this material with higher seriousness.

86. Updike, *Roger's Version*, 50–51.

87. Ibid., 323.

88. John Updike, "Three Talks on American Masters," *Hugging the Shore*, 73.

89. John Updike, *S.* (New York: Alfred A. Knopf, 1988).

90. Updike, "Three Talks on American Masters," *Hugging the Shore*, 80.

91. John Updike, "Emersonianism," *The New Yorker* (4 June 1984): 131–32.

92. Joseph Campbell, *The Hero with a Thousand Faces* (Princeton, N.J.: Princeton University Press, 1949), 19–20.

7. *Boston's Sphere of Influence*

1. Emily Dickinson, "I like to see it lap the Miles," *Final Harvest: Emily Dickinson's Poems*, ed. Thomas H. Johnson (Boston: Little, Brown, 1961), 149.

2. Henry David Thoreau, *A Week on the Concord and Merrimack Rivers*, in *Henry David Thoreau* (New York: Library of America, 1985), 65.

3. Robert F. Dalzell, Jr., *Enterprising Elite: The Boston Associates and the World They Made* (Cambridge, Mass.: Harvard University Press, 1987), x.

4. Ibid., 36.

5. Charles Dickens, *American Notes for General Circulation* (1842; Harmondsworth: Penguin Books, 1972), 114.

6. Ibid., 117–118.

7. Lucy Larcom, *A New England Girlhood, Outlined from Memory* (Gloucester, Mass.: Peter Smith, 1973), 202.

8. Ibid., 8–9, 101.

9. Ibid., 145, 155.

10. Ibid., 163.

11. Ibid., 193, 200, 196.

12. Ibid., 215–16.

13. Ibid., 226.

14. Anthony Trollope, *North America*, ed. Donald Smalley and Bradford Allen Booth (New York: Da Capo Press, 1986), 249–50.

15. Van Wyck Brooks, *The Flowering of New England* (1936; New York: E. P. Dutton, 1952), 408.

16. John Greenleaf Whittier, in Donald Hall, *Introduction to Whittier* (New York: Dell Publishing Co., 1967), 9.

17. Miriam Levine, *A Guide to Writers' Homes in New England* (Cambridge: Apple-wood Books, 1984), 129–36.

18. Whittier, "Massachusetts to Virginia," *Whittier*, 93.

19. Whittier, "Ichabod," *Whittier*, 77.

20. Whittier, "Snow-Bound," *Whittier*, 117, 120.

21. Whittier, "The Barefoot Boy," *Whittier*, 112.

22. Donald Hall, introduction to *Whittier*, 18.

23. Henry Wadsworth Longfellow, "My Lost Youth," *Longfellow* (New York: Dell Publishing, 1959), 42.

24. Robert Frost, in Lawrence Thompson, *Robert Frost: A Biography* (New York: Holt, Rinehart and Winston, 1981), 171.

25. Thompson, *Robert Frost*, 171.

26. Robert Frost, *North of Boston Poems*, ed. Edward Connery Lathem (New York: Dodd, Mead, 1983), v–vi.

27. Robert Frost, "Into My Own," *The Poetry of Robert Frost: The Collected Poems Complete and Unabridged*, ed. Edward Connery Lathem (New York: Holt, Rinehart and Winston, 1975), 5.

28. Robert Frost, "The Death of the Hired Man," *The Poetry of Robert Frost*, 38.

29. "What I am most interested in emphasizing in the application of this belief to art is the sentence of sound, because to me a sentence is not interesting merely in conveying a meaning of words. It must do something more; it must convey a meaning by sound." Robert Frost, ". . . getting the sound of sense," in *Robert Frost Poetry & Prose*, ed. Edward Connery Lathem and Lawrance Thompson (New York: Henry Holt, 1972), 261.

30. Thompson, *Robert Frost*, 102–10.

31. Lawrance Thompson, "Robert Frost's Affection for New Hampshire," (Annual Meeting Address, New Hampshire Historical Society, 1967), 10–14.

32. Thompson, "Robert Frost's Affection for New Hampshire," 10.

33. Thompson, *Robert Frost*, 120–21, 126.

34. Frost, "The Pasture," *The Poetry of Robert Frost*, 1.

35. Frost, "Design," *The Poetry of Robert Frost*, 302.

36. Frost, "Mowing," *The Poetry of Robert Frost*, 17.

37. Frost, in William H. Pritchard, *Frost: A Literary Life Reconsidered* (New York: Oxford University Press, 1984), 82.

38. Frost, "After Apple Picking," *The Poetry of Robert Frost*, 68–69.

39. Frost, in "Robert Frost's Farm," publication of New Hampshire Division of Parks and Recreation.

40. Frost, "What Became of New England?," *Robert Frost Poetry & Prose,* 385–89.

41. Frost, "The Oven Bird," *The Poetry of Robert Frost,* 348.

42. Frost, in Thompson, *Robert Frost,* 482.

43. John Updike, on dustjacket of Andre Dubus, *Selected Stories* (Boston: David R. Godine, 1988).

44. Dubus, "Townies," *Selected Stories,* 360.

45. Dubus, "The Pretty Girl," *Selected Stories,* 106.

46. Maxine Kumin, "A Sense of Place," *In Deep: Country Essays* (Boston: Beacon Press, 1987), 173.

47. Ibid., 158–59, 173.

48. Frost, "Mending Wall," *The Poetry of Robert Frost,* 33.

49. Kumin, "Stones," *Up Country: Poems of New England,* 21.

50. Kumin, "A Sense of Place," *In Deep,* 174.

51. Maxine Kumin, *To Make a Prairie: Essays on Poets, Poetry, and Country Living* (Ann Arbor: University of Michigan Press, 1979).

52. Kumin, "A Sense of Place," *In Deep,* 170.

53. Ibid., 164.

54. Kumin, "In Deep," *In Deep,* 2.

55. Kumin, "A Sense of Place," *In Deep,* 165.

56. Ibid., 168.

57. Jack Kerouac, in Brian Foye, *A Guide to Jack Kerouac's Lowell* (Lowell, Mass.: Corporation for the Celebration of Jack Kerouac in Lowell, 1988), 11.

58. Ann Charters, in Foye, *Guide,* 1.

59. Jeff McLaughlin, "A Week of Jack Kerouac in Lowell," *Boston Globe,* 20 June 1988.

60. Cited from Jack Kerouac Commemorative.

61. Jack Kerouac, *The Town and the City* (1950; New York: Harcourt Brace Jovanovich, 1978), 3.

62. Gerald Nicosia, *Memory Babe: A Critical Biography of Jack Kerouac* (New York: Penguin Books, 1986), 53.

63. William Bradford, *Of Plymouth Plantation 1620–1647,* ed. Samuel Eliot Morison (New York: Alfred A. Knopf, 1963), 61.

64. Ibid.

65. Ibid., 62.

66. Henry David Thoreau, *Walden,* in *"Walden" and "Civil Disobedience"* (1854; New York: Penguin Books, 1983), 165.

67. Cotton Mather, in *The WPA Guide to Massachusetts* (1937; New York: Pantheon Books, 1983), 327.

68. Donald Wood, *Cape Cod: A Guide* (Boston: Little, Brown, 1973), 254.

69. Robert Finch, *Outlands: Journeys to the Outer Edges of Cape Cod* (Boston: David R. Godine, 1986), 40.

70. Robert Finch, *Common Ground: A Naturalist's Cape Cod* (Boston: David R. Godine, 1981), 4.

71. Finch, *Outlands,* 78–80.

72. Clare Leighton, *Where Land Meets Sea: The Enduring Cape* (1954; Boston: David R. Godine, 1984), 189.

73. Henry David Thoreau, *Cape Cod* (New York: Bramhall House, 1951), 13.

74. Ibid., 14.

75. Henry Beston, *The Outermost House: A Year of Life on the Great Beach of Cape Cod* (1928; New York: Ballantine Books, 1956), 3.

76. The thesis of Richard Lebeaux, *Thoreau's Seasons* (Amherst: University of Massachusetts Press, 1984), 201–3.

77. Robert D. Richardson Jr., *Henry David Thoreau: A Life of the Mind* (Berkeley: University of California Press, 1986), 201.

78. Thoreau, *Cape Cod,* 15, 16–17.

79. Ibid., 51.

80. Ibid., 182.

81. Ibid., 145–46.

82. Ibid., 124.

83. Ibid., 233–34.

84. Henry James, *The Bostonians* (1886; New York: Penguin Books, 1983), 298.

85. Ibid., 331, 342.

86. Henry James, *The American Scene* (Bloomington: Indiana University Press, 1968), 35, 36, 34.

87. Ibid., 38, 35.

88. Bradford, *Plymouth,* 25.

89. Arthur and Barbara Gelb, *O'Neill* (New York: Harper and Brothers, 1962), 303–13.

90. Marshall Brooks, "Remembering Eugene O'Neill's Days in Boston," *Boston Globe,* 13 October 1988.

91. Eugene O'Neill, *A Moon for the Misbegotten* (1952; New York: Vintage Books, 1974), 2.

92. Edmund Wilson, *The Shores of Light: A Literary Chronicle of the Twenties and Thirties* (New York: Farrar, Straus and Young, 1952), 764.

93. Edmund Wilson, *The Thirties: From Notebooks and Diaries of the Period,* ed. Leon Edel (New York: Farrar, Straus and Giroux, 1980), 23.

94. Mary McCarthy, *A Charmed Life* (New York: Harcourt Brace, 1955), 8–14.

95. Irvin Stock, *Mary McCarthy* (Minneapolis: University of Minnesota Press, 1968), 29–35.

96. Norman Mailer, *Tough Guys Don't Dance* (New York: Ballantine Books, 1984), 6.

97. Ibid., 9–10.

98. Melissa Green, "January," *The Squanicook Eclogues* (New York: W. W. Norton, 1987), 27.

99. Mary Oliver, "First Snow," *American Primitive* (Boston: Little, Brown, 1983), 26–27.

100. Mary Oliver, "Morning at Great Pond," *American Primitive*, 46–47.

101. Finch, *Common Ground*, 58.

102. Beston, *Outermost House*, 8, x.

103. Ibid., 95, 72.

104. Ibid., 174.

105. Leighton, *Where Land Meets Sea*, 18.

106. Ibid., 202.

107. Finch, *Common Ground*, ix.

108. Epigraph, Robert Finch, *The Primal Place* (New York: W. W. Norton, 1983).

109. Finch, *Primal Place*, 241–42.

110. Finch, *Common Ground*, 103–4.

111. Ibid., 63, 110, 51.

112. Ibid., xv.

113. Emily Dickinson's Boston visits: in 1844 (one month), 1846 (one month), 1851 (two weeks), 1863–64 (Cambridgeport boarding house, seven months). Millicent Todd Bingham, *Emily Dickinson's Home: The Early Years as Revealed in Family Correspondence and Reminiscences* (New York: Dover Publications, 1955), 433.

114. Richard B. Sewall, *The Life of Emily Dickinson*, 2 vols. (New York: Farrar, Straus and Giroux, 1974), 1:38.

115. Hugh F. Bell and Andrew Raymond, "Early Amherst," *Essays on Amherst's History* (Amherst, Mass.: Vista Press, 1978), 4–6, 29.

116. Alison Lurie, *Love and Friendship* (1962; New York: Avon Books, 1970), 112.

117. *Emily Dickinson: Selected Letters*, ed. Thomas H. Johnson (Cambridge, Mass.: Belknap Press, 1986), 7–9, 53.

118. Dickinson, in Sewall, *Life*, 1:39.

119. Dickinson, *Selected Letters*, 185.

120. Ibid., 171.

121. Thomas Wentworth Higginson, in "Emily Dickinson (1830–1886)," *American Literature: The Makers and the Making*, ed. Cleanth Brooks, R. W. B. Lewis, and Robert Penn Warren (New York: St. Martin's Press, 1973), 2:1228.

122. Richard Chase, *Emily Dickinson* (New York: Delta, 1965), 288–92.

123. Alice James, in Chase, *Emily Dickinson*, 275.

124. Dickinson, *Final Harvest,* 36.

125. Higginson, in "Emily Dickinson (1830–1886)," *American Literature,* 2:1224.

126. Dickinson, *Selected Letters,* 176.

127. Higginson, in Chase, *Emily Dickinson,* 280.

128. Richard B. Sewall, "Emily Dickinson," in *Voices and Visions: The Poet in America,* ed. Helen Vendler (New York: Random House, 1987), 68.

129. Dickinson, in Christopher Benfey, *Emily Dickinson: Lives of a Poet* (New York: George Braziller, 1986), 115.

130. Dickinson, in Richard B. Sewall, "Emily Dickinson," *Voices and Visions,* 60.

131. Jonathan Edwards, *Images and Shadows of Divine Things,* in *Colonial American Writing,* ed. Roy Harvey Pearce (USA: Rinehart, 1959), 382.

132. Alan Tate argues that Dickinson remained enough of a Puritan, in the tradition of Edwards or Mather, to master life by rejecting it. Alan Tate, "Emily Dickinson," in *Critical Approaches to American Literature,* ed. Ray B. Browne and Martin Light (New York: Thomas Y. Crowell, 1965). Perry Miller places Dickinson closer to Emerson ("From Edwards to Emerson," *Errand into the Wilderness* [Cambridge, Mass.: Belknap Press, 1956]). Karl Keller locates Dickinson in the context of the dark Puritanism of the Connecticut Valley (*The Only Kangaroo among the Beauty: Emily Dickinson and America* [Baltimore, Md.: Johns Hopkins Press, 1979]).

133. William Dean Howells, in Benfey, *Emily Dickinson,* 78.

134. Samuel Eliot Morison establishes the Bradstreet-Dickinson comparison (*Builders of the Bay Colony* [1930; Boston: Northeastern University Press, 1981], 36).

135. Tate, "Emily Dickinson," *Critical Approaches,* 67.

136. Frost, "The Oven Bird," *The Poetry of Robert Frost,* 119–20.

137. Dickinson, *Final Harvest,* 45.

138. Ibid., 36.

139. Dickinson, in Chase, *Emily Dickinson,* 255.

140. Dickinson, in "The Dickinson Homestead," publication of the United States Department of the Interior.

141. Dickinson, *Final Harvest,* 36.

142. Thompson, *Robert Frost,* 230, 457.

143. Ibid., 250.

144. Robert Francis, *Frost: A Time to Talk: Conversations & Indiscretions Recorded by Robert Francis* (Amherst, Mass.: University of Massachusetts Press, 1972), 54.

145. Thompson, *Robert Frost,* 291.

146. John F. Kennedy, in Thompson, *Robert Frost,* 515.

147. Francis, *Frost,* 48.

148. Ibid., 11.

149. Robert Francis, "The Black Hood," *Collected Poems 1936–1976* (Amherst, Mass.: University of Massachusetts Press, 1976), 214–15.

150. Robert Francis, *Pot Shots at Poetry* (Ann Arbor: University of Michigan Press, 1980), 218.

151. Robert Francis, *Travelling in Amherst: A Poet's Journal 1930–1950* (Boston, Mass.: Rowan Tree Press, 1986), 50.

152. Ibid., 87.

153. Francis, *Pot Shots*, 172.

154. Robert Francis, *The Trouble with Francis: An Autobiography by Robert Francis* (Amherst, Mass.: University of Massachusetts Press, 1971), 183–84.

155. Ibid., 189.

156. Ibid., 4, 83.

157. Robert Francis, "Juniper," *Come out into the Sun: Poems New and Selected* (Amherst, Mass.: University of Massachusetts Press, 1965), 125–26.

158. Francis, *Trouble*, 213.

159. Francis, *Collected Poems*, 279–81.

160. Francis, *Trouble*, 2.

161. Richard Wilbur, in *The Norton Anthology of Modern Poetry*, ed. Richard Ellmann and Robert O'Clair (New York: W. W. Norton, 1973), 1000.

162. Richard Wilbur, "April 5, 1974," *New and Collected Poems* (San Diego: Harcourt Brace Jovanovich, 1988), 78.

163. Frost, "Mowing," *The Poetry of Robert Frost*, 17.

164. Richard Wilbur, in Carol Flake, "Wilbur: A Poet of This World," *Boston Globe*, 9 May 1989.

165. Wilbur, "On Having Mis-Identified a Wild Flower," *New and Collected Poems*, 12.

166. Henry David Thoreau, in Richardson, *Henry David Thoreau*, 181.

167. Henry David Thoreau, "Walking," *The Portable Thoreau*, ed. Carl Bode (New York: Penguin Books, 1975), 604.

168. Ibid., 604.

169. Ibid., 603, 593, 609.

170. D. H. Lawrence, *Studies in Classic American Literature*, quoted in *The Shock of Recognition: The Development of Literature in the United States Recorded by the Men Who Made It*, ed. Edmund Wilson (New York: Farrar, Straus and Cudahy, 1955), 912–13.

8. A New England Genius

1. T. S. Eliot, "Tradition and the Individual Talent," *Selected Essays* (New York: Harcourt, Brace and World, 1960), 4.

2. Francis Russell, "T. S. Eliot: Harvard Loyalist," *Harvard Magazine* (September-October 1988):55.

3. T. S. Eliot, *Four Quartets, The Complete Poems and Plays 1909–1950* (New York: Harcourt, Brace and Company, 1958), 144.

4. "T. S. Eliot," *Writers At Work*, ed. Malcolm Cowley, 2d ser. (New York: Viking Press, 1963), 110.

5. T. S. Eliot, "Henry James," in *The Shock of Recognition: The Development of Literature in the United States Recorded by the Men Who Made It*, ed. Edmund Wilson (New York: Modern Library, 1955), 859.

6. Robert Lowell, "Writers 1 T. S. Eliot," *Notebooks* (New York: Farrar, Straus and Giroux, 1971), 119.

7. Eliot, "Henry James," *Shock of Recognition*, 859.

8. Ibid., 860, 861.

9. Lyndall Gordon, *Eliot's Early Years* (New York: Farrar, Straus and Giroux, 1977); *Eliot's New Life* (New York: Farrar, Straus, Giroux, 1988).

10. Gordon, *Eliot's Early Years*, 2, 11, 14. "What that date meant to Eliot must be a guess. It was soon after that Eliot's grandfather left Boston for the frontier. It was also then that the civilized elite of the Eastern seaboard lost its power in the bitter election of 1828, when John Quincy Adams fell before the rude, uncultivated Andrew Jackson." Gordon, *Eliot's New Life*, 271–72.

11. T. S. Eliot, "Portrait of a Lady," *Collected Poems 1909–1935* (New York: Harcourt, Brace, 1952), 11.

12. Eliot, "The Boston Evening Transcript," *Collected Poems*, 16.

13. Eliot, "Cousin Nancy," *Collected Poems*, 17–18.

14. Gordon, *Eliot's Early Years*, 101.

15. Gordon holds "Prufrock" is about Boston, but Denis Donoghue disagrees, noting "that she identifies the historical T. S. Eliot with the imagined J. Alfred Prufrock and concludes that 'Prufrock finds no woman in the Boston of 1911 in whom he can confide.' The poem mentions neither Boston nor 1911." Denis Donoghue, "The Temptation of St. John," *The New York Times Book Review* 16 (October 1988):40.

16. Eliot, "The Love Song of J. Alfred Prufrock," *Collected Poems*, 3–7.

17. Eliot, in Gordon, *Eliot's Early Years*, 30.

18. Ibid., 126.

19. Gordon, *Eliot's Early Years*, 133.

20. Gordon, *Eliot's New Life*, 12.

21. Eliot, *East Coker, Complete Poems and Plays*, 123–29.

22. Picking up a hint from Edmund Wilson, Lyndall Gordon develops the thesis of Eliot's grounding in Boston Puritanism and sees his work as a spiritual autobiography.

The American aspect of Eliot is still neglected, but the dominant forms of American writing, soul history and sermon, give a curious backing to Eliot's impenetrability. He shares with Emerson, Thoreau, Whitman, and Dickinson a guarded mode of confession. . . . Their confessions, like *The Waste Land*, are fragmentary, and, left so deliberately incomplete, demand a reciprocal effort. The point lies not in their content so much as in the act of self-discovery and judgment. Its ultimate purpose is not to expose the speaker but to create the reader. In short, it is a form of sermon: a call to a new life.

Gordon, *Eliot's New Life*, 234–35.

23. Eliot, "Tradition and the Individual Talent," *Selected Essays*, 7.

24. Helen Gardner, *The Art of T. S. Eliot* (New York: E. P. Dutton, 1959), 88.

25. T. S. Eliot, "The Waste Land," *Complete Poems and Plays*, 39.

26. Gordon, *Eliot's Early Years*, 87, 90.

27. Helen Vendler, "Contemporary American Poetry," in *Contemporary American Poetry*, ed. Vendler (Cambridge, Mass.: Belknap Press, 1985), 15.

28. Robert Lowell, "Antebellum Boston," *Robert Lowell: Collected Prose*, ed. Robert Giroux (New York: Farrar, Straus, Giroux, 1987), 291.

29. Ibid.

30. Elizabeth Bishop, in Jeffrey Meyers, *Manic Power: Robert Lowell and His Circle* (New York: Arbor House, 1987), 36.

31. Seamus Heaney, "Robert Lowell," in *Robert Lowell: Interviews and Memoirs*, ed. Jeffrey Meyers (Ann Arbor: University of Michigan Press, 1988), 245.

32. Lowell, "Antebellum Boston," *Collected Prose*, 302.

33. Lowell, in "A Conversation With Ian Hamilton," *Robert Lowell: Collected Prose*, 276.

34. Ian Hamilton, *Robert Lowell: A Biography* (New York: Random House, 1982), 37–43.

35. Lowell, in "A Conversation With Ian Hamilton," *Robert Lowell: Collected Prose*, 276.

36. Robert Lowell, "91 Revere Street," *Robert Lowell: Collected Prose*, 336, 337.

37. Jean Gould, *Amy: The World of Amy Lowell and the Imagist Movement* (New York: Dodd, Mead, 1975), 54.

38. Robert Lowell, in Hamilton, *Robert Lowell*, 25.

39. William Dean Howells, *Literary Friends and Acquaintance: A Personal Retrospect of American Authorship*, ed. David F. Hiatt and Edwin H. Cady, Selected Edition of W. D. Howells (1900; Bloomington and London: Indiana University Press, 1968), 191.

40. John Freely, *Blue Guide: Boston and Cambridge* (New York: W. W. Norton, 1984), 374–75.

41. James Russell Lowell, *A Fable for Critics*, in *The Shock of Recognition*, 70–71.

42. Martin Duberman, *James Russell Lowell* (Boston: Houghton, Mifflin, 1966), 62, 170–71. "I look upon a great deal of the modern sentimentalism about Nature as a mark of disease." James Russell Lowell, "Thoreau," in *"Walden" and "Civil Disobedience,"* ed. Owen Thomas (New York: W. W. Norton, 1966), 289.

43. James Russell Lowell, "Ode Recited at the Harvard Commemoration," *The Complete Poetical Works of James Russell Lowell*, ed. Horace A. Scudder (Boston: Houghton, Mifflin, 1925), 340–47.

44. Discussed in Steven Gould Axelrod, *Robert Lowell: Life and Art* (Princeton, N.J.: Princeton University Press, 1978), 165–66.

45. Stephen J. Whitfield, " 'Sacred in History and in Art': *The Shaw Memorial*," *The New England Quarterly* 60 (March 1987), 24.

46. Richard Benvenuto, *Amy Lowell* (Boston: Twayne Publishers, 1985), 2.

47. Gould, *Amy*, 89.

48. Amy Lowell, in Gould, *Amy*, 73.

49. Benvenuto, *Amy Lowell*, 7.

50. Amy Lowell, "The Boston Athenaeum," *The Complete Poetical Works of Amy Lowell*, ed. Louis Untermeyer (Boston: Houghton, Mifflin, 1925), 21–23.

51. Robert Lowell, *Life Studies* (1956; New York: Farrar, Straus and Giroux, 1966).

52. Lowell, "91 Revere Street," *Robert Lowell: Collected Prose*, 313.

53. Ibid.

54. Ibid., 309, 311, 343. I am indebted to the attention given to these family portraits in an unpublished essay by Joel Blair, "Robert Lowell's '91 Revere Street': The Mapping of a Psyche."

55. Robert Lowell, "New England and Further," *Robert Lowell: Collected Prose*, 180.

56. Jean Stafford, in Eileen Simpson, *Poets in Their Youth: A Memoir* (New York: Vintage Books, 1983), 124.

57. Lowell, "91 Revere Street," *Robert Lowell: Collected Prose*, 329–30.

58. Ibid.

59. Robert Lowell, in Axelrod, *Robert Lowell*, 158.

60. Lowell, "The Public Garden," *Life Studies*, 26–27.

61. Robert Lowell, "At the Indian Killer's Grave," *Selected Poems*, rev. ed. (New York: Farrar, Straus and Giroux, 1977), 25.

62. Axelrod, *Robert Lowell*, 179. Robert Lowell, *Endecott & the Red Cross*, in *The Old Glory* (New York: Farrar, Straus & Giroux, 1965).

63. Robert Lowell, *My Kinsman, Major Molineux*, in *The Old Glory*.

64. John Andrew, in Freely, *Blue Guide: Boston and Cambridge*, 220.

65. Peter Burchard, *One Gallant Rush: Robert Gould Shaw and His Brave Black Regiment* (New York: St. Martin's Press, 1965), 147.

66. Sidney Kaplan, "The Black Soldier of the Civil War in Literature and Art," The Chancellor's Lecture Series, 16 October 1979, University of Massachusetts, Amherst, Massachusetts.

67. William James, in Kaplan, "The Black Soldier of the Civil War," 3.

68. Michael Dukakis, in Chris Black, "Bay State Black Union Troops Are Laid to Final Rest in South," *Boston Globe*, 30 May 1989.

69. Kaplan, "The Black Soldier of the Civil War," 38.

70. John Berryman, "Boston Common: A Meditation upon the Hero," *"Homage to Mistress Bradstreet" and Other Poems* (New York: Farrar, Straus, and Giroux, 1968), 75.

71. James Russell Lowell, in "Notes," *Robert Lowell's Poems,* ed. Jonathan Raban (London: Faber and Faber, 1974), 175.

72. Allen Tate, "Ode to the Confederate Dead," *The Norton Anthology of Modern Poetry,* ed. Richard Ellmann and Robert O'Clair (New York: W. W. Norton, 1973), 607–10.

73. Hamilton, *Robert Lowell,* 277–78.

74. Lowell, "For the Union Dead," *For the Union Dead* (New York: Farrar, Straus and Giroux, 1964), 70–72.

75. Here Lowell recasts the Latin inscription of the Shaw Memorial: "OMNIA RELINQUIT / SERVARE REMPUBLICAM." The inaccurate Latin derives from the motto to the Society of Cincinnati, a group composed of descendants of the Revolutionary War officers, of which Shaw was a member. See Whitfield, " 'Sacred in History and in Art': *The Shaw Memorial,*" 10.

76. Lowell, "For the Union Dead," *For the Union Dead,* 70–72.

77. Lowell, "New England and Further," *Robert Lowell: Collected Prose,* 181.

78. Lowell, in Hamilton, *Robert Lowell,* 279.

79. Elizabeth Hardwick, in Hamilton, *Robert Lowell,* 140.

80. Lowell, in Hamilton, *Robert Lowell,* 199.

81. Ibid., 223–24.

82. Lowell, "Waking in Blue," *Life Studies,* 81–82.

83. Lowell, "Home after Three Months Away," *Life Studies,* 83–84.

84. Lowell, "Memories of West Street and Lepke," *Life Studies,* 85–86.

85. Elizabeth Hardwick, "Boston: The Lost Ideal," in *The Penguin Book of Contemporary American Essays,* ed. Maureen Howard (New York: Penguin Books, 1984), 249.

86. Elizabeth Hardwick, *Sleepless Nights* (New York: Vintage Books, 1980), 4.

87. Elizabeth Hardwick, "The Genius of Margaret Fuller," *The New York Review of Books* 33 (10 April 1986), 14.

88. Ibid., 18.

89. Elizabeth Hardwick, in Hamilton, *Robert Lowell,* 222.

90. Hardwick, "Boston: The Lost Ideal," in *Contemporary American Essays,* 249–61.

91. Robert Lowell, "The Mills of the Kavanaughs," *"Lord Weary's Castle" and "The Mills of the Kavanaughs"* (Cleveland: World Publishing, 1964), 75–94.

92. David Roberts, "The Failed Escape," *New England Monthly* (August 1987):64–67.

93. Jean Stafford, *Boston Adventure* (Garden City, N.Y.: Sun Dial Press, 1944), 36.

94. Ibid., 124, 127.

95. Ibid., 128.

96. Ibid., 247.

97. Hardwick, "Boston: The Lost Ideal," in *Contemporary American Essays,* 250.

98. Meyers, *Manic Power,* 146.

99. Adrienne Rich, in Linda W. Wagner-Martin, *Sylvia Plath: A Biography* (New York: Simon and Schuster, 1987), 153.

100. Sylvia Plath, in Meyers, *Manic Power,* 146.

101. Ibid., 147.

102. *Anne Sexton: A Self-Portrait in Letters,* ed. Linda Gray Sexton and Lois Ames (Boston: Houghton, Mifflin, 1979), 70.

103. Sexton, "A Story for Rose, on the Midnight Flight to Boston," *To Bedlam and Part Way Back* (Boston: Houghton Mifflin, 1964), 47.

104. Lowell, "New England and Further," *Robert Lowell: Collected Prose,* 190.

105. Hardwick and Lowell, in Hamilton, *Robert Lowell,* 304.

106. Robert Lowell, "Candlelight Lunchdate," *Notebook* (New York: Farrar, Straus and Giroux, 1971), 86.

107. Lowell, "Henry and Waldo," *Notebook,* 91.

108. Lowell, "Writers 1 T. S. Eliot," *Notebook,* 119.

109. Lowell, "Dawn," *Notebook,* 92.

110. Ibid.

111. Helen Vendler, "Robert Lowell's Last Days and Last Poems," *Robert Lowell: Interviews and Memoirs,* ed. Meyers, 298.

9. Boston, City of Spirit and Flesh

1. Samuel Eliot Morison, *Builders of the Bay Colony* (1930; Boston: Northeastern University Press, 1981), 3.

2. M. A. De Wolfe Howe, *Boston: The Place and the People* (New York: Macmillan, 1912), 377.

3. Austin Warren, *The New England Conscience* (Ann Arbor: University of Michigan Press, 1967), viii.

4. "Boston's artists, as well as her historians, were proud of this [artistic] heritage: the studio of John Smibert, the city's first professional painter, became virtually an academy of the fine arts in the late eighteenth century, for after his death it was occupied, and its contents studied, by leading painters of several successive generations, among them [John Singleton] Copley, [John] Trumbell, and [Washington] Allston. In the seventeenth century, despite the myth of Puritan hostility to the arts, Boston was the new world's most influential artistic community." Carol Troyen, "The Boston Tradition: Painters and Patrons in Boston 1720–1920," *The Boston Tradition: American Paintings from the Museum of Fine Arts* (New York: American Federation of Arts, 1980), 6.

5. Samuel Sewall, *Phaenomena quaedam Apocalyptica*, in *The Puritans in America: A Narrative Anthology*, ed. Alan Heimert and Andrew Delbanco (Cambridge, Mass.: Harvard University Press, 1985), 293. Writing on Sewall, David D. Hall says "he thought in terms of wonders and life crises; he yearned to protect his family and New England even as he struggled to accept the lesson of affliction" (*Worlds of Wonder, Days of Judgment: Popular Religious Beliefs in Early New England* [New York: Alfred A. Knopf, 1989], 214).

6. Perry Miller and Thomas H. Johnson, eds., *The Puritans* (New York: Harper and Row, 1963), 2:461.

7. Ralph Waldo Emerson, "Self-Reliance," *The Essays of Ralph Waldo Emerson* (Cambridge, Mass.: Belknap Press, 1987), 51.

8. Dan Wakefield, "An Improper Bostonian Writ Large," *Neiman Reports* 40 (Spring 1986):10.

9. Daniel Aaron, "Introducing Arthur Inman," *The Inman Diary: A Public and Private Confession*, ed. Aaron (Cambridge, Mass.: Harvard University Press, 1985), 1:5, 11.

10. John Winthrop, *Journal*, in *The Puritans*, 1:142–43.

11. Edward Johnson, *Wonder-Working Providence of Sions Savior*, in *The Puritans*, 2:145.

12. Andrew Delbanco, *The Puritan Ordeal* (Cambridge, Mass.: Harvard University Press, 1989), 137.

13. Keith W. F. Stavely, *Puritan Legacies: Paradise Lost and the New England Tradition 1630–1890* (Ithaca, N.Y.: Cornell University Press, 1987), 27. "Antinomianism was but the emergence into discrete doctrine of the tendency of all Protestantism to affirm inner experience in defiance of external and traditional authority. It insisted that imposed rules and regulations were not binding on regenerate Christians" (20).

14. Delbanco, *The Puritan Ordeal*, 236, 242.

15. G. Thomas Couser sees the spiritual autobiography as "religious literature" which holds prophesies, a literature by writers who make "analogies between their own experience and that of the community," a literature which will define character and community (*American Autobiography: The Prophetic Mode* [Amherst: University of Massachusetts Press, 1979], 4–5). Robert F. Sayre sees autobiography in more formal terms (*The Examined Self: Benjamin Franklin, Henry Adams, Henry James* [Madison: University of Wisconsin Press, 1988]).

16. Michael T. Gilmore cites Lewis P. Simpson, in *The Man of Letters in New England and the South: Essays on the History of the Literary Vocation in America* (Baton Rouge: Louisiana State University Press, 1973), 3–31. Simpson sees a nineteenth-century "clerisy" in the Boston-Concord writer. "The wise and learned, it was felt, had a special obligation to educate the nation; through the practice of literature, they were to provide moral guidance and enlightenment." *Walden* is "a reforming text." Michael T. Gilmore, *American Romanticism and the Marketplace* (Chicago: University of Chicago Press, 1985), 43.

17. Sacvan Bercovitch, *The American Jeremiad* (Madison: University of Wisconsin Press, 1978), 9. The New England colonist saw a symbolic landscape. "Thus they personified the New World as American microchrista. . . . [thus] colonial histories read like spiritual biographies of an elect land." Sacvan Ber-

covitch, *The Puritan Origins of the American Self* (New Haven: Yale University Press, 1975), 114–15.

18. Alexis de Tocqueville, in Bercovitch, *The American Jeremiad*, 19. Tocqueville saw New England divided between "the *spirit of religion* and the *spirit of liberty.*" "The settlers of New England were at the same time ardent sectarians and daring innovators. Narrow as the limits of some of their religious opinions were, they were free from political prejudices." Alexis de Tocqueville, *Democracy in America* (New York: Vintage Books, 1945), 1:45.

19. Anne Bradstreet, "To My Dear Children," *The Works of Anne Bradstreet*, ed. Jeannine Hensley (Cambridge, Mass.: Belknap Press, 1967), 241.

20. Bradstreet, "To My Dear Children," *Works*, 243.

21. Morison, *Builders of the Bay Colony*, 331–32.

22. Anne Bradstreet, "Contemplations," *Works*, 210–11.

23. Anne Bradstreet, "Meditations Divine and Moral," *Works*, 283.

24. John Berryman, in *The Norton Anthology of Modern Poetry*, ed. Richard Ellmann and Robert O'Clair (New York: W. W. Norton, 1973), 894.

25. John Berryman, *Homage to Miss Bradstreet*, in *The Norton Anthology of Modern Poetry*, 895. Helen Vendler identifies Berryman's Bradstreet with the alter ego of his *Dream Songs*. *Part of Nature, Part of Us: Modern American Poets* (Cambridge, Mass.: Harvard University Press, 1980), 120–21.

26. Berryman, in Vendler, *Part of Nature*, 120.

27. Barbara Meil Hobson and Paul Wright suggest the Bradstreet-Sexton pairing. "For Anne Sexton . . . the voyage to the wilderness was a spiritual one" (*Boston, A State of Mind: An Exhibition Record* [Boston, Mass.: Boston Public Library, 1977], 82–86).

28. Anne Sexton, "Gods," *The Death Notebooks* (Boston: Houghton, Mifflin, 1974), 1–2.

29. Ibid.

30. Leonard W. Labaree, Ralph L. Ketcham, Helen C. Boatfield and Helene H. Fineman, introduction to *The Autobiography of Benjamin Franklin* (New Haven: Yale University Press, 1964), 14–16.

31. Franklin, *Autobiography*, 43, 158.

32. Samuel Eliot Morison, *One Boy's Boston 1887–1901* (Boston: Northeastern University Press, 1983).

33. Nat Hentoff, *Boston Boy* (New York: Alfred A. Knopf, 1986), 93.

34. Morison, *One Boy's Boston*, 62, 63, 17, 68.

35. Mary Antin, *The Promised Land* (Boston: Houghton, Mifflin, 1912), 195. "*The Promised Land* was an appeal for sympathy and a testament of immigrant pride and patriotic American pride" (Sam Bass Warner, Jr., *Province of Reason* [Cambridge, Mass.: Belknap Press, 1984, 28).

36. Antin, *The Promised Land*, 290.

37. Isaac Goldberg, "A Boston Boyhood," in *The Many Voices of Boston: A Historical Anthology 1630–1975*, ed. Howard Mumford Jones and Bessie Zaban Jones (Boston: Little, Brown, 1975), 354.

38. Ibid., 355.

39. Charles Angoff, *When I Was a Boy in Boston* (USA: Ruttle, Shaw and Wetherill, 1947), 95–96.

40. Mark Mirsky, *Blue Hill Ave.* (Indianapolis: Bobbs Merrill, 1972).

41. Theodore H. White, *In Search of History* (New York: Warner Books, 1981), 39.

42. Ibid., 78.

43. Hentoff, *Boston Boy*, 4.

44. Ibid., 12.

45. Ibid., 122.

46. Frazier was particularly effective at striking a plangent note of mourning for all that Boston had lost, as he did in 1961. "For those years—the years when the Ritz Roof was a hanging garden festooned with the stars of a summer night— were, we realize now, the best years of Boston's life. And now, like the flash of Goodman's clarinet in the warm dark, they have fled. And so, Got wot, has much, much else that was Boston at it most blessed." Cited in Charles Fountain, *Another Man's Poison: The Life and Writing of Columnist George Frazier* (Chester, Conn.: Globe Pequot Press, 1984), 160.

47. Hentoff, *Boston Boy*, 134.

48. Ibid., 175.

49. Henry David Thoreau, *Walden, in "Walden" and "Civil Disobedience"* (1854; New York: Penguin Books, 1983), 382.

50. M. A. De Wolfe Howe, *Boston,* 388.

51. Carolyn G. Heilbrun, introduction to May Sarton, *Mrs. Stevens Hears the Mermaids Singing* (New York: W. W. Norton, 1975), x.

52. May Sarton, *Faithful are the Wounds* (1955; New York: W. W. Norton, 1983), 141.

53. Ibid., 47.

54. May Sarton, *The Education of Harriet Hatfield* (New York: W. W. Norton & Company, 1989), 12, 18.

55. Ibid., 69, 106, 102.

56. May Sarton, *The Small Room* (New York: W. W. Norton, 1961); *A Reckoning* (New York: W. W. Norton, 1978); *Anger* (New York: W. W. Norton, 1982); *The Magnificent Spinster* (New York: W. W. Norton, 1985).

57. May Sarton, *Plant Dreaming Deep* (New York: W. W. Norton, 1968), 23, 182.

58. May Sarton, *Journal of a Solitude* (New York: W. W. Norton, 1973).

59. May Sarton, *The House by the Sea* (New York: W. W. Norton, 1981), 14.

60. Ibid., 287.

61. Alfred Alcorn, *Vestments* (Boston: Houghton, Mifflin, 1988); Dan Wakefield, *Returning: A Spiritual Journey* (New York: Doubleday, 1988); John Updike, *Self-Consciousness* (New York: Alfred A. Knopf, 1989).

62. Updike, *Self-Consciousness,* 218.

63. Alcorn, *Vestments*, 23, 56.

64. Ibid., 29.

65. Ibid., 78–79.

66. Ibid., 109.

67. Dan Wakefield, *Starting Over* (New York: Delacorte Press, 1973); *Home Free* (New York: Delacorte Press, 1977); *Selling Out* (Boston: Little, Brown, 1985).

68. Wakefield, *Returning*, ix.

69. Wakefield, *Returning*, 5–6.

70. Wakefield, *Returning*, 27. Robert Frost, "The Road Not Taken," *The Poetry of Robert Frost*, ed. Edward Connery Lathem (New York: Holt, Rinehart and Winston, 1975), 105.

71. Wakefield, *Returning*, 224.

72. Updike, *Self-Consciousness*, 6.

73. Ibid., 24.

74. Updike, *Self-Consciousness*, 253–54.

75. Updike, in *Current Biography* (October 1984), 38.

76. Updike, *Self-Consciousness*, 221–22, 253.

77. Updike, *Self-Consciousness*, 218n.

78. Updike, *Self-Consciousness*, 232.

79. Edward Bellamy, *Looking Backward: 2000–1887* (1888; New York: New American Library, 1960).

80. John Winthrop, "A Model of Christian Charity," in *The American Puritans: Their Prose and Poetry*, ed. Perry Miller (Garden City, N.Y.: Anchor Books, 1956), 79–80.

81. Margaret Atwood, *A Handmaid's Tale* (Boston: Houghton, Mifflin, 1986).

82. Margaret Atwood, in Mervyn Rothstein, "No Balm in Gilead for Margaret Atwood," *The New York Times*, 17 February 1986.

83. Eudora Welty, "Place in Fiction," *The Eye of the Storm: Selected Essays and Reviews* (New York: Vintage Books, 1970), 122.

84. Samuel Eliot Morison, *Three Centuries of Harvard 1636–1936* (Cambridge, Mass.: Belknap Press, 1936).

Bibliography

Boston: The New England Mind and the Spirit of Place

A Book for Boston: in which are Gathered Essays, Stories, and Poems by Divers Hands Especially Written in Honor of the City Upon the Occasion of the Three Hundred and Fiftieth Anniversary of its Incorporation the Twentieth Day of September Anno Domini Sixteen Hundred and Thirty. Boston: David R. Godine, Publisher, 1980.

Bahne, Charles. *The Complete Guide to Boston's Freedom Trail.* Cambridge, Mass.: Newtowne Publishing, 1985.

Black Heritage Trail. Boston: Museum of Afro-American History, n.d.

Brown, Thomas N. "Boston's Past: History as Common Ground." *Boston Sunday Globe,* 29 December 1985.

Burchard, Peter. *One Gallant Rush: Robert Gould Shaw and His Brave Black Regiment.* New York: St. Martin's Press, 1965.

Bibliography

Carlock, Marty. *A Guide to Public Art in Greater Boston: From Newburyport to Plymouth*. Harvard and Boston: Harvard Common Press, 1988.

Carruth, Frances Weston. *Fictional Rambles in and about Boston*. New York: McClure, Phillips, 1902.

Chametzky, Jules, and Sidney Kaplan, eds. *Black and White in American Culture: An Anthology from the "Massachusetts Review."* Amherst, Mass.: University of Massachusetts Press, 1969.

Coleman, Terry. *Passage to America: A History of Emigrants from Great Britain and Ireland to America in the Mid-nineteenth Century*. Harmondsworth: Penguin Books, 1972.

Dalzell, Robert F., Jr., *Enterprising Elite: The Boston Associates and the World They Made*. Cambridge, Mass.: Harvard University Press, 1987.

Daniels, John. *In Freedom's Birthplace: A Study of the Boston Negroes*. New York: Negro University Press, 1968.

Dickens, Charles. *American Notes For General Circulation*. 1842. Harmondsworth: Penguin Books, 1972.

Diner, Hasia R. *Erin's Daughter in America: Irish Immigrant Women in the Nineteenth Century*. Baltimore: Johns Hopkins University Press, 1983.

Duhamel, P. Albert. *After Strange Fruit: Changing Literary Taste in Post-World War II Boston*. Boston: Trustees of the Public Library of the City of Boston, 1980.

Fairbrother, Trevor J., ed. *The Bostonians: Painters of an Elegant Age, 1870–1930*. Boston: Museum of Fine Arts, 1986.

Freely, John. *Blue Guide: Boston and Cambridge*. New York: W. W. Norton, 1984.

Goodwin, Doris Kearns. *The Fitzgeralds and the Kennedys: An American Saga*. New York: Simon and Schuster, 1987.

Green, Martin. *The Problem of Boston: Some Readings in Cultural History*. New York: W. W. Norton, 1966.

Handlin, Oscar. *Boston's Immigrants: 1790–1880; A Study in Acculturation*. 1941. Cambridge, Mass.: Harvard University Press, 1969.

Holbrook, Stewart H. *The Old Post Road: The Story of the Boston Post Road*. New York: McGraw-Hill, 1962.

Horton, James Oliver, and Lois E. Horton. *Black Bostonians: Family Life and Community in the Antebellum North*. New York: Holmes and Meier Publishers, 1979.

Howe, M. A. De Wolfe. *Boston: The Place and the People*. New York: The Macmillan Company, 1912.

———. *The Atlantic Monthly and Its Makers*. Westport, Conn.: Greenwood Press, 1919.

Kaplan, Sidney. "The Black Soldier of the Civil War in Literature and Art." The Chancellor's Lecture Series, University of Massachusetts, Amherst. 16 October 1979.

Kaplan, Sidney, and Emma Nogrady Kaplan. *The Black Presence in the Era of the American Revolution*. rev. ed. Amherst, Mass.: University of Massachusetts Press, 1989.

Kay, Jane Holtz. *Lost Boston*. Boston: Houghton, Mifflin, 1980.

Kenny, Herbert. *Newspaper Row: Journalism in the Pre-television Era*. Chester, Conn.: Globe Pequot Press, 1987.

Kidder, Tracy. *The Soul of a New Machine*. New York: Avon Books, 1981.

Lukas, J. Anthony. *Common Ground: A Turbulent Decade in the Lives of Three American Families*. New York: Alfred A. Knopf, 1985.

Lupo, Alan. *Liberty's Chosen Home: The Politics of Violence in Boston*. 1977. Boston: Beacon Press, 1988.

McIntyre, A. McVoy. *Beacon Hill: A Walking Tour*. Boston: Little, Brown, 1975.

Miller, Kerby A. *Emigrants and Exiles: Ireland and the Irish Exodus to North America*. New York: Oxford University Press, 1985.

Miller, Perry. *The Responsibility of Mind in a Civilization of Machines*. Ed. John Crowell and Stanford J. Searl, Jr. Amherst: University of Massachusetts Press, 1979.

Morison, Samuel Eliot. *Builders of the Bay Colony*. 1930. Boston: Northeastern University Press, 1981.

―――. *Three Centuries of Harvard 1636–1936*. Cambridge, Mass.: Belknap Press, 1936.

O'Connor, Thomas H. *Bibles, Brahmins and Bosses: A Short History of Boston*. Boston: Trustees of the Public Library of the City of Boston, 1976.

―――. *Fitzpatrick's Boston 1846–1866*. Boston: Northeastern University Press, 1984.

―――. *South Boston: My Home Town*. Boston: Quinlan Press, 1988.

Piersen, William D. *Black Yankees: The Development of an Afro-American Subculture in Eighteenth-century New England*. Amherst: University of Massachusetts Press, 1988.

Potter, George. *To the Golden Door: The Study of the Irish in Ireland and America*. Boston: Little, Brown, 1960.

Powell, Sumner Chilton. *Puritan Village: The Formation of a New England Town*. Middletown, Conn.: Wesleyan University Press, 1963.

Richardson, Marilyn with Edward Clark. *Black Bostonians: Two Hundred Years of Community and Culture: An Exhibition of Books, Paintings, and Sculpture by and about Blacks in Boston; Drawn Chiefly from the Collections of the Boston Athenaeum*. Boston: Atheneum, 1988.

Ruchames, Louis, ed. *Racial Thought in America: From the Puritans to Abraham Lincoln, A Documentary History*. Amherst, Mass.: University of Massachusetts Press, 1969.

Russell, Francis. *The Knave of Boston & Other Ambiguous Massachusetts Characters*. Boston: Quinlan Press, 1987.

Rutman, Darrett B. *Winthrop's Boston: A Portrait of a Puritan Town, 1630–1649*. New York: W. W. Norton, 1972.

Bibliography

Ryan, Dennis P. *Beyond the Ballot Box: A Social History of the Boston Irish, 1845–1917.* Amherst, Mass.: University of Massachusetts Press, 1989.

Shand-Tucci, Douglass. *Built in Boston: City and Suburb 1800–1950.* Amherst, Mass.: University of Massachusetts Press, 1988.

Shannon, William V. *The American Irish: A Political and Social Portrait.* New York: Collier Books, 1966.

Solomon, Barbara Miller. *Ancestors and Immigrants: A Changing New England Tradition.* Boston: Northeastern University Press, 1989.

Thernstrom, Stephan. *The Other Bostonians: Poverty and Progress in the American Metropolis, 1880–1970.* Cambridge, Mass.: Harvard University Press, 1973.

Trollope, Anthony. *North America.* Ed. Donald Smalley and Bradford Allen Booth. New York: Da Capo Press, 1986.

Troyen, Carol. *The Boston Tradition: American Paintings from the Museum of Fine Arts, Boston.* New York: American Federation of Arts, 1980.

Warner, Sam Bass, Jr. *Streetcar Suburbs: The Process of Growth in Boston (1870–1900).* Cambridge, Mass.: Harvard University Press, 1978.

Warren, Austin. *The New England Conscience.* Ann Arbor: University of Michigan Press, 1967.

Warner, Sam Bass, Jr. *Province of Reason.* Cambridge, Mass.: Belknap Press, 1984.

White, Morton, and Lucia White. *The Intellectual versus the City: From Thomas Jefferson to Frank Lloyd Wright.* Cambridge, Mass.: Harvard University Press and the MIT Press, 1962.

Whitehill, Walter Muir. *Boston: A Topographical History,* 2d ed. Cambridge, Mass.: Belknap Press, 1982.

———. *Boston in the Age of John Fitzgerald Kennedy.* Norman, Okla.: University of Oklahoma Press, 1966.

The WPA Guide to Massachusetts. 1937. New York: Pantheon Books, 1983.

Zuckerman, Michael. *Peaceable Kingdoms: New England Town in the Eighteenth Century.* New York: Alfred A. Knopf, 1970.

Selected Literary Works

Aaron, Daniel, ed. *The Inman Diary: A Public and Private Confession.* 2 vols. Cambridge, Mass.: Harvard University Press, 1985.

Adams, Henry. *The Education of Henry Adams: An Autobiography.* Boston: Houghton, Mifflin, 1918.

———. *The Life of George Cabot Lodge.* In *The Shock of Recognition: The Development of Literature in the United States Recorded by the Men Who Made It,* ed. Edmund Wilson. New York: Farrar, Straus and Cudahy, 1955.

Alcorn, Alfred. *Vestments.* Boston: Houghton, Mifflin.

Alcott, Louisa May. *Little Women.* 1868. Boston: Little, Brown, 1968.

———. *Work: A Story of Experience.* New York: Shocken Books, 1977.

Bibliography

Angoff, Charles. *When I Was a Boy in Boston*. USA.: Ruttle, Shaw and Wetherill, 1947.

Antin, Mary. *The Promised Land*. Boston: Houghton, Mifflin, 1912.

Atwood, Margaret. *A Handmaid's Tale*. Boston: Houghton, Mifflin, 1986.

Bellamy, Edward. *Looking Backward: 2000–1887*. 1888. New York: New American Library, 1960.

Berryman, John. *"Homage to Mistress Bradstreet" and Other Poems*. New York: Farrar, Straus and Giroux, 1968.

Beston, Henry. *The Outermost House: A Year of Life on the Great Beach of Cape Cod*. 1928. New York: Ballantine Books, 1956.

Bradford, William. *Of Plymouth Plantation 1620–1647*. Ed. Samuel Eliot Morison. New York: Alfred A. Knopf, 1963.

Bradstreet, Anne. *The Works of Anne Bradstreet*. Ed. Jeannine Hensley. Cambridge, Mass.: Belknap Press, 1967.

Braithwaite, William Stanley. *"The House of Falling Leaves": With Other Poems*. Boston: John W. Luce, 1908.

———. *The William Stanley Braithwaite Reader*. Ed. Philip Butcher. Ann Arbor: University of Michigan Press, 1972.

Brodsky, Joseph. *A Part of Speech*. New York: Farrar, Straus, Giroux, 1980.

Carroll, James. *Mortal Friends*. Boston: Little, Brown, 1978.

Cheever, John. *The Wapshot Chronicle*. 1957. New York: Ballantine Books, 1986.

———. *The Wapshot Scandal*. 1963. New York: Harper and Row, 1964.

———. *The Stories of John Cheever*. New York: Alfred A. Knopf, 1987.

Child, Lydia Maria. *Hobomok*. Boston: Cummings, Hilliard, 1824.

———. *An Appeal in Favor of That Class of Americans Called Africans*. Boston: Allen and Ticknor, 1833.

Curley, James Michael. *I'd Do It Again: A Record of All My Uproarious Years*. Englewood Cliffs, N.J.: Prentice-Hall, 1957.

Dickinson, Emily. *Final Harvest: Emily Dickinson's Poems*. Ed. Thomas H. Johnson. Boston: Little, Brown, 1961.

Dineen, Joseph F. *Ward Eight*. 1936. New York: Arno Press, 1976.

Douglass, Frederick. *Narrative of the Life of Frederick Douglass An American Slave, Written by Himself*. Ed. Benjamin Quarles. Cambridge, Mass.: Belknap Press, 1960.

Dubus, Andre. *Selected Stories*. Boston: David R. Godine, 1988.

Eliot, T. S. *Collected Poems 1909–1935*. New York: Harcourt, Brace, 1952.

———. "Henry James." In *The Shock of Recognition*, ed. Edmund Wilson. New York: Modern Library, 1955.

———. *The Complete Poems and Plays 1909–1950*. New York: Harcourt, Brace, 1958.

———. *Selected Essays*. New York: Harcourt, Brace and World, 1960.

Emerson, Ralph Waldo. *Selected Writings of Emerson*. Ed. Donald McQuade. New York: Modern Library, 1981.

Bibliography

————. *Ralph Waldo Emerson: Selected Essays*. Ed. Larzer Ziff. New York: Penguin Books, 1982.

————. *The Essays of Ralph Waldo Emerson*. Cambridge, Mass.: Belknap Press, 1987.

Finch, Robert. *Common Ground: A Naturalist's Cape Cod*. Boston: David R. Godine, 1981.

————. *The Primal Place*. New York: W. W. Norton, 1983.

————. *Outlands: Journeys to the Outer Edges of Cape Cod*. Boston: David R. Godine, 1986.

Forten, Charlotte L. *The Journal of Charlotte L. Forten*. New York: the Dryden Press, 1953.

Francis, Robert. *Come Out into the Sun: Poems New and Selected*. Amherst, Mass.: University of Massachusetts Press, 1965.

————. *The Trouble with Francis: An Autobiography of Robert Francis*. Amherst, Mass.: University of Massachusetts Press, 1971.

————. *Collected Poems 1936–1976*. Amherst, Mass.: University of Massachusetts Press, 1976.

————. *Pot Shots at Poetry*. Ann Arbor: University of Michigan Press, 1980.

————. *Travelling in Amherst: A Poet's Journal 1930–1950*. Boston, Mass.: Rowan Tree Press, 1986.

Franklin, Benjamin. *The Autobiography of Benjamin Franklin*. Ed. Leonard W. Labaree, Ralph L. Ketcham, Helen C. Boatfield, and Helene H. Fineman. New Haven: Yale University Press, 1964.

Frost, Robert. *Robert Frost Poetry & Prose*. Ed. Edward Connery Latham and Lawrance Thompson. New York: Henry Holt, 1972.

————. *The Poetry of Robert Frost: The Collected Poems, Complete and Unabridged*. Ed. Edward Connery Lathem. New York: Holt, Rinehart and Winston, 1975.

————. *North of Boston Poems*. Ed. Edward Connery Lathem. New York: Dodd, Mead, 1983.

Green, Melissa. *The Squanicook Eclogues*. New York: W. W. Norton, 1987.

Haley, Alex, and Malcolm X. *The Autobiography of Malcolm X*. New York: Grove Press, 1966.

Hardwick, Elizabeth. *Sleepless Nights*. New York: Vintage Books, 1980.

————. "Boston: The Lost Ideal." In *The Penguin Book of Contemporary American Essays*, ed. Maureen Howard. New York, Penguin Books, 1984.

————. "The Genius of Margaret Fuller." *The New York Review of Books* 33 (10 April 1986).

Hawthorne, Nathaniel. *The Scarlet Letter*. 1850. New York: Penguin Books, 1983.

————. *Twice-Told Tales*. 1851. Boston: Houghton, Mifflin, 1879.

————. *The House of the Seven Gables*. 1851. Boston: Houghton, Mifflin, 1964.

————. *A Wonder-Book for Girls and Boys*. Boston: Houghton, Mifflin, 1851.

————. *The Blithedale Romance*. 1852. New York: Penguin Books, 1983.

———. *Mosses from an Old Manse*. 1854. Boston: Houghton, Mifflin, 1882.

———. *The American Notebooks*. Ed. Claude M. Simpson. Centenary Edition of the Works of Nathaniel Hawthorne. Vol. 8. USA: Ohio State University Press, 1972.

———. *"The Celestial Railroad" and Other Stories*. New York: New American Library, 1963.

———. *Our Old Home: A Series of English Sketches*. Boston: Houghton, Mifflin, 1963.

Heimert, Alan, and Andrew Delbanco, eds. *The Puritans in America: A Narrative Anthology*. Cambridge, Mass.: Harvard University Press, 1985.

Hentoff, Nat. *Boston Boy*. New York: Alfred A. Knopf, 1986.

Hopkins, Pauline E. *Contending Forces: A Romance Illustrative of Negro Life North and South*. New York: Oxford University Press, 1988.

Howe, Julia Ward. *Reminiscences 1819–1899*. Boston: Houghton, Mifflin, 1988.

———. *At Sunset*. Boston: Houghton, Mifflin, 1910.

Howells, William Dean. *A Modern Instance*. 1882. Boston: Houghton, Mifflin, 1957.

———. *The Rise of Silas Lapham*. 1885. New York: Penguin Books, 1985.

———. *Literary Friends and Acquaintance: A Personal Retrospect of American Authorship*. Ed. David F. Hiatt and Edwin H. Cady. Selected Edition of W. D. Howells. Vol. 32. Bloomington and London: Indiana University Press, 1968.

———. *A Chance Acquaintance*. Selected Edition of W. D. Howells. Vol. 6. Bloomington and London: Indiana University Press, 1971.

———. *Suburban Sketches*. 1871. Freeport, New York: Books For Libraries Press, 1898.

———. *The Minister's Charge; or, The Apprenticeship of Lemuel Barker*. 1886. Selected Edition of W. D. Howells. Vol. 14. Bloomington and London: Indiana University Press, 1978.

Jacobs, Harriet A. *Incidents in the Life of a Slave Girl: Written by Herself*. Ed. Maria Child. Cambridge, Mass.: Harvard University Press, 1987.

James, Alice. *The Diary of Alice James*. New York: Dodd, Mead, 1964.

James, Henry. *The American*. New York: Charles Scribner's Sons, 1907.

———. *The Complete Notebooks of Henry James*. Ed. Leon Edel and Lyall H. Powers. New York: Oxford University Press, 1987.

———. *The American Novels and Stories of Henry James*. Ed. F. O. Matthiessen. New York: Alfred A. Knopf, 1964.

———. *"A New England Winter" and "The Europeans."* In *The American Novels and Stories of Henry James*, ed. F. O. Matthiessen. New York: Alfred A. Knopf, 1964.

———. *The American Scene*. 1907. Bloomington and London: Indiana University Press, 1968.

———. *Henry James Letters, 1843–1875*. Ed. Leon Edel, 4 vols. Cambridge, Mass.: Belknap Press, 1974.

————. *The Bostonians*. 1886. New York: Penguin Books, 1983.

Jewett, Sarah Orne. *"The Country of the Pointed Firs" and Other Stories*. New York: W. W. Norton, 1981.

Jones, Howard Mumford, ed. *The Many Voices of Boston: A Historical Anthology 1630–1975*. Boston: Atlantic Little, Brown, 1975.

Kerouac, Jack. *The Town and the City*. 1950. New York: Harcourt Brace Jovanovich, 1978.

Kumin, Maxine. *In Deep: Country Essays*. Boston: Beacon Press, 1987.

————. *Up Country: Poems of New England*. New York: Harper and Row, 1973.

————. *To Make a Prairie: Essays on Poets, Poetry, and Country Living*. Ann Arbor: University of Michigan Press, 1979.

Larcom, Lucy. *A New England Girlhood, Outlined from Memory*. Gloucester, Mass.: Peter Smith, 1973.

Leighton, Clare. *Where Land Meets Sea: The Enduring Cape*. 1954. Boston: David R. Godine, 1984.

Longfellow, Henry Wadsworth. *Selected Poems*. New York: Penguin Books, 1988.

————. *Longfellow*. New York: Dell, 1959.

————. *Tales of the Wayside Inn*. New York: E. P. Dutton, 1952.

Lowell, Amy. *The Complete Poetical Works of Amy Lowell*. Ed. Louis Untermeyer. Boston: Houghton, Mifflin, 1925.

Lowell, James Russell. *A Fable for Critics*. In *The Shock of Recognition*, ed. Edmund Wilson. New York: Farrar, Straus and Giroux, 1955.

————. *The Complete Poetical Works of James Russell Lowell*. Ed. Horace A. Scudder. Boston: Houghton, Mifflin, 1925.

Lowell, Robert. *"Lord Weary's Castle" and "The Mills of the Kavanaughs."* Cleveland: World Publishing Company, 1964.

————. *"Life Studies" & "For the Union Dead."* New York: Farrar, Straus and Giroux, 1964.

————. *The Old Glory*. New York: Farrar, Straus and Giroux, 1965.

————. *Notebooks*. New York: Farrar, Straus and Giroux, 1971.

————. *Robert Lowell's Poems*. Ed. Jonathan Raban. London: Faber and Faber, 1974.

————. *Robert Lowell: Collected Prose*. Ed. Robert Giroux. New York: Farrar, Straus and Giroux, 1987.

Lurie, Alison. *Love and Friendship*. New York: Avon Books, 1970.

Mailer, Norman. *Tough Guys Don't Dance*. New York: Ballantine Books, 1984.

Manning, Mary. "Go Lovely Rose." An Entertainment at the John F. Kennedy Library (unpublished). 20 September 1987.

Marquand, John P. *The Late George Apley*. 1937. New York: Pocket Books, 1971.

————. *Wickford Point*. 1939. Alexandria, Va.: Time-Life Books, 1966.

————. *H. M. Pulham, Esquire*. 1941. Chicago: Academy Chicago Publishers, 1986.

Bibliography

———. *Point of No Return*. 1949. New York: Bantam Books, 1961.

———. *Sincerely, Willis Wayde*. Boston: Little, Brown, 1955.

McCarthy, Mary. *A Charmed Life*. New York: Harcourt Brace, 1955.

Melville, Herman. *Piazza Tales*. 1856. New York: Hendrick House, 1962.

———. "Hawthorne and His Mosses." In *The Portable Melville*, ed. Jay Leyda. New York: Viking Press, 1959.

———. *Moby-Dick: or, The White Whale*. New York: Hendrick House, 1962.

Miller, Perry, ed. *The Transcendentalists: An Anthology*. Cambridge, Mass.: Harvard University Press, 1960.

———. and Thomas H. Johnson, eds. *The Puritans*. 2 vols. New York: Harper and Row, 1963.

———. ed. *The American Puritans: Their Prose and Poetry*. New York: Anchor Books, 1956.

Mirsky, Mark. *Blue Hill Ave*. Indianapolis: Bobbs Merrill, 1972.

Morison, Samuel Eliot. *One Boy's Boston 1887–1901*. Boston: Northeastern University Press, 1983.

O'Connor, Edwin. *The Last Hurrah*. New York: Bantam Books, 1967.

———. *The Edge of Sadness*. New York: Bantam Books, 1967.

———. *All in the Family*. New York: Bantam Books, 1970.

———. *The Best and the Last of Edwin O'Connor*. Ed. Arthur Schlesinger. Boston: Atlantic Monthly Press, 1970.

Oliver, Mary. *American Primitive*. Boston: Little, Brown, 1983.

O'Neill, Eugene. *Long Day's Journey into Night*. New Haven: Yale University Press, 1955.

———. *A Moon for the Misbegotten*. New York: Vintage Books, 1974.

Ossoli, Margaret Fuller. *Life Without and Life Within*. Upper Saddle River, N.J.: Literature House/Gregg Press, 1970.

Pearce, Roy Harvey, ed. *Colonial American Writing*. USA: Rinehart, 1959.

Santayana, George. *The Last Puritan: A Memoir in the Form of a Novel*. New York: Scribner's Sons, 1937.

———. *Persons and Places: Fragments of Autobiography*. Ed. William G. Holzberger and Herman J. Saatkamp, Jr. Cambridge, Mass. and London, England: MIT Press, 1986.

Sarton, May. *The Small Room*. New York: W. W. Norton, 1961.

———. *Plant Dreaming Deep*. New York: W. W. Norton, 1968.

———. *Journal of a Solitude*. New York: W. W. Norton, 1973.

———. *A Reckoning*. New York: W. W. Norton, 1978.

———. *The House by the Sea*. New York: W. W. Norton, 1981.

———. *Anger*. New York: W. W. Norton, 1982.

———. *Faithful Are the Wounds*. New York: W. W. Norton, 1983.

———. *The Magnificent Spinster*. New York: W. W. Norton, 1985.

Bibliography

————. *The Education of Harriet Hatfield*. New York: W. W. Norton, 1989.

Sexton, Anne. *To Bedlam and Part Way Back*. Boston: Houghton, Mifflin, 1964.

————. *Live or Die*. Boston: Houghton, Mifflin, 1966.

Stafford, Jean. *Boston Adventure*. Garden City, N.Y.: Sun Dial Press, 1944.

Stowe, Harriet Beecher. *Three Novels: "Uncle Tom's Cabin; or, Life among the Lowly," "The Minister's Wooing," "Oldtown Folks."* New York: Library of America, 1982.

Thoreau, Henry David. *The Portable Thoreau*. Ed. Carl Bode. New York: Penguin Books, 1975.

————. *Henry David Thoreau: "A Week on the Concord and Merrimack Rivers," "Walden; or, Life in the Woods," "The Maine Woods," "Cape Cod."* New York: Library of America, 1985.

Updike, John. *Couples*. 1968. New York: Fawcett Crest, 1969.

————. *A Month of Sundays*. New York: Alfred A. Knopf, 1975.

————. *The Witches of Eastwick*. New York, Alfred A. Knopf, 1984.

————. *Roger's Version*. New York, Alfred A. Knopf, 1986.

————. "Personal History: At War with My Skin." *The New Yorker* (2 September 1985).

————. *S*. New York: Alfred A. Knopf, 1988.

————. *Self-Consciousness*. New York: Alfred A. Knopf, 1989.

Wakefield, Dan. *Returning: A Spiritual Journey*. New York: Doubleday, 1988.

West, Dorothy. *The Living Is Easy*. 1948. New York: Feminist Press, 1982.

Wharton, Edith. *A Backward Glance*. New York: Charles Scribner's Sons, 1964.

————. *Ethan Frome*. 1911. New York: Penguin Books, 1987.

————. *Summer: A Novel*. New York: Harper and Row, 1979.

————. *The Age of Innocence*. New York: Charles Scribner's Sons, 1968.

Wheatley, Phillis. *The Collected Works of Phillis Wheatley*. Ed. John C. Shields. New York: Oxford University Press, 1988.

————. *The Poems of Phillis Wheatley*. Ed. Julian D. Mason, Jr. Chapel Hill: University of Carolina Press, 1966.

White, Theodore H. *In Search of History: A Personal Adventure*. New York: Warner Books, 1978.

Whittier, John Greenleaf. *Whittier*. New York: Dell, 1967.

Wilbur, Richard. *New and Collected Poems*. San Diego: Harcourt Brace Jovanovich, 1988.

Wilson, Harriet E. *Our Nig; or, Sketches from the Life of a Free Black, in a Two-Story White House, North. Showing That Slavery's Shadows Fall Even There, by "Our Nig"*. New York: Vintage Books, 1983.

Criticism, Anthologies and Biographies

Allen, Gay Wilson. *Waldo Emerson: A Biography*. New York: Viking Press, 1981.

Bibliography

Axelrod, Steven Gould. *Robert Lowell: Life and Art*. New Jersey: Princeton University Press, 1978.

Baer, Helene G. *The Heart is Like Heaven: The Life of Lydia Maria Child*. Philadelphia: University of Pennsylvania Press, 1964.

Bedell, Madelon. *The Alcotts: Biography of a Family*. New York: Clarkson N. Potter, 1980.

Bell, Millicent. *Marquand: An American Life*. Boston: Little, Brown, 1979.

Benfey, Christopher. *Emily Dickinson: Lives of a Poet*. New York: George Braziller, 1986.

Benvenuto, Richard. *Amy Lowell*. Boston: Twayne Publishers, 1985.

Bercovitch, Sacvan. *The American Jeremiad*. Madison, Wis.: University of Wisconsin Press, 1978.

———. *The Puritan Origins of the American Self*. New Haven: Yale University Press, 1975.

Bingham, Millicent Todd. *Emily Dickinson's Home: The Early Years as Revealed in Family Correspondence and Reminiscences*. New York: Dover Publications, 1955.

Birmingham, Stephen. *The Late John Marquand: A Biography*. Philadelphia: J. B. Lippincott, 1972.

Blanchard, Paula. *Margaret Fuller: From Transcendentalism to Revolution*. Reading, Mass.: Addison-Wesley, 1987.

Broderick, Francis L. *W. E. B. Du Bois: Negro Leader in a Time of Crisis*. Stanford, Calif.: Stanford University Press, 1959.

Brooks, Paul. *The Old Manse and the People Who Lived There*. The Trustees of Reservations, 1983.

Brooks, Van Wyck. *The World of Washington Irving*. New York: E. P. Dutton, 1950.

———. *The Flowering of New England*. New York: E. P. Dutton, 1952.

———. *Howells: His Life and World*. New York: E. P. Dutton, 1959.

———. *New England: Indian Summer*. New York: E. P. Dutton, 1965.

Buell, Lawrence. *New England Literary Culture: From Revolution through Renaissance*. Cambridge: Cambridge University Press, 1986.

Campbell, Joseph. *The Hero with a Thousand Faces*. Princeton, N.J.: Princeton University Press, 1949.

Chase, Richard. *The American Novel and Its Tradition*. Garden City, N.Y.: Doubleday Anchor Books, 1957.

———. *Emily Dickinson*. New York: Delta, 1965.

Cheever, Susan. *Home before Dark: A Biographical Memoir of John Cheever by His Daughter*. New York: Pocket Books, 1985.

Clifford, Deborah Pickman. *Mine Eyes Have Seen the Glory: A Biography of Julia Ward Howe*. Boston: Little, Brown, 1979.

Couser, G. Thomas. *American Autobiography: The Prophetic Mode*. Amherst: University of Massachusetts Press, 1979.

Bibliography

Crews, Frederick C. *The Sins of the Fathers: Hawthorne's Psychological Themes.* New York: Oxford University Press, 1966.

Davis, Merrell R., and William H. Gilman, eds. *The Letters of Herman Melville.* New Haven: Yale University Press, 1960.

Delbanco, Andrew. *The Puritan Ordeal.* Cambridge, Mass.: Harvard University Press, 1989.

Dineen, Joseph. *The Purple Shamrock: The Hon. James Michael Curley of Boston.* New York: W. W. Norton, 1949.

Donaldson, Scott. *John Cheever: A Biography.* New York: Random House, 1988.

Donovan, Josephine. *New England Local Color: A Woman's Tradition.* New York: Continuum, 1988.

Duberman, Martin. *James Russell Lowell.* Boston: Houghton, Mifflin, 1966.

Du Bois, W. E. Burghardt. *Dusk of Dawn: An Essay toward an Autobiography of a Race Concept.* New York: Harcourt, Brace, 1940.

Edel, Leon. *Henry James: The Untried Years: 1843–1870.* London: Rupert Hart-Davis, 1953.

———. *Henry James: The Conquest of London: 1870–1881.* Philadelphia: J. B. Lippincott, 1962.

———. *Henry James: The Middle Years: 1882–1895.* Philadelphia: J. B. Lippincott, 1962.

———. *Henry James: The Treacherous Years: 1895–1901.* Philadelphia: J. B. Lippincott, 1969.

———. *Henry James: The Master: 1901–1916.* Philadelphia: J. B. Lippincott, 1972.

Elbert, Sarah. *A Hunger for Home: Louisa May Alcott's Place in American Culture.* New Brunswick, N.J.: Rutgers University Press, 1987.

Ellmann, Richard, and Robert O'Clair, eds. *The Norton Anthology of Modern Poetry.* New York: W. W. Norton, 1973.

Foye, Brian. *A Guide to Jack Kerouac's Lowell.* Lowell, Mass.: Corporation for the Celebration of Jack Kerouac in Lowell, 1988.

Fountain, Charles. *Another Man's Poison: The Life and Writing of Columnist George Frazier.* Chester, Conn.: Globe Pequot Press, 1984.

Francis, Robert. *Frost: A Time to Talk: Conversations & Indiscretions Recorded by Robert Francis.* Amherst, Mass.: University of Massachusetts Press, 1972.

Gelb, Arthur, and Barbara Gelb. *O'Neill.* New York: Harper and Brothers, 1962.

Gardner, Helen. *The Art of T. S. Eliot.* New York: E. P. Dutton, 1959.

Gilmore, Michael T. *American Romanticism and the Marketplace.* Chicago: University of Chicago Press, 1985.

Gordon, Lyndall. *Eliot's Early Years.* New York: Farrar, Straus and Giroux, 1977.

———. *Eliot's New Life.* New York: Farrar, Straus, Giroux, 1988.

Gould, Jean. *Amy: The World of Amy Lowell and the Imagist Movement.* New York: Dodd, Mead, 1975.

Bibliography

Hall, David D. *Worlds of Wonder, Days of Judgment: Popular Religious Beliefs in Early New England*. New York: Alfred A. Knopf, 1989.

Hamilton, Ian. *Robert Lowell: A Biography*. New York: Random House, 1982.

Hawthorne, Julian. *Nathaniel Hawthorne and His Wife: A Biography*. 1884. USA: Archon Books, 1968.

Hobson, Barbara Meil, and Paul Wright. *Boston, A State of Mind: An Exhibition Record*. Boston, Mass.: Boston Public Library, 1977.

Howarth, William. *The Book of Concord: Thoreau's Life as a Writer*. New York: Penguin Books, 1982.

Howe, Helen. *The Gentle Americans 1864–1960: Biography of a Breed*. New York: Harper and Row, 1965.

Howe, Julia Ward. *Margaret Fuller*. New York: Haskell House, 1968.

Howe, M. A. De Wolfe. *Memoirs of a Hostess: A Chronicle of Eminent Friendships Drawn Chiefly from the Diaries of Mrs. James T. Fields*. Boston: Atlantic Monthly Press, 1922.

————. *Barrett Wendell and His Letters*. Boston: Atlantic Monthly Press, 1924.

Howells, Mildred, ed. *Life in Letters of William Dean Howells*. 2 vols. Garden City, N.Y.: Doubleday, Doran, 1928.

James, Edward T., ed. *Notable American Women 1607–1950: A Biographical Dictionary*. 3 vols. Cambridge, Mass.: Belknap Press, 1971.

James, Henry. *Hawthorne*. In *The Shock of Recognition*, ed. Edmund Wilson. New York: Farrar, Straus and Cudahy, 1955.

————. "Nathaniel Hawthorne." In *The American Essays of Henry James*, ed. Leon Edel. Princeton, N.J.: Princeton University Press, 1989.

————. "The Art of Fiction." *Henry James: Literary Criticism: Essays on Literature, American Writers, English Writers*. New York: Library of America, 1984.

————. "William Dean Howells." In *The Shock of Recognition*, ed. Edmund Wilson. New York: Farrar, Straus and Cudahy, 1955.

Johnson, Thomas H., ed. *Emily Dickinson: Selected Letters*. Cambridge, Mass.: Belknap Press, 1986.

Kaplan, Justin. *Mr. Clemens and Mark Twain*. New York: Simon and Schuster, 1966.

Karl, Frederick R. *American Fictions 1940–1980: A Comprehensive History and Critical Evaluation*. New York: Harper and Row, 1983.

Kazin, Alfred. *On Native Ground: An Interpretation of Modern American Prose Literature*. Garden City, N.Y.: Doubleday, 1956.

————. *An American Procession*. New York: Alfred A. Knopf, 1984.

————. *A Writer's America: Landscape in Literature*. New York: Alfred A. Knopf, 1988.

Keller, Karl. *The Only Kangaroo among the Beauty: Emily Dickinson and America*. Baltimore, Md.: Johns Hopkins Press, 1979.

Bibliography

Klinkowitz, Jerome. *The New American Novel of Manners: The Fiction of Richard Yates, Dan Wakefield, and Thomas McGuane*. Athens: University of Georgia Press, 1986.

Lang, Amy Schrager. *Prophetic Woman: Anne Hutchinson and the Problem of Dissent in the Literature of New England*. Berkeley and Los Angeles, Calif.: University of California Press, 1987.

Lawrence, D. H. *Studies in Classic American Literature*. In *The Shock of Recognition*, ed. Edmund Wilson. New York: Farrar, Straus and Cudahy, 1955.

Lebeaux, Richard. *Young Man Thoreau*. Amherst, Mass.: University of Massachusetts Press, 1977.

———. *Thoreau's Seasons*. Amherst, Mass.: University of Massachusetts Press, 1984.

Levine, Miriam. *A Guide to Writers' Homes in New England*. Cambridge: Applewood Books, 1984.

Lewis, R. W. B. *Edith Wharton: A Biography*. New York: Harper and Row, 1975.

Light, Martin, ed. *Critical Approaches to American Literature*. New York: Thomas Y. Crowell, 1965.

Lynn, Kenneth S. *William Dean Howells: An American Life*. New York: Harcourt Brace, Jovanovich, 1971.

Mallow, James R. *Nathaniel Hawthorne in His Times*. Boston: Houghton, Mifflin, 1980.

Marshall, Megan. "Three Sisters Who Showed the Way." *American Heritage* (September/October, 1987).

Martin, Theodora Penny. *The Sound of Our Own Voices: Women's Study Clubs 1860–1910*. Boston: Beacon Press, 1987.

Marx, Leo. *The Machine in the Garden: Technology and the Pastoral Ideal in America*. New York: Oxford University Press, 1964.

———. *The Pilot and the Passenger: Essays on Literature, Technology, and Culture in the United States*. New York: Oxford University Press, 1988.

Matthiessen, F. O. *American Renaissance: Art and Expression in the Age of Emerson and Whitman*. New York: Oxford University Press, 1941.

McCormick, John. *George Santayana: A Biography*. New York: Paragon House, 1988.

McNamara, Leo. "Irish and American Politics in the Eighteenth Century and Nathaniel Hawthorne's "My Kinsman, Major Molineux." *Eire-Ireland* 24 (Fall 1989): 20–32.

Meltzer, Milton, and Patricia C. Holland, eds. *Lydia Maria Child: Selected Letters, 1817–1880*. Amherst: University of Massachusetts Press, 1982.

Melville, Herman. "Hawthorne and His Mosses," *The Portable Melville*, ed. Jay Leyda. New York: Viking Press, 1959.

Miller, Perry. *Errand into the Wilderness*. Cambridge, Mass.: Belknap Press, 1956.

Bibliography

————. *The New England Mind: The Seventeenth Century*. Boston: Beacon Press, 1961.

————. *The New England Mind: From Colony to Province*. Boston: Beacon Press, 1961.

Meyers, Jeffrey. *Manic Power: Robert Lowell and His Circle*. New York: Arbor House, 1987.

————, ed. *Robert Lowell: Interviews and Memoirs*. Ann Arbor: University of Michigan Press, 1988.

Myerson, Joel. *The New England Transcendentalists and the "Dial": A History of the Magazine and Its Contributors*. London: Associated University Presses, 1980.

Myerson, Joel, and Daniel Shealy, eds.; Madeleine B. Stern, assoc. ed. *The Selected Letters of Louisa May Alcott*. Boston: Little, Brown, 1987.

Nicosia, Gerald. *Memory Babe: A Critical Biography of Jack Kerouac*. New York, Penguin Books, 1986.

O'Neill, Thomas P., Jr., with William Novak. *Man of the House: The Life and Political Memoirs of Speaker Tip O'Neill*. New York: Random House, 1987.

Osborne, William S. *Lydia Maria Child*. Boston: Twayne Publishers, 1980.

Pritchard, William H. *Frost: A Literary Life Reconsidered*. New York: Oxford University Press, 1984.

Porte, Joel, ed. *Emerson in His Journals*. Cambridge, Mass.: Belknap Press, 1982.

————. *Representative Man: Ralph Waldo Emerson in His Time*. New York: Columbia University Press, 1988.

Rank, Hugh. *Edwin O'Connor*. Boston: Twayne Publishers, 1974.

Reynolds, David S. *Beneath the American Renaissance: The Subversive Imagination in the Age of Emerson and Melville*. Cambridge, Mass.: Harvard University Press, 1989.

Richardson, Robert D., Jr. *Henry Thoreau: A Life of the Mind*. Berkeley, Los Angeles, and London: University of California Press, 1986.

Roche, James Jeffrey. *Life of John Boyle O'Reilly, Together with His Complete Poems and Speeches*. Ed. Mrs. John Boyle O'Reilly. New York: Cassell, 1891.

Ronda, Bruce A., ed. *Letters of Elizabeth Palmer Peabody: American Renaissance Woman*. Middletown, Conn.: Wesleyan University Press, 1984.

Rossi, Alice S., ed. *The Feminist Papers: From Adams to de Beauvoir*. New York: Columbia University Press, 1973.

Russell, Francis. "T. S. Eliot: Harvard Loyalist." *Harvard Magazine* (September-October 1988).

Samuels, Ernest. *Henry Adams*. Cambridge, Mass.: Belknap Press, 1989.

Sayre, Robert F. *The Examined Self: Benjamin Franklin, Henry Adams, Henry James*. Madison: University of Wisconsin Press, 1988.

Bibliography

Sewall, Richard B. *The Life of Emily Dickinson*. 2 vols. New York: Farrar, Strauss and Giroux, 1974.

Seymour, Miranda. *Henry James and His Literary Circle 1895–1915*. Boston: Houghton, Mifflin, 1989.

Sexton, Linda Gray, and Lois Ames, eds. *Anne Sexton: A Self-Portrait in Letters*. Boston: Houghton, Mifflin, 1979.

Shannon, Catherine. "John Boyle O'Reilly, Irish Prophet of Progressivism." Paper delivered at New England Regional American Committee for Irish Studies Conference, Salve Regina College, Newport, Rhode Island, October 1988.

Shealy, Daniel. "Miss Alcott of Boston." Paper delivered at Northeast Modern Language Association Meeting, Boston, April 1987.

Showalter, Elaine, ed. *Alternative Alcott*. New Brunswick: Rutgers University Press, 1988.

Sickerman, Barbara, and Carol Hurd Green. *Notable American Women: The Modern Period: A Biographical Dictionary*. Cambridge, Mass.: Belknap Press, 1980.

Simpson, Eileen. *Poets in Their Youth: A Memoir*. New York: Vintage Books, 1983.

Stavely, Keith W. *Puritan Legacies: Paradise Lost and the New England Tradition, 1630–1890*. Ithaca, N.Y.: Cornell University Press, 1987.

Stock, Irvin. *Mary McCarthy*. Minneapolis: University of Minnesota Press, 1968.

Strouse, Jean. *Alice James: A Biography*. Boston: Houghton, Mifflin, 1980.

Taylor, Robert. *Fred Allen: His Life and Wit*. Boston: Little, Brown, 1989.

Tharp, Louise Hall. *The Peabody Sisters of Salem*. Boston: Little, Brown, 1950.

Thompson, Lawrance. *Robert Frost: A Biography*. New York: Holt, Rinehart and Winston, 1981.

Updike, John. *Assorted Prose*. New York: Alfred A. Knopf, 1965.

———. *Hugging the Shore: Essays and Criticism*. New York: Alfred A. Knopf, 1983.

———. "Emersonianism." *The New Yorker* (4 June 1984).

———. "Howells as Anti-Novelist." *The New Yorker* (13 July 1987).

Van Doren, Mark. *Nathaniel Hawthorne*. 1949. New York: Viking Press, 1957.

Vendler, Helen, ed. *Voices and Visions: The Poet in America*. New York: Random House, 1987.

———, ed. *Contemporary American Poetry*. Cambridge, Mass.: Belknap Press, 1985.

Wagner-Martin, Linda W. *Sylvia Plath: A Biography*. New York: Simon and Schuster, 1987.

Wakefield, Dan. "An Improper Bostonian Writ Large." *Neiman Reports* 40 (Spring 1986).

Washington, Mary Helen. *Invented Lives: Narratives of Black Women 1860–1960*. Garden City, N.Y.: Anchor Press, 1987.

Bibliography

Welty, Eudora. "Place in Fiction." *The Eye of the Storm: Selected Essays and Reviews*. New York: Vintage Books, 1970.

Whitfield, Stephen J. " 'Sacred in History and in Art': *The Shaw Memorial*." *New England Quarterly* 60 (March 1987).

Wills, Garry. *The Kennedy Imprisonment: A Meditation on Power*. Boston: Little, Brown, 1982.

Wilson, Edmund, *The Shores of Light: A Literary Chronicle of the Twenties and Thirties*. New York: Farrar, Straus and Young, 1952.

————, ed. *The Shock of Recognition: The Development of Literature in the United States Recorded by the Men Who Made It*. New York: Farrar, Straus and Cudahy, 1955.

————. *Patriotic Gore: Studies in the Literature of the American Civil War*. New York: Oxford University Press, 1962.

————. " 'Baldini': A Memoir and a Collaboration." *The Best and the Last of Edwin O'Connor*. Boston: Atlantic Monthly Press, 1970.

————. *The Thirties: From Notebooks and Diaries of the Period*. Ed. Leon Edel. New York: Farrar, Straus and Giroux, 1980.

Wilson, Helen M. *Literary Boston of To-Day*. Boston: L. C. Page, 1902.

Wolff, Cynthia Griffin. *A Feast of Words*. New York: Oxford University Press, 1977.

Young, Philip. *Hawthorne's Secret: An Un-told Tale*. Boston: David R. Godine, 1984.

Credits

Grateful acknowledgment is made for permission to reprint the following:

Excerpt from "Elegy: For Robert Lowell," from *A Part of Speech* by Joseph Brodsky. Translation copyright © 1973, 1974, 1976, 1977, 1978, 1979, 1980 by Farrar, Straus and Giroux, Inc. Reprinted by permission of Farrar, Straus and Giroux, Inc.

Excerpts from "I like to see it lap the Miles" and "A certain Slant of light," from *The Poems of Emily Dickinson* edited by Thomas H. Johnson, Cambridge, Mass.: Belknap Press of Harvard University Press. Copyright © 1955, 1979, 1983 by the President and Fellows of Harvard College. Reprinted by permission of the publishers and the Trustees of Amherst College.

Excerpts from *Emily Dickinson: Selected Letters* edited by Thomas H. Johnson, Cambridge, Mass.: Belknap Press of Harvard University Press. Copyright © 1958, 1971 by the President and Fellows of Harvard College and copyright © 1914,

Index

Aaron, Daniel, 136, 307
Abolitionism, 54–56, 58, 97, 167, 214
Adams, Abigail, 52–53, 143
Adams, Charles Francis, 175
Adams, Henry, 66, 188, 196, 212, 258, 268; and Boston, 267, 295; *Democracy*, 178; *The Education of Henry Adams*, 12, 174–78, 271, 275, 319, 321; *Esther*, 178; *The Life of George Cabot Lodge*, 178; his novels of manners, 174, 178; and Quincy, 190; and George Santayana, 179
Adams, John, 52, 142, 143, 148
Adams, Samuel, 4, 147
Advocate, 267

African Meeting House, 168, 171
Agassiz, Louis, 81
Aiken, Conrad, 239, 246
Alcoholics Anonymous, 197
Alcorn, Alfred, *Vestments*, 323, 324–25
Alcott, Abba, 69
Alcott, Amos Bronson, 59, 60, 66, 69; *Concord Days*, 34, 38
Alcott, Louisa May, 33, 52, 69, 72, 97; *Flower Fables*, 67; "How I Went Out to Service," 67; *Little Men*, 67; *Little Women*, 66, 67, 68, 69; *Work: A Story of Experience*, 67–68
Allen, Fred, *Treadmill to Oblivion*, 108
American Revolution, 142, 143, 276

393

Amherst, MA: Emily Dickinson and, 248–54; Robert Francis and, 256–60; Robert Frost and, 255–56
Amherst Academy, 251
Amherst College, 249, 251, 254, 255–56, 257, 261; Robert Frost Library at, 256, 260
Andover Academy, 34
Andover Theological Seminary, 11
Andrew, John, 287
Anglicanism, 11
Angoff, Charles, *When I Was a Boy in Boston,* 315
Antin, Mary, *Promised Land,* 315
Appleton, Nathan, 208
Arbella, 8, 193, 194, 309
Arnold, Matthew, 117; "Discourses in America," 113
Athenaeum, *see* Boston Athenaeum
Atlantic Monthly, 14, 65, 78, 79, 197, 279; and William Dean Howells, 83, 90, 109; and Edwin O'Connor, 108–9, 137
Attucks, Crispus, 142, 143, 144, 162, 169; public monument to, 147–48, 160, 168
Atwood, Margaret, *The Handmaid's Tale,* 329–30
Auden, W. H., 318
Augustine, St., 273; *City of God,* 3; *Confessions,* 3, 33

Baker, George Pierce, 237–38
Balzac, Honoré de, 88
Bates, Arlo: *The Pagans,* 165; *The Puritans,* 165
Beecher, Henry Ward, 56; "Patriotism," 150
Beecher, Lyman, 56, 111
Bellamy, Edward, *Looking Backward: 2000–1887,* 329
Benson, Frank, 6
Bercovitch, Sacvan, 309
Berenson, Bernard, 88
Berryman, John, 261; "Boston Common," 288; *Homage to Mistress Bradstreet,* 309, 311–12
Beston, Henry, 232, 246, 247, 264–65; and Cape Cod, 244–45; *The Outermost House,* 230, 244–45

Bishop, Elizabeth, 275
Black Heritage Trail, 170–71
Blanchard, Paula, 63
Boston and Albany Railroad, 175
Boston Anti-Slavery Office, 149
Boston Associates, 187, 208
Boston Athenaeum, 30, 58, 170, 184, 187, 321; and Waltham-Lowell system, 208
Boston City Reporter, 318
Boston College, 181, 227
Boston Company, 208, 209
Boston Evening Transcript, 163, 271
Boston Globe, 9, 124–25, 197, 318, 321
Boston Herald, 108
Boston Ladies' Anti-Slavery Society, 55
Boston Latin School, 316, 317
Boston Manufacturing Company, 208
Boston Massacre, 142, 144, 147
Boston *Post,* 122
Boston Public Library, 104, 119, 316
Boston Red Sox, 200–202, 204
Boston Stereotype Foundry, 151
Boston University, 157, 162, 169, 197, 291; Robert Lowell's teaching at, 291, 299
Bradford, William, 229, 236–37, 240, 241; and landing of Pilgrims on Cape Cod, 227–28, 231, 242, 248
Bradstreet, Anne, 254, 309–10, 313; John Berryman on, 309, 311–12; "Contemplations," 311; "Meditations Divine and Moral," 311; "To My Dear Children," 309, 310
Braithwaite, William Stanley, 162–63, 169–70; *The House Under Arcturus: An Autobiography,* 164, 166; "In the Public Garden," 163, 168; *Lyrics of Life and Love,* 164; works of, 163–68
Bridge, Horatio, 24
Brodsky, Joseph, 302; "Elegy: For Robert Lowell," 266
Brook Farm, 24, 26–27, 28, 34, 39, 42; Elizabeth Peabody's account of, 60
Brooks, Preston, 55
Brooks, Van Wyck, 87–88, 213; *The Flowering of New England,* 13, 219
Brown, John, 55, 65, 76
Brown, Thomas N., 6, 111

Brown, William Wells, 149–50, 156, 169; and William Braithwaite, 165–66, 167; *Clotelle*, 149, 156; *Narrative of W. W. Brown, a Fugitive Slave*, 149
Bryant, Louisa, 237
Bulfinch, Charles, 114, 115
Burchard, Peter, 287
Burns, Robert, 213

Calvinism, 11, 56, 57, 232, 272
Campbell, Joseph, *The Hero with a Thousand Faces*, 204
Cape Cod literature, 227–48
Cape Cod National Seashore, 230–31
Cape Cod School of Art, 229
Carlin, Terry, 237
Carney, William, 287, 288
Carroll, James, *Mortal Friends*, 123
Catholic church, 114, 118, 296
Catholicism, 11, 111–12, 181, 221, 224; and Lyman Beecher, 56, 111; and Robert Lowell, 269, 272, 296
Century magazine, 86, 96
Channing, William Ellery, 11, 28, 38, 54, 63, 64; and Margaret Fuller, 60; and Elizabeth Peabody, 59; and Thoreau's *Cape Cod*, 232–33
Charters, Ann, 224
Chase, Richard, 173
Chauncey, Charles, 144
Cheever, Daniel, 194
Cheever, David, 195
Cheever, Ezekiel, 193–94, 195
Cheever, Federico, 194
Cheever, Frederick Lincoln, 195
Cheever, John, 194–95, 197; death of, 197; "The Death of Justina," 195–96; "Expelled," 195; his novels of manners, 173, 174; *Oh What a Paradise It Seems*, 197; *The Wapshot Chronicle*, 192–93, 194, 195, 196; *The Wapshot Scandal*, 192–93, 195, 196
Cheever, Mary, 195
Cheever, Susan, 195; *Home before Dark*, 194
Child, David Lee, 53
Child, Lydia Maria, 52, 53, 58, 151; antislavery opinions of, 54–56; *Appeal in Favor of That Class of Americans Called Africans*, 54–55, 56; *First Settlers of New England*, 53; and *Freedman's Book*, 55; *The Frugal Housewife*, 53–54, 56; *Hobomok*, 53; *The Rebels*, 53; *Souvenir of New England*, 53
Christ Church, 11
Ciardi, John, 261
"City upon a Hill," Boston as, 4–5, 9, 15, 17
Civil Liberties Union, 321
Civil War, 71, 84, 106, 142, 143, 177; and Henry Adams, 178; black soldiers in, 164–65, 168; Lincoln's policies in, 280; tributes to black heroism in, 148
Clarke, J. C., 63
Clay, Henry, 175
Collins, Patrick A., 116, 119
Colorado, University of, 296
Colored American Magazine, 156
Colored Co-operative Publishing Company, 156
Columbia University, 226–27
Congregationalism, 10, 11, 249, 251
Conrad, Joseph, *The Heart of Darkness*, 51
"Conversations," 54, 62, 64, 321
Cook, George Cram "Jig," 237, 239
Cooke, Rose Terry, 57
Coolidge, John T., 33
Cotton, John, 70, 308
Coughlin, Father, 317
Craige House, 92, 102–3, 208
Cummings, E. E., 239
Curley, Frank, 124–25
Curley, James Michael, 108, 121, 130, 135, 318; house of, 121–22, 124, 125; *I'd Do It Again*, 121, 124, 127; legend of, 122–25, 139
Curzon, Samuel, 190
Curzon's Mill, 190
Cushing, Richard Cardinal, 115, 118–19

Dalzell, Robert F., Jr., 187, 208
Daniels, Conky, 177
Daniels, John, *Freedom's Birthplace*, 146–47

Dartmouth College, 216
Davis, Jefferson, 155
Delbanco, Andrew, 308
Dial, 59, 61–62, 63
Dickens, Charles, 211, 212, 213, 225; *American Notes*, 209–10
Dickinson, Austin, 250, 252
Dickinson, Edward, 249, 251
Dickinson, Emily, 165, 198, 256, 257; and Amherst, 248–54 *passim*, 264; and Boston, 248, 249; and Robert Francis, 260–61; "I like to see it lap the Miles," 206–7; poetry of, 253–55, 265
Dickinson, Vinnie, 250
Dineen, Joseph F.: *The Purple Shamrock*, 123; *Ward Eight*, 123
Dinesen, Isak, 180
Donahue, Patrick, 116
Donovan, Josephine, 53, 57
Dos Passos, John, 239
Dostoevsky, F. M., *Notes from the Underground*, 307
Douglass, Frederick, 148, 149–50, 151, 166, 167, 169; *Narrative of the Life of Frederick Douglass*, 149
Du Bois, W.E.B., 151–55, 156, 162, 169; *Autobiography*, 153; and William Braithwaite, 165; *The Souls of Black Folk*, 155, 166
Dubus, Andre, 220–22; "The Pretty Girl," 221; "Townies," 221
Duhamel, P. Albert, *After Strange Fruit*, 13
Dukakis, Michael, 288
Dunbar, Paul Lawrence, "We Wear the Mask," 288
Duyckinck, Evert, 44

Eberhart, Richard, 261, 278
Edel, Leon, 77, 78
Edwards, Jonathan, 253
Eliot, Andrew, 270, 273
Eliot, Charles W., 154, 270
Eliot, Charlotte Champe, 270
Eliot, Christopher Rhodes, 270
Eliot, Henry Ware, Jr., 270
Eliot, T. S., 15, 190, 210, 319; *Ash Wednesday*, 272; and Boston Idea, 267–68; centennial of, 267; "Cousin Nancy," 271; *The Dry Salvages*, 273; *East Coker*, 273; family of, 270–71; *Four Quartets*, 267; and Hawthorne, 269–70, 273; and Henry James, 268, 269, 271, 273; "The Love Song of J. Alfred Prufrock," 271–72; and Robert Lowell, 268–69, 270, 272, 274, 301–2; "Portrait of a Lady," 271; "Tradition and the Individual Talent," 267, 273; "Unreal City," 273; *The Waste Land*, 273–74, 302
Eliot, William Greenleaf, 270
Ellicott, Nancy, 271
Elmwood, 102–3, 278–79
"Emerald Necklace," 121
Emerson, Edward, 34
Emerson, Lidian, 39
Emerson, Ralph Waldo, 11, 18, 29, 30, 150, 157; "Boston Hymn," 36–37, 148; and Concord, 30, 31–34, 36, 38, 39; "Concord Hymn," 32; "Discourse on Emancipation," 37–38; *Essays*, 63, 319; and Robert Francis, 257; and Robert Frost, 218; and Margaret Fuller, 61, 63; Harvard Divinity School Address of, 14; and Hawthorne, 44; "Historical Discourse," 32; and William Dean Howells, 76, 77; on Irish newcomers, 112; *Nature*, 30, 32–33, 35; Old Manse of, 30, 105; "Self-Reliance," 306; and Thoreau, 37–40; and Transcendental Club, 58; and John Updike, 204; his view of Boston, 34–37
Emerson, William (father of Ralph Waldo), 30
Emerson, William (grandfather of Ralph Waldo), 32

Fairbrother, Trevor, 7
Farrell, James T., *Studs Lonigan*, 139
Faulkner, William, 2; *Absalom, Absalom!*, 15
Federal Street Church, 11
Feminism, 54, 55, 58–59, 62, 97, 98; and Lowell mills, 211
Fenway Park, 200, 201

Fields, Annie (Mrs. James T.), 44, 98, 185
Fields, James T., 44, 67, 83, 98, 185
Finch, Robert, 229–30; and Cape Cod, 243–44, 246–47, 248; *Common Ground*, 244, 246; *Outlands*, 246; *The Primal Place*, 246–47
First Church of Boston, 30, 31
Fisk University, 154, 155
Fitzgerald, F. Scott, 1
Fitzgerald, John Francis ("Honey Fitz"), 115, 119–20, 121, 135, 138
Fitzpatrick, John Bernard, 118
Flaxman, John, *Designs for Dante*, 92
Flynn, Raymond L., 125, 129–30
Ford, Henry, 3
Forten, Charlotte L., 150
Francis, Robert, 256–59; *Collected Poems*, 260; *The Trouble with Francis*, 259–60; "Two Ghosts," 260–61
Franklin, Benjamin, 166; *Autobiography*, 313
Frazier, George, 318
Frederick Douglass' Paper, 149
Freedman's Book, 55
Freedom Trail, 170, 171
Freeman, Mary E. Wilkins, 49, 57; *A New England Nun*, 57
Free Press, 213
French, Daniel Chester, 118
Frost, Elinor, 217, 218
Frost, Robert, 9, 213, 214, 277; "After Apple-Picking," 219; and Amherst, 255–56; *A Boy's Will*, 215, 216, 219; and William Braithwaite, 163, 165; death of, 220, 256; "The Death of the Hired Man," 216; "Despair," 217–18; and Emily Dickinson, 254, 255, 256; and Robert Francis, 256–57, 260–61; "The Gift Outright," 220; "Into My Own," 216; and Maxine Kumin, 222, 223, 224; "Mending Wall," 216, 222–23; "Mowing," 218; *North of Boston*, 215, 216, 219; "The Pasture," 218; "The Road Not Taken," 326; and Richard Wilbur, 263
Fruitlands, utopian community at, 66–67, 69

Fugitive Slave Act, 37, 55, 214
Fuller, Margaret, 18, 29, 52, 72, 97, 269; and Boston, 14, 63–64, 68; and Lydia Child, 54; "Conversations" of, 54, 62, 64, 321; death of, 28, 63, 64, 232, 233; and the *Dial*, 61–62, 63; "The Great Lawsuit," 62; Elizabeth Hardwick on, 293–94; and Hawthorne's *Blithedale Romance*, 27; her life of letters, 60–61; and Robert Lowell, 301; *Memoirs*, 63; and Elizabeth Peabody, 92; trans., *Eckerman's Conversations*, 61; *Women in the Nineteenth Century*, 63
Fuller, Timothy, 60

Gage, Thomas, 143
Gardner, Helen, 273
Gardner, Isabella Stewart, 104
Garrison, William Lloyd, 149, 150, 213
Garrity, J. Arthur, 113
Goethe, Johann Wolfgang von, 54
Goldberg, Isaac, 315
Goodwin, Doris Kearns, 115, 134
Gordon, Lyndall, 272
Gorham Press, 238
Grant, U. S., 116
Great Awakening, 253
Great Famine (Ireland), 13, 112, 136, 232
Greeley, Horace, 63
Green, Martin, *The Problem of Boston*, 13
Green, Melissa, *Squanicook Eclogues*, 242–43
Griswold, Rufus, *The Female Poets of America*, 144
Grund, Francis J., 112
Guardian, 159

Hale, Edward Everett: *James Russell Lowell and His Friends*, 165; *Letters on Irish Emigration*, 112; *The Man Without a Country*, 165
Hale, Emily, 272–73
Hall, Donald, 215
Hampshire College, 257
Hancock, John, 144
Handlin, Oscar, 113, 114

Hardwick, Elizabeth, 291, 301; "Boston: A Lost Ideal," 12, 292–93, 294–95, 299; "The Genius of Margaret Fuller," 293–94; *The Ghostly Lover,* 291; *Sleepless Nights,* 293
Harper's, 15
Harte, Bret, 81
Harvard Club, 124
Harvard Divinity School, 14
Harvard Law School, 161, 162
Harvard University, 138, 169, 279, 314, 331; and Henry Adams, 177–78; and W.E.B. Du Bois, 152, 154–55; and T. S. Eliot, 267, 270, 272; and Robert Francis, 258; and Robert Frost, 216–17; and Robert Lowell, 301–2; and Eugene O'Neill, 237–38; and George Santayana, 179; and May Sarton, 320–21; and John Updike, 326, 327–28; and Waltham-Lowell system, 208; and Barrett Wendell, 152, 153, 185; and Theodore White, 316; and Richard Wilbur, 261, 262
Hassam, Childe, *Boston Common at Twilight,* 7, 293, 324–25
Hathorne, John, 21
Hathorne, William, 21
Hawthorne, Charles W., 229
Hawthorne, Elizabeth, 23
Hawthorne, Julian, 29
Hawthorne, Nathaniel, 2, 14, 31, 173, 265; as American Consul at Liverpool, 70; *The Blithedale Romance,* 26–28, 49, 69, 95; and Concord, 28–30, 38, 69, 70; at Custom House, 42, 59, 72; "The Custom-House," 19, 21–22, 318–19; death of, 71–72, 103; and T. S. Eliot, 269–70, 273; and Emerson, 44; "Ethan Brand," 72, 312; *The House of the Seven Gables,* 24, 42–44, 46, 47; and William Dean Howells, 75–76, 77, 83, 91, 107; and Henry James, 42, 91–94, 105–6, 107; in Lenox, 42–47, 68–69; and Robert Lowell, 73, 286–87; *Marble Faun,* 76; and Melville, 18, 44–47, 72; *Mosses from an Old Manse,* 42; "My Kinsman, Major Molineux," 25, 88, 287, 298; "The New Adam and Eve," 25; Old Manse of, 28–30,

42, 105; *Our Old Home,* 70, 71; and Elizabeth Peabody, 60; "Pilgrimage to Old Boston," 70; in Salem, 21, 22, 23–24, 42, 44; *The Scarlet Letter,* 10, 11, 15, 19–23, 24, 30, 35, 42, 43, 50, 51, 54, 91, 93, 198, 202, 203, 204, 318–19, 329, 330; *Septimus Felton,* 71; "Sights from a Steeple," 25–26; and Harriet Beecher Stowe, 57; "Tanglewood Porch," 45–46, 47; *Tanglewood Tales,* 49, 69; and Thoreau, 41–42, 71; his view of Boston, 18–19, 24–26, 27, 37; Wayside home of, 69, 70–71, 75; and Edith Wharton, 48, 49, 52; *A Wonder-Book for Girls and Boys,* 45–46, 69
Hawthorne, Sophia Peabody, 27, 28–29, 44, 58–59, 68
Hawthorne, Una, 70
Hay, John, *The Great Beach,* 246
Hayes, Rutherford B., 279
Heaney, Seamus, 275–76
Hecker, Isaac, 39
Hector, 194
Heilbrun, Carolyn G., 320
Hentoff, Nat, 317–18; *Boston Boy,* 314
Higginson, Henry, 177
Higginson, Thomas Wentworth, 65, 112, 117, 164–65; *Army Life in a Black Regiment,* 165, 251; *Cheerful Yesterdays,* 251; and Emily Dickinson, 250–53, 254
Hoar, Elizabeth, 29
Holmes, Oliver Wendell, 4, 44, 80, 83, 84–85; *Autocrat of the Breakfast Table,* 36; "Harvard College in the War," 289; and John Boyle O'Reilly, 117
Homer, Winslow, 6–7
Hooker, Thomas, 248
Hopkins, Pauline E., *Contending Forces,* 155–57
Howarth, William, 39
Howe, Helen, 184
Howe, Julia Ward, 52, 61, 64, 68; *The Battle Hymn of the Republic,* 65; and William Braithwaite, 165; and Margaret Fuller, 64; role of, in Boston, 65

Howe, Mark A. De Wolfe, 165, 184–85, 304; *Barrett Wendell and His Letters*, 184, 185; *Boston: The Place and the People*, 319–20; *Memoirs of a Hostess*, 185; *A Partial (And Not Impartial) Semi-Centennial History of the Tavern Club 1884–1934*, 185
Howe, Molly Manning, *Go Lovely Rose*, 120–21
Howe, Samuel Gridley, 64
Howells, William Dean, 14–15, 57, 74–75, 173, 278–79, 328; and *The Atlantic*, 83, 90, 109; and William Braithwaite, 165; in Cambridge, 80–83; *A Chance Acquaintance*, 79–80; and Emily Dickinson, 253; and Emerson, 76, 77; and Hawthorne, 75–76, 77, 83, 91, 107; and Henry James, 77–79, 83, 84, 97, 103, 104; *The Minister's Charge*, 88–89; *A Modern Instance*, 84; *The Rise of Silas Lapham*, 12, 74, 77, 84–87, 100, 106, 109, 173; *Suburban Sketches*, 82; and Thoreau, 76, 77; and Mark Twain, 89–90; and John Updike, 204
Hughes, Ted, 299
Hutchinson, Anne, 31, 52, 64, 70, 308, 318; banishment of, 11, 19, 310; and Emily Dickinson, 254; murder of, 308, 310
Hutchinson, Thomas, 144

Immigrants, 12, 13–14, 82–83, 89, 104, 232–33
Inman, Arthur Crews, *Diary*, 306–7
Integration, federal court-ordered, of Boston public schools, 6, 113, 147
Irish-Catholic Americans, 109, 110, 111–22. *See also* O'Connor, Edwin
IWW, 213

Jackson, Helen Hunt, 251; *Esther Wynn's Love-Letters*, 252; *Mercy Philbrick's Choice*, 251–52
Jackson, Patrick Tracy, 208
Jacobs, Harriet A. ("Linda Brent"), *Incidents in the Life of a Slave Girl*, 55, 151
James, Alice, 97–98, 252

James, Henry, 44, 49, 57, 74–75, 180, 277; *The Ambassadors*, 102; *The American*, 94–95; *The American Scene*, 16, 77, 102, 235–36, 319; *The Bostonians*, 12, 60, 77, 92, 96, 98–102, 106, 141, 173, 185, 235, 236; on Boston Marriage, 98, 185, 321, 322; and Cape Cod, 235–37; in Concord and Salem, 104–6; *Daisy Miller*, 97; and T. S. Eliot, 268, 269, 271, 273; *The Europeans*, 95; *The Golden Bowl*, 102; and Hawthorne, 42, 91–94, 105–6, 107; and William Dean Howells, 77–79, 83, 84, 97, 103, 104; "A New England Winter," 96, 97; *The Portrait of a Lady*, 97; *The Princess Casamassima*, 88; his view of Boston, 94, 96–97, 103–4, 295; *The Wings of the Dove*, 102
James, William, 99, 154–55, 287, 289; *Psychology*, 217; *The Will to Believe*, 217
Jewett, Sarah Orne, 49, 57, 98, 185; *The Country of the Pointed Firs*, 57
Jewish American writers, 314–18
Johnson, Edward, *Wonder-Working Providence of Sions Savior*, 308
Johnson, Thomas H., 306
Joyce, James, 295
Joyce, Robert Dwyer, *Ballads of Irish Chivalry*, 116

Kakutani, Michiko, 196
Kavanagh, Patrick: "Epic," 135–36; *The Great Hunger*, 136; *Tarry Flynn*, 136
Kavanaugh, Anne, 297
Kavanaugh, James, 296–97
Kazin, Alfred, 14, 33
Keats, John, "On a Grecian Urn," 164
Kemp, Harry, 238–39; *Love among the Cape-Enders*, 239
Kennedy, John F., 9, 115, 121, 124, 220, 256; assassination of, 125, 199; election of, 125, 127; and O'Connor's *All in the Family*, 133
Kennedy (John F.) Library, 120, 121
Kennedy, Joseph P., 120, 134–35, 138
Kennedy, Robert, 121
Kennedy, Rose Fitzgerald, 120–21

Kennedy family, 120, 230
Kerouac, Jack, 214, 224–27; *Book of Dreams*, 225; *Doctor Sax*, 225; *Lonesome Traveler*, 225; *Maggie Cassidy*, 225, 226; *Mexico City Blues*, 225; *On the Road*, 225; *The Scriptures of the Golden Eternity*, 225; *The Town and the City*, 225, 226; *Vanity of Duluoz*, 225; *Visions of Gerard*, 225
King, Martin Luther, Jr., 162, 169
King's Chapel, 182, 286, 325, 326
Kitteridge, George Lyman, 154–55, 217
Kumin, Maxine, 222–24; "A Sense of Place," 222, 223–24; "Stones," 223; *To Make a Prairie*, 223; *Up Country*, 222, 223

Larcom, Lucy, 209, 213; *A New England Girlhood*, 210–12
Lawrence, D. H., 44, 264, 313; "The Spirit of Place," *Studies in Classic American Literature*, 1
Leighton, Clare, 231, 245
Lesbianism, 98, 321–22
Lewis, Sinclair, 2
Liberator, 149
Lincoln, Abraham, 78, 103, 148, 280
Literary World, 44
Little, Malcolm, *see* Malcolm X
Little Review, The, 268
"Local color" literature, 52, 53, 57
Lodge, George Cabot, 178
Lodge, Henry Cabot, 112, 178, 317
Longfellow, Henry Wadsworth, 71–72, 81, 178, 269; and Craige House, 92, 208; "The Herons of Elmwood," 279; "My Lost Youth," 215; *Tales of a Wayside Inn*, 3
Loring, Katharine, 98
Lowell, A. Lawrence, 276
Lowell, Amy, 12, 165, 276, 286; and Boston Athenaeum, 281–82; poetry of, 277–78; Sevenels home of, 281
Lowell, Charlotte Wilson, 276
Lowell, Francis Cabot, 208
Lowell, James Russell, 12, 36, 81, 83, 178, 268; *The Bigelow Papers*, 280; death of, 278; and Elmwood, 278–

79; *A Fable for Critics*, 279; and Robert Lowell, 276, 277, 280–81; "Memoriae Postum," 280; "Ode Recited at the Harvard Commemoration," 280, 288
Lowell, MA: factory system of, 208, 209–12, 277–78; and Jack Kerouac, 224–25, 227
Lowell, Ralph, 124
Lowell, Robert, 4, 15, 35, 176, 179, 319; "Antebellum Boston," 175; "At the Indian Killer's Grave," 286; automobile accident of, 296; and Boston Idea, 267, 274, 302–3; breakdowns of, 291, 292; in Cambridge, 301–2; "Dawn," 302; and T. S. Eliot, 268–69, 270, 272, 274, 301–2; *Endecott and the Red Cross*, 286–87; "For the Union Dead," 16, 280, 285, 288–91, 302; *For the Union Dead*, 12; "Hawthorne," 73; "Home after Three Months Away," 292; identity of, 274–78; *Life Studies*, 12, 282, 286, 291, 299, 300; *Lord Weary's Castle*, 286; and James Russell Lowell, 280–81; marriages of, 12, 291, 295, 296–97; "Memories of West Street and Lepke," 292; *The Mills of the Kavanaughs*, 297; *My Kinsman, Major Molineux*, 287; "New England and Further," 290, 300; "91 Revere Street," 12, 282–85, 290; *Notebooks*, 301, 306; "The Public Garden," 286, 289; and Anne Sexton, 299, 300, 312; his teaching at Boston University, 291, 299; "Waking in Blue," 292; and Richard Wilbur, 261
Lowell, Robert, Sr., 276
Lowell Historic Preservation Commission, Jack Kerouac Commemorative of, 224–25, 227
Lowell Offering, The, 209–10, 211, 212
Lowell Public Art Collection, 225
Lukas, J. Anthony, 113; *Common Ground*, 6, 7
Lurie, Alison, *Love and Friendship*, 249

McCarthy, Joseph, 320

McCarthy, Mary, 239; *A Charmed Life,* 239–40
McCormick, John, 182
McKim, Charles F., 104
McLean Hospital (Belmont), 292, 299
MacLeish, Archibald, 261
Mailer, Norman, 248; and Cape Cod, 240–42; *Tough Guys Don't Dance,* 240–42
Malcolm X, 159–61, 163, 169, 170, 317; *Autobiography,* 162
Mann, Horace, 59, 69
Mann, Mary Peabody, 58–59; *Christianity in the Kitchen,* 59; *The Flower People,* 59
Manning, Margaret, 197
Manning, Robert, 109, 197
Marquand, Adelaide Hooker, 190
Marquand, Christina Sedgwick, 190
Marquand, John P., 173, 190, 191–92, 193, 195; *H. M. Pulham, Esquire,* 190–91; *The Late George Apley,* 12, 183–84, 185–89, 295; his novels of manners, 173, 174; *Point of No Return,* 191; *Sincerely, Willis Wayde,* 191; *Wickford Point,* 190
Marx, Leo, 39
Massachusetts, University of, 249, 257
Massachusetts Bay Company, 10–11
Massachusetts General Hospital, 208, 314
Mather, Cotton, 185, 228–29, 254; *The Negro Christianized,* 142
Matthiessen, F. O., 43, 321; *American Renaissance,* 14, 320
Mayflower, 228
Meiklejohn, Alexander, 255–56
Melville, Herman, 43, 265, 313; and Hawthorne, 18, 44–47, 72; "Hawthorne and His Mosses," 44–45, 47; *Moby-Dick,* 18, 46–47, 234–35; "The Piazza," 47–48; *Piazza Tales,* 47
Merrimack River/Valley, literature of, 207–27 *passim*
Millay, Edna St. Vincent, 239
Miller, Kerby A., 125
Miller, Perry, 9–10, 15, 63, 306; "The New England Conscience," 304
Mirsky, Mark, *Blue Hill Ave.,* 315–16

Miscellany, 54
Mitchell, Margaret, 2
Montclair, 244–45
Monthly Anthology, The, 30
Moody, William Vaughn, "Ode in a Time of Hesitation," 288
Morison, Samuel Eliot, 19, 304, 311, 317; *One Boy's Boston,* 314
Mount Holyoke College, 257
Mount Holyoke Female Seminary, 251
Moynihan, Daniel Patrick, 125
Munsterberg, Hugo, 217
Museum of Fine Arts, 314; *The Bostonians: Painters of an Elegant Age, 1870–1930,* 6–7
Myers, Mordecai, 283

National Anti-Slavery Standard, 55
New England Anti-Slavery Society, 55
New England Suffrage Association, 65
New England Women's Club, 65
New Hampshire Division of Parks and Recreation, 217
New Yorker, The, 327, 328
New York *Tribune,* 63
Nixon, Richard, 139
North American Review, 279, 280
North of Boston, literature from, 207–27
Norton, Charles Eliot, 81, 154–55, 279

Oberlin College, 219
O'Brien, Hugh, 119
O'Connell, William Cardinal, 118, 119–20, 121
O'Connor, Edwin, 114, 136, 181, 183; *All in the Family,* 110, 126–27, 132–35; "The 'Cardinal' Fragment," 136–37; death of, 108, 109, 136; early life of, 109–10; *The Edge of Sadness,* 110, 126–27, 130–32; *The Last Hurrah,* 12, 108, 109, 110, 122–34 *passim,* 139–40, 189
Old Corner Bookstore, 55
Oliver, Mary: *American Primitive,* 243; "Morning at Great Pond," 243
Olmstead, Frederick Law, 121
O'Neill, Carlotta, 238
O'Neill, Eugene, 239; *Ah, Wilderness,* 238; *Bound East for Cardiff,* 237–

Index

O'Neill, Eugene (*continued*)
38; and Cape Cod, 237–38; death of,
238; *Desire under the Elms*, 238;
Long Day's Journey into Night, 238;
A Moon for the Misbegotten, 238;
"Thirst" and Other One Act Plays,
238
O'Neill, Thomas P. "Tip," 122–23; *Man
of the House*, 108, 137–39
Operatives' Magazine, 211
O'Reilly, John Boyle, 115–16; "Amer-
ica," 116–17; death of, 118; "The
Exile of the Gael," 117; "A Philis-
tine's View," 117; values of, 117–18
Orwell, George, *1984*, 330
Osgood, Ellen Sewall, 232–33
Oxford University, 328

Parker, Theodore, 61, 150
Parkman, Francis, 97
Park Street Church, 11
Parnell, Charles Stewart, 280
Paxton, William, 6
Peabody, Elizabeth Palmer, 29, 52, 58–
60, 68, 72, 97; bookshop of, 60, 62,
321; *Record of a School*, 59; *Remi-
niscences of the Rev. William Ellery
Channing*, 59; satirized in *The Bos-
tonians*, 60, 92, 99–100
Peabody, Mary, *see* Mann, Mary
Peabody
Peabody, Sophia, *see* Hawthorne, So-
phia Peabody
Perkins Institute for the Blind, 64
Perry, Thomas Sergeant, 96
Phelps, Elizabeth Stuart, 57
Phillips, Wendell, 55, 149, 154
Pierce, Franklin, 69–70, 71
Piersen, William D., 147, 169
Pierson, George W., "A Study in De-
nudation," 2
Pilgrim's Progress (John Bunyan), 68,
82, 210
Pilot, The, 116, 118
Pittsburgh Courier, 165
Plath, Sylvia, 197, 299–300
Plunkett, George Washington, 127
Poe, Edgar Allan, *The Fall of the House
of Usher*, 86
Poets' Theater (Cambridge), 120, 261

Polk, James K., 42, 175
"Pope's Day," 111
Prendergast, Maurice, 7
Provincetown Players, 230, 237, 238,
239
Pue, Jonathan, 19
Puritanism, 90, 270, 272, 304–5; Em-
ily Dickinson and, 253–55; Ralph
Waldo Emerson and, 31, 32; Robert
Francis and, 258, 259, 261; Robert
Frost and, 255–56, 261; Nathaniel
Hawthorne and, 19–23, 31, 32, 54,
72, 91, 182; Julia Ward Howe and,
65; Robert Lowell and, 261; George
Santayana and, 181–83; Richard
Wilbur and, 261

Reagan, Ronald, 108, 139
Reed, John, *Ten Days That Shook the
World*, 237
Revere, Paul, 114
Rich, Adrienne, 299
Richardson, Marilyn, 162
Ripley, Ezra, 31, 32, 42
Ripley, Samuel, 42
Robinson, Edward Arlington, 163
Roethke, Theodore, 261
Roosevelt, Teddy, 269
Royce, Josiah, 154–55
Ryan, Dennis P., 126

Saint-Gaudens, Augustus, 16, 148, 287
St. John, 232–33, 234
Saint Stephen's Church, 114–15
Salem witch trials, 21, 270
Sandburg, Carl, 165
Sanders Theater (Cambridge), 267
Santayana, Augustin, 179
Santayana, George, 154–55, 179–80,
183, 295; autobiography of, 179,
180; death of, 180; and Robert Frost,
217; *The Last Puritan*, 12, 180, 181–
83, 189, 257, 263, 264; and John
Marquand, 184; his novels of man-
ners, 173, 174; *Persons and Places*,
180, 319; his view of Boston, 180–
81
Sarton, May, 320; *Anger*, 322; *The Ed-
ucation of Harriet Hatfield*, 321–22;
Faithful Are the Wounds, 320–21,

322; *The House by the Sea*, 323; *Journal of a Solitude*, 323; *The Magnificent Spinster*, 322; *Mrs. Stevens Hears the Mermaids Singing*, 322; *Plant Dreaming Deep*, 322; *A Reckoning*, 322; *The Small Room*, 322

Savoy, The, 317

Schlesinger, Arthur, Jr., 137

Scott, Sir Walter, 55

Second Church of Boston, 11, 31

Sewall, Richard B., 248, 252

Sewall, Samuel, 193–94; *Diary*, 305; "The Selling of Joseph," 142

Sexton, Anne, 197, 222, 299, 300, 312; *An Awful Rowing toward God*, 300; *The Death Notebooks*, 309, 312; "Gods," 312–13; "A Story for Rose, on the Midnight Flight to Boston," 300; *To Bedlam and Part Way Back*, 300, 312

Shakespeare, William, 37, 45

Shaler, Nathaniel Southgate, 217

Shannon, William V., 123; *The American Irish*, 121

Shaw, Robert Gould, 55, 65, 280, 289–90; Saint-Gaudens' monument honoring, 16, 148–49, 168, 171, 287–88, 303

Shepard, Thomas, 310

Smith College, 257, 299

South of Boston, literature from, 227–48

Stafford, Jean, 284, 295–96; automobile accident of, 296; *Boston Adventure*, 12, 296, 297–99; Damariscotta Mills home of, 296–97; "An Influx of Poets," 297

Starbuck, George, 299

Stark, John, 276

Stegner, Wallace, 2

Stowe, Calvin, 56, 57

Stowe, Harriet Beecher, 52, 55, 56, 65, 68; *The Minister's Wooing*, 56; *Oldtown Folks*, 56–57; *Uncle Tom's Cabin*, 56

Stuart, Gilbert, 4

Sturgis, George, 179

Sullivan, James J., 113

Sullivan, John L., 114

Sumner, Charles, 55, 150

Sweeney, Frances, 218

Tarbell, Edmund C., 6

Tate, Alan, 254; "Ode to the Confederate Dead," 289

Tavern Club, 117, 118, 184–85

Taylor, Edward, 253

Temple School, 59, 60, 66

Thayer Academy, 195

Thayer and Eldridge, 151

Thompson, Lawrance, 255

Thoreau, Henry David, 11, 14, 18, 29, 198, 213; and Louisa May Alcott, 67; *Cape Cod*, 231–35, 244, 263; "Civil Disobedience," 319; and Concord, 31, 32–33, 38–41; death of, 71, 232; and Emerson, 36, 37–40; and Robert Finch, 246, 247; and Robert Francis, 258–59; and Robert Frost, 218, 219; and Hawthorne, 41–42, 71; and William Dean Howells, 76, 77; and Jack Kerouac, 225, 226; "Ktaadn," 263; and Maxine Kumin, 222, 223, 224; *The Maine Woods*, 263; his view of Boston, 37, 248; *Walden*, 38, 39–41, 76, 218, 242, 244, 247, 319, 322; "Walking," 263–64; *A Week on the Concord and Merrimack Rivers*, 207–8, 220, 233

Thoreau, John, 207, 232–33

Thoreau, Sophia, 232

Thornton, John, 145–46

Ticknor, William, 55, 71

Ticknor and Company, 55

Time magazine, 184

Tocqueville, Alexis de, 309

Todd, Mabel Loomis, 252

Transcendental Club, 58

Transcendentalists, 29, 61–62, 66

Trinity Church, 11

Trollope, Anthony, 212–13, 225; *North America*, 212

Trotter, William Munroe, 158–59

Truman, Harry S, 124

Twain, Mark, 89–90

Unitarianism, 14, 59, 90, 182, 251, 270; and William Ellery Channing, 11; and Ralph Waldo Emerson, 30, 31

Updike, John, 15, 197–98, 203–4, 220, 326–29; *Assorted Prose*, 200; *Couples*, 198–200; and Hawthorne, 203, 204; and William Dean Howells, 74–75, 77; "HUB FANS BID KID ADIEU," 200, 201; *A Month of Sundays*, 198; "New England Churches," 200; his novels of manners, 173, 174, 198; *Roger's Version*, 198, 202–3; *S.*, 198, 203; *Self-Consciousness*, 306, 323, 327

Ursuline Convent, burning of, 112

Vanderbilt, Kermit, 86
Vendler, Helen, 274, 302
Vietnam war, 275, 286
Virgil, 217

Wakefield, Dan: *Home Free*, 325; *Returning: A Spiritual Journey*, 323, 325–26; *Selling Out*, 325; *Starting Over*, 325
Wakefield, John, 326
Walker, David, 162
Waltham-Lowell system, 187, 208
Warren, Austin, 304–5; *The New England Conscience*, 13
Washburn, Mrs. (former slave), 167–68
Washington, Booker T., 155–56, 288
Washington, George, 111, 315
Waugh, Evelyn, 129
Weber, Max, 313
Webster, Ben, 317
Webster, Daniel, 37, 55, 148, 214
Weeks, Edward, 108
Wellesley College, 120–21
Welty, Eudora, 330
Wendell, Barrett, 112, 152, 153, 184, 185; *A Literary History of America*, 185
West, Dorothy, 169, 170; *The Living Is Easy*, 157–59
West of Boston, literature from, 248–65
Wharton, Edith, 18; *The Age of Innocence*, 51–52; *A Backward Glance*, 48; *Ethan Frome*, 48, 49–51; and Hawthorne, 48, 49, 52, 72; Lenox home of, 48–49; *Summer*, 48, 49, 50, 51

Wheatley, John, 144
Wheatley, Phillis, 143–46, 151, 162, 169, 315; and Charlotte Forten, 150; "On Being Brought from Africa to America," 145; *Poems on Various Subjects, Religious and Moral*, 144–45
Wheatley, Susanna, 144
Wheaton Seminary, 211
White, E. B., 328
White, Theodore H., 316–17; *In Search of History*, 316
Whitehill, Walter Muir, 10–11, 14; *Boston: A Topographical History*, 5
Whitman, Walt, 2; *Leaves of Grass*, 5
Whittier, John Greenleaf, 55, 89–90, 116–17, 211; "The Barefoot Boy," 214–15; and Robert Frost, 217, 218; "Ichabod," 214; and Jack Kerouac, 225; *Leaves from Margaret Smith's Journal*, 213; *Legends of New England*, 213; "Massachusetts to Virginia," 214; *Snow-Bound*, 213, 214; *The Tent on the Beach*, 213, 215
Whorf, John, *North End, Boston*, 7
Wigglesworth, Michael, *Day of Doom*, 329
Wilbur, Richard, 261; "April 5, 1974," 262–63; *Ceremony*, 261; "On Having Mis-Identified a Wild Flower," 263; *Things of This World*, 261
Wilde, Oscar, 65
Williams, Ted, 200, 201–2
Williams, William Carlos, 291
Wills, Gary, 135; *The Kennedy Imprisonment*, 133
Wilson, Edmund, 65, 110, 133; and Cape Cod, 238–39, 240; *The Crime in the Whistler Room*, 238
Wilson, Elena Mumm Thornton, 239
Wilson, Harriet E., *Our Nig*, 150–51
Wilson, Margaret Canby, 239
Wilson, Mary Blair, 238
Wilson, Mary McCarthy, *see* McCarthy, Mary
Winthrop, John, 10, 11, 16, 145, 307–8, 331; and *Arbella*, 8, 194; on Boston as "City upon a Hill," 4, 34; and Emerson, 30; and Anne Hutchinson, 31; his ideal of "justice and

mercy," 53, 329; "A Model of Christian Charity," 8–9

Woodward, C. Vann, "The Search for Southern Identity," 2

Wordsworth, William, *Prelude,* 33

World War I, 157, 230, 316

World War II, 161, 239, 259, 261, 286

Yeats, William Butler, 318

Zuckerman, Michael, 10